THE BELL MODERN HISTORIES

THE EUROPEAN WORLD

1870–1961

By T. K. Derry

THE CAMPAIGN IN NORWAY (*H.M.S.O., History of the Second World War*)

A SHORT HISTORY OF NORWAY (*Allen and Unwin*)

By T. L. Jarman

THE RISE AND FALL OF NAZI GERMANY (*Cresset Press*)

——— ☆ ———

THE BELL MODERN HISTORY SERIES

Other volumes in the series
When ordering mention the series title above

HISTORY OF EUROPE, 1450–1660
by P. J. Helm

SEVENTEENTH-CENTURY EUROPE
by Leonard W. Cowie

EIGHTEENTH-CENTURY EUROPE
by Leonard W. Cowie

THE EUROPEAN WORLD, 1870–1961
by T. K. Derry and T. L. Jarman

THE FOUNDATIONS OF MODERN EUROPE
1789–1871
by M. E. Barlen

BRITAIN AND THE STUARTS, 1603–1714
by D. L. Farmer

HANOVERIAN ENGLAND, 1714–1837
by Leonard W. Cowie

In preparation
ENGLAND UNDER THE YORKISTS
AND TUDORS
By P. J. Helm

THE
EUROPEAN WORLD
1870-1961

By

T. K. DERRY

and

T. L. JARMAN

LONDON
G. BELL & SONS LTD

First Published 1950
Reprinted 1951, 1958
New Edition 1962
Reprinted 1964, 1965, 1968

Printed in Great Britain by
William Clowes and Sons, Limited, London and Beccles

PREFACE

THE Battle of Sedan as the starting-point for a study of modern times needs no apology: but to attempt to carry the story down to the close of the year 1961, as we now do, is clearly somewhat presumptuous. However, experience has led the authors to believe that the gaps in our education as Europeans are never so painfully obvious to ourselves and to others as when the knowledge that is required to shed light on the problems of the hour is a knowledge of contemporary or near-contemporary history. They therefore hope to make up for any misplaced emphasis or over-hasty judgements in dealing with the immediate past by their efforts to relate the narrative more completely to present needs.

The new edition includes various minor amendments to the text, but the principal change is the replacement of the epilogue, written in 1949, by two chapters to cover the period from 1945 to 1961.

T. K. D.
T. L. J.

ACKNOWLEDGMENTS

Permission has been kindly granted as follows for the inclusion of various copyright passages on the pages named:

By Martin Secker & Warburg Ltd. for a passage on p. 17 from *Essays of Three Decades* by Thomas Mann; by The Cambridge University Press for a passage on p. 24 from *The Economic Development of France and Germany* by Sir John Clapham; by Macmillan & Co. Ltd. for a passage on p. 240 from *Economic Consequences of the Peace* by Lord Keynes; by Charles Scribner's Sons, Ltd. for a passage on p. 196 from *The Coming of the War* by B. E. Schmidt; by Sir Arthur Salter for three passages from *Recovery* (G. Bell & Sons, Ltd.) on pp. 237 and 347; by George Allen & Unwin Ltd. for two passages on pp. 263 and 334 from *Bolshevism, Fascism and Democracy* by F. Nitti; by Ernest Benn Ltd. for two passages on pp. 263 and 338 from *Italy* by L. Villari; by Hamish Hamilton Ltd. for a passage on p. 295 from *U.S. Foreign Policy* by Walter Lippmann; by the Oxford University Press for a passage on p. 306 from *The Growth of the American Republic* by Morison & Commager and also for the passage on p. 351 from *Survey of International Affairs* by Dr. Toynbee (published for the Royal Institute of International Affairs); by Routledge and Kegan Paul Ltd. for a passage on p. 323 from *Soviet Economic Development Since 1917* by M. Dobb; and by Mrs. R. M. Hewitt for the translation by R. M. Hewitt on p. 325.

CONTENTS

LIST OF MAPS

I

CHAPTER 1

EUROPE IN 1870

The Franco-Prussian War Marks a New Era

CLEARLY defined periods exist in history-books rather than in history itself. Yet the events of the summer and autumn of 1870 seemed even to the casual newspaper-reader of the day to mark a decisive change in the fortunes of Europe. The glittering and apparently powerful French Empire of Napoleon III lightheartedly declared war on Prussia and was quickly overwhelmed by the massed guns at Sedan (September 2); the Third Republic was proclaimed in France, stirring up memories of Danton, Carnot, and the national recovery of 1792; but the new Government saw its remaining army surrendered as the result of political intrigue at Metz (October 28), and Paris itself laid under siege. Europe, it was said, had lost a mistress and gained a master. To us looking back upon the event it appears to have been decisive only in a more limited sense, since the German mastery of Europe was to be overthrown in half a century. It is true that France in the 1920's no longer had the resources of population and industry to make an effective mistress of Europe, and Hitler's Germany quickly took her place for the second time; but this was only the prelude to a catastrophe after which neither Germany nor France is likely to reappear with the kind of ascendancy which they once enjoyed. At all events, the history of two and a half generations, leading up to Europe as we know it now, though it has its roots far back in the French Revolution of 1789 and the roughly contemporary Industrial Revolution in Britain, springs in many ways from the decisive campaign of 1870.

Decisive as that campaign was, at the close of the year France still struggled on. The eyes of Europe were fixed on Paris, which had been under siege since September 19. The capital was now approaching the double climax of its fate—conditions of starvation in what was then the second largest city in the world and bombardment of the crowded area within the fortifications. For bombardment the Germans had ready the huge siege-train which their commander-in-chief, von Moltke, had patiently accumulated. Meanwhile the heroic Gambetta had made his famous escape from Paris by balloon, to stage a final attempt to save the capital by an attack on the German lines of communication from the direction of Orleans. In France and Germany, therefore, big internal changes, resulting from the war, were not consummated until 1871, and the present chapter may more conveniently be given to those countries and aspects of European life in general for which 1870 itself is a representative year.

Events of 1870 in Italy

We may take first those Powers on which the actual war had an important influence. To the youthful Kingdom of Italy it meant a further stage towards unification in the transfer of the capital from Florence to Rome. Rome, the last remnant of the once large Estates of the Church, had for twenty years been preserved for the Pope mainly by the almost continuous presence of a French garrison, kept there by Napoleon III to conciliate the Catholic party in France. Its existence gave the Italians an excuse for their failure to help France at the outset in 1870, as France had helped them in 1859: when it was finally withdrawn, a month after the outbreak of war, the French had already suffered their first serious defeats and Italy was not tempted to join the losing side. Without the French Pope Pius IX could offer only token resistance. On September 20 the walls were breached to achieve the entry of Italian forces into the city, which was shortly afterwards incorporated with the Kingdom by vote of its inhabitants. But although Rome duly became the capital and King Victor Emmanuel established his court on the Quirinal, the Pope did not desist from his antagonism towards the new temporal Italian power. In this same summer of 1870 he had held in Rome the Vatican Council, the first such synod of the Catholic Church to be summoned since the Council of Trent, which launched the Counter-Reformation in the sixteenth century. Its objects included the denunciation of modern liberalism with all its works, such as the attack on the Papal possessions. Its outstanding achievement was the formal extension of the power of the Pope, when the representatives of world-wide Catholicism after bitter discussion voted by a large majority that the Pope is infallible when 'he defines by his apostolic authority that which should be held in the matter of faith or morals.' The Decree of Papal Infallibility of July 18, 1870, has not been used to make new declarations, but its existence has greatly helped the tendency towards centralisation in the Catholic Church, which has so largely preserved its power in a rapidly changing world. Accordingly, the Law of Papal Guarantees, by which the Kingdom of Italy tried to obtain recognition from the Pope in return for full sovereignty over the Vatican Palace and its environs and the provision of an annual income, was not accepted by the Papacy, and for the next two generations the Popes regarded themselves as prisoners confined to their palace and threw the influence of the Church against the struggling Italian monarchy. The Italian government even feared that its possession of Rome might be challenged by a foreign Power.

Papal hostility, which both France and Germany were at first inclined to encourage, was not the only factor which caused united Italy to fall short of the success which European Liberals had hoped for it. The monarchy itself was far from secure, since the followers of Mazzini and many of the Garibaldians remained republicans at heart. These and other malcontents continued to attack the government for its failure to get from Austria-Hungary the Trentino and Trieste, where a largely Italian-speaking population constituted an *Italia Irredenta* until 1919. More serious was the division of the existing Italian territory into two widely dissimilar halves—the progressive north, which was already to some extent industrialised as the seat of the largest silk manufacture in Europe, and the feudal south, which had no considerable industries, a barren soil, and a backward peasantry. The constitution, which was a development of that which had been granted to Piedmont, the nucleus of the new Kingdom, in the revolutionary year 1848, did little to promote true unity. It was modelled upon England, but the property qualification for a vote was very high (the electorate was only

EUROPE
IN 1871

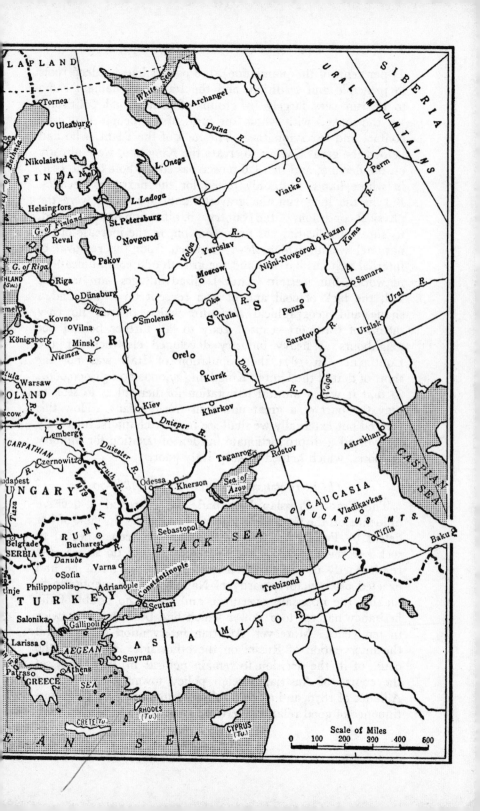

2½ per cent. of the population), the parties had no deep roots in principle and tradition, and the Italian parliament came to be run very largely by groups of professional politicians 'on the make,' with whom the mass of the people had little contact and less sympathy. The men of the Right, who had helped the great Cavour to create the Kingdom, were already on the decline; and in 1876 power passed to those of the Left, in whose hands it mainly rested for the next two decades. But in the long run the gravest handicaps of all were the physical conditions of the country. Unification found, indeed, its surest justification, as time went on, in the increase of the national wealth which slowly resulted from the removal of internal customs barriers and the growth of a communications network. But certain natural disadvantages—an infertile soil, the lack of coal and of iron (except on Elba), and a shape and geographical structure which offered no easy means of transport—caused Italy to fall further behind her neighbours as heavy industry developed elsewhere on the Continent. In 1871 the population of Italy was not far short of that of the United Kingdom (27,000,000 : 31,000,000), so that it was a natural temptation for her rulers to seek to play the part of a great power in world affairs. How this worked out externally we shall see in later chapters; internally it involved a disproportionate burden of taxation for military purposes, which helped to keep Italy poor.

The Reorientation of Austria-Hungary, 1867–70

The Franco-Prussian War had also exercised a decisive influence on the fortunes of Austria-Hungary. In view of her defeat by Prussia in 1866 she might have been expected to seek her revenge in 1870. That she did not do so was the result partly of Bismarck's moderation in the terms he had exacted after victory, partly of Napoleon III's ineptitude in making the necessary overtures, and partly no doubt of the hesitancy natural to a Power which had been defeated twice in ten years. Moreover, Austrian intervention might entail the intervention of Russia on the other side. Whatever the cause of it, the decision to remain neutral in July 1870, set the course of Austrian foreign policy towards the German Alliance of 1879, and made possible in domestic policy the continuance of good relations between Austrians and Hungarians.

For good relations could not have continued if there had been a fresh embroilment in the affairs of Germany, as Austria-Hungary, like Italy, was a state established upon a new foundation. An unsuccessful attempt had been made, after the suppression of the revolutionary outbreak of 1848, to subject the entire Austrian Empire to centralised control by the German-speaking Austrians of Vienna and Austria proper. This was undermined by the failure of Austrian arms against France in the Italian war of 1859, and a new settlement was already under discussion with the Hungarians when the second failure, against Prussia in 1866, made the settlement more urgent. Hence the *Ausgleich* or Compromise of 1867, which governed the affairs of the Danube basin and the rest of the wide lands of the Hapsburg monarchy for the next half-century.

By this instrument the monarchy became a Dual Monarchy: the Emperor Francis Joseph of Austria was crowned a second time as King of Hungary, and his empire divided into two halves at the River Leitha. Each half had complete control over its internal affairs, with an independent parliamentary system, administration, and Cabinet. For external affairs there were to be common ministers for foreign policy, war, and finance, acting in the name of the Emperor-King but responsible to the Delegations, committees nominated by the two Parliaments to meet separately but simultaneously, one year in Vienna, the next in the Hungarian capital of Budapest, and authorised to communicate with each other in writing only (such was their mutual distrust!). These Delegations were to vote the money needed for common purposes, of which Austria as the wealthier partner paid seven-tenths. Where necessary, as in the case of military organisation, the two Parliaments enacted identical laws, and they also maintained identical tariffs. Thus the industries of Bohemia, the financial resources of Vienna, and the corn-growing areas of the Hungarian plain and Transylvania remained effectively linked together, helped to develop by the growth of a single network of railways radiating from Austria.

The Ausgleich was, indeed, more beneficial to the economic than to the political life of the peoples concerned. Politically, it guaranteed that there should be constitutional laws in both halves of the Monarchy. This meant in Austria the Patent of 1861—a Parliament (Reichsrat) elected by a complicated system to represent not individuals but the four great interests, one of which, the large landowners, was intended to have a permanent majority, and a Cabinet which was specifically absolved from responsibility to the Parliament when the latter was not in session. In Hungary it meant the restoration of the ancient Diet, as modified in 1848 by the substitution of a middle-class franchise for the old privileges of the nobility. But in both cases the masses were left virtually unrepresented, and political life was largely influenced by the skill of the Emperor Francis Joseph in playing off one interest against another, in which he was helped by the absence of a single imperial Parliament. Industrious, wary, cynical, the last but one of the long Hapsburg line, in a reign of nearly seventy years (1848–1916) he showed himself the most resourceful politician of his variegated dominions.

To keep the balance among his subjects and so maintain his own prerogatives the Emperor-King made much use of the fundamental injustice of the new system—the fact that it provided for the claims of only two races, the German-speaking Austrians and the Hungarian Magyars. The Slav and Latin peoples, who made up the majority of the empire's population, were left at the mercy of these two triumphant aristocracies, though even so they did not all suffer alike. Thus the Polish nobles of Galicia, who constituted a regular part of the governing class in Austria, had been given full charge of their own province and its subject Ruthenians in 1869; and the Bohemian Czechs, though they had no such home rule privilege as loyalty had earned for the Polish lords, formed a group in the Reichsrat which it was worth while to conciliate. In the same way the Croats were allowed an important share in the Hungarian Diet and a large measure of home rule. But national sentiment, which had first made itself strongly felt in 1848, continued to grow, spreading slowly from the educated middle class to the peasantry, from Czechs, Croats, and Austro-Italians to Serbs, Rumanians, and the down-trodden, inarticulate millions of Slovaks and Ruthenians. Thus the policy of the Dual Monarchy at home and abroad came to be dominated more and more by the purely negative consideration of how best to avert or postpone its dissolution into its many component parts.

Russia and the Abrogation of the Treaty of Paris

Russia, like Austria-Hungary, had stood aside from the war, but unlike the Dual Monarchy, she was strong enough to exact a price. Since 1856 her influence in the Balkan Peninsula had been diminished by the clauses of the Treaty of Paris, under which she bound herself to refrain from keeping any naval vessels or establishments on the Black Sea coast. In October, 1870, with the connivance of Prussia, her government denounced its obligations, arguing correctly enough that France could not, Britain would not, and Turkey alone dare not, bring her to book. The denunciation was regularised at the Conference of London in the following year, at which Russia accepted the British principle that there could be no unilateral repudiation of an international treaty, on the strict understanding that there was no interference with her act of repudiation in practice. Thus Russia found herself once more in a position to take up a forward policy in south-eastern Europe, to which the Czar turned the more readily in relief from domestic problems and in enthusiasm for a new idealistic programme.

The early years of the reign of Alexander II (1855–81) had been devoted to the internal reforms, long overdue, which it was imperative to make in order to counteract the shock given to the purely autocratic government of Russia by its failures in the Crimean War. The greatest reform was the emancipation of the serfs (1861), nearly 40,000,000 in all, both from the obligation to work the estate of their lord, whether a private proprietor or the State itself, and from restrictions on their personal liberty. Socially, this was a huge advance, for the Russian peasantry were the last in Europe to linger in conditions of personal subjection worse than those of the English villein in the Middle Ages. Economically, it was less satisfactory, for the division of the land between lord and peasant left the latter in most cases with an insufficient share, a fact which became more evident as population grew (it doubled between 1850 and 1900), and for this share he was required to make compensation payments over a period of fifty years. Moreover, control of the land was vested in the village commune or Mir, which usually tended to preserve the old-fashioned, uneconomic 'strip' system of cultivating the fields.

B

The Mir was also the traditional basis of local self-government: it was responsible for the payment of taxes and dues by the village, and was therefore empowered to refuse the passport without which the ex-serf still could not move from place to place.

Then local government at a higher level was the subject of the second great reform, the institution of elected councils (Zemstva) for districts and provinces, which controlled local affairs and appointed local magistrates. This measure was accompanied by a judicial reform, which remodelled the regular law courts and methods of trial in general accordance with the practice of Western Europe; by modernisation of the military system; improvements in education; and—a big step for an autocratic government to take—some relaxation in the iron censorship of the Press. In 1870 elected councils were also set up in the towns, but by this time Alexander had lost his enthusiasm for the reforming policy, startled to see that each concession on his part, so far from producing tranquillity, emboldened the more enlightened of his subjects to ask for more, and that each relaxation of the police régime meant increased activity among the small but formidable groups of Narodniki or 'Men of the People' (so called because they tried to spread their ideas by going to live among the peasants), nihilists, and anarchists. It was, indeed, only too easy to show how limited the reforms were. The local councils, for instance, were elected on the Prussian three-class system so as to ensure a preponderant vote to the larger landowners. The censorship of the Press, again, was weakened but not abolished; and the judicial reforms were never allowed to interfere too drastically with the despotic powers of the police. In 1878 trial by court-martial was formally restored for political offences. Nevertheless, the reforms of the 1860's settled the general basis of Russian life for the next forty years: and Russia, though the most backward, was also the most populous, the most incalculable, and the most feared of the European Powers.

Alexander turned with relief from the innovation of domestic reform, which had caused him so much trouble, to the forward policy in foreign affairs, which was traditional and popular and had been suspended only on account of the reverse suffered by Russian arms in the Crimea. But he clothed the old policy with a new pretext—the championship of the Slav races in

accordance with the ideals of the Pan-Slav movement. Pretext it was, as appeared in the case of the Poles, the Slav
brothers who had been made the special charge of the Russian
Crown since 1815. The suppression of a Polish rebellion in
1863 had resulted in the removal of the last traces of self-
government and the imposition of a police régime, with
special features of martial law, russification of the schools,
oppression of the Catholic Church, and persecution of every
class of Pole except the peasants, that made the treatment of
Slav by Slav a byword in Europe. Nevertheless, as a
movement, Panslavism could be exploited. Panslavism arose
out of the revival of the study of the Slav languages and history
by the more advanced elements among the seven Slav races
subject to the Austrian Empire, and became a prominent
factor in Prague and elsewhere during the revolutions of
1848; it was now seen to offer great political advantages. It
gave to Russia a position of natural leadership, as was demonstrated when every Slav people (except the Poles) sent its
representatives to a great ethnic exhibition, held at St.
Petersburg in 1867. It lent to an aggressive foreign policy the
romantic aura of a crusade. It would enable Russia (which
had saved the Austrian Empire by its intervention in Hungary
in 1849, only to be opposed by Austria at the time of the
Crimean War) to weaken and perhaps destroy her Austrian
rival, whenever she chose, by intrigue. More immediately, it
opened a new path to leadership in the Balkans as the champion
of brother Slavs against the Turk.

Institution of the Bulgarian Exarchate

On the military side this programme was advanced in
October, 1870, by the return of the Russian war-flag to the
Black Sea, on the political by the establishment of the Bulgarian
Exarchate or Headship of the Orthodox Church in Bulgaria, a
few months earlier. Two of the existing Balkan States found
little favour in Russian eyes. Greek nationalism, which
centred upon a rather artificial revival of the language and
other glories of ancient Greece, was an independent force,
though the new Kingdom had led a very struggling life since
its formation in 1832. The politicians concentrated their
attention upon the enlargement of the frontiers, for these shut
out more than half the nation. But in this matter they had

had no success, and the country itself, apart from Athens, remained lawless and undeveloped. Russia's nearest neighbour, Rumania, likewise built up its nationality upon a non-Slav foundation; the Latin tradition held that modern Rumania was the ancient Roman colony on the lower Danube. Though formed as recently as 1859, Rumania had the advantage of a flourishing wheat trade and of its new German Prince, Carol I, who was an expert in the manipulation of politicians and elections without any open breach of the constitution, which was modelled on that of liberal Belgium. There remained of the Balkan states the tiny principality of the Black Mountain, where the Montenegrins had never given up the struggle against the Turks; there remained also Montenegro's larger neighbour, Serbia. Serbia had received Russia's help in 1867, when her influence secured the removal of the last practical evidence of Turkish suzerainty in the shape of a garrison in the capital, Belgrade: but Serbia, though indubitably Slav, was economically very backward, a land of wild tribesmen, torn by a dynastic struggle between the reigning family of the Obrenovici and their rivals, the Karageorgevici, under whose leadership the first blow for freedom had been struck in 1804.

The significance of the new Bulgarian Exarchate was therefore twofold. It detracted from the importance of the Greeks by withdrawing the Slav members of the Orthodox Church inside the Turkish Empire from the authority of the Greek Patriarch at Constantinople, who was their traditional head. Conversely, it added to the importance of the Bulgars by giving them, while still subject to the Turks, the status of a distinct religious community. They were the last of the historic Christian kingdoms of the Balkans to re-emerge from the twilight of Turkish rule, to which they had all been subjected at the close of the Middle Ages—their first school dated only from 1835 and the modern literature of the language was scarcely older. But the Bulgarians, whose deadly quarrel with the Greeks dates from the first actual appointment of an Exarch in 1872, were to play a very active part in the events of the next few years—establishing an independent state, extending its boundaries, and reaching out towards the debatable lands of Macedonia, for which Bulgar and Greek have struggled ever since.

The Vacancy on the Spanish Throne filled

Europe was entering upon a period in which the most backward of its lesser component states, those of the Balkans, were to attract great attention as pawns in the conflicts of Great Powers. The most advanced of the lesser states, on the other hand, those of the west and north, were to be left for nearly half a century to develop unobtrusively and in peace. But this could never have been guessed from the situation in 1870. Spain, for instance, had provided the immediate pretext for the Franco-Prussian War, because France saw a threat to her security in the proposal that a scion of the Prussian royal family should ascend its throne, left vacant by the expulsion of the scandalous Queen Isabella. After the abandonment of the Hohenzollern candidature the place was filled by an Italian princeling, Amadeus of Savoy, whose accession was followed within two years by the establishment of a republic, which again within two years was followed by the restoration of the Bourbon dynasty in the person of Isabella's son, Alfonso XII. But neither in Spain nor in Portugal, where the position of the royal house was less obviously insecure, was there any further interference from outside, except as regards their colonial empires, relics of an earlier age of expansion, which newer Great Powers grudged to their traditional owners. In each portion of the peninsula power was shared between the Court, the grandees, the generals, and the leaders of the Catholic Church, who between them controlled the Parliament and the electorate without difficulty.

Effects of the War of 1870 in Belgium and Denmark

The war had also impinged upon the fortunes of Belgium and of Denmark. Although Belgium had a model constitution and a prudent monarchy, the newness and artificiality of the Kingdom made its survival uncertain. Just after the outbreak of hostilities Bismarck published evidence which seemed to show that Napoleon III had contemplated annexing it to France; but Britain, which could not afford to see either France or Prussia in possession of Antwerp, made a treaty with each belligerent, to side against whichever of them should violate Belgian neutrality, which accordingly remained

unviolated until 1914. The independence and integrity of
Belgium had in any case been guaranteed by the Powers in
1839. Denmark was less fortunate. Having lost Schleswig-
Holstein to Prussia and Austria by the war of 1864, she now
saw in the triumph of Prussia the disappearance of her last
chance of securing at least some rectification of the frontier.
But even for dismembered Denmark the most important fact
was that she was now to enjoy two generations of undisturbed
peace, fraught with political and economic progress: so also
for Belgium's neighbour, Holland, with her rich colonial
empire, and for Denmark's Scandinavian kinsmen in Sweden-
Norway, then two separately governed kingdoms under a
single crown. All five countries were constitutional monarchies,
having a considerable middle class based on trade, and because
of that middle class having a parliamentary system which was
expressive of the articulate public opinion of the country and
controlled its laws. The franchise was rather narrower than
in England and the Cabinet less directly responsible to the
more popular chamber of the legislature: but the important
thing is that these countries—to which we may add the
Swiss republic, then just beginning to attract the attention of
mountain climbers and tourists—unlike Iberia and the
Balkans, had each of them a constitution which was not a
sham and a standard of living for the masses which was not
wholly dissimilar to that of France or Germany.

The Ideas of the 'Seventies

With the exception of the more mountainous inland districts,
all western and north-western Europe was by 1870 subject in
varying degrees to the influence of the great industrial changes
—the development of steam-power, the factory system, and the
increased dependence on iron and steel—which had become
conspicuous in north-east France and in Belgium soon
after the end of the Napoleonic Wars and had spread
between 1850 and 1860 to the coal-bearing districts of
Germany. These changes will be considered in the next
chapter.

Closely interrelated with the political and economic changes
of the nineteenth century were the social and intellectual
movements which necessarily accompanied them. We are
still close enough in time to the Europe of 1870 to have direct

personal links.[1] Yet so fast has been the movement of events,
so great the changes since, that already it is difficult for us to
form a clear impression of the life of the 'seventies, what
people did, what interested them, how they lived and thought.
It was a great period not only in the development of states
but also in the intellectual and artistic life of peoples. A
universal body of thought, the property of all civilised nations,
was fast growing up. Scientific thought especially was
becoming international. This was partly due to the increased
facilities for communication, and partly to the growth of
two marked tendencies in method. Science had established
a mathematical method, with exact ways of counting, measur-
ing and calculating; philosophy, theology and history were
themselves becoming scientific with the development of a
scientific method of logical, philological and historical criticism.
With the growing command over nature which science brought
came an optimism as to the future and a belief in the progress
of man which were characteristic of a period of unparalleled
material expansion.

In 1870 America was still undeveloped, and the cult of the
large was in its infancy. But the nineteenth century was
already an age of the large, in western Europe, both in
material things already achieved and also in man's hopes of
achieving still more in the future. The nineteenth century was
an age of materialism; but it was also an age of idealism, in
its faith in human progress and in its liberalism. The period
has been called not unjustly the age of 'the liberal experiment';
in 1870 liberalism in the sense of constitutional monarchy and
representative parliaments was established in western Europe.
Although it was to develop much further in Great Britain and
western Europe generally, it received a check in Germany in
1871 indicative of Germany's future development along
autocratic, and later totalitarian, lines.

Liberalism was limited to western Europe and the New
World; it was kept in check by Germany, Austria-Hungary,
Russia and the Ottoman Empire. In the intellectual and
spiritual sphere it was opposed by the Papacy, the great

[1] In 1937 one of the authors was present, at the Petersberg on the Rhine,
at the review by Field-Marshal von Mackensen of the surviving veterans of 1864,
66 and 70. Von Mackensen himself had fought in 1870. It was difficult to
believe that these venerable, white-haired men who reminisced in gentle tones
about Bismarck and Napoleon III had actually fought at Sadowa and Sedan.

remaining pillar of European conservatism. The Pope stood
out against the modernising tendencies of the age.[1]

Laissez-faire individualism and free trade had been worked
into a body of principles by the great British economists of
the early nineteenth century; they had been given an ethical
association in Bentham's 'the greatest happiness of the greatest
number' and a political philosophy in John Stuart Mill's
Liberty and *Representative Government*. J. S. Mill lived until
1873 and forms a link with the 'seventies. But already a
reaction had been provoked. Ruskin and Carlyle had both
attacked *laissez-faire*; the German Jew, Karl Marx, living in
London and working in the British Museum library, was
producing a new interpretation of economics and history in
terms of social class which was to become the gospel of revolutionary socialism on the Continent.[2]

Another current of intellectual change was started by the
work of Darwin in biology. The *Descent of Man* appeared
in 1871 (his *Origin of Species by Means of Natural Selection* had
come out in 1859). A new interpretation was given to the
human story; the theory of evolution began to take the place
of belief in a creation. And the evolutionary theory was
seized on by economic and philosophic writers to support the
ideas of individualism. Most influential was Herbert Spencer;
he had a following all over Europe. He was typical of
the changing character of this age; he was a mining engineer,
forthright and blunt, radical and agnostic, and caring nothing
for the older education of Latin and Greek. He was progressive, scientific, modern; he both reflected and himself directed
the tendencies of his time. He was optimistic in that he saw
human history as progress, as social evolution; human society,
previously despotic and military, was passing, he thought, into
an industrial period of democracy and reason.

A Great Era in the Arts

Many of the great figures of the intellectual and literary
life of the century were at the height of their powers in 1870:
Renan, Flaubert, Zola in France; Wagner, Nietzsche in
Germany; Ibsen in Norway; Dostoievski, Tolstoi in Russia.
Manet, chief of the French Impressionist painters, closed his
studio to serve in the national guard during the siege of Paris.

[1] See p. 171.   [2] See also pp. 183 and 222.

The German novelist and critic, Thomas Mann, speaking in the University of Munich just after Hitler came to power, looked back nostalgically to the 'seventies and 'eighties: 'The enchanted garden of French impressionistic painting, the English, French and Russian novel, German science, German music—no, it was not such a bad age; in fact, it was a perfect forest of giants.' The civilisation of the late nineteenth century to which Mann looked back was a bourgeois one; it gave great opportunities and expanding possibilities to the new middle classes. They regarded machinery as a means of making a better and a higher life possible for an ever-increasing number of people. Democracy together with industry would be the means of winning this higher life of culture and philosophy. But the bourgeois ideal declined. Mann complained in 1937 that these bourgeois ideas had come to be regarded, under the pressure of communist and fascist totalitarianism, as 'idealistic rubbish from the nineteenth century.'

The Concert of Europe and the Preservation of Peace

There remains one more way in which the Franco-Prussian War was a dividing-line, though it could not have been apparent at the time. It was the fifth considerable European war in less than two decades, but was to be followed by four and a half decades of uninterrupted European peace, to which the only exception was the wars arising out of the decline of Turkey; and Turkey was generally regarded as an excrescence upon the body politic, non-European and unprogressive, and not to be controlled even by the best of political machinery, though the Concert of Europe, to whose protection Turkey had been nominally admitted in 1856, was in fact almost continuously occupied by Turkish affairs. From 1871 onwards it was generally accepted that the five Great Powers, to which Italy made a feeble sixth, had an interest both in the avoidance of war and in the preservation of the existing balance of power. Therefore, whenever any change affected international relations, they made a common effort to restrict the area of change, to substitute diplomacy (and intrigue) for open clashes of rivalry, and to compensate a Great Power, often by indirect means, when its prestige suffered through the gains of another. The method was rough and ready, but for a time it worked—forty-three and a half years was the longest period of peace European soil had known since the fall of the Roman Empire. Our knowledge of what happened in the end, when the rival alliances forming within the Concert precipitated the catastrophe of 1914, does not render altogether valueless the system which staved off catastrophe for so long.

What kind of a thing was this Concert of Europe? It is in fact something quite difficult to define, and it is remarkable that it worked so effectively over so long a period. The expression 'Concert of Europe' is used by different writers to apply to different periods during the nineteenth century.[1] There had been indeed, on many occasions an attempt at concerted action. The Congress of Vienna is an example of the Concert at work; it was followed by a series of international congresses. In the period 1848-70 the ideas of nationalism and constitutional government led to revolutions and wars; international negotiation played a smaller part. But by 1870 the nationalist movements in Italy and Germany had achieved success. The wars had attained their immediate objects. It was now possible to use the method of international discussion and compromise to settle matters important, but not of vital importance, to the Great Powers. Thus, in the period after 1870, it was again possible to speak of the Concert of Europe. It was possible because, as Gladstone put it in a speech of 1879, 'Common action means common objects; and the only objects for which you can unite together the Powers of Europe are objects connected with the common good of them all.' The great objects, about which disagreement was fundamental, had been settled for the time being by war. The only really dissatisfied Power, France, was powerless. The remaining Great Powers were ready to compromise. Thus Gladstone could think that he was indeed seeking 'to develop and mature the action of a common, or public, or European opinion, as the best standing bulwark against wrong.' To this he had referred in a dispatch of 1869. Again, in the speech of 1879 he defines as a sound principle of foreign policy—'to strive to cultivate and maintain, ay, to the very

[1] H. G. Schenk, *The Aftermath of the Napoleonic Wars—The Concert of Europe*, uses the term of the period after the fall of Napoleon. R. B. Mowat, *The Concert of Europe*, deals with the period 1870-1914. J. A. Spender, *Fifty Years of Europe*, studies the same period without using the term Concert of Europe.

uttermost, what is called the Concert of Europe; to keep the
Powers of Europe in union together.'

This Concert of Europe was not an organised and clearly
defined system. It rested upon a certain will of sovereigns and
heads of governments to maintain peace and so prevent an
upset by war of the prevailing balance of power, an upset
which might well have been dangerous to themselves. The
Concert showed itself in the normal and frequent international contacts through ambassadors; it took tangible form
in the various international conferences and congresses, such
as the great gathering at Berlin in 1878.[1]

Yet Bismarck had no real belief in Europe and the Concert.
He wrote on the margin of a dispatch from the Russian
Chancellor, Prince Gortchakoff, the note: 'Anyone who speaks
of Europe is mistaken,' with the ironic comments, 'Geographical notion' and 'Who is Europe?' And again Bismarck
laid it down categorically that 'it is necessary for us earnestly
to hold far from us this charlatanism with regard to Europe'
(*Spiegelfechterei mit dem Europäertum*). 'Nothing but our own
interests' was the German guide to foreign policy, as summed
up by one of Bismarck's colleagues at the German Foreign
Office.

Once Bismarck had achieved his object of the unification
of Germany by the defeat of France he was haunted by the
fear of a war of revenge. To protect Germany he built up
a series of alliances—the *Dreikaiserbund* and later the Triple
Alliance—and these in turn led to the formation of counter-
alliances. Thus Europe became an armed camp, and the
period 1870–1914 is often called, and rightly, the period of
the Armed Peace, characterised by the growth of armaments,
mutual distrust, and recurrent international crises. But during
these years peace was at least maintained, and for this the Concert
of Europe, such as it was, proved in a rough and ready way
effective. What was not generally realised was the dependence
of the Concert for its success upon three special factors—the
improvement in agricultural, and especially in industrial
techniques, which made for a general rise in the standard of
living; the safety-valve of emigration (about 45,000,000
dissatisfied Europeans entered the United States between 1815
and 1914); and the existence of two huge land masses, darkest

[1] See p. 67.

Africa and the declining Chinese Empire, where the same
amount of effort would produce far richer rewards for European
capital than in the border-lands of Europe itself.

SUGGESTIONS FOR FURTHER READING

Encyclopædia Britannica (14th edition), article on *Europe: History* by Charles
Seignobos, with cross-references to other articles.

W. L. Langer: *European Alliances and Alignments 1871–1890*, c. 1.

R. Albrecht-Carrié: *Diplomatic History of Europe since the Congress of Vienna*,
c. 5.

C. J. H. Hayes: *A Generation of Materialism*, cc. 1 and 2.

CHAPTER 2

THE ECONOMIC BASIS

The Economic Ascendancy of Germany

THE campaigns of the Franco-Prussian War, which were of decisive significance in the political development of France and Germany, were also of significance in the economic sense, for they indicated a change in the relative economic power of those two states. The events of 1870 followed by the formation of the new German Empire at the beginning of 1871 made Germany the pre-eminent country in continental Europe. It was a political pre-eminence founded on a solid basis of economic strength. The steady growth of German industry was the necessary economic support of Prussian military power and Prussian political ambition. 'The German Empire has been built more truly on coal and iron than on blood and iron.' The words of Britain's leading economist, Lord Keynes, written in 1919, were more than a clever parody of Bismarck; they expressed a real economic truth. The year 1870 revealed the economic strength of the new Germany, a strength which was to increase rapidly and vastly after 1870 and to enable the German Empire on two occasions to pit itself against the world. The rise of Germany to a position of economic dominance in Europe was accompanied by the relative decline of France. It was not that France had retrogressed: she had in fact made a great material advance. A network of railways had been built, and during the Second Empire a considerable industrial and commercial expansion had taken place. But German industrial expansion was greater still. The year 1870 appears as a year of division between the old Europe of France and the new Europe of Germany. In 1870 events made it clear that Germany had already surpassed France; the following decades were to see Germany greatly increase her lead, and far out-distance France in population, industrial production and technical skill.

Characteristics of the New Era

The German Empire was founded on coal and iron, but the year 1870 may well be regarded as opening for the world the age of steel. For the production of cheap steel was a further development of the growing iron industry. Iron is perhaps the most useful metal known to man, and simple iron-smelting is a human art of great antiquity. The process consists of heating the iron ore (iron oxide) until the iron runs off, leaving behind the impurities of the ore. Smelting produced pig or cast iron, which has a high carbon content and is hard and brittle; by a refining process, soft or malleable iron was produced. Neither this wrought iron nor the cast iron had the strength of steel. Steel—which is almost pure wrought iron to which a limited quantity of carbon has been added—could only be made by a difficult and expensive process. The next step was to be cheap steel. In 1856 Sir Henry Bessemer found that a cold blast of air could be introduced at the bottom of the smelting furnace to cause combustion so intense as to burn out the carbon present. To the residue of wrought iron the necessary determined amount of carbon could then be added to produce steel. This process was improved and extended. If the iron ore contained phosphorus, however, the system did not work well. But in 1878 this difficulty was overcome by Thomas and Gilchrist, who found that if the furnace were lined with magnesium limestone, the phosphorus was turned into waste which could be run off as slag. Another steel-producing process—the open-hearth—was developed in the 'sixties by Siemens (a British subject of German birth) and the Frenchmen Emile and Pierre Martin. Molten iron was poured into a shallow pan and a mixture of gas and air played upon it.

The production of steel on a larger scale was made possible by these technical developments, and the stronger and longer-lasting steel steadily took the place of iron. Steel hulls and more effective engines were now built for ships; steel rails began to replace iron in the 'seventies and gave the railway track a longer life. The importance of steel in the growth of European industry after 1870 is shown by the fact that its production between 1870 and 1875 more than doubled in Germany and in Great Britain, and between 1875 and 1880 nearly doubled again; in France, though output was less than in Germany, it trebled during the years from 1870 to 1875, and made a further substantial, though smaller, increase from 1875 to 1880.

The improvements in the means of transport which the use of steel made possible brought about further great increases in world trade, and, most important of all, the opening in 1869 of the transcontinental railway through America led within a few years to the bulk export of corn from the Middle West to Europe. The result was a change in European fiscal policies. Earlier in the century industrialism had been accompanied by a free trade movement. It was supported by the leading economists (except List in Germany), and it had led to the *Zollverein* (Customs union) between the German states, the repeal of the Corn Laws in England, and the important Anglo-French commercial treaty of 1860. With the fall of its French sponsor, Napoleon III, the triumph of German nationalism and the increasing economic competition of distant parts of the world as transport became easy, safe and cheap, there began a long era of protection. Neither France nor Germany with their large conscript armies could allow their peasantry to be ruined. Protective duties against the import of foreign corn were therefore necessary; new industries also called for protection against English competition, for England was still by far the greatest industrial and commercial nation in the world. Thus Germany passed a tariff law in 1879, and France in 1881. Tariffs were still low when compared with tariffs later on, after 1900. But nearly all the European states turned to tariffs for protection against foreign competition in the decades following 1870. Britain, in her position of exceptional economic strength, clung to free trade. Her agriculture suffered, but the large industrial population welcomed cheap imported food.

The period from 1871 to 1914 was one of peace, and the development of industry was accompanied by the growth of the new middle class, or *bourgeoisie*. This period was the heyday of capitalism. The new industries were created and built up by the initiative, thrift and hard work of individuals taking advantage of the opportunities offered by the circumstances of the time. The joint stock company with limited liability offered a convenient means for investment, and in days of expanding economy brought large profits to those who had money available to invest. As industrial profits were large, there was surplus capital available—particularly in Great Britain—for investment abroad, and European capitalists financed the development of the more backward parts of the world, Russia, South America and the Far East. The development of capitalism encouraged imperialism. States whose subjects had opened up foreign markets and exported capital goods in the form of machinery, rails and locomotives and dock equipment, were tempted to seek for political control over the territories concerned whenever these were not already part of or controlled by some strong sovereign state. Thus there was a scramble for colonies, and this is described in a later chapter.

With peace in Europe and government probably more efficient and less corrupt than ever before, with increasing output and increasing world trade, there was a development of urban life and of a more civilised form of existence. General improvement made possible a great increase in population throughout Europe, and expansion everywhere and a rising standard of life in the industrial countries made for a very general optimism in western Europe.

Direct Economic Effects of the Franco-Prussian War Small

The economic effect of the Franco-Prussian War, as distinct from its significance in the economic development of Germany and France, was slight—although it did saddle France with a war indemnity and give to Germany the iron ores of Lorraine. But the war of 1870, as Sir John Clapham has said, 'was short and cannot be called devastating, when compared with those of any other century. It did not divert the course of civilisation; cripple or destroy great industries; completely ruin populous cities; throw wide stretches of land out of cultivation; or impose a fearful strain on the population of the combatants. The great wars of other centuries have done some or all of these things. Recovery from them has often been a matter not of years but of decades and generations.' The war of 1870, though bitter and though leaving behind it a legacy of hatred and suspicion, struck no crippling blow at the economy of either of the combatants. It did not hamper, but encouraged, the growth of heavy industry.

The Industrialisation of Europe a Long-Continuing Process

Increasing industrialisation was dividing the countries of Europe—as also the countries of the world—into two groups: the industrial countries and the non-industrial or agricultural countries. Industry was transforming the north and west of Europe and creating a new kind of material and social life, but the countries of south and east remained agricultural and their people, apart from the handicraft workers congregated mainly in the capitals, were predominantly peasants whose standard of life was poor and primitive. A new economic division was added to the old divisions of race, language and religion. Industry created a new working class of factory hands in western Europe, whose urban lives, corporate interests and familiarity with machinery and scientific processes separated them from the peasantry of the south and east. Indeed, the economic development of modern Europe can be summed up in one word—industrialisation.

The development of industry is perhaps the greatest change in history: it marks off clearly the last 150 years from the previous history of the world; it divides to-day the industrialised countries of north-western Europe and North America from the still materially backward countries of the Orient; it has made possible the high standard of life characteristic of western Europe and the New World. Machine production meant mass production, and mass production meant plenty where before there had been scarcity. Machine production and steam power gave man a new means of exploiting natural reserves. But industry developed most easily near the coal and iron; it did not therefore spring up equally everywhere. If it is almost impossible to exaggerate the importance of industry, it is also important to remember that, even to-day, large parts of Europe remain agricultural. Industry spread rapidly in the north and west after 1870, but it barely touched the Balkans, and was slow to develop in Russia. In fact, the desperate effort to industrialise a backward country has been the outstanding feature of Soviet policy. Great Britain was already advanced industrially by 1870; in the following decades industry developed still further in western Europe. But it was in Germany that it made its greatest advance. Though Germany surpassed France in 1870, that year was

C

the beginning rather than the end of the German Industrial Revolution. Germany was still medieval in character at the beginning of the nineteenth century, still divided into numerous kingdoms, principalities and free cities. By 1860 industry was beginning to develop, and a railway system was already in existence; by 1870 the movement of industry was gaining pace; in the 'seventies and 'eighties the new German Empire went through a process of industrialisation that transformed the backward, medieval country into the dominant industrial and political power in continental Europe.

The Economic Condition of France in 1870

Before the war of 1870 France was still regarded as the greatest Power in Europe. Her long supremacy had rested on the firm foundation of a fertile soil and hence, for those times, a large population, factors which were decisive economic advantages in days before industrialism. As a result of her long predominance—from Richelieu to Napoleon I—France was enabled to take advantage early of the economic changes going on in England. The geographical position of France favoured the spread of a knowledge of the new industrial machinery and methods. Proximity also favoured Belgium and Holland. At the end of the Napoleonic wars, contacts were resumed and industrial information spread. Thus it was not surprising that France was early affected—though never to the same degree—by the industrialisation which was already transforming Britain. By 1870 the growth of industry had advanced considerably in France.

The use of machinery in factories, the application of steam power to drive the machinery, the growth of an iron and steel industry, and the development of railways and steamships were all outstanding characteristics of the new industrial age. All had been developed to some extent in France by 1870, the period since 1848 having been one of rapid industrial expansion. Thus the figures for the production of coal and iron reveal an ever-increasing resort to steam power and the machine.

	FRENCH COAL PRODUCTION (IN METRIC TONS)	FRENCH IRON PRODUCTION (IN TONS)
1840	3,003,000	348,000
1850	4,433,000	405,000
1860	8,309,000	967,000
1870	13,179,000	1,178,000

Imports of raw materials grew rapidly; the import of raw cotton more than doubled, and that of wool increased six times. The import and export trade increased by 206 per cent. in the period between the beginning and end of the Second Empire.

To this great industrial and commercial development, the growth of the railway system contributed. In England the building of railways was one of the outstanding features of the Industrial Revolution; but rails, locomotives and rolling stock could be imported, and thus railways could be laid and used in countries in an early stage of industrialisation, or even in countries still predominantly agricultural in character. The great English contractor, Thomas Brassey, in the years 1840–70, had railway contracts in many European countries and also in South America, India and Australia. Railways were first built on the Continent long before 1870, before either France or Germany had advanced far in the process of industrialisation. In 1870 France had already a network of railways, which had been much more carefully planned than in England. Whereas the British railways were built by private enterprise, in France there was a larger measure of State control and both State and private enterprise shared in the work of creating railways. The country was divided into a number of areas each to be served by a trunk line radiating from Paris. By 1870 the great trunk lines were completed, and the Government was encouraging the companies to extend the network of branch lines by guaranteeing a minimum return on such lines.

France was still in 1870 the equal of the other western Powers in population. France had a population of 38,440,000 in 1870; the United States at that date had only a few thousands more, and Germany about 400,000 more. Britain (the United Kingdom) with 31,000,000 had considerably less.

France in 1870, therefore, was not economically a weak Power. She had made great industrial progress; she was probably stronger than she had ever been before. It is the relative position of France which had declined, as the war of 1870 demonstrated; a new and economically stronger Power was moving ahead. French industrial expansion continued steadily in the decades following 1870 but it was less rapid and less widespread than in Germany. This is illustrated by comparative figures for railway building and coal, iron and steel production.[1]

The Economic Condition of Germany

In Germany, the development of industry, slower at first than in France, became much more rapid and far-reaching after 1870. Germany in the 'seventies and 'eighties grew into the leading industrial nation on the Continent. The German talent for careful planning and painstaking organisation down to the last detail was bound to bring a large return in the fields of both war and industry. During the nineteenth century a combination of favourable factors enabled Germany to advance from the position of impotence which had been the lot of the German states at the end of the Middle Ages and during the first centuries of modern times. Germany had not lacked great men in the past, and the Hanseatic cities had developed a flourishing Baltic and inland trade; Germany during the Renaissance and Reformation had produced a breed of northern humanists and reformers with the vitality and courage of a Luther to stand out against the orthodox way of the past and break away from Rome. But the weakness of the central power of the Holy Roman Emperors (of Germany) had encouraged the fatal division of their territory into many states—almost 300 at the end of the Middle Ages. A still more fatal division was that caused among these states by the Reformation. The savage and destructive Thirty Years' War laid Germany waste and prevented its political and economic development. With the wars of Frederick the Great and of Napoleon, Germany again became a battlefield. It was not until the nineteenth century that circumstances developed favourable to the growth of a powerful Germany. The defeat of France in 1815, the gain of new territories by Prussia, enabling that state to emerge as the rival of Austria in competition for leadership in Germany, the sudden appearance of German inventive talent in almost every field, the opportunity which industrialism offered to her industries and disciplined people, and the ruthless determination and political sagacity of Bismarck resulting in the unification of Germany—all these contributed to the rise of Germany to a position of dominance in Europe.

[1] See p. 31.

The year 1870, as events demonstrated, was the turning point. Quietly, but effectively, German power had grown until, when mobilised for action, it was more than the equal of the more showy might of the French Empire, although that Empire had behind it the genuine and considerable industrial expansion which we have already observed. But the French showed themselves unable to make use of their advantages: their army, still generally considered to be the first in Europe, was not effectively used because of bad staff work, lack of an adequate plan of mobilisation and the breakdown of communications and the railway system; their fleet, the second in Europe, to which Prussia could have opposed practically nothing to counter an invasion of its coasts, could not be used to the full because the ships were not ready for war. Prussia, on the other hand, was fully prepared. Moltke had his plan ready in 1867, and it was kept revised in detail by the General Staff. The Germans had more detailed information on the French railway capacity than the French had themselves; the German troops had better maps of the district between the Rhine and Paris than were available to the French staffs. Thus in Germany careful planning went side by side with the growth of industrial resources. These two factors must both be considered when assessing the strength of a nation. It is one thing to possess economic strength. But this, so far as war is concerned, may well be potential rather than actual; it is another thing to be able to mobilise economic resources quickly and to use them to the full.

The foundations of German industrial power had been laid by 1870; the building of railways was making it possible for people to move from the countryside and concentrate in new industrial areas. As Treitschke put it, the railways first dragged Germany out of economic stagnation, and with the development of railways the expansion of coal-mining was very closely connected. Great Britain was in 1870 easily the first industrial nation, but by that time Germany had already surpassed France in railway-building and coal-production. The railways both burned coal and carried coal; their early development put Germany far ahead of France and Belgium as a producer of coal. Germany was mining in 1870 more than twice the amount of coal produced by France; the great coalfields in the Ruhr, the Roer, the Saar and in

Saxony were already opened up, although the Silesian coal-
field was not effectively worked until later in the 'seventies. In
addition to coal proper, Germany was producing lignite, or
brown coal—more easily mined than coal, but of lower heating
power.

Germany was also making rapid progress in the large-
scale smelting of iron; she had already surpassed France
by 1870. With the acquisition from defeated France of the
ores and ironworks of Lorraine, the development of the metal
industries in Germany proceeded at a great pace. Between
1871 and 1874, it is said that more iron-smelting and engineering businesses were set up in Prussia than in all the foregoing
years of the century put together. The development by 1878
in England of the Thomas-Gilchrist process of making steel
from iron ore of a high phosphorus content was particularly
favourable to Germany, where much of the ore was of
this kind. Solingen was already the Sheffield of Germany. A
vast variety of metallurgical industries grew up, and it was not
long before Germany became a considerable exporter of
iron, steel and machinery.

In other directions, too, Germany was moving ahead in
1870. Her mercantile marine was beginning, but the sailing
ship predominated, and as late as 1880 both France and
Spain had more steam tonnage than Germany. In the next
decades, however, the building of steel ships driven by steam
increased rapidly. The textile industries were growing fast,
and were changing over to machinery. The processes of
spinning wool by machinery were taken over from England
and France in the years 1866–70. In weaving hand labour
persisted much longer, and hand-loom weavers were still
common in the 'nineties. Few Germans wore cotton clothes
before 1850, but spinning and weaving of cotton grew as
time went on, although the introduction of machinery was
not widespread until after 1870. Cotton-weaving was still in
1871 predominantly a hand industry. Two other industries
must be mentioned which were in their infancy at this time,
but were destined to become of the first importance—the
chemical and the electrical. For the former, Germany was
favourably endowed by nature with deposits of rock salt and
of potash. Werner von Siemens invented the dynamo in
1867 and experimented with electric traction in 1879. The

development of both these industries depended upon the growth of scientific and technical knowledge. Germans during the nineteenth century gave especial attention to these branches of education, and leaders of French thought could only admit in 1871 that the better educated people had won.

European Industrial Output in and after 1870

At this point some comparative figures will best illustrate how, in 1870, Germany had already surpassed France and was moving forward as one of the leading industrial nations of the modern world.

RAILWAYS (KILOMETRES OF LINE OPEN FOR TRAFFIC)

	Germany	France	U.K.	Italy	Spain
1850	6,000	3,000	10,500	400	28
1870	19,500	17,500	24,500	6,000	5,500
1910	61,000	49,500	38,000	17,000	15,000

PRODUCTION OF COAL (IN METRIC TONS)

	Germany		France	U.K.
	Coal	Lignite (or Brown Coal)		
1871	29,400,000	8,500,000	13,300,000	118,000,000
1900	109,300,000	40,500,000	33,400,000	228,800,000

PRODUCTION OF PIG IRON AND STEEL (IN METRIC TONS)

	Germany		France		U.K.	
	Pig Iron	Steel	Pig Iron	Steel	Pig Iron	Steel
1865	882,000	97,000	989,000	41,000	4,892,000	225,000
1870	1,391,000	169,000	1,178,000	83,000	6,060,000	286,000
1875	2,029,000	370,000	1,416,000	258,000	6,469,000	723,000
1880	2,729,000	660,000	1,725,000	388,000	7,875,000	1,320,000
1905	10,987,000	10,066,000	3,077,000	2,110,000	9,746,000	5,983,000

These figures for railway construction and the production of coal, iron and steel, all of which are of basic importance to modern industrial development, illustrate the fact that in 1870 the United Kingdom was easily the leading industrial nation. But on the Continent Germany was already becoming the dominant Power. Modern Germany took over her industrial system from England, profited by English mistakes and learnt from English experience; in a few decades Germany was to become an industrial and commercial rival. Industry was also affecting a number of other countries and was developing rapidly in the United States. Of the European countries, Belgium in 1870 was mining slightly more coal than France, and was a not inconsiderable producer of iron and steel; Belgium, though small, had long since become highly industrialised, densely populated and prosperous. Holland, though possessing no ores and not mining coal until the end of the century, was able to gain economic advantage from the general advances of western Europe by reason of her highly developed agriculture, shipping, commerce and the development of her overseas colonies. Norway was also able to use her geographical position and mercantile marine to good advantage in the general expansion of world trade. Austria-Hungary, Sweden and Italy (mainly the north) were also able to industrialise to a certain extent. The following table gives some impression of the location of industry in Europe in the decades subsequent to 1870.

ANNUAL CONSUMPTION OF PIG IRON (IN POUNDS PER CAPITA)

					1866	1900
U.K. .	.	.	.	.	110·0	292·0
U.S.A.	.	.	.	.	110·0	351·3
Germany	.	.	.	.	41·8	289·7
France	.	.	.	.	58·3	152·4
Austria-Hungary		.	.	20·9	68·2
Belgium	.	.	.	.	71·5	205·9
Sweden	.	.	.	.	57·2 (1864)	127·6
Italy .	.	.	.	.	17·6	39·8
Russia	.	.	.	.	8·8	56·9

Russian industrialisation was late, as might be expected from her geographical position and backwardness. With French and Belgian capital, railway building commenced in 1868; it was not until the last decade of the century that industrialisation really set in. There followed a big expansion in the production of oil, pig iron, coal and cotton manufactures.

Agriculture and the Agrarian Worker

The industrial changes in modern Europe were accompanied by considerable changes in agriculture. We are inclined to contrast industry and agriculture in our minds; we think of the Middle Ages as a period when society depended upon agricultural production and of the nineteenth and twentieth centuries as a period of industry. This is a justifiable distinction, but we must always remember that the distinction is a relative one. Human society has always depended upon agriculture, and in all the great industrial states of to-day agriculture is still very important—in the U.S.A., Great Britain, Germany, Soviet Russia. What happened during the Industrial Revolution was not that agriculture was replaced by industry, even in the industrial countries. In fact, agriculture was also revolutionised and developed to feed the growing industrial population; many parts of Europe are still predominantly agricultural. But the development of industry was so novel, so rapid and so far-reaching in its social and political effects that it gave a new character to western Europe and made political power henceforth dependent upon industrial strength.

By 1870, improved methods of farming had found their way into France and Germany. Some of these had come long ago from the Low Countries into England. In the case of agricultural development, as in that of the transformation of industry, the pioneering efforts were made in Great Britain during the eighteenth century. The rotation of crops which avoided a fallow year by making use of winter roots, such as turnips, or special grasses like clover, improvements in animal breeding, new methods of draining and the application of machinery to farming, these together had made a revolution in agriculture. The German chemist, Liebig, in 1840 was already making possible the manufacture of artificial manures. France, Germany and Denmark all had agricultural research stations before 1870. The work of Pasteur on the diseases of silkworms, on anthrax in animals and on hydrophobia made him internationally famous. Between 1861 and 1881 there was a rapid growth in the number of research stations in Germany; most were attached to universities, though under close government control, and they studied the problems of soils, fertilisers, seeds and feeding-stuffs. Machinery was invented or brought from America, such as the reaper and later the combined reaper and binder.

Meanwhile, with the steady growth of population there was an increasing demand for food and hence a continuous urge to the farmer to extend his production. In the third quarter of the nineteenth century farming was a profitable business. British farming reached a high degree of excellence, and foreigners came over to visit farms in England. After 1874 a

decline in European farming began. The competition of the
New World was beginning to have effect. The coast-to-coast
railway across the United States was linked up in 1869; the
import of wheat from the great Middle West into Europe
lowered prices; in 1880 came the first cargo of frozen beef
from Australia. In the economic sphere, as formerly in the
political, a new world was coming in to redress the balance of
the old. The vastly increased agricultural production of the
world was bringing cheap food to the industrial workers of
Europe.

By 1870 not only had agriculture developed technically,
but the peasantry throughout Europe had been personally
emancipated. During the French Revolution feudalism had
disappeared in France, the estates had been broken up and
the peasants had become owners of the land. Thus to-day
France, in its countryside, is a nation of peasant proprietors.
This did not happen in England. During the eighteenth and
early nineteenth centuries the landlords had enclosed land,
taken in the commons wherever possible, and made the big
farm the main field of agricultural improvement. The small
man found himself forced out, became a labourer or went off
to work in the new factories. Emancipation of the peasantry
took place in Belgium and Western Germany during the
French wars under the influence of French ideas. But on the
great estates of the landlords or Junkers of eastern Prussia
serfdom, or something very like it, lingered on. Not until
about 1860 had it virtually disappeared—though East Prussia
remained a district of large estates. In Russia, too, for long
the most backward part of Europe, the year 1861 had seen an
Emancipation Edict—but the peasants, though they gained
their personal freedom, had to give up a part of their land
to the landlords and pay dues to the State. They were still
dissatisfied.

The Growth of Population

One of the most striking features of the industrialisation of
Europe has been the vast growth in population; almost as
striking is the concentration of population in large cities and
urban areas. The following approximate figures illustrate
the growth in population in the leading countries of
Europe:

	U.K.	France	Germany	Russia	Italy
1800	16,000,000	27,000,000	25,000,000	38,000,000	18,000,000
1870	31,000,000	38,000,000	39,000,000	78,000,000	27,000,000
1900	42,000,000	39,000,000	57,000,000	112,000,000	32,000,000

We observe that in the course of the nineteenth century the population has doubled itself in Britain and Germany; in France the growth has been much slower. In 1870 we see that this rapid growth was in full tide. It is one more factor in the full development of industrialism; more people mean more workers and more industrial production; more people also mean more soldiers. Population, like industry, is a factor in military power. And in this respect Russia must be mentioned. Because of her vast size her population, though sparse over most of the country, is large, and in spite of the late development of industry in Russia it has grown rapidly. Had she had anything comparable to the industry of Germany and the German ability to make use of it, Russia would have been the dominant power in the Europe of 1870. It must be pointed out, however, that the increase in Russian population is partly accounted for by additions to her territories; she expanded considerably during the nineteenth century. Nevertheless, Russian population growth was remarkable, and it is also to be noted that her birth-rate is calculated to have been higher than the European average of thirty-six per thousand. Between 1891 and 1900 the Russian rate is put as high as forty-nine. But population growth was general throughout Europe—the only country to show a fall between 1870 and 1900 being Ireland, from which emigration had been especially heavy. Industrial expansion, improved agriculture and the development of overseas territories all helped to provide for the increase in numbers. It is generally held that advances in sanitation and improved medical skill by reducing the death-rate led to population growth in the industrialised countries which enjoyed a rising standard of life. But population also grew in the agricultural and backward regions of Europe, even if not to the same extent. Between 1870 and 1900 there were very considerable increases in Bulgaria, Rumania, Serbia and Greece.

Emergence of 'Modern' Ideas and Institutions

A feature of population growth in the industrial countries was the concentration of the population into cities, towns and often groups of towns covering whole industrialised regions. Thus grew up during the nineteenth century a new class—the industrial working class. Karl Marx (1818–83) and the socialists who followed him divided society into two—the *bourgeoisie* or capitalist class and the proletariat or working class. By their analysis the socialists thought they discovered a constant war between these two classes which would lead to revolution, the taking over by the workers of the capitalist means of production (i.e. mines, railways, factories, etc.) and the setting up of a communist State. But the outcome has not proved so simple. The class structure is more complex than supposed—one class shades into another. Capitalism brought a rising standard of life and the State has provided social services to ease the worker's lot. In the provision of social services the new German Empire was to the fore: Bismarck declared that 'only the hungry labourer is dangerous.'

In 1870, many of the characteristic features of modern life were already in existence or fast coming into existence. Banks and commercial policy were developing to keep pace with the growth of industry and agriculture. Economic theory was already a subject of study, and economists analysed and attempted to explain the vast economic transformation going on around them. The struggle over tariff policy was on; the free trade of Cobdenite England and the internationally minded Napoleon III was soon to suffer a setback with the adoption of a protectionist policy in the new German Empire of Bismarck. *Laissez-faire* was beginning to come under criticism even in England; on the Continent in many countries the State was exercising a measure of control over economic development. The State was beginning also to organise national systems of education: in England the Education Act of 1870 provided for setting up rate-aided elementary schools; defeat in war stimulated France to create an elementary education 'obligatory, gratuitous and secular'; in Prussia the principle of compulsory school attendance had been accepted since the time of Frederick the Great. Socialism was already agitating the industrial workers of France and Germany, and trade unions were being organised to bargain with the employer on behalf of the worker. Transport and communication were improving fast. Cook's tours were already making Continental travel available to a growing middle class. Europe was being more and more covered by a network of railways and the greatest natural obstacles were being overcome. The Mont Cenis tunnel through the Alps was opened in 1871; in the following year work commenced on the St. Gotthard. Europe was also being linked up with the most distant parts of the world: the American cable was laid in 1866, the Suez Canal was opened in 1869, Bell demonstrated his telephone in 1876.

Urban life was becoming the lot of more and more of the people of western Europe. London was already an immense city; Paris had been replanned during the Second Empire; Berlin, in the decades after 1870, became one of the world's great capitals. Life, too, was becoming a little easier and more comfortable; a proper sewerage system was constructed in London in 1864; street lighting by gas had existed since early in the century, and electric lighting was to begin in the 'eighties. In 1871 Gladstone at a public ceremony referred to the great part played by underground railways in solving London's traffic problem; the first electric Tube was opened in 1890. The Paris Métro came towards the end of the century. Large shops, like the Bon Marché, had been set up in Paris; multiple stores were beginning. Tea-shops started in London with the 'ABC' before 1870, but Lyons does not come until 1894. Camille Pissaro was painting in France in 1870, and in his picture of the 'Boulevard des Italiens: Effet de Nuit' he gives also an effect of the busy movement and striking brilliance of a great city in the new age of industry. The other side of the story is told by Van Gogh, who in his 'Sketch at Cuesmes' shows the miners returning from work with drawn faces and bent backs against the squalid drabness of a mining town.

All this is the result of the development of industry. By 1870 industry was becoming fast the dominant characteristic of western and north-western Europe. South and eastern Europe—especially the Balkans and Russia—were still incredibly primitive. In the Middle Ages peasant workers everywhere were not dissimilar in their kind of life. By 1870 the Albanian

or Serb peasant, for example, had been left behind by the
new industrial workers of the west. Industry brought power;
industry brought a rising standard of life; industry led to the
development of a society and a kind of life in western Europe
and the New World unknown before in history.

Suggestions for Further Reading

Sir John Clapham: *Economic Development of France and Germany, 1815–1914*, cc. 8–13.

L. C. A. Knowles: *Economic Development in the Nineteenth Century*, Part I, cc. 1 and 2; Part III, cc. 1–3.

W. H. Dawson: *Evolution of Modern Germany*, c. 3.

Bertrand (Lord) Russell: *Freedom and Organisation, 1814–1914*, c. 30.

W. Bowden, M. Karpovich, and A. P. Usher: *Economic History of Europe since 1750*, c. 24.

New Cambridge Modern History, Vol. XI, c. 2 (by C. H. Wilson) and c. 3 (by T. I. Williams).

CHAPTER 3

THE NEW GERMAN EMPIRE AND FRENCH REPUBLIC

End of the Franco-Prussian War

THE early months of 1871 saw the laying of new foundations both in victorious Germany and in vanquished France. An armistice was signed on January 28, by which date all Gambetta's efforts to relieve the siege of Paris were seen to have failed, and the last French army, that which was to have saved heroic Belfort, was being driven over the frontier into Switzerland. Ten days earlier, in the splendid and significant setting of Louis XIV's Hall of Mirrors at Versailles, the new German Empire had been proclaimed—the empire which was to dominate European history until the dethronement of its third Emperor, Kaiser William II, in November, 1918. The Third French Republic, which was to have twenty years' longer life, seemed a much flimsier structure—in January, 1871, it consisted of no more than a revolutionary Government of National Defence, approved in the previous November by plebiscite in Paris only. Indeed, the German Emperor, by the conclusion of the armistice with the French republican government, decided indirectly the political future of France. He renounced any restoration of Napoleon III or his dynasty and made possible the preparation of a definite republic in France. The first object of the armistice was to enable elections to be held for a new National Assembly. This Bordeaux Assembly, under the guidance of the elder statesman, Thiers, who had been Prime Minister in the days of the Orleans Monarchy (1830–48), accepted the inevitable in the shape of the peace terms Germany was in a position to impose (March 1), and two months later these terms were converted into the formal Peace of Frankfort.

The main feature of the settlement was the cession of Alsace-Lorraine by France to the new German Empire. This cession was important in several ways: militarily, because it gave south Germany security in peace and advantage in

war through possessing the line of the Vosges mountains and
the fortresses of Strassburg and Metz; economically, because
of the iron ores of Lorraine (and of the nominally independent
Duchy of Luxemburg, which was brought more closely within
the orbit of Germany when Lorraine changed hands); and
politically, because France neither forgave nor forgot the loss
of these territories, which had not indeed always formed an
integral part of France, but were claimed as French on the
grounds of language and culture. Bismarck, a firm believer
in the expediency of moderation, would have been willing
to forego the city of Metz, whose sympathies were overwhelmingly French, but the soldiers insisted on its retention; and the
third great fortress of south-eastern France, Belfort, was only
saved for France by the cession of an additional strip of
territory in the Thionville district of Lorraine and consent to
a triumphal entry of the German troops into surrendered
Paris. France was also compelled to promise to pay
£200,000,000 as a war indemnity (reduced from £240,000,000
by the efforts of Thiers), a German garrison to be maintained
in the country at French expense pending discharge of the
debt. The whole sum was raised as a Government loan with
such rapidity that the last German soldiers left French soil in
September, 1873. Contemporaries noted this chiefly as
striking evidence of the economic stability of France and of
the relatively small havoc wrought by the campaign; but
later generations can see that the easy exaction of her war
costs by Germany confirmed the deadly teaching of the
Danish and Austrian wars of 1864 and 1866—that war can
be a paying proposition for the efficient aggressor.

Revolt of the Paris Commune

Meanwhile, the first steps had already been taken which
were to shape the course of political life under the new régime
in France. The Bordeaux Assembly, whose mandate from
the electors was for the task of peace-making only, had nevertheless set up a new provisional government under Thiers
(Pact of Bordeaux, February 16) and, once the peace prelimin-
aries had been settled, transferred its sessions to the historic
Palace of Versailles with the intention of making a new
constitution. Its membership included as many as 400 mon-
archists and 30 Bonapartists against 200 republicans: in other

words, it was more representative of property and the conservative peasantry than of the industrial masses. Against this Paris struck in the historic revolt of the Commune, which was touched off on March 18, 1871, when the Government sent from Versailles to remove some guns from the Butte (or hill) on Montmartre and the people both resisted the order and murdered the Government's emissaries in defiance of the youthful Mayor of Montmartre, the little-known Radical physician Clemenceau. For nearly two months Paris was in the hands of the Communards, so called because their main demand was for the absolute autonomy of the commune— that is to say, they claimed the widest powers of local self-government for all areas and especially for the great cities, such as their own and Lyons and Marseilles (where similar outbreaks occurred, though on a smaller scale and of a much shorter duration).

Behind the formal constitutional claim, which derived its inspiration from the first phase of the original Revolution of 1789, lay a great variety of motives for discontent, ranging from indignation at the loss of the war, through feelings outraged at the triumphant German entry into the capital (which had taken place on March 1), to the conviction that heroic Paris had been betrayed by unheroic provincials in the war, and that the unemployment and financial hardships of the peace revealed a second betrayal of honest Paris workers by dishonest Paris capitalists in league with the Assembly at Versailles. During the war 'capitalist' had been identified in the minds of the people with 'capitulator,' and now the groupings in the Assembly showed that property was the enemy of republicanism. These facts enabled a small number of leaders, mostly foreigners, who had advanced socialist views, to give the rising the semblance of a proletarian communist revolt, which it in fact was not. Its 'communist' measures went no further than the re-starting on a co-operative basis of factories which had been abandoned by their owners.

The events of the Commune are less important than its consequences. After the episode at the Butte of Montmartre Thiers withdrew his troops from Paris, leaving it militarily in the hands of the National Guard, the Home Guard which had been raised to fight the Germans and now refused to recognise his authority—authority which had been used to

D

stop their pay.   Politically, power rested with the Commune
or municipal council, for which new elections were held a
fortnight after Thiers' withdrawal, and with a Central Committee representing the National Guard, an uneasy combination
which it taxed the skill of even Delescluze, a veteran of
two earlier revolutions and the outstanding figure in the
Commune, to keep in working order.   In any case, amateur
soldiers had no chance against regulars brought from all
parts of France and against the artillery with which MacMahon
prepared their re-entry into the city.   The western suburbs
were entered on May 21.   The streets were blocked by barri-
cades and fired buildings (including the historic Palace of the
Tuileries), but within a week the troops had fought their way
through to the eastern outskirts in a hand-to-hand conflict,
which was made all the more savage by the action of the
insurgents in killing the Archbishop of Paris and other hostages
in retaliation for the maltreatment of their men when taken
prisoner.   But after May 28 there were no more hostages and
no more Commune, and there followed a long period of
judicial reprisals.   Some 20,000 persons had lost their lives
in street-fighting and by summary court-martial; another
13,000 were convicted subsequently—the courts-martial were
in session for five years—of whom about half were transported
and 270 condemned to death.   If we include those who fled
and the dependants of the victims, it seems likely that the
working population of Paris was reduced by about 100,000
souls at a date when its total inhabitants numbered 1,800,000.

Abroad, the main effect of the Commune was to lower still
further the damaged prestige of a defeated country—it was
viewed as an outburst of primitive savagery equally shocking
to the respectable classes everywhere.   Only a few small
groups of working-class leaders saw it through the eyes of
Karl Marx, watching and writing from exile in London, as
an instructive example of revolutionary technique, the establishment for a first brief period of that dictatorship of the proletariat
of which the world was to hear more in 1917.   At home, the
immediate effect, apart from the economic loss, which French
thrift and enterprise quickly made up, was to paralyse the
working-class movement.   It was nine years before the
Communards were amnestied, and a much longer period
before the last leader had completed his term of transportation

and drifted back to France—and there were many leaders who never returned. More permanent was the rift between parties and classes, for the workers never forgot the cruelty of the 'men of Versailles' and the propertied classes never forgot the suddenness, savagery, and success of the original revolt: these factors have not ceased to influence French political life to-day. Lastly, the events of the Commune had an immediate positive effect in tilting the balance in favour of a republican form of government, because it was under republican auspices that a movement which threatened private property had been so firmly repressed. Thus a monarchy no longer appeared to be indispensable for the defence of property; and, in any case, no one wished to provoke a revival of that movement which had based itself partly upon the suspicion that the men of Versailles intended to destroy the republic.

The Establishment of the Republic, 1871–9

The issue was, indeed, long in doubt. From August, 1871, the Assembly, having conferred new powers upon itself by the Rivet Law, sat as a constitution-making body, with Thiers, who had negotiated the peace, destroyed the Commune, and restored the national finances, using all his eloquence and experience to create a republic on the lines of the British Constitution but with an elected President in place of the King. He was duly promoted from his original position as Chief of the Executive Power to be President for the duration of the Assembly, but after nearly two years of inter-party intrigue the Royalists united to replace him by Marshal MacMahon. As an honest soldier, who had been wounded at Sedan and had commanded against the Commune, MacMahon was the right President to prepare the way for a monarchy; yet his term of office (May, 1873–January, 1879) actually saw the establishment of the Republic both in constitutional theory and in political practice. Of the three royalist claimants one, the Prince Imperial, heir to Napoleon III (who died in England in 1873), was a boy of seventeen; the second, the Count of Paris, grandson of Louis Philippe, represented the younger branch of the Bourbons; the third, the true legitimist heir to the throne of France, the Count of Chambord, was over 50, childless, unambitious, and uncompromising. He used his refusal to substitute the tricolour for the white flag of the Bourbons to symbolise his unwillingness to shed the strict principles of a legitimate and absolute monarchy, thus wrecking a scheme to unite Bourbon and Orleanist supporters through the adoption of the Orleanist Count of Paris as his heir. This intransigeance, combined with the eloquence of Gambetta, the great champion of republicanism after the fall of Thiers, and the tacit but weighty support given by Bismarck to the republican institutions, which he hoped would keep France permanently isolated and divided, led to the vital decision of January 30, 1875, when the Assembly resolved by a majority of one vote upon the final establishment of the executive office of 'President of the Republic.'

It remained for MacMahon to determine by a process of trial and error whether the presidential office was to be a strong one, such as might, in the hands of a less honourable holder than himself, still prepare the way for monarchy, or weak and innocuous. In 1876 the first elections under the new constitution produced results which were too democratic for the President's taste—a royalist Senate but a republican Chamber of Deputies. He therefore adjourned the Chamber, chose his own Prime Minister, ignored all protests, and held a new election the following year, in which he used his personal influence and his control over officials to manipulate the results. He failed completely to get his way in the elections or in the democratic Chamber whose meetings could no longer be postponed. By January, 1879, the Republicans had achieved a majority in the Senate as well, whereupon MacMahon resigned office. During his six years it had been settled that France should be not merely a republic, but a republic sharply distinguished from many others, and notably from the American model, by the weakness of the Presidency.

The French Constitution

The constitution of the Third Republic, which remained substantially the same until its betrayal by Marshal Pétain in 1940, differed from its shorter-lived predecessors in its piecemeal construction and incompleteness. There was no preliminary Declaration of the Rights of Man. The judicial system, the civil service, and the highly centralised plan of

local government, which left little real freedom of action even
to Departmental Councils, to say nothing of the 36,000
communes, remained very much as Napoleon I had left them.
No logical remedy was provided even for the obvious contingency of a deadlock between the two chambers of the
Legislature. In comparison with Britain the basis was more
democratic, as there was manhood suffrage at the age of
twenty. The Legislature was broadly speaking similar, the
Chamber of Deputies, elected at four-yearly intervals, having
the same functions as the House of Commons, and the Senate,
which shared the legislative power with the Chamber, having
the same conservative and restraining influence as our House
of Lords. The Senate was not, however, composed of
hereditary peers, but of persons elected for nine years by an
electoral college in each Department, composed of its Deputies,
Departmental and major district councils, and one representative of each minor district council or commune, however
small. One quarter of the senators were to be co-opted for
life, according to the original plan, but this provision was
dropped in 1884 by a democratic amendment to the constitution, though the senators continued in fact to exercise a highly
conservative influence.

The French Presidency proved to be nothing more than a
pale imitation of British constitutional monarchy. In one
respect the President's powers exceeded the King's, since he
did not merely nominate a Prime Minister in accordance
with the wishes of the Legislature, but himself presided at the
formal meetings of the Council of Ministers or Cabinet. But
the fact that he was elected for a seven-year period, his
election being the function of the National Assembly (the
name given to the two Houses when they sat together for this
purpose or to amend the Constitution) meant that he could
hardly ever accumulate the experience of a King; the custom
of electing a politician meant that the President could not
stand above the bickerings of parties. Royalists, who continued
to enjoy great social influence, viewed his office with open
contempt; and Republicans, fearing that a successful President
might aspire to dictatorship, with jealousy and suspicion.
In addition to all this, the President in effect lacked what is
by far the most important part of the royal prerogative,
namely, the power of dissolution. In legal theory he could

dissolve the Chamber of Deputies, given the concurrence of the Senate, but the circumstances of MacMahon's dissolution in 1877 caused the power to fall into immediate and complete disuse.

This partly explains the outstanding difference between French and British political history in the democratic era. The relationship between the Cabinet and the Legislature was in theory the same, but in France the Cabinets proved to be hopelessly unstable.   In the first forty years, for instance, there were fifty changes of government, though serious changes of policy were much less frequent.   This may have been due in part to the historical accident that France lacked two firmly rooted parties whose principles could be applied to each new political question as it arose; in part to the keen sense of logic which so often caused French parties to break up into splinter formations; and in part to central control of local affairs through the Departmental Prefect, which tempted French politicians to concentrate on putting individual schemes through parliament and influencing ministerial patronage so as to benefit constituents.   But the instability of French governments, each dependent on the support of a number of groups in the Chamber to maintain a majority, which was lost when one group almost lightheartedly changed sides, was primarily due to the fact that the Prime Minister could not appeal to the President for a general election as a means of punishing dissidents and perhaps recreating his majority.

Republican Politics and Boulangism

Thus the constitution was so framed as to accentuate the weakness which was almost bound in any case to mark the political life of a defeated France in a Europe where her triumphant enemy was the predominant power. As early as 1872 France introduced the Prussian system of conscription in place of the long-service recruitment of the Army on which Napoleon III had so unsuccessfully relied, and in 1889 the system became one of three years' compulsory service for all. The nation indeed never ceased to dream of the recovery of the lost provinces, but knew in its heart that it could never again tackle Germany alone. As for the prospect of allies, her weakness made France an unattractive partner, and

Bismarck used all his diplomatic skill to keep her isolated. Consolation and compensation—including a source of additional manpower for the French Army at which the rest of Europe looked very much askance—were therefore sought in the colonial field, where Bismarck encouraged French aspirations so as to separate her from any potential ally. Tunis was occupied in 1881, Madagascar began to be brought effectively under French control in 1883, and a series of military operations were conducted to develop the opening which Napoleon III had made for a French empire in Indo-China. But there was no great enthusiasm for imperialist expenditure in men or money, and in 1885 a minor defeat in the Far East (Lang-Son) was enough to overthrow the ministry and wreck the career of Jules Ferry, the outstanding French statesman of the period, author of a new educational system and the man who in the preceding year had brought France a step nearer to normality by restoring the trade unions. The President, Grévy (1879–87), was an elderly free-thinker who could be trusted to keep royalism at bay, and in his time the Catholic Church rather than the monarchy provided the rallying-point for the forces of conservatism—there was even a new cult of the Sacred Heart sedulously fostered as atonement for the impieties of the Commune. The first stone of the famous Parisian church of the Sacré-Cœur had been laid in 1875.

Against conservatism, the Republicans were disunited. They had lost their ablest leaders through the deaths of Thiers in 1877 and Gambetta in 1882, the latter having failed in spite of his reputation as patriot and republican to overcome the jealousies of lesser men, which had put an end to his Ministry of All the Talents earlier in the same year after sixty-six days in office. Gambetta bequeathed to his successors a strong group of Republican Opportunists, so called because their programme favoured reform 'when the time was opportune,' but they were never able to absorb the Extreme Left, which called for ever stronger measures against the Church, denounced the colonial policy, and opposed, often in a spirit of sheer faction, any change (such as election by departmental constituencies each returning a list of candidates, which was tried in 1885–90) if it was expected to increase the authority of the ministry of the day. Since 1876 the Extreme Left had been led by Clemenceau, a stronger and more ruthless politician than any of the Opportunists, whose aims may be deduced from his boast that in presidential elections he engineered the choice of the weakest candidate.

The main constructive achievement of the Opportunist ministries was Ferry's reorganisation of education, which he undertook for two reasons. Manhood suffrage could not function properly with illiterate voters: hence his provision of primary schools for all children between six and thirteen years of age. But as regards education at all levels, primary, secondary, and university, he had the further aim of attacking the Catholic Church as directly as he dared. A ban was imposed on most of the Catholic teaching Orders, and on the Jesuits in particular, closing their Houses and forbidding their members to teach in the public schools. While primary education was made free, compulsory, and—by English standards—highly efficient, Ferry also saw to secondary education. In the public Lycées which he set up education was of a standard to compare favourably with that of the schools still run by the Church, and included education for girls, of which the Church had previously had almost a monopoly. Finally, he gave new vigour to the universities, which greatly extended both the scope of their teaching and the numbers of their students, while Catholic colleges were deprived of university status. The institution of civil marriage and reintroduction of divorce into France may be mentioned as further examples of Ferry's indirect attacks upon the power of the Church.

The fall of Ferry in April, 1885, was followed by a period of crisis, in which the republic at one time seemed likely to founder. One cause was the emergence of a popular hero with boundless ambitions in the person of General Boulanger, lately military governor of Tunis and now Minister of War, a protégé of Clemenceau, and a hero inasmuch as he induced the mighty Bismarck to climb down about the seizure of a French agent named Schnaebele, who in April, 1887, had been decoyed across the frontier into Alsace. A few months later point was given to Boulanger's ambitions by the odium which the Presidency incurred, just after Grévy's re-election, when it was discovered that his son-in-law, Daniel Wilson, who resided with him at the Elysée Palace, was receiving bribes to arrange nominations to the Legion of Honour. Grévy was then replaced by Carnot, grandson of the Organiser of Victory, by no means the least successful of Presidents, though he had been run by Clemenceau as the weakest possible candidate. Boulanger demanded a dissolution of the Chamber and revision of the constitution by a specially elected constituent assembly, which might pave the way to a stronger presidential system or a dictatorship or a return to monarchy and might even bring with it, somehow, the glorious foreign policy which was the dream of Déroulède and his League of Patriots, forerunners of Fascism. Clemenceau, seeing that the very existence of the republic was at stake, drew back, but for a time Boulanger united every other element of discontent. At six provincial by-elections he headed the poll, and finally in January, 1889, Paris itself elected him with a majority of 66,000 over all other candidates combined. But there was nothing heroic behind the façade of this hero. When the government proceeded to alter the electoral law so as to stop multiple candidatures, and to impeach him before the Senate for treason, Boulanger fled to Brussels, where, after two years, he died. At a general election later in 1889 less than fifty Revisionists were returned to the Chamber. In 1889 also France was celebrating the great traditions of 1789, a fact which, combined with the fears of the peasantry that constitutional change might somehow precipitate war, assisted the Third Republic to complete its second decade in temporary calm.

The New Germany and the Old Prussia

The German Empire, as it developed between its proclamation at Versailles and the fall of Bismarck just twenty years later, stands in contrast to the French Republic as strength to weakness, a contrast which extends to their constitutions, though the historian may note that the French, unlike the German, system enabled the art of self-government to be learnt by process of trial and error. There was no scope for improvisation in the institutions which Bismarck had designed for the North German Confederation of 1867 and which he now applied with the full force of his constructive genius to the new Reich. The only limitations were the reluctance of his Emperor (who thought there was no higher office than that of King of Prussia), the need to show some regard for the sensitiveness of the three southern states, especially the ancient Bavarian monarchy, and the political urge to keep the support of the National Liberal party in the early stages, because of its voting strength throughout the empire. By 1873 the structure was complete—that of a federation with a single member predominant.

From 1871 until 1945 Prussia dominated Germany. Historically, unification had been achieved by the triumph of Prussian arms in 1866 and 1870. The liberal attempt at unification in 1848, when Germany had so nearly been united by the free will of her various peoples, had failed, although the way had been prepared by another, less spectacular triumph of Prussian organisation, the development of the Zollverein, in which rival states first learnt the advantages of co-operation. Practically, unification meant the leadership of a state which contained some two-thirds of the area and three-fifths of the population of the whole federation, its closest rival being Bavaria, with about a quarter of Prussia's area and a fifth of her population. Constitutionally, Prussia's position was secured in two ways. The King of Prussia, as hereditary German Emperor, controlled imperial civil administration through the Chancellor and the army through his separate Military Cabinet and the general staff. Prussia had sufficient voting power in the Federal Council to block any unwelcome constitutional amendment. And quite apart from the federal constitution there was always the fact that on many ordinary subjects, such as police, local government, education, and religion, the separate states alone had legislative power, which meant that Prussia, preponderant in size and wealth, would inevitably give the lead. This was especially important because the Prussian electoral law, a system of voting by classes, which dated from 1850, was heavily weighted in favour of property. Elections to the lower house of the Prussian Parliament (*Landtag*) were made by a special body of electors in each constituency, of whom one-third were chosen by the largest tax-payers whose assessments made up one-third of the direct taxes, a second third by the medium tax-payers whose assessments likewise made up one-third, and the remaining third by the great mass of small tax-payers, whom this ingenious device placed permanently in a minority. Accordingly, throughout the period of the Second Reich Left Wing parties made far slower progress in Prussian than in Imperial elections.

The Constitution of the Second Reich

As has already been indicated, the constitutional position of the German Emperor or Kaiser was a strong one. His office was to pass by inheritance with the Kingship of Prussia; his person was declared sacrosanct (a useful weapon against republican agitation); as War Lord he effectively controlled the armies of the states, which passed under his direct authority in time of war—and he had power to declare a 'defensive' war; and through his nomination of the Imperial Chancellor, who was responsible to no other person or body, he set the course of civil administration in a country where the administrative zeal of bureaucratic officials had an unusually wide influence on public life. In relation even to the legislature, he had a power of veto and could dissolve the Lower with the consent of the Upper House. But in the long run constitutional strength could not supply the want of personal strength. For twenty years the system worked smoothly under a veteran emperor who supplied prestige to the imperial office while delegating the effective executive power to Bismarck, whose political talents matched the scope of the Chancellorship as he wielded it. His position is said to have been the greatest that any subject had held under a European monarchy since the days of Richelieu. After 1890, however, the direct exercise of power by the Emperor William II and the decline in authority of the later Chancellors, who were weaker men in a weaker office, caused many people bitterly to regret the inferiority of the legislature.

The Federal Council or *Bundesrat*, which deliberated in secret, was the common organ of the federation for policy as well as law-making, having numerous standing committees, the best known, though perhaps the least effective, being a foreign affairs committee, the chairmanship of which was guaranteed to Bavaria as a solace to her pride. Each of the twenty-five states had at least one member among the fifty-eight composing the Council, but the members represented the governments which sent them, and all the votes for one state, which ranged up to a total of seventeen for Prussia, were cast as a single bloc on each occasion of voting. Besides the fact that fourteen negative votes were enough to stop any constitutional change, Prussia enjoyed the advantage that the

Chancellor of the Reich, who would usually be Prussian, was *ex officio* President of the Bundesrat. In constitutional theory the Bundesrat and Reichstag had equal legislative powers, all laws being required to pass both Houses, but as the former was also the policy-making body important measures were usually drafted by it and then sent down to the Reichstag. The Reichstag, elected for five-year periods by manhood suffrage exercised from the age of twenty-five, with secret ballot in single member constituencies of roughly equal proportions throughout the whole of Germany, seemed more than it was. By creating a representative chamber that was considerably more democratic than the British House of Commons of those days, Bismarck had, indeed, 'squared' the National Liberals. But he had not conceded full control of legislation. As regards the army, for instance, the constitution not only laid down the principle of recruitment by conscription but fixed originally its peace-time strength, and it required a bitter struggle before the Reichstag secured the right to review military expenditure once in seven years, when a special Budget known as a Septennate was presented. The same device of making long-term agreements so as to exclude the Reichstag from intervention was applied when the Chancellor negotiated treaties with foreign Powers. More important still, there was no concession of responsible government. The Chancellor was answerable to the Emperor alone, all other ministers to the Chancellor: thus the hostility of the Reichstag meant a hold-up in legislation and some financial difficulty for the Chancellor, since the Budget might not be voted, but never his overthrow. Moreover, a skilful Chancellor could often play off the Reichstag against the Prussian parliament and the generally conservative governments of the smaller states, the more readily as he was almost invariably Prussian Prime Minister himself and his principal subordinates would also hold office in the Prussian Cabinet as well as in the Imperial bureaucracy.

The last of the Imperial institutions to be established was the Supreme Court, with power to hear both civil and criminal appeals from all German states under their several legal codes, which were only gradually superseded by Imperial codes of law and Imperial statutes. The fact that the Supreme Court was located at Leipzig instead of Berlin, in defiance of

Bismarck's wishes, may serve as a reminder that, although Prussia and the revived empire were the two main factors that determined the course of events in Germany after 1871, the twenty-four smaller states kept their ancient constitutions (one of them still had legislation by mediæval estates), loyalties, and cultures. Munich, Dresden, and Stuttgart were still the capitals of three monarchies; and at the other end of the scale the Hanse cities of Hamburg, Bremen, and Lübeck retained something of the democratic civic traditions of their past. All this was helped by the fact that local government was a state, and not an imperial, concern; and Germany became renowned for her town planning and attention to working-class housing and public health.

Bismarck's Conflicts with National Minorities and the Catholics

The age of Bismarck was for Germany a tremendous age of growth, prosperity, and success, marred only by a trade depression in 1873 and by recurrent fears of war with Russia.[1] It was an age in which the empire became established because of the good things it had brought with it. Only three issues seriously disturbed the tranquillity of Bismarck's domestic policy, of which the first was a direct result of the way in which the empire had been built up by him—the discontent of the dispossessed minorities. From his war of 1864 he inherited as Imperial Chancellor the Danish question, the unrest in that area of North Schleswig which had been promised a plebiscite by the Treaty of Prague, to determine whether it should remain with the rest of Schleswig-Holstein, incorporated in Prussia, or should return to Denmark. The desire of North Schleswig to return to Denmark was not in serious doubt; but in 1879 Bismarck obtained Austria's consent to the abrogation of the Treaty of Prague, to which Denmark was not a party, and he adopted a policy of petty persecution to make North Schleswig give up its Danish sympathies. (The plebiscite in 1921 showed that he had failed.) Bismarck was more successful with the inheritance from the 1866 war, when Hanover had been absorbed in Prussia as a punishment for its support of the Austrian cause: he refused to make any concession to the Guelph party, which demanded the restoration of the King of Hanover, and in the early twentieth

[1] See c. 4.

century this cause was seen to die a natural death. From the war of 1870 came the major problem of Alsace-Lorraine with its population of 1,500,000. It was treated as an imperial territory under a Viceroy (*Statthalter*) appointed by the Emperor, and was given representation in the Reichstag, though not in the Bundesrat, as early as 1874. Bismarck aimed at conciliation by such measures as the revival of Strassburg university, but although Alsace at least was partly German-speaking, the only inroad that could be made into past loyalties was through the slow infiltration of German business interests. Fifteen representatives from Alsace-Lorraine joined the handful of Danes and Guelphs as a nucleus of opposition to the empire in the Reichstag, where they were joined by the Poles, irreconcilable victims of the eighteenth century partitions and the general European settlement which gave back Posen to Prussian rule in 1815. All in all the national minorities could muster nearly 10 per cent. of the Reichstag.

Bismarck's efforts at germanisation of the border lands were linked up, in the case of Poland, with a wider effort to germanise an element which in all parts of the empire stood out against the absolute claims of the new Reich to loyalty, namely, the Catholic Church, which among the Poles in particular had come to be the badge of their nationality. A pretext was given by the cleavage in the Church which resulted from the Decree of Papal Infallibility of 1870. A considerable group of German Catholic divines and scholars, headed by the historian, Dr. Döllinger, of Munich, resisted the decision of the Vatican Council, formed a contumacious group of Old Catholics, and gave the lay authorities a chance to intervene on their behalf against the ecclesiastical authorities of their Church. The Old Catholics proved in the long run to have a smaller following than had been expected, but Bismarck for seven years pursued an anti-Catholic policy designed to put the Papacy in its place. He believed that in an empire where Protestants outnumbered Catholics by two to one he could put down the claims to independence of a Church which was associated with Polish (and Alsatian) disloyalty. In so doing he would also strike at the Catholic Centre Party, the only political organisation that seriously threatened the power of Bismarck's alliance with the National Liberals. The

Kulturkampf or ideological struggle was therefore in a special sense the National Liberal programme. It began in July, 1871, with the suppression of the separate government department in Prussia for Catholic Church affairs and the recognition of Old Catholics as entitled to teach in Catholic schools, etc., in defiance of the unanimous protest of the Catholic bishops of Germany from their annual assembly at Fulda. In November the Reichstag endorsed Bismarck's policy for Germany as a whole by enacting the Kanzel paragraph, which provided as part of the new criminal code special penalties against politically inspired sermons, by making civil marriage compulsory, and by expelling the Jesuits and other Orders from the empire. In 1872 diplomatic relations with the Pope were severed.

However, the struggle was mainly fought out in Prussia, both because the imperial constitution reserved religious legislation to the separate states and because Prussia contained two key areas—the Polish provinces and the Catholic Rhineland, whose loyalty to Prussia was also uncertain. It was therefore the Prussian Minister of Education, the Liberal Falk, who took prime responsibility for the May Laws of 1873, 1874, and 1875, which tried to extend the authority of the state into the churches themselves as well as the church schools. Lay inspection of church schools had already been instituted: now there was to be control of Church discipline (such as excommunications), a German university course was to be required of all ordination candidates, seminaries for training priests were to be inspected, and all appointments in the Church were to be submitted for state approval. The result was the biggest failure in Bismarck's career. Out of 10,000 priests in Prussia only 30 submitted; forfeiture of salary and imprisonment made martyrs of bishops and priests alike; and the solidarity of Catholic lay opinion was shown by the growth of the Centre Party from fifty-eight to nearly a hundred strong at the Reichstag election of 1874. Bismarck made no admission of defeat, but negotiations were quickly opened when the more conciliatory Pope Leo XIII succeeded Pius IX in 1879, and in the course of the following decade most of the anti-Catholic laws were repealed or modified, though the Church never regained its former position of privilege under the Prussian constitution, and the empire did not give up the ban on Jesuits until 1917.

At the end of his life Bismarck justified the Kulturkampf
on the ground of its intimate relation with his Polish policy,
but the one was not allowed to drop with the other. The
Polish Archbishop Ledochowski, whose see was kept vacant
for twelve years, was the most prominent victim of the religious
conflict, and in Poland the institution of lay inspection of church
schools was followed up in 1874 by insistence on German as
the language of all instruction, including even religious
instruction given in primary schools, except where it could be
certified that only Polish was understood. In 1886 a German
was appointed Archbishop of Posen in Ledochowski's place,
and about the same time Bismarck inaugurated a new project
of colonising Polish lands with Germans. Some 35,000
Polish-speaking aliens, who had filtered in from Russian and
Austrian Poland, were expelled from the region of the lower
Vistula. This made some land vacant, and more was to be
freed by setting up a commission for colonisation to buy
Polish estates for German farmers with German wives.
Bismarck had fallen before it became apparent that competition
had been aroused and that Poles bought faster than Germans.
But as a final indication of the heaviness with which his hand
lay on the subject nationalities we may note that not until
1889 was Posen included in the general scheme of local self-
government established for the other Prussian provinces in
1872.

The 1879 Tariff a Turning-point:
Bismarck's Domestic Policy in Later Years

In most other respects the year 1879, when the Kulturkampf
began to decline, marks a turning-point in the domestic
history of the empire.   The alliance with the National Liberals
came to a sudden end, because the Chancellor had decided
to abandon the free trade policy towards which Germany had
moved fairly steadily under the Zollverein and which had
been crowned by the abolition of duties on iron as recently as
1873. The reasons for this momentous decision were only
partly economic. The trade crisis of 1873 had created alarm
about the future prospects of the iron industry; the inclusion
in the empire of Alsace-Lorraine, with its iron ores, increased
the attractiveness of a closed home market; and German
agriculture was worried by the loss of its export trade to

England (which was beginning to be flooded with American wheat) and by the competition of Austrian wheat and Russian rye on the home market. There was also a compelling constitutional motive: Bismarck wanted a steady and sufficient source of revenue for the Reich which, if it could not make do with Customs duties, had to ask for direct taxation in subsidies from the states, and this gave the states a claim to interfere with his policy on which the money was spent. But perhaps the most important factor was the spirit of nationalism. Neighbouring Powers, such as Russia, Austria-Hungary, and France, were all beginning to turn their backs on free trade in what they believed to be the pursuit of national self-sufficiency and strength, so it was natural that the new, self-confident Germany should follow their example—and by so doing make the trend decisive.

The new tariff, which was moderate, gave more protection at first to the agricultural interest (the Junkers of the big estates east of the Elbe, the substantial peasant proprietors of south and west Germany) than to the captains of industry; but the long-term political result was that the Chancellor now found his natural supporters among the conservatives. To these might be added, as time went on, a grouping of the Centre party (which, once the Kulturkampf was abandoned, tended to be a party of order) and some Right Wing Liberals who preferred a share of power to the dim prospect of a free trade revival. The original Junkers and the so-called 'Junkers of the Chimneys' provided the officer and managerial classes in an increasingly prosperous and powerful empire, so until 1916 relations between Chancellor and parties remained harmonious. In shaking off the National Liberals, Bismarck had shaken off the one party which never lost sight of the importance of constitutional evolution towards a system in which the Chancellor should be, not allied with, but responsible to, a party majority.

In making his breach with the Liberals Bismarck, who was a past master of the art of managing the gutter Press, arranged for their leaders to be denounced as Jews, which was perhaps the first use of anti-Semitism as a major weapon in a modern political campaign. But at the moment interest centred rather upon his employment of the anti-socialist cry. Two attacks had been made upon the Emperor's life by persons

E

who were not, but might credibly be represented as being, socialists, and after the first attack Liberal influence had been exerted in the Reichstag to prevent the passage of an anti-socialist law. The second attack was used by Bismarck to secure a patriotic vote against the Liberals as the men who had failed to defend their Emperor. Accordingly, the new phase in domestic politics was also marked by the passage of the Exceptional Law of 1878, outlawing the Social Democratic Party, which had won twelve seats in the Reichstag election the year before. Founded by Marx's disciple Liebknecht at the Eisenach Congress of 1869, it had become formidable through its absorption of the older German Workers' Association which had been formed on less dogmatic lines by Ferdinand Lassalle. The party itself, its meetings, and its propaganda were all now heavily proscribed, and agitators found themselves liable to be deported. This régime lasted until 1890; but the party continued to hold periodic congresses abroad, its newspapers were smuggled into Germany in large quantities, and its representatives in the Reichstag made full use of their official immunity to speak in the one place where the voice of socialism was not silenced. By 1890 the Social Democratic vote had trebled.

Thus Bismarck's repressive measures enjoyed little more success against the socialists in the long run than against the Catholics. More lasting importance attaches to the positive measures by which he tried to kill socialism with kindness. Although he did not ever achieve his primary object, his introduction of social insurance set an example which the rest of Europe slowly followed. Beginning with a partial return to gild organisation, at least in the smaller industries, Bismarck went on to set up nation-wide systems of insurance for workers in all main industries, under direct State control. Sickness insurance came first, on the basis of compulsory contributions by employer and employee. Then insurance against accidents, which was based on contributions by employers only. Finally, in 1888, old age pensions insurance was started, with contributions by employer and employee and with a government subsidy to augment the benefits paid out. It is very hard to estimate the extent to which Bismarck succeeded in reconciling the workers to things as they were, though he himself would no doubt have regarded their loyalty to the empire in 1914 as proof positive. In any case, a system which offered no protection against the hardships of unemployment would placate no worker who had once accepted the socialist theory of the growing Social Democratic Party.

One other important departure in Bismarckian policy was directly due to the requirements of his latest allies, who found in the new tariff arguments in favour of the acquisition of colonies. They would be a protected market for German manufacturers, a secure source of raw materials, and, it was hoped, a field for German emigration (100,000 Germans a year were leaving the homeland for America). There was also the desirability of giving maximum employment to Germany's growing mercantile marine. Bismarck was better aware than the colonial propagandists of big business, who formed a powerful Colonial Union in 1882, that their policy would involve dangerous international friction and increasing commitments. He preferred to regard Germany as a 'satisfied country' with no further claims to advance. But in 1884 he yielded on this issue, and the main German positions in Africa were obtained the same year. In 1885 the German flag was raised in New Guinea and at least four groups of Pacific Islands. In 1890 negotiations had also been begun to define the limits of the East African claims (the modern Tanganyika), when the replacement of Bismarck by Caprivi closed an era in the colonial as well as the general domestic history of Germany—an era which, as the next chapter will show, was no less clearly marked as Bismarck's in the diplomatic history of Europe.

SUGGESTIONS FOR FURTHER READING

F. Jellinek: *Paris Commune of 1871*, Part II, cc. 9–12.

J. E. C. Bodley: *France*, Books II and III.

Cambridge Modern History, Vol. XII, c. 5 (by E. Bourgeois).

Sir Charles Grant Robertson: *Bismarck*, c. 6.

G. P. Gooch: *Germany*, c. 2.

E. Ludwig: *Bismarck*, Book 4.

E. Eyck: *Bismarck and the German Empire*, c. 4.

J. P. T. Bury: *France, 1814–1940*, pp. 131–81.

CHAPTER 4

BISMARCK'S DIPLOMACY
AND THE TRIPLE ALLIANCE

Bismarck's Ascendancy in Europe

THE success which had crowned Bismarck's foreign policy in the 'sixties gave him in the 'seventies and 'eighties a far higher degree of unchallenged control in this sphere than he was ever permitted to enjoy in domestic affairs. The same cause, plus the high state of efficiency in which the German Army was seen to be kept, gave him an ascendancy in the field of international relations such that his attitude was the prime factor in connection with each problem that arose, even where German interests were not directly affected. In general, Bismarck used his ascendancy for widely approved objects. Regarding Germany as a satisfied Power, he promoted peace. Representing the Junker class, he sympathised with autocratic and aristocratic governments against liberal, and especially against socialist, influences. Making the isolation of France the very basis of his policy, so that her desire to revenge the war of 1870 might remain an ineffectual passion remote from reality, he was adroit enough to achieve his object indirectly. Thus he supported the establishment of the republic because republicanism was suspect in the eyes of France's possible allies—in 1874 he broke the career of Count von Arnim, the ambassador in Paris, for countenancing the intrigues of the French royalists—and he encouraged the expansion of the French empire because imperialism made quarrels with possible allies almost inevitable. So far from appearing to keep France down, Bismarck from time to time made moves towards a rapprochement with Germany's traditional enemy to induce her to abandon the hope of revenge. Never forgetting that Germany's position in central Europe was an exposed one, Bismarck sought to be the prime mover in an organisation of powers, or failing that of an alliance, which would preserve not only the peace of Europe but such an equilibrium among the greater states as was incidentally a strong protection to the liberties and territories of the lesser states. Between 1871 and 1914 no state was extinguished, and the only extensive changes were achieved at the expense of the Ottoman Empire, of which any proposed liquidation was widely approved on grounds of religion and humanity.

In practice, Bismarck's main task was to make and keep good relations with Austria-Hungary and with Russia. Their rivalry over the Eastern Question, which came to a head in 1878, forced him to choose between them: for a variety of reasons, he chose Austria, and the Dual Alliance followed accordingly. Then came a prolonged and very skilful attempt to re-establish close relations with Russia, which was complicated in 1887 by a second crisis in the Eastern Question, when Bismarck sided perforce with his ally, Austria. But at the time of his fall from power in 1890 Germany was still secretly linked with Russia, while the official alliance with Austria-Hungary had been expanded to include Italy, and the whole of the Mediterranean and Balkan area was covered by a further network of special relationships under ultimate German control, to which even Britain was within limits a party.

At the close of the Franco-Prussian War relations with Russia were already good, so a ceremonial visit by the German to the Austrian Emperor at Ischl in August, 1871, was used to remove some of the soreness resulting from Austria's defeat in the war of 1866. A year later all three emperors met in Berlin, accompanied by their chief ministers, and came to a general understanding which, though an unwritten agreement, is commonly styled the League of the Three Emperors (*Drei-kaiserbund*). The main points were the acceptance of the existing territorial settlement, an acknowledgement of a common interest in the suppression of subversive socialist movements, and provision for mutual consultation in all international difficulties. The understanding also envisaged an agreed settlement of the Eastern Question, which was to prove impossible. In 1873 and 1874 meetings of the sovereigns recalled the days of the Holy Alliance, but in 1875 a short-lived war scare, the nature of which has never been wholly cleared up, showed that the League did not in all circumstances achieve the first aim of Bismarck's diplomacy, namely the isolation of France.[1]

War Scare of 1875

The speed with which France was recovering from the war was emphasised to the world by measures taken to strengthen the French Army, and Bismarck appeared for a time to be considering whether to launch a second war so as to crush France beyond all possibility of revenge.   The irreconcilability of the Francophil population of Alsace-Lorraine and the support which the French Catholic bishops gave to Bismarck's opponents in the Kulturkampf also disposed him at least to teach France a sharp lesson.   In April, 1875, a Berlin newspaper published an article headed, 'Is War in Sight?' and the subject was taken up in other newspapers which were more definitely under Bismarck's influence.   The French government believed that this propaganda was to prepare the way for heavy demands—a fine twice as large as the indemnity which had just been paid, and a new German occupation of eastern France to exact it.   But this time the Russians, whom the Germans had sounded about their attitude in the event of a second Franco-German war, realised that the permanent disablement of France would weaken their own position vis-à-vis Germany, and readily responded to a French appeal to use their influence against war.   The Russian attitude had strong support from the British government, Queen Victoria having been warned by her daughters, the German princesses, that an aggressive policy was contemplated.   Accordingly, the Czar Alexander II and his Minister Gortchakoff on a visit to Berlin in May were assured that no move against France was contemplated.   The war scare then died away, leaving it uncertain whether Bismarck had ever intended to do more than frighten the French, even if there had been no prospect of a Russian intervention backed by Britain.   What is certain is that Bismarck never forgave Gortchakoff for the triumphant dispatch he dated from

[1] In 1873 there was a written agreement—the Schönbrunn Convention—for consultation in case of crisis.   The story of the *Dreikaiserbund* is complicated but is vividly told in W. L. Langer: *European Alliances and Alignments 1871–90.*   It should be remembered that the *Dreikaiserbund* was far from being a hard and fast alliance. Each country was intriguing for its own hand against the others; Russia was already looking hopefully towards France as a possible support against Germany, and Austria was anxious to maintain friendly relations with England.

Berlin, giving himself the credit for the fact that 'Now peace is assured.'

The Eastern Question Reopened

In the course of the same year, 1875, an insurrection against the Turks in Herzegovina turned the attention of the three Powers to the complexities of the Eastern Question, which by 1878 was to force Germany to choose between support of Austria and of Russian interests, with the result that Gortchakoff and his master were left out in the cold. In essence the problem was a simple one—how to maintain the *status quo* in the Ottoman Empire consistently with some regard for the welfare of its Christian subjects; how to localise conflicts arising from the collapse of the *status quo*; and, above all, how to arrange that any new settlement should yield equivalent gains in territory or influence to the two Powers most closely interested, Russia and Austria-Hungary, while not ignoring British fears for the independence of Constantinople. In detail, however, the problem was complicated by racial, religious, and traditional rivalries among the Balkan peoples. Serbia and Montenegro were certain to support their fellow Slavs in Herzegovina and the larger Bosnian province, which was soon involved in the rebellion. Rumania, on the other hand, as a small Latin state bordering the greatest of Slav states, was hampered by anxieties about Russian policy. Greece, which had developed very slowly since liberation, viewed the situation solely in accordance with her chances of winning Epirus and Thessaly. Thus the small neighbours of the Turk were in any case disunited, when the events now to be described added an independent Bulgaria to their number in circumstances which gave this least civilised and most warlike of Balkan peoples the maximum incentive to struggle on for a further accession of territory in Macedonia, which had been snatched at the last moment from its grasp.

The first result of the insurrection was an attempt by the three Empires, with the partial support of Britain, to get the Turkish system of rule in Bosnia-Herzegovina radically improved; but the insurgents refused to lay down their arms and Britain refused to support the other Powers (including Italy and France) in enforcing an armistice. When nearly a year had passed in this way the conflict widened: a further revolt began among the Slav Christians of Bulgaria, and Serbia and Montenegro went to war on behalf of Bosnia-Herzegovina. The Bulgarian revolt threatened the right flank of any Turkish army operating in the northern provinces, so it was quickly stamped out in blood—the Bulgarian Atrocities with their 12,000 victims in one month (May, 1876), of which Gladstone made the story ring through the civilised world. The Serbian Army was badly beaten by October, when the Russians intervened diplomatically to make Turkey concede an armistice to the Serbians, and the second phase of the struggle and the year 1876 closed with a further attempt by the Powers to get radical improvements for the revolted Turkish subjects. But a new Sultan, Abdul Hamid, rendered this Constantinople Conference wholly abortive by announcing the voluntary concession of a parliamentary constitution for all his dominions, but this concession was only a temporary victory for the Turkish liberal reformers, and was soon abandoned by the reactionary Sultan. So far the least impermanent result was a secret convention between Russia and Austria, signed at Reichstadt in July, 1876, in which Bosnia and Herzegovina for the first time were named as appropriate compensation for Austria if Russia were to regain part of Bessarabia which she had lost in 1856.

The Russo-Turkish War

In April, 1877, by which date the Sultan had already rid himself of the minister who was responsible for the new constitution, the Russians lost patience with Turkish wiles and declared war. As six years had not been long enough to restore her naval strength in the Black Sea, Russia launched her attack across the Danube, securing her right flank by an alliance with Rumania and having also the support of the Montenegrins, who readily reopened a campaign in which they (unlike the Serbs) had already won some independent successes against the Turk. At the end of July the advance of the main Russian Army, which laboured under the handicap of an uncompleted reorganisation on the Prussian model, was held up at Plevna. There, halfway between the Danube and the Balkan mountains, Osman Pasha stood a heroic siege of five months, until the town had been completely invested by Todleben, famous for the construction of the

THE BALKANS 1876-87

defences of Sebastopol in the Crimean War. But further south
Russian forces had already seized the Shipka Pass, so Osman's
eventual surrender to Prince Carol—for the check had caused
the Russians to welcome the active help of the despised
Rumanians—was the signal for a rapid advance to Sofia
and Adrianople, where an armistice was signed on January 31,
1878. The Serbs had re-entered the war in its final stages;
the Montenegrins had penetrated from their mountain fast-
nesses to the Adriatic; the Greeks were busily fomenting
rebellion against the Turks in Thessaly and Crete; and on

the farther side of the Black Sea the fall of Kars in November
had put all Armenia in Russian hands.

The Turks' position seemed desperate, but this was not the
first or last time they were able to count on the rivalries of
Christian Powers for partial deliverance. Britain had from the
outset viewed the handling of the situation by the three empires
with suspicion, from which Gladstone's impassioned appeals
for action against the Turks had only partly distracted attention.
She now feared for Constantinople and the Straits, and before
the armistice had been converted into the treaty of San
Stephano (March) the bringing of the Mediterranean squadron
into Turkish waters had shown her intention to challenge
the gains of the Russian Army with her fleet.   In this challenge
Britain enjoyed the support of Austria, who had assembled an
army in the Carpathians as a strategic threat to the Russian
flank, so that Bismarck was forced to choose between members
of the *Dreikaiserbund*.

The treaty had two main aspects—Russia's direct gains
from Turkey and the gains obtained for the Balkan states.
The former consisted of the Dobrudja (between the great
northern bend of the Danube and the sea), which Russia
proposed to hand to Rumania in exchange for the Bessarabian
territory forfeited at the end of the Crimean War, and, to the
east of the Black Sea, Kars and Batum, but not the whole
conquered area of Armenia.   Such moderation was designed
to conciliate Britain.   The gains accruing to the Balkan states
varied greatly.   For Greece, nothing; for Rumania, a forced
exchange, even though she had borne a large share in the
fighting: these were not Slav states.   More remarkable was
the discomfiture of Serbia, which was given an extension
southwards to include Nish, but not the great prize of Bosnia
with its Slav population, since Bosnia-Herzegovina had
already at Reichstadt been secretly assigned to Austrian
occupation.   Montenegro, on the other hand, was doubled
in population and received a small strip of sea coast with two
minor ports, while this tiny but ancient principality shared with
Serbia the advantage of having its formal independence at
last recognised by the Porte.   But the main beneficiary of
Russia's treaty-making was to be Bulgaria, erected into a
self-governing principality with lavishly extended boundaries.
This Greater Bulgaria was to stretch from the Danube to the

Aegean and from the Black Sea to within fifty miles of the Adriatic, swallowing up Macedonia and leaving to the Turks only their Thracian province west of Constantinople and a much larger but detached territory in Albania, Thessaly, and Epirus. Owing its very existence to Russian arms and Russian diplomacy, the new principality might be expected to welcome, or at least to tolerate, Russian control in domestic and foreign affairs.

The Congress of Berlin

England saw in this project the prospect of an eventual Russian advance to Constantinople, Austria the disappearance of her influence from the Balkans, where Serbia was her chief protégé. But their demand that the treaty should be referred to a European congress might have been ignored at this juncture, had Bismarck come down on the side of Russia. But when Russia asked that Germany should 'contain' Austria so as to free Russia's hands against England, as Russia had 'contained' her eight years earlier[1] to free Prussia for her war against France, Bismarck refused. The proposed congress therefore duly assembled at Berlin in June and, what was more important, the main issues had been settled in advance by secret Anglo-Russian negotiations and ancillary arrangements, also of a secret character, between England and Turkey and Austria respectively. It took one month to confirm the settlement, which determined the main lines along which the Eastern Question was to develop up to 1914.

Russia had agreed to the trisection of 'Big Bulgaria,' so that only the area between the Danube and the Balkan Mountains formed the new Bulgarian state under a Christian Prince. The area south of the Balkans, for which the name Eastern Rumelia was invented, remained under Turkish military control as a bulwark for Constantinople, though it was to have self-government—a precarious arrangement which was to cause a further European crisis only eight years later. Macedonia returned completely into Turkish hands, to be disputed in later generations by Greek and Serb as well as Bulgar. Bulgaria might reasonably have been compensated for the change in her prospects elsewhere by the retention of the Dobrudja in her north-east frontier, but Russia persisted

[1] See pp. 6 and 9.

in her plan to allot two-thirds of this to Rumania, as a forced exchange for those parts of Bessarabia which Russia had ceded to her at the end of the Crimean War. In the long run, however, the Anglo-Austrian agreement, confirming the Treaty of Reichstadt, was to influence history more. By the political occupation of Bosnia-Herzegovina and the additional military occupation of the Sanjak of Novibazar, which separated Serbia from Montenegro and provided what was then believed to be the best route for a railway to the much coveted Macedonian port of Salonika, Austria acquired a hold on a new Slav province and brought independent Serbia within her sphere of influence. It was when the latter arrangement came to an end in 1903 that Serbian nationalism, contesting the former arrangement as well, became a direct menace to the existence of the Dual Monarchy and consequently to the maintenance of European peace. The Anglo-Turkish agreement also has its direct connection with the events of 1914. The British occupation of Cyprus was designed to protect the Turkish Empire in Asia against further encroachment by the Russians, if, as was correctly foreseen, they insisted at Berlin on the retention of Kars, Ardahan, and Batum. Russia did not in fact advance further into Armenia and the approach to the Suez Canal was not threatened; but the ancillary agreement, by which Turkey undertook to govern the Armenians humanely, was utterly ignored. This behaviour provoked British remonstrances which, coupled with the loss of Cyprus, began a change in Turkish policy. It now moved towards friendship with Germany, for Germany made no demands on Turkish territory or humanity.

Bismarck's Alliance with Austria and Subsequent Agreements, 1879–1884

All this lay far in the future. For the time being the Eastern Question had been solved or shelved, and we may turn to consider its repercussions upon Bismarck's wider policy. At the Congress he had refused to champion either Russian or Austrian claims to the point of war, and it was Russia that had been the chief loser by his moderation. The Czar was the more indignant because of the recent debt of gratitude which Germany owed him for his action in containing Austria in 1870. In the early months of 1879, therefore, a rapprochement between Russia and France seemed quite likely, so Bismarck was impelled to secure his country's safety by turning to Austria for a definite alliance. Andrassy, the Foreign Minister of the Dual Monarchy, saw that Bismarck was for once in a weak position and raised his terms accordingly, a direct alliance against France being actually refused. Instead, the Treaty which created the Dual Alliance, signed after some two months' negotiation on October 7, 1879, gave protection only against attack on either signatory by Russia or by some other Power assisted by Russia. In the event of attack by one Power other than Russia, the only obligation upon the other signatory was to observe a benevolent neutrality. Periodically renewed up to the fateful year 1914, this Dual Alliance was the fundamental combination in European politics, in relation to which the other Powers one by one took their stand. We may therefore ask why Bismarck made this choice, bitterly opposed by his king, contrary to a long-standing Prussian tradition of friendship with Russia, and involving Germany in the fortunes of a partner far weaker than Russia would have been. Bismarck had at least three good reasons and one bad. He chose the less adventurous Power, not wishing Germany to be involved in crises arising out of Pan-slav and Asiatic ambitions; he chose the weaker Power, because more readily controllable; he chose the German rather than the Slav Power, because German opinion would welcome the association on grounds of history and sentiment; and, we may suppose, he chose also the course which would involve the discomfiture of his old enemy, the Russian Minister, Gortchakoff. The Alliance became known in Russia before the end of the year; her attitude grew less threatening; and in the course of 1880 Bismarck was in a position to start work on a renewal of his original League of the Three Emperors under other forms.

It will be more convenient to notice first, however, the expansion of the Dual into a Triple Alliance by the inclusion of Italy (May, 1882). The existence of an *Italia Irredenta* in the Tyrol disinclined Italy for permanent friendship with Austria, but as the weakest of Great Powers (or greatest of weak ones) she was reluctant to stand alone, and she was alienated from France by the fact that French Clericals made common cause with the Pope, to which was added the burning grievance of the French occupation of Tunis, where Italian settlers were numerous and ambitious—an occupation to which Bismarck had instigated the French with this very object in view. By the Triple Alliance all three Powers were pledged to fight if one of them were attacked by any two other Powers, and there were specific provisions for the case of a French attack on Italy, which would involve Germany and Austria, or on Germany, which would involve Italy. In no case, however, could Italy be required to fight Britain. Having acquired status by this purely defensive alliance, Italy was later to demand support for her interests both in the Mediterranean area and in the Balkans. Meanwhile, the Triple Alliance had two further ramifications. Since 1881 Austria had been closely allied with Serbia, and in 1883 an Austro-Rumanian alliance was made against the eventuality of a Russian attack, Germany acceding at once and Italy in 1888.

Thus the Dual Alliance of Germany and Austria-Hungary had expanded into what was virtually a Quintuple Alliance. Nevertheless, Bismarck knew that his main problem was still the keeping of Russia apart from France. Hence the importance of the negotiations with the new Czar, Alexander III, who succeeded his murdered father in March, 1881. These negotiations renewed the former understanding among the three emperors, known as the *Dreikaiserbund*, and defined it by treaty (June, 1881). The treaty had two main features. Benevolent neutrality was promised in the event of one party being involved in war against a fourth Power, so that Germany was safeguarded against a Franco-Russian combination and Russia—we may note in passing—was likewise safeguarded against an Anglo-Austrian or Anglo-German combination in case she found herself at war with Britain, a contingency which rivalries in the east made not unlikely. In the second place the treaty tried to minimise the risk of a further quarrel between Russia and Austria over the Eastern Question. Austria's gains at the Congress of Berlin were explicitly recognised by agreeing that she might turn the occupation of Bosnia-Herzegovina into an outright annexation when she chose, and the gains of which Russia had then been deprived were to some extent restored to her by agreement that Bulgaria and

Eastern Rumelia (about two-thirds of 'Big Bulgaria') might be united when she chose. It was further agreed that benevolent neutrality in the event of one party engaging in war against Turkey should be conditional upon prior agreement among the three empires as to the peace terms which would be imposed upon Turkey. The treaty was renewed at a meeting of the emperors at Skiernwicze after the first three-year period, but when it became due for renewal a second time in 1887 Russia refused, as the Eastern Question had again exposed her fundamental conflict of interest with Austria.

The Bulgarian Crisis, 1885

For some years after the Congress of Berlin events in the Near East followed on the whole the expected course. In May, 1881, the Treaty of Bardo made Tunisia a French protectorate, thus completing, in accordance with both German and British suggestions, the list of annexations from Turkish territory with which each Power compensated itself for the gains of others at the Berlin settlement. In the same month the kingdom of Greece, which had clamoured loudly at Berlin for gains at least equivalent to those of the Balkan states, received by agreement Thessaly and a part of Epirus, but not western Epirus or the 'great Greek island' of Crete, which was to involve the Powers in serious complications later on. But the crucial area was the new Principality of Bulgaria, left after the Congress of Berlin under Russian tutelage. Its prince was the youthful Alexander of Battenberg, Alexander II of Russia's nephew, but the power behind the throne was Stambulov, a ruthless nationalist politician of humble origins and high ambitions, who had already played a big part in the revolt of 1876 and in the war of liberation. Prince Alexander began his reign by suspending the constitution, so that Russian advisers had full play in both the civil and the military administration of the country. But after four years he restored the constitution; Stambulov became President of the Sobranje or Parliament; and it was made increasingly clear that Bulgaria's gratitude to Russia for her liberation was now replaced by nationalist resentment against Russian interference in Bulgarian affairs. Such was the situation in Bulgaria when, in September, 1885, the neighbouring, newly-created Turkish province of Eastern Rumelia expelled the Turkish governor from Philippopolis and proclaimed its union with Bulgaria. On Stambulov's orders Prince Alexander agreed to the sudden doubling of the territory under his rule, and the Powers were confronted by a *fait accompli*.

In this crisis the previous roles were reversed—Russia, having unexpectedly failed to make a permanent satellite or client state of Bulgaria, no longer desired its aggrandisement; Britain for the same reason now viewed it with approval; and Austria likewise approved, subject to the requirement of compensation for her client, Serbia. The Serbians, fully independent since 1878 and having made their principality a kingdom in 1882, looked upon Bulgaria as a rival; an easy triumph would restore the popularity of King Milan Obrenovic; and the withdrawal of Russian instructors from the Bulgarian Army, which was one mark of Russia's displeasure, made an easy triumph seem likely for Serbia's veterans of the 1876 and 1877 campaigns. The result was a complete surprise. War began on November 14, 1885, and within a fortnight the Serbian invasion of Bulgaria had been turned by the Battle of Slivnitsa into a Bulgarian invasion of Serbia, terminated not by Serbian arms but by an Austrian ultimatum in defence of her protégé. No frontier changes resulted directly from the Serbo-Bulgarian war, but it saved the union of Bulgaria and Eastern Rumelia, which Turkey now accepted. It did not, however, save the victorious Prince Alexander from the wrath of his cousin, the new Czar Alexander III, who held him personally responsible for the decline of Russian influence in Bulgaria. In August, 1886, a group of pro-Russian army officers organised a *coup d'état*, in which the Prince was forced to abdicate and was carried off to Russian soil; but Stambulov was stronger than the conspirators and the Prince was quickly recalled, only to lose his throne permanently as the result of an unwise telegram to the Czar, announcing his restoration in submissive terms, which cost him the support of Stambulov without gaining him that of his cousin.

For a year the Russians strove to win back control of Bulgaria, but in August, 1887, a new Prince ascended the throne, Ferdinand of Saxe-Coburg, who was a German and a Roman Catholic and had been brought up in Vienna—in fact, everything that the Russians did not want. The Czar refused to recognise his election (which was technically, but not practically, ignored by the other Powers for diplomatic reasons), but so far as the internal history of Bulgaria was concerned the crisis then ended with the triumph of Stambulov, hailed as the 'Bulgarian Bismarck,' who suppressed all pro-Russian activities with a rod of iron and governed as a virtual dictator up to 1894, by which time the young prince had learnt enough of Balkan politics to make himself master.

The Reinsurance Treaty with Russia (1887) and Overtures to Britain

Meanwhile, the complications of these years had produced the most serious threat of a general European war of any that occurred between 1871 and 1914, which was surmounted by Bismarck's diplomatic skill in its last and most tortuous phase. For on this occasion the crisis of Russian indignation over the Eastern Question, which Bismarck could not mollify without losing his Austrian alliance, coincided with—and in part stimulated—the crisis of French bellicosity which was reached in the movement of Boulangism.[1] The fall of the Ferry Ministry in 1885 marked a revulsion of feeling in France against letting colonial aspirations replace the hope of revenge against Germany; in 1886 Boulanger became Minister for War; and the tide of passion began to run which was to reach its climax in the episode of Schnaebele's arrest in April, 1887. Because of the Bulgarian imbroglio the Czar encouraged France, the idea of a Russo-French alliance being canvassed in the carefully controlled Russian Press. The arrest of Schnaebele led to a direct appeal from the Czar to the Kaiser, which formally stated that the Treaty of 1881 was at an end and frightened the aged Kaiser into releasing the victim. In January Bismarck had called upon the Reichstag to increase the army estimates because of the danger from both Russia and France, and got what he wanted—a dissolution which resulted in a decisive defeat at the polls for the Left Wing Liberals who had dared to oppose the Septennates. But in June he succeeded in postponing the perhaps inevitable rapprochement between his eastern and western neighbours by the device of a secret Reinsurance Treaty, between Germany and Russia. In this way Bismarck tried to overcome the difficulty caused by Russian refusal in the same

[1] See p. 48.

F

year to renew the *Dreikaiserbund*.[1] This incidentally confirmed
the agreement to keep the Straits closed (which had been enforced against Britain in 1885); and it explicitly recognised, so
far as words went, the preponderant influence of Russia in
Bulgaria and in the Balkans generally; and it agreed to keep
Prince Alexander from resuming the Bulgarian throne.   But
the main point for Germany was the promise of benevolent
neutrality if one party to the treaty were involved in war
against a third Great Power.   Thus Germany was secured
against the possibility of a Franco-Russian combination,
whereas Russia only seemed to be secured against a combination of Germany and Austria, since Germany was already
pledged to Austria by the Alliance of 1879.   The Reinsurance
Treaty was kept strictly secret,[2] but Bismarck justified his
action to himself by the plea that it made it easier for him to
exert a restraining influence on Russia, which (he claimed)
was in Austria's best interests.

In the same year, 1887, Bismarck further secured his position
by bringing Great Britain for the first time within the framework of alliances under his control.   In February Italy signed
a Mediterranean agreement with Britain, to prevent France
from upsetting the *status quo* there.   In December this was
extended, by a transaction of the utmost secrecy, to an agreement among Britain, Italy, and Austria to prevent Russia
from upsetting the *status quo* in Bulgaria or the Ottoman
Empire.   The Triple Alliance also came up for renewal in
1887, and Italy was more firmly attached to it by German
recognition of her claim to Tripoli and Austrian admission
of her interests in the Balkans.

Russia, however, was neither appeased nor intimidated,
and the election of Prince Ferdinand to the Bulgarian throne
produced a final crisis between her and Austria.   As in 1878,
Bismarck was again forced to choose between the two Powers.
Accordingly, in February, 1888, he published the terms of
the German-Austrian Alliance of 1879, which had been
secretly known to the Russians for many years but which by
publication clearly acquired pre-eminence over the Reinsurance Treaty with Russia.   Bismarck flung down his

[1] See p. 71.
[2] It was made public by Bismarck himself in 1896 as part of his unscrupulous
campaign against his successors in office.

challenge in a famous speech in the Reichstag, declaring that 'We Germans fear God and nothing else in the world' and thereby securing financial provision for an extra 700,000 soldiers to make good his boast. The total combination against Russia's aims in Bulgaria was too strong for her and she slowly gave way, so that, when Bismarck's dismissal by the youthful Kaiser Wilhelm II two years later closed this era in diplomatic history, the aged Chancellor was negotiating with Russia for a possible renewal of the Reinsurance Treaty, which was due to expire (1890).

It seems improbable that even Bismarck's virtuosity could have bound Russia permanently to Germany's side, the more so as the refusal of a loan by Germany in January, 1888, had already sent the Russian authorities to the French money market for needs which grew more urgent with the years, needs of economic development and needs of defence. Perhaps his long-term plan was to draw Britain through co-operation in the Mediterranean and Balkan areas into actual member-ship of the Triple Alliance. He had in fact made overtures to Beaconsfield in 1879 and to Salisbury on more than one occasion, the latest and most definite in 1889. In that case a renewal of the Reinsurance Treaty with Russia would have been merely a temporary expedient to tide over the period of negotiation, assuming—and it is a big but by no means an absurd assumption—that Britain would have come to terms with him. But it is more profitable to reflect on what Bismarck did do than on what he might have done. He made Germany great by war, but he kept her great by peace. The wealth, the teeming population, the strong organisation, and the self-confidence which rendered twentieth-century Germany so formidable resulted from the two decades in which Bis-marck's diplomacy kept the peace, as well as from the wars of the 'sixties. The power of the German Army lay always in reserve to strengthen his diplomacy, but that power was also available to German diplomats of the next generation, who proved so much less successful. What rules, then, did Bismarck keep that they failed to keep? He limited the ambitions of his ally, Austria-Hungary. He diverted, to imperialism, the ambitions of his inevitable enemy, France. He avoided ever quarrelling simultaneously with the two Powers that most nearly matched Germany, namely Russia and Britain. Finally, Bismarck never raised the issue of sea-power, which more than any other one cause overthrew the empire of Kaiser William II.

SUGGESTIONS FOR FURTHER READING

Sir Charles Petrie: *Diplomatic History, 1713–1933*, c. 20.

G. P. Gooch: *History of Our Time, 1885–1914* (Home University Library), 2nd edition, c. 6.

Sir J. A. R. Marriott: *The Eastern Question* (4th edition), cc. 12, 13 and 14.

W. L. Langer: *European Alliances and Alignments, 1871–1890*, cc. 6 and 7.

B. Croce: *History of Italy, 1871–1915*, c. 4.

R. W. Seton-Watson: *Britain in Europe*, cc. 13 and 14.

A. J. P. Taylor: *Struggle for Mastery in Europe*, cc. 11–14.

CHAPTER 5

THE EXPANSION OF EUROPE

The Starting-point of a New Era of Empire-building

JUST as Bismarck's diplomacy provides the connecting thread in the diplomatic relations of the Great Powers after 1870, so the expansion of European economic interests into other continents, resulting in the growth of great new colonial empires, becomes the characteristic feature of their national life and aspirations. Colonial empires were, of course, no novelty. The British Empire, to which the French Revolutionary and Napoleonic Wars brought notable additions, had continued to expand, particularly in India and Australasia, during the next two generations. France had acquired Algeria in 1830 and got her first footing in Indo-China under Napoleon III. As for Russia, her colonising activities are too often forgotten because it was a matter of pushing an existing land frontier further and further forward into ill-defined Asiatic territory. By 1870 she had already secured most of Turkestan between the Caspian Sea on the west and Chinese territory on the east and, beyond Manchuria, the Amur province and a Pacific port at Vladivostok, founded in 1860. There were also some stationary colonial empires, relics of past greatness, such as the very valuable Dutch East Indies, the Portuguese settlements along both the west and the east coast of Africa, and the Spanish possessions in Cuba and the Philippines. Nevertheless, for a variety of reasons, 1870 marks a new starting-point in the relations between Europe and less highly developed regions of the world.

In the first place, the attention of Europe was no longer engrossed, as it had been between 1815 and 1870, by the internal struggles of the nationalist and liberal movements: for two short periods (1876–8 and 1885–7) the Eastern Question loomed large, but otherwise the Powers were left free to conduct their rivalries further afield. To some extent the rivalry in empire-building was political, since it was believed that a great empire meant great strength in terms of population and strategic positions. Thus the French were foremost in raising native regiments to help out their declining numbers, the

British in securing lines of development, such as the Cape-Cairo route cutting through Africa. But the main factors were economic—the age-old desire for a profitable trade monopoly, on which most of the world's empires have been founded, and which the circumstances of the 1870's rendered at the same time more acute and more readily capable of fulfilment.

The desire for colonial trade was more acute because Europe's return to protection made each country fear exclusion from markets and sources of raw material, on which its trade depended. Large-scale industry was developing very fast, so that this need for markets and raw materials was very urgent, and its satisfaction in turn created new needs—for foodstuffs to feed an increasing manufacturing population, and for new fields of investment abroad to use the profits which soon outstripped the possibilities of further industrial development at home. Again, the desire for empire was more readily capable of fulfilment because of the great progress in communications, and to a much smaller extent in medicine, which for the first time rendered inland tropical regions accessible to Europeans. The opening of the Suez Canal in 1869 is one landmark, not only because it shortened the voyage to east Africa and the Far East, but also because it gave a great impetus to the general conversion of shipping from sail to steam. Stanley's discovery of Livingstone in the heart of Africa in 1871 is another, for the great journeys of the older man, which the younger was to continue along the Congo, opened up darkest Africa to the railway as well as to the Bible.

The Opening-Up and Partition of Africa

The opening up of Africa is one of the greatest achievements of modern imperialism; in this achievement explorers, traders, missionaries and governments all played a part. Although the coasts of Africa had long been known, the interior was unexplored until recent times. In the early eighteenth century Swift repeated in verse a complaint made first by Plutarch nearly seventeen centuries earlier:

> *'Geographers, in Afric maps,*
> *With savage pictures fill their gaps,*
> *And o'er unhabitable downs*
> *Place elephants for want of towns.'*

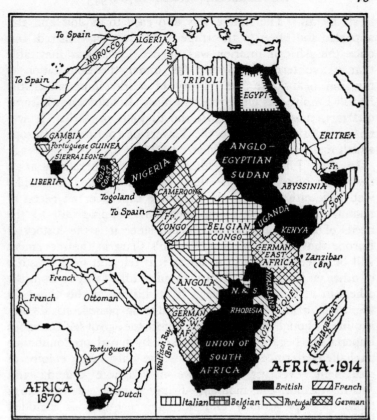

European Expansion in Africa

In the second half of the nineteenth century Livingstone and Stanley made the great journeys of geographical discovery which enabled the modern map of Africa to be drawn. Their explorations also revealed the nature of tropical Africa: its great forests, mighty rivers, and also its vast size. Native life was primitive and marred not only by poverty and disease, but also by such horrors as the slave trade and cannibalism. The native needed help, and this need appealed to the conscience of humanitarians in Europe. In 1873 Britain negotiated a treaty which closed for ever the great Arab slave market in Zanzibar, and this was followed some twenty years later by a comprehensive anti-slavery code which was drawn up by seventeen Powers and accepted, in name at least, by all. The native was also easy to exploit and this appealed too often to the trader. Motives were mixed, but once the African interior was opened up it was inevitable that native territories would fall under the domination of the Europeans. In the history of world imperialism the British Empire has often received most attention and, in some quarters, most criticism. In the division of Africa, it was not only Britain but also the Powers of continental Europe which took an important share.

In 1885 Jules Ferry defined this new imperialism as 'a new form of colonisation—that which is adapted to peoples who have either a mass of disposable capital or an excess of manufactures.' It was thus peculiarly appropriate to the needs of Britain at this period, but since it is the history of Europe that we are tracing, Britain's share in the movement will be discussed only in so far as it is relevant to the history of other empires. The British Empire differs widely from the others in at least three aspects of its history at this time. It was more firmly based upon world-wide possessions already acquired, though little esteemed, before the age of self-conscious imperialism began, and was backed by naval predominance unchallenged since 1805. It was the only great empire of settlement: even in Africa—we may ignore Canada and Australasia for the moment—Britain's base was the farm lands of Cape Colony and her later acquisitions included both Kenya and Rhodesia, which could develop a white population far in excess of those of the German or French African colonies. Thirdly, the British was a free trade empire, which kept on extending its boundaries, not in order to make a closed tariff area (such as the other empires mainly were) but to preserve the open door for trade, being confident of its own success under competitive conditions.

What has been called the 'scramble for Africa' may be dated from the Treaty of Bardo (May, 1881), named from the Bey's summer palace at which a French protectorate was established over Tunis as the result of a military expedition. It precedes by fourteen months the bombardment of Alexandria, by which the British occupation of Egypt was launched without deliberate intention. Both Tunisia and Egypt were Turkish possessions under local rulers who became overwhelmingly indebted to European investors; the native rulers borrowed money at high interest both for productive development and for their private pleasures. In both cases joint financial control by the interested parties preceded occupation, and in both cases the occupation was the cause of a long-continued quarrel, between French and Italians in one and French and British in the other.

These disputes outside Europe (as we have seen) materially helped Bismarck in his primary object of keeping France isolated.[1] Italy, by virtue of her commercial activities and investments, her settlers, and her understanding with the Powers (Austria had suggested the occupation in 1877 as a suitable *quid pro quo* for Bosnia-Herzegovina), had as good a right to Tunisia as France. France, by virtue of close relations dating from the Egyptian expedition of Napoleon Bonaparte and the recent enterprise of de Lesseps in building the Suez Canal (in which English capitalists had deliberately refused to take any part), had as good a right to Egypt as Britain. Hence the bitter feelings. But the facts remained. Tunisia became firmly added to Algeria, giving France a natural encouragement to expand further across the Sahara Desert. Egypt had a less simple history, for the European investors, headed by France, retained considerable powers of control over the finances to ensure payment on their loans. Moreover, the British intervention, though it meant in practice the complete reconstruction of the country by Lord Cromer, 'the great pharaoh of modern Egypt,' was in theory a temporary measure, with Cromer merely advising the Khedive as a glorified consul-general, and the British Army, which gave point to his advice, likely to be withdrawn at any time. Nevertheless, our presence in Egypt acted as a magnet to draw Rhodes northwards, and led more directly to the acquisition of the Sudan in 1898, theoretically an Anglo-Egyptian condominium but in practice a great colonial possession based on British capital and British administration.

While Britain and France were thus fairly launched upon an era of competitive imperialism, and Italy sought consolation for her disappointment by taking various tentative steps towards the establishment of her east African colony of Eritrea (which dates officially from 1890), Germany quite suddenly entered into rivalry with them for the as yet unappropriated territories of the east and west coasts. Bismarck

[1] See p. 47.

had said he was 'no colonies man,' but he also said, when he saw the modern port of Hamburg with its forest of masts and funnels, that this was a new world. The new world required, or seemed to require, a new policy, into which the propaganda of industrial and commercial interests pushed even the Iron Chancellor. Starting from nothing, in less than two years Germany made herself the third greatest Power in Africa. This was no mean feat of diplomacy, even when it is remembered that Britain was at this time at loggerheads with Russia (over the threat to India implied in her advance to Penjdeh)[1] as well as France, and that the British Prime Minister (up to June, 1885) was the pacific and anti-imperialist Gladstone.

First in April, 1884, Bismarck took over possession of South-west Africa (excepting the British enclave of Walfisch Bay) between the Portuguese and British frontiers, an area for which Britain had refused to accept responsibility and where German missionaries stood in need of protection. Less reputable was the seizure of the Cameroons and Togoland, where Bismarck deceived Britain as to his intentions. More important than any of these west coast acquisitions was the work of Dr. Karl Peters on the east coast. By a series of quick negotiations with native chiefs, who claimed to be independent of the Sultan of Zanzibar—the sultanate was under British influence and possessed a kind of suzerainty over the coastal territories—Peters provided Bismarck with the material on which to base a formal protectorate, proclaimed in February, 1885. This was the origin of German East Africa (better known as Tanganyika), valuable alike for its large native population, its raw materials, and its strategic position. In 1890, shortly after the fall of Bismarck, an Anglo-German agreement, which was much criticised in Germany, secured recognition for the existing frontiers of German East Africa at the cost of admitting British claims in Zanzibar and elsewhere, which debarred Germany from further expansion. It was in this settlement that Germany obtained the island of Heligoland.

The years 1884-5 were decisive for the development of another African empire besides Germany's. One of the richest prizes Africa could offer was the valley of the Congo,

[1] See p. 92.

the exploration of which had been completed by Stanle
Snubbed by Disraeli's government, Stanley had gone out
the instigation and expense of King Leopold II of the Belgians.
A conference was now held at Berlin to regularise the position,
resulting in certain rules for the suppression of slavery and
the slave trade and for the avoidance of friction between
Powers by prescribed methods of making and justifying
annexations. This conference resulted in the Berlin Act of
February, 1885, an important instrument to facilitate peaceful
partition of all Africa. But it referred mainly to the Congo
Basin, where the Powers agreed to set up a Congo Free State
controlled by an international association on a free trade
basis. But practice differed widely from theory. The association was entirely in the hands of King Leopold, who created
a gigantic trade monopoly in rubber, ivory, and other valuable
products; and he exploited the natives with a cruelty which
rivalled that of the worst slave dealers. In 1889 he published
his will, bequeathing the Congo State to Belgium, which
already provided the backbone of his administration. In
1908, by which date the Congo atrocities had become a byword, Leopold finally ceded the state to the Belgian people;
but the administration was not effectively reformed until
after his death in December, 1909. He had accumulated,
and largely spent, a vast fortune; but he had also made
Belgium an important colonial Power.

After 1885 Britain under the Salisbury Ministries played the
most active part: the British East Africa Company opened
up Kenya and led the way to Uganda; the Royal Niger
Company on the opposite side of the continent pushed inland
up the Oil Rivers for palm-oil to form Nigeria, the third most
populous element in the whole British Empire; and Rhodes's
South Africa Company thrust northwards to carve out the
two great colonies which bear his name. The main agreement
with Germany, referred to above, was followed in 1891 by
an Anglo-Portuguese treaty, acknowledging the British claim
to what Rhodes had seized, namely the hinterland of the
ancient Portuguese colonies of Angola and Mozambique.
These had been mere coastal settlements, but the Portuguese
had caught the fever of imperialism and were extending their
frontiers: they were held up by lack of manpower, money,
by Rhodes, and the British ultimatum in 1890. In 1898

Britain and Germany made a secret agreement for the division of the Portuguese possessions, if their existing owners became unfortunately unable to maintain them—the wish was no doubt father to the thought, but the contingency never actually arose. Britain also made an agreement in 1891 with Italy, whose interests adjoined ours both by the Red Sea in Eritrea and on the Somali coast further south, the effect of which was to encourage Italian colonial ambitions, then at their height. By the Treaty of Ucciali of 1889 the Emperor Menelek of Abyssinia was believed to have recognised an Italian protectorate over his country; but in 1896 the defeat of the Italian forces at Adowa completely restored the independence of Abyssinia (which Menelek never admitted to have been alienated). The blow to European prestige and the dangerously exposed position of the Italians then provided one of the motives for the Anglo-Egyptian reconquest of the Sudan, which was undertaken in 1896-8.

The Clash of Interests between Britain and France

The Sudan expedition, which was the last main stage in the dividing-up of tropical Africa among the Powers, brought to a head the conflict between Britain and France, the two main beneficiaries of the process, which had been going on since the British entry into Egypt. In 1890, indeed, an agreement was signed which recognised a French protectorate over the great island of Madagascar, to which Britain had not inconsiderable claims; it also recognised French ownership of the huge but barren area between Tunisia and Senegal (the Sahara Desert and French Sudan). In return France accepted British claims in the little known but potentially valuable region between the lower Niger valley and Lake Chad. But the conflict of interest in the last-named area continued, since the French were already established in the remote hinterland of each of the British West African colonies and there were large areas which neither side had as yet effectively occupied. The question was finally settled in June, 1898, by which date the flags of rival forces of 'effective occupation' were in some cases flying in the same bewildered native village.

Scarcely, however, had this critical situation been resolved by a compromise, which gave Britain secure possession of the lower and middle Niger while French territory was expanded further to the north, than the final clash arose. This was over the ambition which the French cherished (as did also the Germans and even the Portuguese) to make their influence effective over a belt of territory stretching right across the continent—and incidentally cutting across the intended all-British belt from north to south. In September, 1898, Major Marchand's party from the French Congo were descending the Nile Valley to effect a juncture with a stronger French party, which was due to meet them from French Somaliland, when they met Kitchener, who had just won control of the Sudan by his victory over the Dervishes at Omdurman. The French action was really a challenge to the British position in Egypt, since our claim to the upper Nile Valley rested upon the fact that Egypt had in some sense owned the Sudan before the era of the Dervishes, as well as upon the stronger basis of conquest. Therefore no compromise was possible with the French at Fashoda, and they eventually yielded to the implied threat of war, though Lord Salisbury was quick to compensate them afterwards over their other interests in central Africa. But the recognition of Britain's superior strength set the French Foreign Minister, Delcassé, thinking of an *entente* as the more profitable alternative to colonial rivalries, in which the British fleet was plainly the trump card.

British, French, and German Colonies Compared

Britain had, indeed, obtained the lion's share. She had secured all the principal areas which were climatically suitable for white settlers; had nearly completed her all-British route from Cairo to the Cape; held (except for Dakar) each of the key-points for the strategic control of the continent from Gibraltar to Simonstown, from Alexandria to Durban; and bestrode three out of the four great African rivers on which the growth of trade and civilisation largely depended. But the French share was the largest in area, though not in population; it included a portion of the fourth river basin, the Congo, and Madagascar, the third largest island in the world; and the north African colonies were ideally situated for the practice of the characteristic French colonial policy of 'assimilation,' that is, treating colonies and their inhabitants as provinces

and citizens of France proper. From this it was an easy
step to tariff assimilation, which was applied by 1900 wherever
France was not bound by treaty to act otherwise. This
practice again treated the colony as a part of France, so
that French goods were imported customs-free and all others
on the terms of the French tariff, though the converse proposition, that colonial goods should be imported customs-free
into France, was applied only in the modified form of a
preference for goods from assimilated colonial areas.

The results were somewhat disappointing, for Algeria, the
nearest colony to France, accounted for more than half of
all French colonial commerce, and the external trade of all
French possessions put together was not one-third that of
India alone. But the French, like the British, were actuated
by political as well as economic motives, and the fact that
they are virtually immune from a sense of the colour bar has
made their general civilising influence and their efforts to
spread a distinctively French culture widely effective. The
experience of the Germans in Africa was more definitely
disappointing. Not one of their colonies there ever paid its
way, which is the more remarkable as Bismarck had made it
clear that he regarded them as a business proposition, in
which the Hanse tradition would provide a model. None
of them proved attractive to German emigrants, who were
flocking to America; in 1914 there were, as Sir Norman
Angell pointed out, more Germans earning their living in one
foreign city, Paris, than in all the German colonies put
together. Serious native wars, such as the rebellion of the
Hereros in South-west Africa in 1904, cost money and damaged
prestige, the Germans being justly accused of cruel treatment
of the native populations. As a market for German goods
the colonies proved negligible. But in 1914 the Germans
were just turning over their colonies to an alternative use as
plantations, which should supply all the needs of German
industry for rubber, oilseeds, cotton, and other raw materials,
and might even achieve a predominant position that
would enable the market to be cornered against the foreigner.
In 1911 the acquisition of two considerable portions of the
French Congo, which might have paved the way for larger
acquisitions from Belgium, had made such schemes more
feasible.

The opening up of Africa to European influences was one of the most important enterprises in European history. Four of the six Great Powers took part in it, while considerable shares were also allotted to two of the smallest Powers of Europe—namely, Belgium and Portugal. They worked in rivalry with each other, as we have seen, but accepted common rules of procedure (the Berlin Act) and a system of peaceful bargaining within the general framework of the Concert of Europe. For Europe, which has fought so many wars for trifling territorial causes, to divide up the entire ill-defined hinterland of a continent three times as large as itself without a European war, was indeed an important achievement. Its immediate results, measured in terms of political power and economic resources gained, were also important. But only time can show whether the most important result of the impact of European civilisation upon the Dark Continent will not be the contribution which Africa, so backward for so long, makes eventually to the common heritage of mankind.

The Islands of the Pacific

The dividing-up of the island groups of the Pacific Ocean was a parallel process to the partitioning of Africa, though it attracted much less attention because the prizes were much smaller. In 1870 the Dutch East Indies, the most valuable of all tropical possessions, India alone excepted, had recently come under a régime of free instead of forced labour, which helped the population of Java to double itself in half a century. The Dutch authorities had sufficient capital, manpower, and administrative experience to make it in the highest degree improbable that these islands would be open to fresh conquerors except in the event of a general war, such as had given Sir Stamford Raffles occasion once to conquer them for Britain in 1811. But the ownership of Ceylon, the coastal regions of Burma, and the Straits Settlements of Singapore, Malacca, and Penang, put Britain in a strong position for further expansion, as did the coming to maturity at this time of her white colonies of Australia and New Zealand. The French had been established in Tahiti since 1843 and had more recently taken possession of New Caledonia. To Germany the impulse to expand in the Pacific came at the same date, 1884, as her expansion in Africa. Indeed, the general course of events was much the

same, though it must be borne in mind that these lesser
prizes had smaller populations, smaller natural resources, and
no areas suitable for large-scale colonisation by Europeans.
Missions again prepared the way for annexation, and the
elements of civilisation spread rapidly in the smaller islands,
which were much more accessible than the hinterland of
Africa; but the plantation system, on which the exploitation
of raw materials largely depended, required the introduction
of indentured coolies from the Asiatic mainland, as South
Sea islanders do not care for industrial discipline.

The outstanding events were these. In 1874 the British
annexation of the Fiji Islands began a process of division
between Britain and France. Ten years later the Germans
joined in, when they took north-eastern New Guinea (the
west being already in Dutch hands)—much to the indignation
of the Australians, who tried to forestall the German action,
received little support from home, and had to be content with
the south-east portion of the island, later known as Papua.
The Germans also secured the offshore islands, which they
named after Bismarck, and within two years the neighbouring
Solomon Islands and the Marshall group further north.

By this time a fifth Power—the fourth being the Dutch,
who were stimulated by rivalry to develop their huge existing
possessions in New Guinea, Borneo, and elsewhere—had come
upon the scene, as American trade interests required the
maintenance at least of coaling stations. This brought the
Americans to Samoa, where intrigues among the native
chiefs created serious trouble between English, American, and
German interests. In 1889 a hurricane dispersed the warships
of the three Powers and perhaps averted an open conflict,
in which the English and Americans would have been ranged
together against the Germans. Friction continued, advertised
and perhaps fomented by the presence of the writer, R. L.
Stevenson, then at the height of his fame, until a treaty was
made in 1899, under which America divided Samoa with
Germany and Britain received compensation elsewhere.
This assertion of American power was the natural sequel to
the Spanish-American War of 1898, which arose out of the
misgovernment of Cuba, but had its roots also in the new
and late development of American imperialism. The rapid
and overwhelming defeat which Spain suffered put her

Pacific colonies in the position that was anticipated more than once for the African colonies of Portugal. The Philippines, where the Americans had won a decisive naval victory at Manila, passed under direct American control, which was the means of educating the population for home rule. America also annexed Guam, but the rest of the Marianas and the Caroline Islands were sold by Spain to Germany, which had been hoping for the reversion of them before the war. Finally, in 1899 the imperialist mood of the American people encouraged the annexation of Hawaii, which became the great American naval base in Pacific waters.

European Expansion in Other Areas

Thus by the close of the century the European Powers and their offspring in the western hemisphere, the U.S.A., had practically extinguished all independent native states in Africa and among the Pacific islands. There were at least four other possible fields of expansion, where the establishment of political control meant assured markets and assured supplies of raw materials. The most attractive of these was South America, because it also offered the chance of great colonies of settlement. But although much European capital was invested there and it became the field for considerable immigration from the Latin countries and even from Germany, the Monroe Doctrine effectively barred the way to European annexations. This was probably fortunate for South America because the chaotic political conditions there would certainly, without the Monroe Doctrine, have invited European intervention. Revolutions, civil wars and wars between the states were frequent. Nevertheless economic development led to a demand for European labour, skill and capital. The President of the Argentine was subsidising immigration in the 1850's. The freeing of the slaves in Brazil in 1888 caused economic dislocation on the coffee plantations but brought a rapid immigration of Italian workers. In the same year 97,000 Italians entered Brazil. Of the non-Latin peoples, the British also went in considerable numbers to South America, especially to the River Plate area. The British were mainly merchants, stock-raisers, engineers and miners. But more important than British settlers was British capital. From the early days of the South American republics, the European nation which

G

played the largest part in their development was Great
Britain.

Britain had made the first public loans to Latin America.
Britain and Latin America were complementary in their
economies: the one a manufacturing country, the other an
area producing raw materials. Britain had introduced into
the Argentine the merino sheep in 1813 and pedigree cattle
in 1848. But the greatest contribution of British capital was
the development of communications: railways, tramways and
steam ships. English railway engineers were at work in
remote parts of Paraguay as early as 1854, and in the following
decades railway development was pushed ahead in South
America generally. In Chile the mining of copper and
nitrates was developed by foreign capital. At the end, in
1883, of the War of the Pacific between Chile and Peru and
Bolivia, Peru was unable to repay her foreign debt to Britain
and later in exchange for its cancellation made a cession of
the state railways to the Peruvian Corporation of British
bond-holders. Though intellectually South America looked
to France rather than Spain or Portugal (because of the
bitter republican feelings aroused against the old empires),
Great Britain retained till the end of the nineteenth century the
commercial and financial preponderance. Even against the
United States, Great Britain held at this time the better cards.[1]

India was the richest area for European expansion, but the
wars of the eighteenth century had permanently ousted
Britain's rivals from power. France and Portugal, however,
retained certain small colonies in India, the most important
being Pondicherry and Goa.

The third region, central Asia, was completely dominated
by Russia, which (as we have already seen) enjoyed the
long-term advantage of an empire stretching right across
Asia with uninterrupted access by land. It is significant that,
though the Russian empire in the eighteenth century had
crossed the sea to Alaska, that was the one region from which
the empire later withdrew; after its sale in 1867 Russia needed
only the development of the railway to give her empire a
coherence which others could not rival. There remained the
Far East.

[1] See *South American Progress* (1934), by C. H. Haring, Professor of Latin-
American History at Harvard University.

The process of partitioning which we have watched elsewhere was set in motion at the same period in the Far East.
But by the end of the century European efforts had done
little more than emphasise the enormous difficulties involved
in the attempt to dominate and westernise an empire with
one-quarter of the world's population and a complex civilisation that long antedated the Christian era.

The Far East

By 1870 the Chinese empire was in an advanced state of
decay. In the two China wars first Britain, and then Britain
and France together, had humiliated the government, forced
open its territories to European trade at the Treaty Ports,
established the Capitulations, so that European residents
were no longer subject to Chinese courts, and, by the pillaging
of the Emperor's Summer Palace in 1860, made it clear that
China's ancient civilisation would not safeguard her from
methods of barbarism when she resisted the West. In 1842
Britain had annexed the island of Hong Kong, which rapidly
became the chief commercial centre of the whole China
coast. In 1860 the Russians had rounded off their Amur
province by the foundation of Vladivostok. A few years
later Napoleon III's annexation of Cochin-China began the
creation of French Indo-China. Meanwhile the government
of the Manchu dynasty had been threatened by a rebellion
which challenged the traditional Chinese religion and the
effeteness of the government in the name of a new Tai-Ping
dynasty. This Tai-Ping rebellion cost China more than ten
years of civil war and (it is said) more lives than were lost by
all the belligerents in the First World War. To put it down
required the help of foreign commanders, such as General
Gordon, and the subsequent record of the Manchus suggests
that their help enabled the wrong side to win.

In the next two decades the most conspicuous advances were
made by France. French influence expanded from Cochin-
China into Cambodia, Tonkin, and Annam, helped to some
extent by her position as the recognised protector of all
Chinese Catholics. In 1885 the Chinese government went to
war in a vain effort to retain Tonkin, and was compelled to
make a formal cession of both Tonkin and Annam, though it
was a small reverse in this war which turned the great French

imperialist Jules Ferry out of office. The population of the new French possession of Indo-China, twenty millions, was not very great, but its area exceeded that of France. Britain made no further direct annexations of Chinese territory, since she was in secure control, through her ownership of Hong Kong and her pre-eminence in the Treaty Ports, of about two-thirds of China's foreign trade, a prize in comparison to which territorial gains were almost insignificant. But she was advancing her flag on the outskirts of the Chinese world in Burma and Malaya, and in 1893, when the French tried to extend their influence from Indo-China to Indo-China's neighbour, Siam, Britain objected to a French naval blockade of Bangkok, the upshot being the agreement which has since preserved the integrity of Siam almost alone among eastern kingdoms.

The Russians in this period were pushing forward their frontiers in central Asia, where in 1880, General Skobelev, hero of the siege of Plevna, completed the conquest of Turkestan, which had been begun in earnest to compensate for Russia's setback in Europe after the Crimean War. So China was threatened from the north-west at the same time as the Russian advance towards Afghanistan threatened India. The latter threat subsided after a British show of firmness at Penjdeh (1885), but China continued to be subject to Russian pressure from every side except the sea, where British sea-power controlled the only practicable route to Vladivostok. In 1892 Russia began to modify the general situation to her great advantage by the construction with French financial help of the Trans-Siberian railway to the Far East, which would give Russia a means of operating over which British naval power had no control and, in consequence, the possibility of directing the trade of Manchuria and most of north China into Russian channels. This promised to be a much more profitable challenge to Britain's position than any descent on India through the Afghan mountains.

The Rise of Japan and the Sino-Japanese War

The break-up of China was then precipitated by an unexpected development, which has no parallel in the partition of Africa. Since 1853 American and European trade had forced its way into the Japanese islands, to which existing trade with China naturally attracted attention. The Chinese giant, perhaps because of his size, did not react at all strongly to western influences. The Japanese, on the other hand, reacted with vigour. They were a disciplined people who possessed along with the culture they derived from China a military and social code not unlike that of mediæval Christendom, with a great emphasis on loyalty, courage, and the worship of tradition; they now determined to add the external trappings of western civilisation to their original basic outlook on life. In 1867 the so-called Era of Enlightenment began with the emergence of the emperor from retirement, in which he had been placed, while an all-powerful Minister, the Shogun, ruled in his stead. The prestige of the monarchy, which the Japanese worshipped as divine in origin, was then used to modernise every institution of the State. A parliament, with Houses of Lords and Commons, made its appearance. Education and health services began. Factory industries and a large mercantile marine enabled the islands to sustain a vastly increased population. Above all, an army modelled on the German and a navy modelled on the British prepared to show the world, which was still laughing at the quaint humour of Gilbert and Sullivan's *Mikado*, that the real Mikado had fully learnt the lesson of European politics in the age of imperialist wars.

In 1894 the Japanese, vastly outnumbered, fought China for the control of Korea, an empire under Chinese suzerainty, the proximity of which to Japan made it a natural object of ambition. The Chinese were quickly defeated, and early in 1895 by the Treaty of Shimonoseki they agreed to the independence of Korea, the cession of the Island of Formosa and the Liao-tung peninsula (with Port Arthur) in south Manchuria, payment of a war indemnity, and—perhaps most significant of all—that Japanese subjects should have the same privileges on Chinese soil as subjects of the Western Powers. Thereupon Russia, France, and Germany, acting together in Far Eastern matters as a league of three (*Dreibund*), forced Japan to give up her Manchurian gains and, when a larger indemnity was fixed in consequence, Russia and Germany lent China the money to pay. The motive was not, except of course in name, their deep concern for the integrity of Chinese territory, but the desire to further their own interests.

Russia was an immediate beneficiary, for the Chinese in gratitude gave them a concession for a Chinese Eastern Railway in Manchuria, which shortened the route to Vladivostok, and signed a secret treaty (1896) promising further concessions, both military and economic, which would have turned China virtually into a Russian sphere of influence. In 1898 China allowed Russia to occupy Port Arthur. The other members of the Dreibund likewise had great expectations; but Britain, which had not taken China's part against Japan, had acquired neither gratitude nor influence by these events and felt that her established predominance in the trade of the Yangtze Kiang basin was now threatened.

The partitioning process, except in China, had gone far towards completion without war and on generally amicable terms; under favourable conditions of expansion open to all, the Concert of Europe had been effective in its working. But the attempted partition of China had achieved three results of an opposite character. China itself was on the verge of a nationalist revolt, the Boxer rising; a Far Eastern Power was preparing to challenge Western predominance in the Russo-Japanese war; and, most immediate issue of all, Britain was being driven by anxiety for her Far Eastern interests, more than by any other single factor, to abandon her established policy of isolation and join one or other of the rival groups of Powers. We must now study the growth of those groups, as it proceeded in Europe after the fall of Bismarck.

SUGGESTIONS FOR FURTHER READING

G. P. Gooch: *History of Modern Europe, 1878–1919*, c. 3.

Ramsay Muir: *The Expansion of Europe*, c. 7.

B. H. Sumner: *Tsardom and Imperialism in the Far East and the Middle East, 1880–1914*.

New Cambridge Modern History, Vol. XI, c. 22 (by R. E. Robinson and J. Gallagher) and c. 23 (by F. C. Langdon).

CHAPTER 6

DUAL ALLIANCE AND *ENTENTE CORDIALE*

The Rapprochement between France and Russia

THE last decade of the nineteenth century, in which the expansion of Europe was proceeding most rapidly and imperialism became a popular cult, is also remarkable for the growth of a counterpoise to Germany's Triple Alliance in the Dual Alliance between France and Russia. Imperialism, as we have seen, involved Britain in serious clashes with other Powers, which were made all the more serious when each of those Powers had behind it the strength of an alliance. Accordingly, the characteristic event of the next decade, the first of the twentieth century, was the inclusion of Britain in the alliance system by the formation of the *Entente Cordiale* with France, which later developed into the Triple Entente, of which Russia was also a member.

France had no great tradition of friendship with Russia and their forms of government were poles apart. But the strength of imperial Germany made it a natural thing for her neighbours to east and west to combine against her, just as France had been the natural ally of Poland in the days of her greatness. They were kept apart by the diplomatic skill which never failed Bismarck to the day of his departure from office in 1890. But he was helped also by temporary circumstances—the lowering of French prestige by the defeat of 1870, which suggested that she was not a worth-while ally for another Great Power, and the warm regard which the two Russian Czars, Alexander II and III, felt for the Emperor William I. Towards 1890, however, the career of General Boulanger seemed to show that, though the political world in France was changeable and excitable, still the country had recovered some of its old passion for military glory; and the system of military conscription which was started in 1872 had had time to take effect. The Russians did not want actual war against Germany and would doubtless have deprecated any *coup* which set Boulanger in power, but it was an important fact that the Germans treated his threats with some respect. At the same time the personal link between the two empires was weakened by the death of the old Emperor William I. His son's reign of three months left no mark on history, while the youthful Emperor William II (1888-1918) was not, at any stage in his eventful career, the man to hold two Powers together by a systematic and sympathetic regard for his neighbour's susceptibilities. In the decisive years 1890-94 the German Chancellor, Count Caprivi, was handicapped by inexperience and the enmity of his fallen rival, as well as by the new Kaiser's reckless determination to shape his own foreign policy.

Much had, indeed, happened before Bismarck's fall: in Russia the inspired press campaign for an understanding with France began in 1886; in 1887 the Czar intervened effectively in the Schnaebele episode; and in 1888 the French subscribed heavily to a Russian loan after the German Reichsbank had been forbidden to accept Russian paper. The first successful loan was probably the turning-point. The government of the third French Republic, though it was founded on the graves of the Communards and had already had a longer life than any other régime in France since 1789, was by no means congenial to the reactionary Czar Alexander III. But his entourage moved more quickly than its master towards friendship on equal terms, for which the French ministers and people were obviously eager. The first loan was so heavily over-subscribed from the pockets of the thrifty French peasantry and *rentiers*, ever willing to invest abroad the savings which French industry was too slow-moving to absorb, that a regular practice was established—five more issues in 1889 and 1890 were supplemented by further loans every two or three years up to the war of 1914. Russia derived a three-fold advantage: she was able to convert the whole of her external debt to an interest rate of only 4 per cent.; she could open up vast territories by railway enterprises like the Trans-Siberian and the Trans-Caspian; and she added to the military strength, which the new railways made it possible to mobilise, by large-scale purchases of French arms and munitions, which constituted yet another link between the two countries. In July, 1891, a French fleet visited Kronstadt and was received with ostentatious cordiality: when the Czar swallowed his prejudices to the extent of having the Marseillaise played in his presence the French felt for the first time since 1870 that they were no longer the pariahs of Europe. Next month the two Powers signed a general political agreement, providing for mutual consultation and the concerting of measures against an aggressor. Two years later came Russia's commercial treaty with France and her nine months' tariff war against Germany (in order to force the latter to reduce its tariff rates for Russian corn exports). Then the Czar finally committed himself by a military convention, signed on December 27, 1893, which put teeth into the alliance. Ratification was completed by January 4, 1894.

The Dual Alliance—Its Terms and Influence

The main provision was for mutual assistance against any attack directed against one of the signatories by Germany with or without the support of Italy (against France) or of Austria-Hungary (against Russia). Subordinate provisions laid down that there should be systematic collaboration between the two general staffs, that mobilisation should follow automatically if any member of the Triple Alliance mobilised, and that for a war against Germany France should employ not less than 1,300,000 and Russia not less than 700,000 of her troops. In addition the principle was formulated of war on two fronts: the promised forces were to engage 'to the full with all speed, in order that Germany may have to fight at the same time on the East and on the West.' In 1906 a French loan of record size induced the Russians to guarantee a larger proportion of their troops to fight against Germany rather than Austria-Hungary. The convention was secret, and the exact terms were not revealed until 1918; France, however, disclosed in 1895 the fact that the diplomatic situation had been thus altered in her favour. The main result was to restore the balance of power in Europe, which had ceased to exist in 1871 because Germany was stronger than any single state and there was then no combination of states in which she was not included.

The new Dual Alliance was probably weaker than Germany's Triple Alliance, but not so weak that Germany dared ride roughshod over its wishes; and if Britain were ever to join it, the prospect for Germany would obviously be formidable.

The effect of the alliance on France was to restore self-confidence and national dignity, so that there were fewer hysterical outbursts of chauvinism such as had temporarily made the fortune of General Boulanger. Its effect on Russia was to encourage her expansionist programme in the Far East—the Trans-Siberian Railway, for instance, could not have been built without the French loans which the alliance facilitated—in which France had to share in order not to risk losing her new-found friend.

The British attitude towards the Franco-Russian Alliance was at first one of ridicule, later of fear. *Punch* reflected the earlier attitude in a cartoon (October, 1893) which stressed the incompatibility of the new partners. A picture representing the Russian Bear dancing with Miss Republic was accompanied by the verse:

> '*Beauty and Beast* vis-à-vis *in the dance*
> *Were scarce funnier partners than Russia and France.*
>
> . . . . .
>
> *Autocrat Bruin, can he really relish*
> *The larkish high-kick, the tempestuous twirl*
> *That risky Republican dances embellish?*
> *And she—a political "Wallflower," poor girl—*
> *Can she truly like the strange partner that fate*
> *Apportions her, lumpish, unlovely and late?*'

But a note of fear and warning was soon struck in England; France was after all the traditional enemy, and Russia at this very time was threatening British interests in the Far East. During the same winter (1893–4) a writer in the *Nineteenth Century* argued that the new alliance was directed 'as much against England and her Eastern Empire as against the Powers of the Triple Alliance' and went on to say that the French hatred of the German was 'faint when compared with that which the French feel, and on every occasion proclaim, to England.' An article in the *Contemporary* predicted 'a resolute squeezing of England by Russia and France in regions a long way off from Charing Cross.' Thus an uncomfortable feeling of isolation grew up in Britain, especially after the winter of 1895–6, when two sudden and short-lived crises about the widely different problems of the Venezuela frontier and the Jameson Raid showed that she alone had no friend on whom to rely. Hence successive attempts to come to terms with Russia, with Germany, and finally with France.

The Diplomatic Isolation of Britain

The agreements for the partitioning of Africa in and around the year 1890 had already involved Britain in hard bargaining, and Lord Salisbury habitually compromised, as in the deal with Germany over Heligoland and Zanzibar, because he knew that, since Britain had no allies, it would be unwise to press the advantage of her naval supremacy too far. In 1894-5, during Lord Rosebery's Government, she had found herself alone over an issue of a rather different kind. Turkey challenged the conscience of Christian Europe by a series of massacres on a larger scale than the Bulgarian atrocities of 1876 and this time perpetrated upon the Armenians of Asia Minor. Their well-being was of particular concern to Britain because our undertaking of 1878 to defend Asiatic Turkey against any further Russian advance was based upon Abdul Hamid's specific promise of reform there. But the massacres went unavenged. Russia refused to join in any measure of coercion; the Germans went further, ingratiating themselves with the Sultan by allowing him their tacit support; and, in default of any action by the Concert of Europe, Britain felt her general isolation too keenly to act alone.

Then on came the two major crises. The boundary dispute between British Guiana and Venezuela was of long standing, but it was brought to a head suddenly in 1895 because the Venezuelans had given a concession in the disputed area to an American syndicate and because the American President, Grover Cleveland, needed a popular cry for the elections coming in the following year. On December 17 he sent a message to Congress, announcing his intention to set up his own boundary commission and enforce its findings, by war if necessary, on the ground that the question came within the scope of the Monroe Doctrine. In other words, he claimed that Britain was seeking new colonies on the American continent, and proposed to stop her. The idea of a war against Britain was popular in America among the masses, but Lord Salisbury refused to be provoked. He even supplied documents of the British case to the American commission, while he and Chamberlain worked privately for an agreement to refer the matter to independent arbitrators. This was eventually done, and the arbitration upheld the British claims. In the meantime, however, this crisis had merged with the crisis in South Africa. Britain's isolation when confronted by Grover Cleveland's demands seemed to strengthen the case for immediate action over the Transvaal, before Kruger received overwhelming support from outside. At the same time our isolation caused the non-British element among the Uitlanders in Johannesburg to doubt whether our action would be allowed, by other Powers, to succeed. The upshot was the mistimed and mishandled Jameson Raid of December 29th–January 2nd, the failure of which emboldened the Boers as much as its wanton aggression embittered them. The results are writ large upon the history of South Africa, but for Europe the episode is important as marking a definite cleavage between Britain and Germany.

The 'Kruger Telegram' was a cabled message from the Kaiser to the Boer President, congratulating him on maintaining the independence of his country against armed hordes 'without appealing for the help of friendly Powers.' Thus it combined a reproof to Britain with an offer of assistance which implied non-recognition of the 1884 Convention between Britain and the Transvaal, whereby Britain reserved control of foreign relations. Coupled as it was with Jameson's humiliating failure, the telegram roused animosity against Germany and against the Kaiser, who was assumed to be personally responsible and was so, though the telegram had the considered support of his then Chancellor, Prince von Hohenlohe. During the preceding quarter of a century Britain had quarrelled almost incessantly about colonial issues with Russia and France, but it was a startling novelty to find Germany ranged against her as well, and our isolation began to seem foolhardy rather than splendid. The immediate situation was met by the formation of a naval 'flying squadron,' which could destroy any other navy afloat. It would have been able to deal with the German plan for intervention, which was to ship troops from German East Africa to the Transvaal through Mozambique: but the Portuguese in any case refused passage. That flying squadron was later to provide one of the arguments for the creation of a powerful German Navy. On a wider view, however, this episode began the preparation of British public opinion as well as of the experts in foreign policy for the problems of a new age, in which the empire could not safely stand alone.

As we saw in the previous chapter, the most serious immediate issue for Britain was her rivalry with Russia in the Far East. This did not greatly interest the general public, which was more familiar with Russian ambitions in the Balkans and on the road to India, and did not realise that when thwarted over the advance to Afghanistan in the Penjdeh crisis of 1885, and again over the control of Bulgaria in 1885–7, Russia had been caused to turn more wholeheartedly to the exploitation of her position in the Far East with the help of the new Trans-Siberian Railway. But Lord Salisbury, foreseeing that the collapse of the Chinese Empire might involve a whole series of inconclusive struggles among the Powers, as the collapse of the Ottoman Empire had done, approached the Russian Government in January, 1898, with a scheme for settling all Anglo-Russian disputes by partition. Unfortunately, this approach coincided with a move by Germany, which started a general policy of grab.

The murder of two German missionaries in Shantung Province was made to serve as the pretext for demanding a lease of the harbour of Kiao-Chau (in Shantung), which the German admiral Tirpitz had previously reconnoitred, on the Kaiser's instructions, and selected as the best military and economic base available. Russia thereupon took the district of Port Arthur, from which she had helped to eject the Japanese less than three years earlier. Thus Russia obtained at a single stroke a great naval base and a commercial port (Dalny) which, unlike Vladivostok, was ice-free in winter. China's third champion of 1895—namely, France—compensated herself with the lease of Kwang-Chau, a port conveniently near to her possessions in Indo-China. Britain obtained partial compensation for Russia's gains, by leasing Wei-hai-wei for a naval base, and the intangible advantage of not incurring the hatred which Japan naturally felt for the three Powers that had joined to protect Chinese territory against her only to seize it for themselves. But the main fact was that the possession of Port Arthur gave Russia a secure base for the exploitation of Manchuria and a prospect of effectively challenging British trade elsewhere in China. Britain therefore turned to Germany.

The Anglo-German Negotiations of 1898–1901

This was a much more natural course of action than appears in retrospect. We had had serious differences of opinion with the German Empire on colonial matters and about the Armenians, and the Kruger Telegram had its smaller parallels in a brusque and almost brutal manner of negotiation which taxed even the equanimity of Lord Salisbury. But our disputes with both Russia and France had been in general more bitter and more prolonged. There was no fundamental conflict of interest between Britain and Germany, since in trade Germany was a great customer as well as a great rival, her army we did not seek to challenge, and our navy we, at this time, thought unchallengeable. The first German Navy law, backed by the popular propaganda of the Navy League, the ambition of Admiral Tirpitz, and the Kaiser's irresponsible enthusiasm, passed through the Reichstag in the same year, 1898. It provided for the building of a considerable battle fleet, and the need to win votes for this expenditure by showing England as a danger may have influenced the German Government against a rapprochement just then; but the German Navy did not at this stage represent a serious conflict of interests in English eyes. Moreover, the British Government was encouraged by past history to think a link-up with Germany practicable. In 1879 and again in 1889 Germany's most admired statesman had made overtures to Britain. In 1887 the Bulgarian crisis had resulted in the signature of two agreements, which in effect guaranteed the preservation of the *status quo* in the Mediterranean area and the Balkans by joining Britain, for that limited purpose at least, to the powerful structure of the Triple Alliance.

Accordingly, the first overtures were made by Chamberlain to the German Embassy in London as soon as the Russian negotiations were seen to fail, and had for their prime object the checking of the Russian advance in China. Chamberlain apparently talked of an alliance, though he may not at this stage actually have envisaged more than a friendly understanding. Whatever it was, he failed to get it, since the German policy at this juncture was not to check, but rather to encourage, the Russian advance in China, which would serve to render France's ally less active in the affairs of Europe.

Instead, by the end of May, 1898, the Kaiser was busy disclosing Chamberlain's secret overtures to the Czar, in order to show who was Russia's true friend. This last fact was not, of course, known to Chamberlain, who continued to use his position as colonial secretary to promote good relations with Germany. In particular, the risk of further trouble about the Transvaal was lessened by a treaty dated August, 1898, by which Germany abandoned her interest in the fate of the Transvaal in return for the promise of a major share in the Portuguese African colonies if Portugal were to renounce their ownership. When the Boer War began in October, 1899, public opinion in Germany, as elsewhere in Europe, was overwhelmingly on the side of the Boers. But the German Government, though it used the chance to drive a hard bargain over Samoa, rejected Russian proposals for a European coalition against Britain; refused to receive Kruger, when he came to Europe in search of help; and kept the door open for further negotiation. To Britain, on the other hand, the need for friends became suddenly more obvious.

In November, 1899, Chamberlain renewed his overtures when the Kaiser, accompanied by his foreign minister Bülow, visited England for Queen Victoria's eightieth birthday. The proposal now was for a triple combination of Britain, Germany, and the United States, which Chamberlain proceeded to expound in a public speech at Leicester. Bülow, whom he believed to have approved the idea at Windsor, replied in the Reichstag and emphatically rejected it. Though Chamberlain was justly indignant at the public rebuff, he made yet a third attempt, in the early months of 1901, when a Convention was actually drafted by the new Foreign Secretary, Lord Lansdowne. This would have joined Britain to the Triple Alliance in the event of an attack by two Powers (i.e. France and Russia) against the Triple Alliance, and *vice versa*. Lord Salisbury thought the terms unduly onerous for Britain, whose frontiers were so much easier to defend than those of the Triple Allies, but his reluctance made the German Government feel that the bargain must be a good one for them, and for a time they were pressing Britain to declare her open adherence to the Triple Alliance. There was even talk of bringing in Japan as well. This last series of Anglo-German negotiations was finally terminated by an altercation between Bülow and Chamberlain, who had been stung by German allegations of British atrocities in South Africa into an attack on the German Army's conduct during the war of 1870.

In any case, in spite of the fact that agreement between Germany and Britain was not fundamentally impossible at this time, there were in practice many differences of temperament and attitude which made negotiation and close relationship difficult. The German Foreign Office (the *Wilhelmstrasse*) was reserved and distant in attitude; it was always bargaining and demanding compensation (a word at which Lord Salisbury 'demurred'); and it held the threat of force in the not distant background. This attitude was particularly unfortunate in dealing with the British. As the German historian, Brandenburg, has pointed out: 'The way in which German policy invariably opened fire at once with its biggest guns was extremely antipathetic to English statesmen, who were more tranquil and tolerant in their diplomatic intercourse and very sensitive to threats.' The German feeling about the British was well expressed in a memorandum written by Bülow in 1899.[1] With characteristic cynicism and realism he sums up the British: 'British politicians know little of the Continent. . . . They are naïve. . . . They believe with difficulty that others have bad motives. They are very calm, very easy-going, very optimistic.' Of the feeling of each people towards the other he says: 'There is no doubt that feeling in England generally is far less anti-German than German feeling is anti-British. Therefore the most dangerous Englishmen for us are those, who, like Chirol and Saunders, know from personal observation how sharp and deep is the German dislike of England.' The two men singled out by name were *Times* correspondents in Berlin.

German professors had already been responsible for developing among the young an exaggerated patriotism. The most influential of them, von Treitschke, became professor of history at Berlin in 1874. He taught that the all-important

---

[1] This memorandum should be read by every student of Anglo-German relations. It is a masterly analysis of the British attitude; many of its points were equally applicable to the British attitude later towards Nazi Germany. The document can be found in E. T. S. Dugdale, *German Diplomatic Documents*, III, p. 113, and is quoted at length by Sir Valentine Chirol, *Fifty Years in a Changing World*, and by J. A. Spender, *Fifty Years of Europe*.

characteristic of the State was force, that war was in the nature of things and that a love of peace was something weak and sentimental. 'The State,' he said, 'is the public force for Offence and Defence.' He spoke of the 'moral majesty of war,' and of the German Army as 'the real and effective bond of national union.'[1]   In his youth Treitschke had been a Liberal and looked forward to a unification of Germany through the formation of a German parliament.   But with the failure of those early hopes, Treitschke was completely carried away by the success of Bismarck and the formation of the German Empire by force of arms.   Thus he came to glorify Prussian militarism, and showed a contempt for foreign states and an especial dislike of England.

It is clear, then, that the Germans did not look in a very friendly spirit at England.   Meanwhile, too, the Kaiser was setting his 'New Course' of expansion south-eastwards with the scheme for a Berlin-Baghdad railway and his firm support for Austria in the Balkans.   The final failure of Chamberlain's plan for agreement with Germany was also due to doubts about Germany's good faith, arising from an actual experiment of co-operation in the Far East.

During 1900 the situation in China had made Britain's need of support in that part of the world more acute than ever.   The Dowager Empress having wrested control of the country from her nephew, who had made some attempts at reform, a society of fanatical reactionaries, known as 'Fists of Righteous Harmony' *alias* Boxers, organised nationalist outbreaks against the foreigners.   These culminated in the siege of the legations at Pekin, which was relieved by an international expeditionary force (in which the six Powers constituting the Concert of Europe were all represented, together with the United States and Japan) under a German commander-in-chief.   British influence helped to secure the appointment of a German, on which the Kaiser's heart was set in order to avenge the murder of his minister in Pekin; and in the more cordial atmosphere resulting an Anglo-German convention was signed to preserve the territorial

---

[1] See H. von Treitschke, *Politics* (2 vols., translated by Mrs. Blanche Dugdale). Writing an introduction in 1916 for the English translation, Balfour referred to Treitschke's description of war as a 'medicine for mankind diseased.'   Since Treitschke lectured that medicine has indeed, as Balfour put it, 'been supplied in overflowing measure.'

H

integrity of China and the 'open door' for the trade of all nations. Britain tried to use this agreement to restrain the Russians, who took advantage of the confused condition of the country. Even after the Boxers had been suppressed and a large indemnity exacted from the imperial government for their outrages, the Russians extended still further their hold over Manchuria. But the Germans promptly declared that this agreement applied only to the Yangtse Basin, which was a limitation stated in the first, but not in the final, draft, and refused to exert any pressure on the Russians.

The Anglo-Japanese Alliance

Nevertheless, it was the Far Eastern question which brought Britain into effective alliance with another Great Power, thereby breaking the long tradition of proud independence or splendid isolation which Canning had been the first to propound. If Germany would not help to curb Russia, Japan would, for her only alternative was to come to terms with the Russians, then in their haughtiest mood. Japan's ambition being rather to humiliate the Russians, to eject them from Manchuria, and above all to secure possession of Korea, her need was for some one to keep the ring in order that Russia might be challenged without the challenger needing to fight France as well. Accordingly, the treaty as signed in January, 1902, provided for the maintenance of the *status quo* in the Far East and for the intervention of the ally by force of arms if the other party were to find itself at war with two Powers in defence of the *status quo*.   Hence the Russo-Japanese War of 1904–5; the defeat of Russia and the further rise of Japan; and the extension of the alliance in 1905 to cover the defence of the *status quo* in India and intervention in future if the other party to the alliance found itself at war with even one Power in the treaty area.

Britain turns from Germany to France

But by the time of the outbreak of the Russo-Japanese War the British position in Europe had undergone a double change—relations with Germany were slowly but definitely worsening, relations with France were improving quickly towards the consummation of the *Entente Cordiale*. In the winter of 1902–3 there was a fresh crisis in the affairs of Venezuela, where frequent revolutions led to outrages against foreigners and refusal to acknowledge debts. Britain and Germany therefore joined in a naval blockade, much to the indignation of the United States, to which Britain deferred a little more readily than Germany, so that the latter got most of the blame for what was alleged to be an infringement of the Monroe Doctrine in spirit if not in letter. Shortly after this the cleavage was made more evident by British refusal to put up money for the Baghdad Railway, a scheme for developing a line through Asia Minor to the Persian Gulf, which would open up the trade of Mesopotamia and other Turkish provinces. The German entrepreneurs were genuinely in need of additional capital and would have welcomed both British and French participation;[1] but Germany's growing friendship with Turkey was believed to portend an ultimate attack on Egypt or even India. The upshot was that the Berlin-Baghdad route remained unopened in 1914. At the same time Joseph Chamberlain's tariff reform campaign was giving wide publicity to German trade competition, not because of its absolute importance but in order to paint an alarming picture of the results of free trade. But the biggest factor was undoubtedly the growth of the German Navy. The first important Navy Law of 1898 had been followed by the authorisation of big increases in 1900, when Britain's ability to isolate the Boers from sea-borne help emphasised the value of a navy. In 1903 our decision to start a naval base at Rosyth showed how seriously Britain regarded the emergence of a new naval power in northern waters; ships began to be concentrated there from other commands, notably the China station, where we relied instead upon the fleet of our Japanese ally; and the building of extra ships to meet the threat soon started to fan the flames of national and sporting rivalry.

The British rapprochement with France was partly a personal achievement. Delcassé worked for it steadily from the time of the trial of strength at Fashoda; and he, unlike most French foreign ministers, had charge for a long continuous

---

[1] Lord Hardinge points out that up to the time of Hitler Germany had never derived any exclusive advantage from the building of the Baghdad Railway (*Old Diplomacy*, p. 47).

period, from 1898 to 1905. On the British side there was the
character of the new King, Edward VII, who was no policy-
maker, but had a flair for personal contacts and a love of
foreign travel, which combined with his life-long preference
for France over Germany to make him the ideal propagandist
for a pro-French policy among the masses on either side of
the Channel. This was the more important because the
failure of the last efforts at co-operation with Germany,
over the Venezuela debt-collecting and the financing of the
Baghdad Railway, had been due to the antipathy of Englishmen towards Germans as much as to that felt by the Germans
for the English.

In May, 1903, Edward's first visit to Paris since becoming
King found the public resentful of Fashoda and by no means
forgetful of the Boer War, but left it captivated by his charm
and adroitness. When President Loubet and Delcassé returned the visit in July, their cordial reception showed the
diplomats that they had the ground on which to work.
German journalists, followed later by German historians,
have made the natural mistake of supposing that King Edward
had some of the power of initiative in policy-making possessed
by his volatile nephew the Kaiser—natural in view of the
German constitution and made additionally plausible in this
particular case by the ill-concealed animosity between King
and Kaiser. Hence the story of Edward VII's *Einkreisungs-
politik*, the encirclement of Germany which was supposed to
provide the motive for all his frequent Continental journeys.
But the *Entente* was actually created by hard diplomatic
bargaining, which was started between Delcassé and Lord
Lansdowne in the autumn and reached fruition in April, 1904.
What was far more important than personalities was the fact
that each side stood to gain by reaching an agreement. To
Britain in her present exposed position it seemed eminently
desirable to settle each outstanding colonial quarrel which
might some day flare up into a war, and in particular to buy
off French hostility in Egypt, where it was a grave impediment
to the work of Lord Cromer. To France there was bigger
game afoot, we may suppose, even at this early stage—namely,
the possibility that the *Entente* might be so handled as not
merely to settle disputes with England, but to range England
on the side of France in her disputes with third parties. It

is doubtful whether British statesmen fully realised this before 1911—perhaps not before 1914.

To the British the new understanding with France was a pacific one. Eyre Crowe of the Foreign Office in a lengthy and important memorandum,[1] written three years later in 1907, stated that 'In England, the wish for improved relations with France was primarily but a fresh manifestation of the general tendency of British Governments to take advantage of every opportunity to approach more closely to the ideal condition of living in honourable peace with all other States.' To German, and indeed to many other foreign politicians, this kind of sentiment in the British was simply naïveté or even hypocrisy. In 1904 the Germans felt that England, consciously or unconsciously, had at last abandoned isolation and taken sides in the European struggle. They felt that the English casting vote had gone to the French group.

Eyre Crowe, in any case, was one of those British who *did* know their Europe. His mother and wife were German; he was in close touch with German thought and feeling, and in this memorandum he ruthlessly exposed the dangerous, aggressive tendencies developing in Germany. Then, as later with the Nazis, the Germans demanded the right to expand at the expense of anyone who stood in their way. The German argument, in the words of Crowe, was: 'A healthy and powerful State like Germany, with its 60,000,000 inhabitants, must expand, it cannot stand still, it must have territories. . . . Necessity has no law. The world belongs to the strong.' The British Foreign Secretary, Grey, marked this memorandum 'most valuable.' Lord Fitzmaurice, Parliamentary Under-Secretary, added a minute on a consideration of personality—'whether the restless and uncertain personal character of the Emperor William is sufficiently taken into account. . . . There was at least method in Prince Bismarck's madness; but the Emperor is like a cat in a cupboard. He may jump out anywhere.' It is not surprising that in a world largely dominated by Germany England should be looking round for powerful friends; it is not surprising also that Eyre Crowe has been described, from the German point of view, as the evil genius of the Foreign Office (*der böse Geist des Foreign Office*).

[1] Gooch and Temperley, *British Documents*, III, pp. 397–420.

The Anglo-French Entente Cordiale

The series of agreements constituting the *Entente Cordiale* covered colonial rivalries in all parts of the world. Thus France surrendered the territorial privileges of her fishermen on the so-called French shore of Newfoundland, dating from 1713, in return for modifications in her favour of the frontiers of Gambia and Nigeria which had been fixed as recently as 1898. Zones of influence were fixed in Siam; Britain gave up her opposition to the tariff which the French had established after their annexation of Madagascar; and a start was made on the problem of the New Hebrides, which was later (1906) turned into a condominium of the two Powers. But the three main provisions were as follows: France agreed that there should be no time-limit demanded for the British occupation of Egypt. Britain agreed in return not to obstruct French activities in Morocco. Thirdly, the most significant provision of all promised mutual support in the event of any modification in the status of Egypt or Morocco: in other words, Britain might keep Egypt, France might take Morocco. This last provision was secret, but as it involved agreement with Spain, to which the Moroccan territory adjoining the Straits of Gibraltar was allocated by special negotiation later the same year, news of the secret provision leaked out long before its publication in 1911. As we shall see in the next chapter, Germany waited no longer than till 1905 to challenge the *Entente* by championing the independence of the Sultan of Morocco, whose affairs, which had been regulated by a conference of all the Powers at Madrid in 1880, were now being forced under the jurisdiction of a group of three or four Powers only. For the Germans had an additional grievance in the fact that Italy had been induced by Delcassé to barter her consent to France's Moroccan project for French consent to her less well matured plans in Tripoli. In 1902, moreover, Italy had formed the intention to remain neutral if France was attacked or 'directly provoked'; and she had long since stated her refusal to be drawn by the Triple Alliance into war against Britain.

The Russo-Japanese War (1904–5)
and the Ensuing Russo-German Negotiations

Accordingly, Germany's first reaction to the *Entente* was to draw closer to Russia. The Japanese campaign in the Far East, to which we must turn for a moment, had proceeded according to plan. In February, 1904, a crippling initial blow was struck at the Russian fleet in Port Arthur by means of a surprise torpedo-boat attack, two days in advance of the Japanese declaration of war. This gave Japan control of the sea, so that her armies could be conveyed in safety to Korea and Manchuria. On January 1, 1905, Port Arthur fell after ten months' siege. A decisive land victory was gained at Mukden in March. There remained only the Russian Baltic fleet, which was sent round the world to meet disaster in the Straits of Tsushima, at the approach to the Sea of Japan, where Admiral Togo won perhaps the most overwhelming naval triumph of modern times.

Britain's share in the war had been to hold the ring for her ally according to the terms of the 1902 treaty: but this was not without danger. The sensational Dogger Bank episode of October 21, 1904, when the Russian fleet, emerging nervously from the Baltic, fired in error upon British trawlers, brought war for a moment very near. The matter was settled in the end by payment of compensation, but it was of ominous significance that Germany gave Russia her diplomatic support, as well as practical assistance in the shape of coaling facilities as the fleet continued its long voyage. In August, 1905, however, by the good offices of President Theodore Roosevelt, the war came to an end with the Treaty of Portsmouth. The Russians forfeited Port Arthur and the southern half of the island of Sakhalin (taken from Japan in 1875); evacuated Manchuria; and agreed to leave the victors a free hand in Korea, which was annexed five years later. But their firm refusal to pay an indemnity showed their disbelief in Japan's capacity to win a prolonged war of attrition, much less to penetrate into Russia proper, however great her successes on the outer periphery of the empire.

During the course of the war some remarkable telegrams— later published in the 'Willy-Nicky Correspondence'—passed between Kaiser and Czar, which criticised English neutrality as unfriendly to Russia. 'The naval battles fought by Togo are fought with Cardiff coal,' said the Kaiser. The Czar referred to 'Anglo-Japanese arrogance and insolence.' While the peace negotiations were on foot the Kaiser tried to restore Germany's position as arbiter of Europe by creating a fresh link with Russia through its disillusioned monarch. He arranged to meet the Czar in the course of a Baltic yachting cruise, when the two monarchs, as it were on the spur of the moment, signed a treaty of which the Kaiser had a draft conveniently ready. The object of this Treaty of Björkö (July, 1905) was to unite both Russia and France with Germany against Britain, the method a Russo-German pact of mutual support against 'any European enemy,' to which France would be induced subsequently to adhere. The agreement between the monarchs was too much of a personal policy to find favour with the German Chancellor Bülow and was completely scouted by his Russian counterpart, Witte, who saw that it would break up the alliance with France and, being limited to Europe, would not even ensure German support for Russia to redress the balance of power in the Far East. It therefore came to nothing, but the history of this dramatic proposal emphasises the fact that it was not the mere formation of the Dual Alliance and the *Entente Cordiale*, but the way in which they stood the rigorous testing of the successive crises of 1905–11, which divided Europe into two well-defined camps and made world war in the end inevitable.

SUGGESTIONS FOR FURTHER READING

Cambridge History of British Foreign Policy, Vol. III, c. 4, by Sir Valentine Chirol, and c. 5 by G. P. Gooch.

J. A. Spender: *Fifty Years of Europe*, cc. 13, 20–2, 24–7.

R. B. Mowat: *History of European Diplomacy, 1815–1914*, cc. 26 and 27.

W. L. Langer: *Diplomacy of Imperialism*, cc. 1–3.

CHAPTER 7

THE EUROPEAN CRISES, 1905–11

The First Moroccan Crisis

THE year 1905 is memorable in European history, not only for the external discomfiture of Russia, as expressed in the Treaty of Portsmouth, but still more for the internal revolutionary outbreaks, foreshadowing the upheaval of 1917, which for the time being made her power a cipher, or at best a question mark, in world affairs. That was why the Kaiser came so near to success with his Björkö Treaty, which offered Czar Nicholas the moral support he so badly needed in return for a scheme which would either have linked the Dual Alliance with Germany against Britain or have disrupted it altogether. But Germany was simultaneously pursuing another plan which hinged on the evident weakness of Russia, and when Björkö failed to produce either of the hoped-for alternative results this other plan was pushed forward to test the new combination more fully. Such a test involved some risk of a general war, but the completion just at this time of the Schlieffen Plan, for holding the Russians while a great wheeling movement of the main German forces across Belgium administered the *coup de grâce* to France, made war in some respects an attractive risk to the military party in Germany.

Accordingly, on March 31, 1905, the Kaiser was induced by his advisers, Bülow and Holstein, to break his Mediterranean cruise by landing at Tangier and making one of his over-emphatic speeches, which could be relied upon to reach the newspaper headlines in all parts of the world. By assuring the Sultan of Morocco that he regarded him as a free and independent sovereign the Kaiser gave his backing to German commercial interests in Morocco, which were not as a matter of fact then in danger, proclaimed Germany's support for the principle of the integrity of Moroccan territory, and above all indicated that Germany did not recognise the agreements for its disposal which had been entered into by France, Britain, and Spain. The Kaiser's speech was followed up

by an official German demand for an international conference on the affairs of Morocco, which the Sultan, hard pressed
by French concession-hunters, readily endorsed.   France had,
in a sense, deliberately asked for trouble by planning to
turn Morocco into a second Tunis by secret agreements
with Britain, Spain, and Italy, over which Germany had
never been consulted, much less compensated.   But the
brusqueness of German methods once again diverted attention
from any reasonableness in her claims.   Indeed, Bülow, without
even informing the Kaiser, rejected a French offer at this
stage to make a general colonial settlement, which might have
developed into a Franco-German *entente*.   It was this brusqueness as much as anything which induced Britain to take the
first steps towards turning the passive 'understanding' with
France into active co-operation.

   The first round, nevertheless, went to Germany.   The
French Foreign Minister, Delcassé, as prime author of the
entente, held out against the German demand for a conference
on Morocco and claimed that he had assurances of British
support in the event of serious trouble.   The Foreign Office
had given no such assurances, though it ventured to warn the
Germans that public opinion might cause us to side with
France if she were attacked: any stronger assertion came
from King Edward as he passed on holiday between Biarritz
and London.   Germany, on the other hand, sent a special
envoy to Paris to insist that Delcassé should be got rid of as a
trouble-maker.   In early June Delcassé found that the Prime
Minister, Rouvier, and the entire Cabinet (though not President Loubet) were against him, primarily because they thought
that any attempt to call Germany's bluff would mean a war
for which France was ill-prepared, Russia incapable, and
Britain unwilling.   He therefore resigned, and the Kaiser
emphasised Germany's triumph over the *Entente* by making
Bülow a prince.

The Algeciras Conference

   The second round, however, went differently to expectation.
The French under pressure agreed to a conference, a little
consoled by President Theodore Roosevelt's promise that, if
they agreed to it, he would see fair play.   A preliminary
arrangement about Morocco was sketched out between the

French and Germans, in return for which the latter now signified their approval of the public clauses of the *Entente*. But relations between the two countries continued to be so strained that at the beginning of January the French pressed the new British Liberal Government for the same general assurance that Britain would help France against an unprovoked attack as their Conservative predecessors had given a few months before. Then, as a corollary to the assurance, the French asked for discussions between the two General Staffs to determine what help *might* be made available. Such discussions were begun; they embraced Belgium as well as France, and brought in the Navy (though discussion of this had been originated by Lansdowne); and their continuance and development until 1914 implicated Britain in French policy in a manner, and to an extent, which were wholly concealed not merely from the man in the street but from all except an inner ring of the Cabinet and the War Office. Constitutionally, such secret arrangements, distasteful to democratic theory, could never commit Britain to war; but in practice they created a position from which it was difficult to back out. Thus the German move at Tangier, which seemed to have discredited the *Entente* to some extent, had actually increased its value to France.

The Conference itself, which met at Algeciras on January 16, also disappointed Germany. Russia, Britain, and Spain all supported the French claims, as might be expected; but France was also backed by the United States (now first emerging on the European scene) and by Italy, while the third member of the Triple Alliance, though thanked by Germany for acting as a 'brilliant second,' gave rather lukewarm support. The maintenance of the territorial integrity of Morocco was one of the principles which France and Germany had agreed upon beforehand, so the main discussions turned on the control of internal arrangements which would give economic power and political influence. On two points France won—the personnel of the police were to be provided by France and Spain (with a Swiss inspector-general); control of Customs and of the traffic in arms was likewise assigned to France and Spain on their Algerian and Riff frontiers respectively. The third point was the more strictly economic question of a State bank, in which Germany obtained an equal share of control with France, Spain, and Britain. But even when we add that Germany's action in requiring a conference to be called had postponed the swallowing up of Morocco by France, the sum total amounted to a diplomatic rebuff of a kind to which imperial Germany was unused. It was the end of the career of Holstein, the counsellor who had chiefly instigated the Kaiser to land at Tangier. Bülow pretended to be well satisfied with the results of the conference; but in reality he and his master were biding their time, first for a diplomatic counter-stroke elsewhere, and then (though not actually during the Chancellorship of Bülow, which came to an end in July, 1909) for a renewal of the struggle for Morocco.

The Anglo-Russian Entente

Two and a half years intervened between the close of the Algeciras Conference and the new crisis over the Eastern Question, years which served to bind Britain more closely to the Dual Alliance. For the prolonged friction of the days of the Russo-Japanese War, when the backwash of the Dogger Bank incident encouraged the Kaiser to plan the abortive Björkö Agreement, began to give place to a sense of common interests, warmly fostered by France. France could exert the maximum pressure upon her ally, because the dissolution of the Duma in 1906, by which action the Czar got back his power, was only made possible by a new French loan, larger than any in the past history of the world. Then the Conference itself tended to improve Anglo-Russian relations, because the two Powers found themselves in the same camp, defending France's position in Morocco. There was also the politic self-restraint shown by the British over the Baghdad Railway scheme, where they opposed German aims more consistently than the French and won the gratitude of the Russians, who, just at this time (1907), were being driven to give a very grudging consent to the activities of the German company, which was still building its line in 1914. Finally, good relations were helped by the men who found themselves in power in both countries at this juncture. Grey, the Liberal Foreign Secretary, was better placed than a Tory minister to overcome the distrust of Russian policy, both foreign and domestic, which was probably more general in Liberal than in Tory circles, though common everywhere in Britain. Izvolsky, who became Russian Foreign Minister in 1906, was pro-British, and wanted to turn Russia's attention from the Far East to ambitions nearer home. This, as we shall shortly see, meant trouble in a new quarter, but the immediate result was the creation of a good impression in Britain by the guaranteeing of the territorial integrity of China, which was undertaken by France and Japan and Russia and Japan severally in June–July, 1907.

Accordingly, the plan of the original Anglo-French *Entente* was followed in an Anglo-Russian Convention, signed on August 31, 1907, which got rid of all the main causes of friction. Tibet was the easiest to settle, for it was only in 1905 that the British mission under Younghusband had penetrated to Lhasa in order to open up trade and secure an exclusive political influence for Britain. These advantages were now forgone, as both Britain and Russia undertook to make political representations to Tibet only through its suzerain, China, and to refrain from seeking economic conces-sions. The second problem was that ancient bone of conten-tion, Afghanistan, control of whose foreign policy Russia now yielded to Britain, subject only to an undertaking to preserve its independence and to allow Russians equal access for trade. Thus the age-long Russian threat to India was at last removed. But the main agreement concerned Persia, which was breaking up rapidly and, but for the British position in India and our sensitiveness to Russian activities on its borders, would almost certainly have passed entirely into Russian hands. As it was, Russia got the lion's share—a sphere of influence in the north-west, which included eleven out of the twelve principal Persian towns, was larger than the British sphere of influence in the south-east along the Persian Gulf, and provided a good base for penetration into the nominally quite independent centre. Russia, aiming at a trans-Persian railway, 'autonomy' for Azerbaijan, and economic concessions everywhere, sub-sequently took every advantage of Grey's reluctance to quarrel. In 1909 matters came to a head in a revolution, which was followed by the appointment of an American financial expert to straighten matters out, whereupon the Cossacks were sent into north Persia and the neutral adviser ejected. Grey tolerated all this for the sake of the *Entente*, and is even believed to have held out hopes, informally and conditionally, that British friendship might eventually enable Russian warships to secure the long-coveted permission to operate from the Black Sea through the Straits.

The Growth of Naval Rivalry between Britain and Germany

For it is most important to realise that the growth of the *Entente* relationship resulted, not only from the crises in French and Russian policies, but also from Britain's steadily increasing need of friends in face of what she regarded as the German naval menace. One of the minor repercussions of the Algeciras Conference was that the German Navy League, which existed to organise public opinion in favour of ever greater naval expenditure, was able to argue that lack of sea power had exposed Germany to a diplomatic rebuff. Then there was the challenge and opportunity with which Germany was confronted by the launching of the *Dreadnought* in February, 1906. Sir John Fisher, who had been First Sea Lord since 1904, was the least discreet of men and even spoke of 'Copenhagening' the German fleet in the manner of 1807. By designing a wholly new type of battleship, outclassing all others by the fire-power of its big guns and the speed of its turbine engines, he gained a long lead over the German shipyards (which took about two years to develop a similar design) and a still longer lead over the German strategists, because it took eight years to widen the Kiel Canal so that Dreadnoughts could pass freely between the Baltic and the North Sea.

However it was a real opportunity as well as a challenge, for the Liberals were indisposed to build the new ships, which were fabulously expensive, at top speed, so that the Germans could take heart from the fact that our accumulation of older ships was obsolete and that only a relatively small number of the new models would be needed to threaten the balance of power at sea. In 1907, accordingly, Bülow brought forward a new naval programme far more ambitious than that of 1900, and rejected as an oblique threat the British Prime Minister's suggestion in a magazine article that all Powers might profit by agreeing to postpone any further naval construction for an agreed period. When naval disarmament came up again a few months later at the Second

Hague Conference it was again scouted by Germany, which rather adroitly gave the naval discussions a very different twist by supporting the American demand for the freedom of the seas—that is, for the abolition of control of private property on the high seas which has always been one of Britain's most cherished uses of naval power. The only practical result of the Conference was the further development of facilities for voluntary arbitration between Powers which had been tentatively organised at the First Hague Conference in 1899.

The German Navy League was not the only important organisation at work in stimulating an extreme and arrogant nationalism among the Germans. The Pan-German Union was also active in the work of nationalist propaganda. A Foreign Office minute (of 1906) stated: 'There can be no doubt as to the immense popularity of the Pan-German move-ment and of the agitation carried on by the German Navy League. Both these organisations are inspired by bitter and often scurrilous hostility to Great Britain.' The minute was written on a dispatch received from the British Minister Resident at Munich (Reginald Tower) which described in detail the aims and activities of the German nationalists. 'The Union aims,' wrote Tower, 'at a revival of German nationalism and patriotism all over the world . . . at a compact union of Germans in all lands.

'To carry out this programme, the Union begins by claiming all German-speaking peoples as of German kith and kin. It aspires to the ultimate inclusion of the German-speaking cantons of Switzerland, of the Baltic provinces of Russia, of parts of Belgium and Luxemburg, and, most important of all, of Holland with her littoral and her Colonies.' There is an almost Marxian (and Marx was a German, and a nationalist, too, in his attitude to the Balkan Slavs) belief in the inevitability of social development about the statement Tower quotes from the weekly publication of the Union: 'The elevation of Germanism into Pan-Germanism is the necessary step in the evolution which has by successive stages witnessed the Branden-burg and Prussian States, the Zollverein, the North German Confederation, and, lastly, the German Empire.'

Further notable exacerbations of Anglo-German relations came in 1908 and 1909. In October of the former year the

Daily Telegraph published an interview with the Kaiser, in which he explained how he had used his influence to restrain France and Russia from active intervention against Britain in the Boer War, had stood out against the strongly pro-Boer opinions of his own subjects, and had even devised the plan by which the British eventually won the campaign. The interview created such a furore in Germany, that the Kaiser talked of abdicating and never again trusted Bülow (who had failed to censor the script of the interview and now took responsibility for his master's errors with ostentatious magnanimity). In Britain it confirmed the impression of the Kaiser's instability, and in addition made the public realise for the first time how definitely hostile the German people had become. On top of this came the discovery in 1909 that Germany was catching up fast in the race for Dreadnoughts, which roused the British people to the cry of 'We want eight and we won't wait.' In practice, we built eighteen ships in the next two years to Germany's nine, so that the Germans gained nothing, and relations were further exacerbated because Bülow's pacifically minded successor, Bethmann-Hollweg, was no more receptive than Bülow to our proposals for a naval holiday.[1]

We can now see why it was that, in the second period of European crisis, the affairs of the *Entente* were complicated by the belief, to which the French Premier Clemenceau gave vigorous expression, that Britain might need to be restrained from picking a quarrel with Germany, in which the French Army would have to bear the brunt of the attack. In part, the French apprehension was based on their natural grudge against the British for the fact that, alone among first-class European Powers, they refused to shoulder the burden of conscription. But in the main it arose from their indifference to the Eastern Question, which was now raising its head once more after a period of quiescence.

[1] Anglo-German naval rivalry, one of the contributory factors in the course of events leading to the First World War, has been exhaustively dealt with by E. L. Woodward, *Great Britain and the German Navy*. Of the long wrangle between British and German statesmen, he remarks: 'Upon these formulæ hung the fate of millions of men.' Germany needed a navy, said Bethmann-Hollweg, for the 'general purposes of her greatness.' But a navy was vital to Britain for the protection of her world trade. The essentials of the issue were well put at the same time by Mr. Churchill when he described the British fleet as a necessity and the German fleet as a luxury.

The Bosnian Crisis

In the first years of the twentieth century Turkey was firmly attached to Germany, while Britain, having secured her aims in Egypt and Cyprus, was consistently anti-Turkish. Another change from the old days was the transference of Serbia from the Austrian to the Russian camp, a change which was signalised by the brutal murder of the last Obrenovic King and his Queen in 1903, a murder to which the Russian Minister at Belgrade was almost certainly privy, and which was followed by the so-called 'Pig War,' when Austria tried in vain to call Serbia to heel by banning her principal export commodity from the Austrian market. But the biggest change of all was the agreement reached between the two great rivals, Austria and Russia, which began in 1897 as an understanding that British intervention in Macedonian massacres must be thwarted in both their interests. In 1903 it had developed into the Mürzsteg Agreement, by which the two Powers went beyond the existing promise to preserve the *status quo* in the Balkans and organised an international gendarmerie to prevent further massacres in Macedonia. This kept the peace for five years, each of the Powers, with the significant exception of Germany, taking police responsibility in one zone.

And then early in the year 1908, Austria and Russia fell foul of each other over rival railway plans to meet the situation resulting from Serbia's recent change of sides—for an Austrian line southwards through the Sanjak towards Salonika and for a Russian line westwards across Serbia towards the Adriatic—which came to nothing in the end, though the immediate effect was to strengthen the Anglo-Russian *Entente*, as spectacularly demonstrated by King Edward's visit to the Czar at Reval in June. But instead of pursuing the quarrel Izvolsky began to negotiate a bargain, by which the Austrians were to allow Russia to pass her warships through the Straits into the Mediterranean, the fulfilment of an age-old ambition which would help to make up for the losses in the Far East, in return for the conversion of the occupation of Bosnia-Herzegovina into outright annexation by Austria. Discussions of a very tortuous character had already begun, when the Turkish revolution of July forced Abdul Hamid to concede the

I

Constitution of 1876 and threw all Europe into a fluster because
the Young Turk leaders, a posse of Army officers who were
really a foretaste of the Fascists, were taken at their face value as
apostles of liberalism. All attempts to reform Macedonia by outside agencies were abandoned as superfluous in a liberal Turkey,
and—what was more important—Izvolsky and the Austrian
Foreign Minister, Aehrenthal, met at Buchlau in September
to push on with their plot before a Turkish revival should
render it unworkable.

Their plot was in all probability a plot against each other
as well as against the Turks. The details of the supposed
agreement between the two statesmen are still uncertain;
but what happened was that Izvolsky had only just begun to
canvass opinion among the Powers about his project for
opening the Straits when the Austrians on October 6 announced
the formal annexation of the provinces of Bosnia-Herzegovina.
Bulgaria by arrangement announced her formal independence
of Turkey the previous day, Ferdinand assuming the title of
Czar, so although Austria now restored the Sanjak (partly to
appease Italy, partly because she had come to prefer the
Morava route for an eventual penetration to Salonika),
Turkey was thrown once more into the melting-pot. The
first consequence was that the British Foreign Secretary,
apparently unaware that the annexation had been secretly
approved by Germany and Russia in 1881 and, more recently
and conditionally, by Italy as well, said that the Bosnian
question ought to be submitted to a conference of the Powers.
What was of more practical importance, he denied Izvolsky
his compensation on the same grounds—the Powers (who were
certain to refuse) must be consulted about any scheme for
opening the Straits to Russian warships only. Grey's attitude,
we may note in passing, disappointed the French, who were
determined not to fight about Bosnia and might have been
glad to see their ally Russia compensated at the Straits. The
second consequence was a heavy diplomatic defeat for Russia,
which was being egged on by the Serbs to offer armed resistance to the formal incorporation in the Austrian empire of
their fellow Slavs, 1,500,000 strong, of Bosnia-Herzegovina.
Austria refused to submit the matter to the decision of any
European conference, though she made it easier for the Turks
to stomach their losses by negotiating financial compensation

for Crown lands in Bosnia and Turkish railway property in Bulgaria, the sum required being in the latter case lent to their Bulgarian friends by the Russians. On the main issue Germany made it clear that she would stand by Austria, with the result that Russia, still weakened by the war with Japan, was forced on March 23, 1909, to capitulate to what was virtually a German ultimatum.

Finally, the crisis had grave consequences for Serbia. The Serbs got no compensation, because all they had lost was a loss of expectation—the expectation that the inhabitants of Bosnia-Herzegovina, who since the turn of the century had been awakening rapidly to the cause of national unity for the southern Slavs (Jugoslavia), would some day and somehow be united with the independent 3,000,000 Slavs of Serbia rather than with the 5,000,000 who were already engulfed in the Austrian Empire. The Serb and Montenegrin Armies were on a war footing throughout the winter of 1908-9, with the rather unbalanced Serbian Crown Prince, George, casting himself for the role of a Garibaldi. But when Russia gave way they were forced to climb down: George himself resigned the succession within a week. This left behind a terrible legacy of Serb irredentism, the more dangerous because the Serbs were one of the most primitive peoples in Europe. The Austro-Hungarian authorities tried to improve upon their victory by launching accusations of high treason against the Serbo-Croat leaders inside the Monarchy, and attempted to show that they were conspiring with the Serbs across the frontier. But the final upshot of the Agram (Zagreb) trial was a scandal which seriously discredited the régime, as Masaryk and other Slav champions proved that the Government was relying upon forged evidence which had been procured by the Austrian Minister at Belgrade. Moreover, the Serbs, when they recovered from the first shock of disappointment, realised that next time the Russians, as they valued their prestige and their leadership of the Slav peoples, would not dare to let them down. Hence in large measure sprang the war of 1914, which Izvolsky, relegated to the Paris Embassy after the 1909 fiasco, but still highly influential in the counsels of Russia, is said to have acclaimed at once as 'his war.'

Relations among the Powers were considerably affected by

the events of 1908–9. Russia strengthened her position slightly by a secret treaty with Bulgaria, building upon a pact made in 1902 and the recent offer of financial assistance. More surprisingly, she gave occasion for further mistrust in France and Britain by negotiating a convention with Germany, which cleared up outstanding points of disagreement very much in the manner of the *Entente Cordiale*. In this Potsdam Accord Germany's Baghdad railway scheme was accepted as a *quid pro quo* for Russia's gains in Persia, a move which the new foreign minister Sazonoff made at the instance of his Premier, Stolypin, on the ground that Russia had too little internal stability and had made too little progress towards military recovery to be able to afford European complications. To Britain, however, it looked as though Russia was bent on getting German support for her encroachments on British interests in Persia.

Italy Encouraged to Invade Tripoli

More lasting significance attached to the change in Italian policy. Italy regarded herself as the victim of, rather than a partner in, the Triple Alliance, since the aggrandisement of Austria in the Balkans both prevented Italian penetration in the same regions and made Austria stronger to resist Italian claims to the Tyrol and the Adriatic littoral. She therefore signed the Racconigi Agreement with Russia in October, 1909, for the purpose of maintaining the *status quo* in the Balkans against Austria and bartering approval for Russian ambitions at the Straits for approval of Italian ambitions in Tripoli. This was a real issue because, whatever the events of 1908–9 meant to other Powers, for Turkey they were disastrous. In April, 1909, Abdul Hamid attempted a counter-revolution, failed, and was deposed, power being left in the hands of a few ambitious militarists. Every pretence of a liberal reform was abandoned; all the outlying parts of the Ottoman Empire were in a ferment; and in September, 1911, Italy demanded the right to occupy Tripoli and went to war to enforce it. Her only excuse, if excuse it was, lay in the belief that German action in Morocco foreshadowed similar action in Tripoli unless it was forestalled. By October, 1912, when the outbreak of the Balkan War forced Turkey to buy her off by making the Treaty of Lausanne, she was in possession of the coastline, though the tribes of the interior of Tripoli kept up the fight long after the formal cession of their country, and she had also occupied the Dodecanese Islands. Thus Italy compensated herself for the Austrian annexation by a further weakening of Turkey.

The Second Moroccan Crisis

Meanwhile Moroccan independence had been finally extinguished. The Algeciras settlement was vague on vital points, as was shown already in the year 1908 in the affair of the Casablanca deserters, when the French relied on their police powers to arrest Foreign Legionaries of German origin who had taken refuge in the German Consulate. This dispute was referred to the new Hague Court, which found that the French had acted within their rights, so in 1909 France and Germany signed an agreement about Morocco, acknowledging the predominant political influence of France subject to the preservation of equal economic opportunity for Germany. But Germany had no intention of conceding the claim to an actual French protectorate, and warned France against the occupation of Fez, the Moroccan capital, to which a French column was nevertheless dispatched in April, 1911, at the request and for the protection of the usurping Sultan, a younger brother whom the French had placed on the throne three years before. In June the column was reported on its way back to the coast, but the weakness of successive French governments favoured the exercise of pressure by Germany on France. Clemenceau, who handled the Casablanca affair, went out in 1909, and this, together with the distraction of Britain by the Parliament Bill and a great wave of industrial unrest, encouraged the German Foreign Secretary, Kiderlen-Wächter, to force the issue. It is doubtful whether he wanted a share in Morocco, which had already caused so much wrangling; more likely, his aim from the outset was colonial compensation, which, at the imminent risk of a general war, Germany finally obtained.

The method was thoroughly German in its brusqueness and ineptness. On July 1 it was announced that the German gunboat *Panther* had been sent to the roadstead of Agadir for the protection of German lives and interests. This was brusque in its disregard of the Act of Algeciras, inept because it led Britain to believe that Germany thought of establishing a west Atlantic naval base corresponding to her Pacific base at Kiao-Chau, a project in which Britain would feel a much more direct interest than in the fate of Morocco as an area of economic exploitation. The immediate sequel was that the Germans negotiated with the French in secret at Berlin, the British being excluded so as to increase the chances both of humiliating France and of splitting the *Entente*. But on July 21 Lloyd George, with Grey's approval, broke the silence in a challenging assertion of Britain's resolve 'at all hazards to maintain her place and her prestige.' The effect of the speech was all the greater because Lloyd George, at that time Chancellor of the Exchequer, had made his name as an anti-imperialist during the Boer War. The Germans promptly disavowed any designs on Agadir, and the world noted that for once Germany did not answer big words with bigger ones. But as between France and her the crisis continued through August and September, when preparations for mobilisation were put on foot in both countries and in Britain and Belgium. Russia, however, was as loath to fight for French claims now as the French had been to fight for hers three years before; Austria-Hungary showed no enthusiasm for war; and both sides may have been influenced by the panic among banking interests. The final result was a comprehensive treaty, signed on November 4, by which Germany definitely abandoned Morocco to France, stipulating only for an open door for her trade. In return, France ceded about one-half of her Congo territory in two strips, which placed Germany in an advantageous position for penetrating into the Belgian Congo, though France refused to include in the treaty any clause about rights of pre-emption there.

Morocco duly became a French protectorate, apart from Tangier (which was finally internationalised in 1923) and a zone allotted to Spain by a new Franco-Spanish treaty of 1912, which tempted the Spaniards into a forward policy that was ultimately to be disastrous. The Russians sought equivalent advantages for themselves: in Persia, where they looked like annexing Teheran, and in the matter of the opening of the Straits, which they now formally demanded. But both Britain and France remained unsympathetic. Italy, as we have seen, seized the chance to launch a war of her own for

Tripoli. But the main result of the Agadir crisis was that it made the peaceful solution of any further crisis on the same scale humanly impossible. The blow to Russian prestige in 1908-9 now had its counterpart in the fact that Germany, having light-heartedly challenged her rivals by the *Panther's* spring, had failed conspicuously to make the challenge good.

The German handling of the Agadir affair has been bitterly criticised by German politicians and historians themselves. Bülow ridiculed the German action—'Like a damp squib, it startled, then amused the world, and ended by making us look ridiculous.' It was, says Brandenburg, 'an ill-considered act inspired by the mere craving for prestige and the desire to wipe out the reverse of Algeciras. The danger of the general position in which we found ourselves was undoubtedly aggravated by it; where the utmost prudence was indicated, a frivolous stroke was made which cost us more in prestige than it brought in.' It seems that Kiderlen-Wächter, the moving spirit in the German Foreign Office, and the Chancellor, Bethmann-Hollweg, had really thought that the sending of the *Panther* would speed up agreement with France over Morocco without provoking awkward international complications. The thought and the action illustrate the typically German belief in the manifestation of armed force as a method of conducting diplomacy.

Once more Great Britain was blamed for her support of France. Feeling was mounting in Germany against the British, and the German Navy League found in the situation added material for its propaganda. The growing hostility in Germany made it all the more difficult for the Kaiser or his Government to exercise restraint. In the Reichstag one of the party leaders had called Lloyd George's speech 'a menace, a challenge, a humiliating challenge' and had attacked the Government for a weak response. It was extremely doubtful if a German government could again give way.

Accordingly, Europe now entered upon the immediate pre-war phase, with the building of additional strategic railways in Russia, strategic canals in Germany, and the drafting of the War Book of mobilisation details in Britain. In the early months of 1912 Germany was encouraged by the friction between Britain and Russia referred to above to make one last effort to split the *Entente*. Lord Haldane was invited to Berlin, to see if some modification of the naval competition with its mounting expense could be accompanied by a declaration of British neutrality 'if war was forced upon Germany.' But the British negotiators fought shy of any formula which might appear to diminish the obligations to the *Entente*. The German naval programme was found to be bigger than had been previously understood; and by September Britain was arranging a concentration of French naval power in the Mediterranean and British in the North Sea. Upon that concentration of forces was based the fateful promise, made during the crisis two years later, that the British Navy would protect the north coast of France.

SUGGESTIONS FOR FURTHER READING

J. A. Spender: *Fifty Years of Europe*, cc. 26–33.

G. Lowes Dickinson: *International Anarchy*, cc. 5–7.

Cambridge History of British Foreign Policy, Vol. III, c. 6 (by G. P. Gooch).

N. Mansergh: *The Coming of the First World War: A Study in the European Balance, 1878–1914.*

New Cambridge Modern History, Vol. XII, c. 11 (by J. P. T. Bury).

II

CHAPTER 8

PRE-WAR EUROPE: WESTERN

The Advance of Liberalism and Nationalism

EUROPE was marked throughout the nineteenth century by a broad general distinction between west and east, the former influenced to a special degree by the politics and civilisation of France and Britain, the latter dominated politically by the three great autocracies of central and eastern Europe. In the east, except in the case of Germany, culture was much less widely diffused among the people. Nevertheless, the kind of progress in which Victorians and Edwardians believed as a law of nature was to be seen in the east as well as in the west during the unique period of peace which began with the Treaty of Frankfort and was now drawing to its close. We may therefore begin by enumerating the common factors.

There had been a genuine advance towards liberalism almost everywhere. Measured by the standards of the French declaration of the rights of man in 1789, the Europe of 1912 had gone a long way towards the establishment of civil liberty and civil equality. Except in Russia the claim of the individual to religious and intellectual liberty was no longer systematically challenged, and the police power was not used publicly to influence political opinion. What went on behind the scenes was another matter, but in the days of Metternich concealment had not been needed. In fine, the police state was beginning to appear an anachronism. After the establishment of the Russian Duma in 1906, laws, apart from laws governing military expenditure, were being made in principle by parliamentary methods in every important state, and the formation of 'pressure groups' to influence voters had replaced methods of dictation and force as the weapon of powerful interests, such as the great landowners. The main political difference was no longer that between autocracies and constitutional régimes; it was now a difference between fully responsible government, where the executive or cabinet was dependent upon the majority in the legislature, and a lesser form of parliamentary government, where a parliament made the laws but did not control their execution.

In the diffusion of a common European culture, it remained true in 1912, as it had been for a thousand years before, that the greatest influence was that of the Churches. Catholic, Orthodox, and Protestant, together they covered Europe and gave to the individual European not only his beliefs about the next world but most of his ideas about the nature and needs of this one. Superimposed upon this influence was the traditional cultural leadership of three Powers—of France, for so many centuries the centre of art and fashion; of Germany, which had spread its groups of cleanly, economical, and industrious colonists to set an example as far afield as Transylvania and even on the banks of the Volga; and of Russia, to which the awakening Slav peoples turned as the repository of their greatest traditions. Nationalism, in almost every corner of Europe, now provided a liberating though not a unifying influence on popular culture, giving to language, literature, and history a highly prized significance as the badge and evidence of the separateness of the nation. Lastly, and most characteristic of the period after 1870, there was the growth of universal elementary education, in which Germany and France led the way, enabling new elements in the common culture, such as developments in applied science and public health, to spread with unheard-of rapidity and ease.

Economic progress had been very great, in spite of mounting tariff walls. The population of Europe was increasing fast, as it had done ever since 1815. The peasantry were still in many parts pressed against the margin of subsistence, but even they could purchase a wider range of manufactured goods than before. As for those who flocked into the growing towns or rose by their own efforts into the middle class—to say nothing of migrants journeying overseas—they were on an average getting an altogether higher standard of living as the reward of enterprise. This did not of course prevent a marked increase in class antagonisms, fostered by the opportunity which town life and factory work gave for effective combination. Economic progress was also associated with an international struggle for raw materials, commercial privileges, and so forth; but financial interests were pacific except in very extreme cases and international relations were often helped, as in the example of Britain and Germany, by the knowledge that one's chief competitor might also be one's chief customer.

The danger of a general war, which was becoming grave in both east and west, sprang not from economic competition but from nationalist emotion. This was most obvious in the east, where the rivalry of Slav and Teuton and the internal stresses of suppressed nationalities influenced every event. In the west, France and Italy alone had serious irredentist ambitions, but the same emotional attitude coloured the minds of men in most countries over questions of colonial expansion or the vindication of the 'national honour.' Another common feature of the age was therefore the building-up of armaments and an increasing stringency in conscription arrangements—a cult of national preparedness. This became more serious as Anglo-German rivalry developed and the Triple *Entente* took shape, because there was no unattached power of sufficient importance left in Europe to mediate. But even so this age witnessed a parallel growth of anti-war propaganda and activity, basing itself variously on religious, ethical, and social-economic arguments, to which the governments paid assiduous lip-service on suitable occasions such as the two Hague Conferences.[1] Those conferences were on the whole a disappointment to world opinion, perhaps because they aimed too high. On a less idealistic basis the task of preserving peace still rested with the Concert of Europe. The diplomatic machinery which the Concert provided for the pacific settlement of disputes was noticed least when it succeeded most: but without it the Powers could not have remained free for a whole generation to give their main attention to internal developments and domestic problems. Space for a full treatment, country by country, is necessarily lacking, even if such a treatment did not involve much wearisome repetition: but a short survey may remind the reader of what occupied the forefront of men's minds far more frequently than the normal workings of international relations or even the crises of diplomacy.

[1] See p. 176.

France in the 'Nineties

In France there was a remarkable contrast between the continuity of her foreign policy, never seriously distracted from the one great hope of a second encounter with Germany under more favourable conditions than the first, and the recurrent crises and kaleidoscopic changes of ministry which made up her domestic history. Thus Boulanger was scarcely laid in his grave when the parliamentary system was again threatened with destruction, this time through its own rottenness. De Lesseps in his old age had floated a company for the construction of a second great canal, at Panama. It failed, mainly on account of the natural difficulties, but partly also because the United States regarded the enterprise as an infringement of the Monroe Doctrine. With its failure the ugly fact came to light that about one-third of the entire capital of the company had been spent on bribing politicians and such other persons as might have exposed its affairs to the investing public—that is, to the thrifty French peasantry. Opportunists and Radicals shared the guilt, and Clemenceau was among the prominent men whose constituents rejected them on this account at the next election. But perhaps the most important result was the stimulus given to anti-Semitism by the fact that the bribery of politicians was mainly the work of two German-Jewish financiers. The feeling against the Jews in France dated from the Second Empire and had provided part of the stock-in-trade of Boulanger's royalist partisan, Déroulède, but now it crystallised in the *cause célèbre* of the Dreyfus case.

Captain Dreyfus was an unprepossessing Alsatian Jew, employed in the French War Office, upon whom certain officers of clerical and royalist tradition decided to fasten a charge of high treason, probably because leakage from other quarters in the War Office was in danger of discovery. On the strength of a forged document, he was found guilty of selling secrets to a foreign Power (i.e. Germany), degraded, and sent to Devil's Island. This was in 1894, and it is highly probable that nothing more would have been heard of his innocence, which Dreyfus consistently protested, if his case had not been taken up by a powerful combination between the politician, Clemenceau, and the great writer, Zola. Although

the forgery was exposed to the War Minister by the head of
his Intelligence Department in 1896, and although the real
criminal admitted his authorship of the disputed document
in 1899, it was not until September, 1899, that Dreyfus
received a grudging pardon, and he was not fully reinstated
until 1906. For the anti-Dreyfusards included, not only the
Army and the Church, but the hysterical Paris mob, a good
many Cabinet Ministers (who identified the Dreyfusards
with the socialists, of whose reviving strength they were
inordinately afraid), and the President himself. Indeed,
the climax of this last great effort against the republic came
with the death of this President, Félix Faure, in February,
1899, his funeral being made the occasion for a plot by
Déroulède, in which the soldiers were to seize power. It
failed and he was banished, though the new President Loubet
remained in a very insecure position for his first few months,
until the formation of the Waldeck-Rousseau ministry restored
the fortunes of the Republic.

The Triumph of Radicalism and the Emergence of the Socialist Party

The Army having at last been duly subordinated to the
civil power, there remained, apart from anti-Semitism, two
problems still to be faced—clericalism and socialism. There
had been a temporary reconciliation between the Church and
the Republic in the early 'nineties under the benign influence
of Pope Leo XIII, whose Encyclical of 1892 induced the
majority of royalists to accept the Republic; but the Dreyfus
case had brought the issue back to where it stood when
Gambetta had proclaimed that clericalism was *the* enemy.
As for socialism, which had begun slowly to revive after the
debacle of the Commune, it included in France a strong
element of anarchists and syndicalists, who preferred direct
and often violent action to the slow working of parliamentary
forms. But socialism was for the most part only a danger
to the stability of the community because the middle-class
republicans had sought to exclude it from any share of political
power. Waldeck-Rousseau and his successor, Combes, whose
ministries of republican defence made the years 1899–1905
'the spring-tide of Radicalism,' tried to conciliate republicans
of all kinds, including the much-dreaded socialists, and to
lead them in a final onslaught upon the clerical power. The

moderate socialist Millerand, and later Briand, were members of the government, which enjoyed the support of the principal socialist leader, Jaurès, though not of the extremists. The establishment of the ten-hour day and a rudimentary public health act went some way towards bringing France abreast of other industrial Powers in social welfare legislation. The new military service law, making two years' service universal in place of the old arrangement of three years with exemption for large classes, such as students, also did something to reconcile the socialists to the maintenance of the Army, which they disliked as a bulwark of the middle class in its defence of private property. But the main thing was the attack on the Church.

First the greater religious Orders, which had increased their membership six times over since Ferry had tried to suppress them some two decades before, were all required to submit their rules for approval; then the unapproved Orders were suppressed, including the powerful Assumptionists; and finally all Orders were forbidden to teach in France. The State, through the *Université*, undertook the control of all teachers. So far, the attack had been directed against the monastic and other Orders, which were believed with some justice to have provided the backbone of the anti-Dreyfusards, and had deliberately spared the parish priests. But when the Radical Combes found himself confronted by a new and less conciliatory Pope, a quarrel quickly developed about the whole basis of the Concordat between Church and State, negotiated by Napoleon I in 1802. A visit by the French President to the King of Italy in 1904 resulted in the severance of diplomatic relations between France and the Vatican, and in the course of the following year the Separation Law terminated all connection between Church and State. Apart from pensions for the older priests (and for Protestant and Jewish ministers) the State gave up all financial responsibility, while Church property was to be managed by bodies of trustees known as *Associations Cultuelles*. The Pope refused to recognise such a breach with tradition as the use of lay trustees implied, and after a period of deadlock the Catholic Church was allowed its own methods of administration, as the Radicals had established their main point—namely, that the religion of which most Frenchmen were at least nominal adherents should receive no official recognition in France.

The Separation Law was actually passed after the fall of the Combes ministry, but it was carried out as a measure which gave a quietus to both royalism and clericalism by the two chief ministries of the pre-war era, those of Clemenceau (1906–9) and Briand (1909–11). The main domestic problem of these years was the growth of the Unified Socialist Party, founded by Jean Jaurès in 1905, formidable to other parties because it succeeded in composing the quarrels which had previously rendered modern French Socialism ineffective. It was still more formidable to the parliamentary State because its syndicalist programme was built upon direct action, by methods ranging from sabotage of machinery in the factory to the nation-wide general strike. By the use of such methods it was thought the workers need not wait for a parliamentary majority before seizing control of the means of production.

Clemenceau, as member of the opposition, had been a factious Left Wing critic of the Opportunist republicans who were in power; however in office he proved to be an Opportunist himself. When his government nationalised the Western Railway, the shareholders were bought out at great profit to themselves; an income tax bill was dropped in deference to the Senate; Clemenceau even conceded a cut in the budget for the armed forces. While thus conciliating the bourgeoisie, he took stern measures against strikers, and when the C.G.T. (Confédération Générale du Travail, a more revolutionary equivalent of the British T.U.C.) proclaimed a general strike, he had its leaders arrested. Briand, still nominally a socialist, took the same general line, breaking a railway strike by calling the railway men to the colours, so that military discipline could be enforced upon them.

The unrest can be exaggerated. Only half of the trade unions supported the C.G.T., and the resolute syndicalists were estimated at 400,000 of a working-class population totalling 11,000,000 in 1912. Moreover, the growth of the trade unions, which doubled their membership between 1900 and 1914, was a natural accompaniment of a record industrial expansion, in which the steel and iron of the north-east and the output of its coalfields caught up with the older-established textile industries. Thus it was an age of progress and optimism, when the town worker shared to some extent in the increased prosperity of industry and the peasant profited by the rising tariff on agricultural produce. It was even argued that the steady internal market, stable population, and scattered industries of France made social welfare legislation, in which she remained notoriously backward, less necessary than in countries which depended upon one or two main industries and the fluctuating world market. Nevertheless, the anti-socialist feelings of the peasantry combined with the living memory of the Commune and, perhaps, the unidealistic philosophy of the republican Radicals, made the cleavage between classes and consequent embitterment of political life a characteristic feature of the French scene that long outlived the world of 1912.

By that date the needs of national defence were tending to blot out other questions. A scandal in the administration of the army, when freemasons were employed to spy on the religious activities of Catholic officers, had overthrown the Combes ministry; later in the same year the first Morocco crisis forced Delcassé out of the Foreign Office; and in 1911 Clemenceau was busy attacking Caillaux, who had been his own finance minister, for the secret treaty by which Congolese territory had been bartered to Germany. After 1910 a powerful influence was also being exerted in Paris by Izvolsky, thirsting for revenge after the Bosnian fiasco, and able to make his presence felt through the newspapers, to many of which Russian advertisements were an important consideration. In January, 1912, the Lorraine lawyer Poincaré formed a 'national' government, and although the extension of the military service period from two to three years actually took effect under Briand the following year, when Poincaré had succeeded to the Presidency, yet it may fairly be regarded as a typical result of the spirit of national alertness and increased self-confidence of which he was the embodiment. Besides, it was Poincaré as President who refused to allow the Radicals, predominant in the new Chamber of 1914, to go back upon the three-year service law, which had given France a peace-time army larger than that of Germany.

Italy Under the Rule of Crispi and Giolitti

The history of Italy is marked by certain constant factors which rendered her always the least effective of Great Powers.

The lack of important natural resources, such as coal, and the infertility of the soil made emigration necessary; and the stream of emigrants, to the United States and South America, to Tunisia and France, while it provided a handsome flow of remittances home, stripped the country of much of its best youth. The cleavage between the progressive north and the backward south, already noted, grew no less with the passage of time. In 1912 what had once been the Kingdom of the Two Sicilies was still poverty-stricken, priest-ridden, and apathetic, with the ancient secret societies of the Camorra and the Mafia, prototypes of the American gang, as its most characteristic institution. Rome remained a dual-purpose capital, though relations between the Quirinal and the Vatican became less hostile under Pius X, who substituted Italy for anti-clerical France as the titular protector of Catholics in the Middle East. Good Catholics were no longer forbidden by their Church to take part in political life. As for the north, it had if anything drawn still further away from the feudal, agricultural society of the southern provinces. Since the 1880's there had been large-scale industrial development in textiles, metallurgical manufactures, and other branches, culminating after 1900, when hydro-electricity supplied the want of coal. But a high tariff kept the purchasing power of wages very low, so industrialisation was accompanied by a rapid growth of socialism, syndicalism, and anarchism. North Italy was notorious for its revolutionary outbreaks of violence, such as a general strike in 1904, and for an imitation, with no greater success, of Bismarck's war against the Socialist Party.

Once the constant factors have been appreciated, three main periods may be distinguished in the history of the peninsula as a whole. From 1887 to 1896 was the age of Crispi, an ambitious Sicilian who had been one of Garibaldi's Thousand. Though the high property qualification for the franchise had been abolished in 1882, it was still restricted by a literacy test, while the senators in the upper house were nominated by the Crown for life. Crispi was a regular party boss, who used all the power of the governmental machine to secure his majority, but he is chiefly remembered for his forward policy in foreign and colonial affairs, which ended in disaster for himself and his country on the stricken

K

field of Adowa.[1] This event was the more catastrophic because a previous, smaller defeat at the hands of the Abyssinians, at Dogali in 1887, had been one of the main factors that brought Crispi into power. After Adowa the next few years were a period of unrelieved gloom, marked by abandonment of the long-planned colonial venture in Abyssinia, riots amounting to open rebellion in Milan and other cities, and the assassination of King Humbert by an anarchist. His son and successor, Victor Emmanuel III (1900–46), saw his country rise again from the trough of the wave—more prosperous (in spite of the terrible Messina earthquake of 1908), united enough for manhood suffrage to be introduced, and above all, able to resume her colonial ambitions with the war for Tripoli. The leading politician, less violent but no less corrupt than Crispi, was now Giolitti, under whose guidance Italian foreign policy, from about the beginning of the new century, aimed at good relations with the Dual Alliance as well as with her own partners in the Triple Alliance. What has been said about internal conditions should explain why the kingdom had no desire for a major war, even to satisfy the irredentist claims to the Trentino and Trieste.

Spain and Portugal

The life of Spain and Portugal at this time bears some resemblance to that of Italy. In international affairs they played only a minor part. Spain only comes into the limelight in 1898, when chronic misrule in Cuba gave the United States occasion to disrupt the whole of what still remained of the proud empire of Philip II. Portugal comes into the limelight not at all, though secret bargains as to the ultimate disposal of her African possessions were twice attempted between Britain and Germany, in 1898 and 1914, and in 1890 her claim to a hinterland for her two colonies, stretching right across the continent, was disposed of by a British ultimatum, before which she was bound to retire.[2] The domestic scene also had common features, such as a constitutional monarchy exercising considerable authority both directly and indirectly; a parliamentary system entirely under the domination of coteries of professional politicians, who 'made' the elections and held office by mutually agreed

[1] See p. 84.　　　　　　　　　[2] See p. 83.

rotation; and powerful interests, the Church, the Army, the landowning nobility, and latterly the great industrialists, which were the real repositories of power. As for the great mass of the peasantry, their plight rivalled that of their fellows in south Italy, while industrial development rendered Barcelona a more formidable centre of unrest even than Milan, since anarchism was there combined with the separatist ambitions of the ancient Kingdom of Catalonia.

The long reign of Alfonso XIII of Spain, a posthumous son born to the throne in 1886, was marked by the introduction of manhood suffrage in 1890, during his mother's regency; but the change was nominal rather than real, and in 1907 a Conservative government actually made the exercise of the franchise compulsory because they believed that, if the peasantry voted at all, they would vote as their landlords directed—and so counteract the growth of radicalism in the towns. In 1895 a new rebellion in Cuba, where rebellion was almost endemic, followed by a smaller rising in the Philippines, advertised the government's incompetence and brought about the Spanish-American War.[1] The rapid collapse of the Spanish Empire exposed the ineptitude of the ruling class to the eyes of the whole world. But the poorer classes in Spain were more interested in the gradual improvement in economic conditions after 1898, to which the loss of the colonies, a cause of distraction rather than profit, undoubtedly contributed.

In 1909 popular discontent, never far below the surface of Spanish politics, came to a head. A serious war with the Riff tribesmen of north Morocco grew out of their attack on Melilla, one of the ancient Spanish possessions on the coast, where minerals had begun to be exploited. Turbulent Barcelona revolted against conscription for the Riff war; there was heavy street-fighting and some sacking of churches and monasteries. When order was restored the clericals exacted stern retribution, which included the execution under martial law of the great educator and anarchist theorist, Ferrer. In the following year, therefore, the Conservatives, who had been in office almost continuously since 1898, gave place to a Liberal group, who did something to reduce the religious houses to order and hastened the growth of religious

[1] See p. 297.

toleration, in which Spain and Portugal notoriously lagged
behind most other European countries.

In Portugal the régime collapsed more rapidly. King
Luis, who had been on the throne since 1861, was succeeded
in 1889 by his son Carlos, who was dictatorially inclined and
took a more active part in politics; he enhanced his unpopularity by his extravagance. The humiliation of the British
ultimatum in 1890 brought about a formidable but unsuccessful
rising in Oporto; the introduction of manhood suffrage (1901)
made no difference to the machinations of the professional
politicians; and in 1906 the king appointed an 'independent'
minister named Franco, who rapidly obtained the powers of
a dictator. In February, 1908, the assassination of King
and Crown Prince in the streets of Lisbon destroyed the
dictatorship, but a coalition of the traditional parties proved
unable to establish the surviving Prince, Manoel, on the throne.
After two and a half uneasy years an almost bloodless revolution completed the overthrow of the House of Braganza,
which gave place to a middle-class republic of strong anti-
clerical tendencies, modelled upon contemporary France.
The workers and peasants did not gain greatly by the
change.

The Swiss Confederation—Referendum and Initiative

While Portugal thus became a republic after years of tumult,
the first such creation in Europe since the abortive Spanish Republic of 1873, the Swiss Confederation, Europe's most ancient
republic and most complete democracy, had a history amounting to little else than the slow and peaceful evolution of the established institutions. The constitution of 1848 had equipped
the country with a properly organised central government
—a federal assembly of two houses, which elects a federal
executive of seven members. The distinctive feature of the
constitution continued to be the very wide powers of self-
government reserved to itself by even the smallest canton.
In 1874 popular control over the central government was
strengthened by the adoption of the Referendum, enabling a
small minority of voters or cantons to require any new federal
law to be submitted to a plebiscite for approval or disapproval.
This was followed seventeen years later by the adoption of the
Initiative, by which a minority can require the federal

government to consider and vote upon any project for partial revision of the constitution.

Divided in language and religion (though each of the twenty-two cantons is by itself fairly homogeneous) and held together so loosely by their federal constitution, the Swiss nation were fortunate in having virtually no foreign policy. Being surrounded by high-tariff states, they were forced to adopt a tariff, which was obviously to their disadvantage since, apart from Britain, Switzerland was in all Europe the country most dependent on imports. Otherwise, the calm was disturbed by nothing more serious than Bismarck's fulminations against the right of asylum, which the Swiss gallantly maintained for German socialists as for all other political underdogs. But in the last analysis their stability resulted chiefly from their prosperity, based upon well-organised pasture farming; upon industries, such as high-grade textiles and watch-making, in which skilled labour was an important factor and the availability of hydro-electricity a new incentive; and upon the entertainment of tourists and semi-permanent foreign residents. Travel to Switzerland was stimulated by the great railway developments, such as the completion of the St. Gotthard line in 1882 and of the Simplon Tunnel in 1906.

The Low Countries

Belgium shared with Switzerland the privilege of a guaranteed neutrality: the guarantee for Switzerland dated from 1815, that for Belgium from 1839. What was to prove more important was the fact that while the former covered an Alpine area, admirably suited for defence (to which the peaceful Swiss devoted much thought, money and manpower), the latter guaranteed for the most part the levels of the North Sea littoral, where no mere chain of artificial fortresses could prevent the German army from deploying. Belgium also resembled Switzerland in having a language problem. In Belgium's case it was a serious danger to unity, as the Flemings of the north might be tempted to co-operate with a foreign invader to secure an ascendancy over the French-speaking Walloons of the more industrialised and generally wealthier southern provinces, and attempts to conciliate the Flemings by giving their language equal official status (which date from 1898) were never wholly successful. But the importance of these considerations lay in the future.

In 1912 her industrialisation and the activities of her monarchy made Belgium conspicuous among the smaller nations of western Europe. An abundance of coal had encouraged Belgium to make a successful transition from the skilled handicrafts in which she had excelled in the Middle Ages to the great iron-works and textile factories of her modern economy. In the whole continent of Europe this people of 7,000,000 came second only to Germany and France in industrial output; its foreign trade exceeded that of Italy; and its railway network was the densest in the world. As might be expected, the densely populated urban areas had given birth to an important Socialist Party, led by Vandervelde, which had used the threat of a general strike to get manhood suffrage in 1893. But there were additional votes for heads of families, property owners, and the better educated, which helped the Catholic Party to remain continuously in power from 1884 to the outbreak of the First World War. It may be noted that in this intensely Catholic country the Catholic Party was a far more democratic body than the Liberals, and strongly championed social welfare legislation. As for the monarchy, although it was modelled upon the English pattern, it was the long reign, business acumen, and ambition of Belgium's second sovereign, Leopold II (1865–1909), that enriched Belgium with her Congolese Empire.[1]

The Kingdom of the Netherlands or Holland resembled her southern neighbour in the middle-class ascendancy, based on restriction of the franchise, and the long period of economic prosperity, which made that ascendancy tolerable. For Holland the colonial empire in the East, a survival from her days of maritime supremacy, was still of great importance as one of the two supports on which her commercial wealth and mercantile marine rested. The other was her advantageous geographical position, which made Rotterdam and Amsterdam the natural entrepôt markets for Germany. There was agricultural development, too, which required heavy preliminary expenditure on dyking and draining in a country so largely below sea level, but had its reward in the export of food and garden products to Germany and Britain. In

[1] See p. 83.

1890 the accession of Queen Wilhelmina in the absence of
any male heir to the House of Orange ended the personal
union between Holland and Luxemburg, but this had little
practical importance, since the Grand Duchy already formed
part of the German Zollverein or Customs union. But her
marriage (in 1901) to a German prince did arouse serious
fears that Holland might also be swept into the German orbit,
especially as the Boer War created a strong anti-British
prejudice. However, Dutch politics in the early years of
the twentieth century continued to be dominated by domestic
issues, such as the franchise, the costs and technique of colonial
administration, and the vexed problem of religious instruction
in the schools of a Protestant country with a 40 per cent.
Catholic minority.

The Three Scandinavian Kingdoms

Of the three Scandinavian kingdoms, Denmark and Norway
had by 1912 reached a point in their political evolution at
which they differed little from Switzerland, except in the
possession of a royal figure-head. Sweden, on the other hand,
inspired by the example of her German neighbours across
the Baltic, still accorded considerable influence to the King
and the nobility, which was among the most ancient in
Europe, and retained in her constitution a royal veto on
proposed laws and a property qualification for all members
of the Upper Chamber. It was partly in consequence of
this difference that Sweden and Norway in 1905 disturbed
the tranquillity of western Europe by the threat of war.
The union of crowns, imposed upon Norway by the Powers
in 1814, had never been popular west of the Kjölen, where
there was no aristocracy but a democratic, parliamentary
constitution drawn up in 1814 by its officials, merchants, and
peasant farmers; and as the century wore on the spectacular
growth of her mercantile marine gave Norway additional
pride, a name in the world, and divergent economic interests.

The ablest King of the house of Bernadotte, Oscar II, who
reigned from 1871 to 1907, carried on a losing struggle against
the tide of Norwegian nationalism, helped as elsewhere by a
literary renaissance, of which (from the political standpoint)
the key figure was not so much Ibsen as Björnson. In 1884
the Liberals under Sverdrup's leadership won a decisive

victory by impeaching the members of a Conservative ministry who were trying to uphold the royal veto on constitutional changes against the Norwegian Parliament. After this, the ministry in Norway came to be entirely dependent upon the parliamentary majority, so that it was merely a question of time before matters were brought finally to a head over the demand for a separate consular service, plausible by reason of Norway's huge carrying trade but fatal to the union because it implied the possibility of a separate foreign policy. In April, 1905, the Norwegian Ministry resigned when King Oscar, strongly supported by his Swedish subjects, refused any further concession on this issue. He was unable to form an alternative ministry; and the Norwegian parliament thereupon declared that he had ceased to exercise his functions as king so that the union was at an end. This was confirmed by a referendum of the Norwegian people, in which the republicans made a strong showing: but to convince the Powers that the new state would be respectable a king was sought and found in the person of a Danish prince, who had married a daughter of Edward VII and now ascended the ancient Norwegian throne as Haakon VII. More remarkable was the self-restraint shown by the Swedes, who outnumbered the Norwegians by more than two to one, yet refrained from any violent action. Later the common frontier was de-militarised, and the new kingdom got its territorial integrity guaranteed by a four-power treaty in 1907.

For Sweden there remained the great problem of her eastern frontier, where the Grand Duchy of Finland, joined by a personal union to the Russian crown in 1809, was now being forcibly absorbed into Russia. The Swedes felt deeply for the fate of their ancient province, where the upper classes still spoke Swedish and looked to Sweden. But the Swedes were powerless to help and could only look with fear upon their neighbours, the Russians, and turn to Germany as their only possible champion in the event of trouble. The long reign of Gustav V began with the concession of manhood suffrage, which at length gave the second chamber of the Swedish Parliament greater authority than the first chamber, which was of an aristocratic complexion: but as late as 1914 the royal power was sufficient to enable him to dismiss a ministry which differed from the royal policy and to get his policy endorsed at the ensuing election.   It is significant that the royal policy in question was an armament programme inspired by the mounting fear of Russia.

Denmark lagged behind Norway, but by 1912 had advanced further than Sweden towards democracy. The immense discouragement of the loss of Schleswig-Holstein in the war of 1864 had caused the liberal constitution of 1849 to be revised so as to strengthen the upper house of the legislature, and for many years the reactionary King Christian IX (1863–1906) ruled through ministers in opposition to a majority in the democratically elected lower house.   It was not until 1901 that he was finally obliged to yield to the pressure of the Left, of which the strength had been steadily increasing with the economic fortunes of the country.   These likewise had been despaired of after the war of 1864, but were restored by the systematic changing over of rural Denmark from a grain-exporting to a dairying and pig-farming country, a change to which producers' co-operation (that is, co-operative societies for marketing the product) has largely contributed.   Hardly less remarkable ingenuity was shown in the introduction of new industries to the towns, although Denmark has virtually none of the raw materials.   Finally, in 1915, a new constitution made the upper as well as the lower house of the Danish Parliament dependent upon universal suffrage.   For the ensuing generation Denmark and its remote European dependency of Iceland, which after a long and obstinate struggle was on the verge of attaining the equivalent of dominion status under the Danish Crown, rivalled Norway in their exposition of social democracy under the conditions most favourable to its achievement—namely, a strong national sentiment, a rising standard of life, and an absence of foreign distractions.

Intellectual and Artistic Developments

In the history of European culture the years immediately preceding the First World War are a period of widespread talent and activity rather than of outstanding genius.   In the 'seventies (briefly surveyed from the cultural angle in Chapter 1) some of the great intellectual movements of the nineteenth century were at their height.   The years between 1900 and 1914 did not beget giants: there was not another

Flaubert, Ibsen or Tolstoi. But popular education was producing a wider class of readers than ever before and also enlarging the field of those likely to interest themselves in art and music. New, experimental groups of artists followed the Impressionism of the nineteenth century: the post-impressionists used glaring contrasts of crude colour, the cubists tried to reduce the curves found in nature to a series of blocks, the futurists aimed at suggesting movement rather than the static. In the prolific literature of an age of growing mass-production it is difficult to sum up tendencies or movements in a word or a phrase, but scepticism, realism and also an increasing interest in the problems of political and social life are all to be found.

The last-named tendency is especially marked in the drama and novel of Great Britain. The plays of Bernard Shaw and the novels of H. G. Wells and Galsworthy are all marked by social criticism and a feeling of urgency in the need for social reform. The Russian, Maxim Gorki, friend of Lenin, studied in his novels both the life of Russia and social problems in general. His revolutionary activities made him the literary idol of the proletariat. Less serious, but far-reaching in its influence, was Conan Doyle's creation of Sherlock Holmes (1891), prototype of the modern detective novel with its vast public in Europe and America.

In France Romain Rolland's *Jean Christophe* was outstanding among the work of novelists. The philosopher Bergson, a naturalised Frenchman of Anglo-Jewish parents, won a reputation far beyond the confines of France. He studied the problem of existence behind evolutionary phenomena in *L'évolution créatrice*, his most famous work, published in 1907. But the greatest literary figure in France, perhaps in Europe, was Anatole France: deeply sceptical, steeped in classical learning, and with all the urbanity and polish of the Latin tradition. Pirandello, the Italian dramatist, another sceptic, was imbued with the tragedy of human existence. In Benedetto Croce, Italy produced a philosopher of wide influence, who sought for reality in the nature of history. The Spaniards Unamuno and Ibañez were both critics of the existing order in Spain. Unamuno's novels were philosophical not realist in character, and in his mysticism he has been compared with Blake. Ibañez' *Four Horsemen of the Apocalypse* (1916) became, soon after the war, internationally famous as a film. The Belgian writer, Maeterlinck, passed through a period of pessimism to one more hopeful. The German Thomas Mann in his best-known novel, *Buddenbrooks* (1903), brilliantly portrayed period and character in his study of a Lübeck family. Germany's foremost lyric poet of the time, Rainer Maria Rilke, was a great stylist and his work was coloured with religious mysticism. Sweden possessed in Strindberg its greatest literary figure, whose unhappy life provided ample material for his dramas, novels and poems.

Apart from literature, pre-war Europe saw developments in every direction, but especially in science. What was almost a new subject—Psychology—was being developed by the researches into the sub-conscious of Freud, Jung and Adler in Vienna. The Russian Pavlov was also contributing to this study by his research into 'reflex action' showing how the living organism reacts automatically to external stimuli. Medical investigation was revealing the functions of glands and hormones, and the importance in diet of vitamins. Frazer's *Golden Bough* had an influence far beyond the bounds of anthropology, and modified the outlook of philosophers and theologians. In chemistry and physics momentous changes were taking place. Röntgen's discovery of X-rays and Professor and Mme. Curie's of radium and radio-activity started important lines of research. The atom came no longer to be pictured as a rigid unit, and matter was interpreted in terms of energy. In short, the earlier postulates of physics and chemistry were undergoing fundamental modification, while in mathematics Einstein, a German Jew, was in the early stages of developing his theory of relativity and approaching thereby a new view of space and time by bringing them together into a four-dimensional framework.

SUGGESTIONS FOR FURTHER READING

J. Hampden Jackson: *Clemenceau and the Third Republic.*

E. Wiskemann: *Italy* (World To-day Series), cc. 1–6.

R. C. K. Ensor: *Belgium* (Home University Library).

G. M. Gathorne Hardy: *Norway* (Modern World Series), cc. 5, 9, 10, 11.

J. P. T. Bury: *France 1814–1940*, cc. 11–13.

T. K. Derry: *Short History of Norway*, cc. 9 and 10.

CHAPTER 9

PRE-WAR EUROPE: CENTRAL AND EASTERN

Illiberal Characteristics of the Three Great Monarchies

WESTERN EUROPE was a region of parliamentary governments presided over by constitutional monarchies, in which the urban middle class was the generally predominant element: since 1870 it had developed fairly steadily towards the fulfilment of liberal ambitions. Central and eastern Europe, on the other hand, consisted (with the partial exception of the Balkan Peninsula) of three great authoritarian states, ruled over by semi-autocratic monarchies, in which landowning families of the nobility and the squirearchy were generally predominant: since 1870 it had developed towards the use of parliamentary forms, but the spirit of the administration was far from being liberal. The domestic history of the three states was dominated by three events, each in its own way highly characteristic— the fall of Bismarck in 1890, the suppression of the Russian Revolution in 1905, and the introduction of manhood suffrage for his Austrian dominions, with separate constituencies for each racial element, by the hard-pressed Hapsburg emperor in 1907.

The Wilhelmine Era in Germany

In Germany the Wilhelmine era, as it was called, was preceded by two short but dramatic episodes—the reign of the Emperor Frederick and his youthful successor's quarrel with Bismarck, which ended in his 'dropping the pilot.' The death of the aged William I should in the normal course of events have put the German Liberals in power, since Crown Prince Frederick was their life-long champion. But the cancer of the throat, which had struck him down the previous year, limited his reign to ninety-nine days, sufficient for the dismissal of Puttkamer, Bismarck's highly reactionary subordinate at the Prussian Ministry of the Interior, but not for the more fundamental changes in German politics which might have altered the course of world history. The accession of William II in the same year, 1888, at the age of twenty-nine,

148

at first put back the clock to the days and ways of his grand-father. But a gulf opened between the young ruler and Bismarck. Officially, the new Kaiser insisted on modifying Prussian constitutional practice, so that he might deal with ministers directly instead of through the Chancellor; unofficially also, the Kaiser was at least toying with the idea of conciliatory treatment of the Social Democrats and labour movement, long alienated from the throne by the anti-socialist laws. For such reasons Bismarck's long period of power came to an end.

Bismarck lived for eight years longer, writing and in-triguing against his successors, but they were not foemen worthy of his steel. For the first four years the Chancellor was General Caprivi, a soldier with very little political or even diplomatic experience, who merely took his orders from the Kaiser. Prince Hohenlohe, who succeeded him for the period 1894–1900, was a very eminent Bavarian statesman whose personal rank entitled him to address the Kaiser as man to man, but he was seventy-five years of age and was brought into office mainly to assuage the resentment of the agricultural interest at a trade treaty with Russia, which temporarily facilitated the importation of cheap corn for the masses. In his last three years Hohenlohe had with him as Foreign Minister the plausible, unscrupulous, and ambitious Bülow, who, as Chancellor (1900–9), came nearest to making the relationship with the monarchy a partnership such as it had been before 1888. It is said that it was expressly because he wished to retain control of foreign policy in his own hands that the Kaiser chose as Bülow's successor, Bethmann-Hollweg, an honest civil servant much respected by the Reichstag, but no leader of men.

William II was, in fact, to a great extent his own Chancellor. It will be remembered that he had a separate military cabinet in his capacity as war lord and a separate dignity as King of Prussia. He was thus in a position to keep even a strong Chancellor in check, and by choosing a weak one he could give full play to those qualities of inconsistency and self-assertiveness, brutality and nervousness, generosity and the artistic temperament, in virtue of which the last German Kaiser held the centre of the European stage for so long. Some of his gestures in foreign affairs, which have already been mentioned, suggest that this was the sphere in which his actions were most untrammelled. But they were in practice restricted for many years by the power which Holstein, the mystery man of German political life, exercised behind the scenes. Embittered against the world by Bismarck, who forced him into his own sinister schemings against Arnim in the 'seventies, Holstein became the relentless exponent of a policy of opposition and hostility towards Great Britain. It was he, for instance, who sent the Kaiser to Tangier in 1905. His basic argument was that Britain would never be able to form a common front with France and Russia; therefore there was no need to conciliate her. Time showed the argument to be unsound, but he was still consulted behind the scenes in the last years between his resignation in 1906 and death in 1908, as the Kaiser and his ministers always went in fear of Press campaigns which Holstein had devious ways of inspiring.

Fundamentally, the Kaiser was always unsure of himself. At the outset he had tried to conciliate labour, but without much success. Social insurance, educational facilities, and municipal enterprise in Germany continued to be the admiration of her neighbours; but the Social Democratic Party, though perpetually in opposition in the Reichstag, polled more votes at each election and by 1912 was numerically the most important of the political parties, so that the ascendancy of the upper classes came to depend upon the retention of the antiquated electoral system in Prussia. Moreover, although the Kaiser's personality aptly and accurately reflected the national cult of power for power's sake, into which Germany relapsed as soon as the common-sense influence of Bismarck was removed, there was never a time when important sections of the loyal middle and upper classes did not laugh at his flamboyant posturings upon the world stage. In 1908 this came to a head over the *Daily Telegraph* interview, when William lost his balance and self-confidence so completely as even to contemplate abdication.

German Ambitions and Policies

The Kaiser's one great popular success was his propaganda for the Navy and the support he consistently gave to Tirpitz's demands as Minister of Marine, which were opposed by both

the Foreign Office and the general staff. The naval budget
was not protected like that of the Army by an agreement to
vote seven years' supplies at once, nor was the Admiralty as
remote from civilian control as either the general staff or the
military cabinet: so the Kaiser's personal enthusiasm for
their cause was of real importance in helping the Navy League
to carry the day for ever-mounting expenditure. This was
linked up with two other propaganda movements that received
the imperial blessing—the Colonial Union, which agitated for
the seizure of every chance of aggrandisement in the Far East
and the Pacific, and the Pan-German League, which cast
greedy eyes upon those areas of Europe where migrant
German settlers had once staked claims and modern finance
might reap advantage.[1]

For Germany in the early twentieth century was above all
a land of economic prosperity and self-confidence, based
upon discipline and hard work in all classes of society and the
skilful exploitation of political strength for commercial advantage. Moreover, her success could not be gainsaid at a time
when her steel output, that touchstone of industrial strength,
was increasing seven times as fast as that of Britain, while
the German system of industrial monopolies or cartels was
being imitated more or less covertly by all her chief rivals.
Germany had much but wanted more—the search for profits
had much to do with her Moroccan policy, while in south-
eastern Europe the Foreign Office was secretly subsidising
the Pan-German organisation to stake out claims for future
reference. As the World War was soon to show, the mass of
the German people may have criticised its rulers in detail,
may perhaps have looked forward eagerly to the achievement
some day of a genuine parliamentary régime, but they were
reasonably satisfied in the present and hopeful for the future.

The one glaring exception was the national minorities. The
Danes of North Schleswig, after two generations of Prussian
rule, continued to look longingly northwards to their fatherland. Much more, the people of Alsace-Lorraine, which
had not been trusted with the rank of a state within the German
Empire, never ceased to hope that some new European
conflagration might restore them to France, which for the
Alsatians at least stood as the symbol of their culture as well

[1] See p. 119.

as of their political liberty. In 1911 they had been given
representation in the Bundesrat and a modest instalment of
home rule. Yet in 1913 the tenseness of the situation in
Alsace was to be revealed to the world when the military
authorities, backed by the Crown Prince, made a hero of a
German lieutenant who had been reprimanded for knocking
an Alsatian cripple out of his way with his sword in the
streets of Zabern. As for Poland, William II revived the
programme of Germanisation which he had let Caprivi
suspend. During the years of Bülow's Chancellorship an
attempt was made to suppress the Polish language in the
schools, resulting in a strike of 100,000 schoolchildren; the
Germans also tried to prevent its use in meetings and assemblies.
Powers were taken to stop the Poles subdividing estates for
the benefit of Polish peasants, and to expropriate estates for
the benefit of German peasants supplanting them. But all in
vain. A high birth-rate, agricultural prosperity, the comparatively good relations between gentry and peasants, and the
self-discipline of the increasing middle class of the towns
combined to defeat every effort of the German Empire to
digest its prey. Most significant feature of all, the national
hopes were strong enough for Poles to migrate steadily into
Germany from across the Russian frontier.

Russia under Czar Alexander III and Pobiedonostzeff

For imperial Russia Polish nationalism was only one of a
host of problems, any one of which would have taxed the
energies and brains of a government far cleverer and more
alert than that which ruled at St. Petersburg. The Czar
Alexander II had been murdered by revolutionaries in 1881,
upon the very day when he had signed a project to give
elected representatives of his people a share in making the
laws. Alexander III, throughout his reign of thirteen years,
did nothing to build upon this or upon the foundations laid
in the earlier years of his father's reign. The peasants,
though no longer bound by the chains of serfdom, were kept
in order by a new type of official called the Land Captain and
in a state of misery by two continuing grievances—the scarcity
of land for a rapidly growing rural population and the burden
of payments to landowners for that portion which had been
transferred to the peasants by the edict of emancipation.

Farming on the strip system under communal control by the Mir also made productivity low and the producer poor.

Meanwhile, the other great reform institution, the Zemstvo, was weakened by an edict of 1890, which restricted the rights of the peasants to the choosing of a list of candidates, from which the provincial governor picked their so-called representatives for them.   In any case these local councils had little influence upon the official class or bureaucracy, which actually ruled the country in accordance with the reactionary principles that were known to find favour at court.   The court lived in strict seclusion, remote from the opinions of its subjects. The most influential minister was Pobiedonostzeff, the procurator (or lay head) of the holy synod of the Russian Church. His typical policy was the persecution of Jews, who were forbidden to reside anywhere outside the towns of the western border territories, especially Poland, and were there subjected to pogroms organised with the tacit approval of the police, such as the once-famous outrage in which hundreds perished at Kishinev in Bessarabia.   In general, Russia suffered from a complete police régime, ruthlessly controlled by Plehve, who made his name originally by tracking down the conspirators of 1881.   To such conditions the intellectual life of the Press and the universities largely succumbed, so that Tolstoi was led to preach the anarchical doctrine that all coercion is bad.

The first decade of the reign of Nicholas II, the least intelligent, least significant, and probably the best intentioned Czar of the century, saw the continuance of Pobiedonostzeff's policy of repression.   In one respect, indeed, it was intensified, for the campaign to Russify all nationalities which differed in language or religion, of which the Jews had been the first victims, now pressed very hardly on the Poles.   They had slowly recovered from the repression of 1863 and were now demanding the conditions of self-government enjoyed by their fellow countrymen across the border in Austrian Galicia.   Repression also fell upon the humbler peasantry of the Baltic provinces, and most notoriously upon the people of Finland.   In 1898 Bobrikoff was sent there as Governor-General to turn the Grand Duchy into the likeness of a Russian province.   In 1904 his assassination roused the ineffective interest of Europe in the losing battle which the Finns were

L

waging for the preservation of their liberal parliamentary system and constitutional rights, guaranteed at the time of the annexation of the Grand Duchy by the Czar in 1809.

Economic Development: the Work of Witte

But the main feature of the decade lay in the achievements of Witte, Minister of Finance from 1892 to 1903 and Prime Minister in 1905–6. He began the industrialisation of modern Russia, which a hundred years before had led the world in iron output, but had then fallen so far behind that only the textile manufactures were in any sense commensurate with the size of the home market. Count Witte had begun as director of railways: by their purchase for the State and systematic development he made further improvements possible. Other State monopolies, such as the spirit trade, increased the resources of government. A financial system which was primarily dependent on foreign (especially French) loans for both public and private enterprise was strengthened by bringing the rouble on to the gold standard. Above all, Witte gave a new impetus to the growth of industry by instituting the highest tariff in Europe to keep foreign goods out, encouraging the employer by State subsidies for new branches, and enticing the employee by the protection of a factory code. Russia remained economically the most backward of the Powers, because she was not strong enough to shake off her dependence on Germany in such matters as tariff treaties and because her international position prevented her from reducing the heavy burden of military expenditure, which included the provision of strategic railways. Nevertheless, with the help of cheap labour made available by the rapid growth of population, large-scale manufactures now became established in St. Petersburg, Moscow, and elsewhere in Russia proper, and in Warsaw, Lodz and other Polish centres, while the coal of the Donets Basin and the oil of the Caucasus were exploited on a scale which at least foreshadowed the industrial development of more recent years.

The Growth of Bolshevism and the 1905 Revolution

Hence there grew up a new Russian revolutionary movement, pregnant with importance for world history. The anarchism preached by Bakunin had made its converts chiefly

abroad.   The other main revolutionary group of intellectuals,
once known as the Narodniki, was revived in 1898 as the
Social Revolutionaries, who preached to the peasants with
land distribution as object and terrorism as method.   It was
chiefly due to the Social Revolutionaries that accusations of
political crime were multiplied sixfold in the first nine years
of the reign, and their hold on the peasants made them the
largest revolutionary party until their virtual suppression by
Lenin at the end of 1917.   But the revolutionary peasants
were hard to organise, and the future lay with the more
malleable revolutionary proletariat of the urban centres.
In 1896 the first big strike on Marxist lines was organised
among the workers of St. Petersburg.   Out of this grew the
Social Democratic Labour Party (1898), a party led by suspects
and exiles, with whom the name Bolsheviki ('Majority')
originated.   The name was used because a majority vote was
obtained at a party conference held in London in 1903
denouncing the moderate, evolutionary, and non-political
programme of the Mensheviki ('Minority').   Thus the Bolsheviks were distinguished by their absolute adherence to the
Marxian gospel of class revolution and the dictatorship of the
proletariat, their strict subordination of means to the great
revolutionary end, and their strong sense of party discipline.
While such movements were brewing beneath the surface of
Russian society, the Czar was content to snub the middle-class
liberals and reformers within the constitutionally appointed
zemstvos.   In 1903 Witte was dismissed from office because
certain local committees, which he formed to enquire into the
shrinkage of the arable area under cultivation, had dared to
discuss political reforms.   In 1904, after the outbreak of the
war against Japan, the reactionary Plehve, whose power had
increased with the fall of Witte, was assassinated, and a
champion of the zemstvos succeeded him.   But the year ended
without any firm decision by the court in face of popular peti-
tions which asked for the liberties of the subject to be formally
recognised and for a parliament to be established.

On January 22, 1905, a mass deputation of strikers went to
the Winter Palace, headed by a certain Father Gapon, who
may well have been an *agent provocateur*.   The Czar had left
St. Petersburg, but there was an indiscriminate massacre,
resulting in a thousand deaths and leading to a slow but sure

separation between the constitutional and the revolutionary reform movements. Red Sunday was followed by widespread attacks on rural manor houses and the wealthier proprietors, which culminated in November when Witte, on his return to power, had to consider the possibility of a general expropriation of landowners to restore order. In October the town workers, more dangerous than the peasants, proclaimed a general strike. Workers' soviets (or councils) made their first appearance, and the St. Petersburg Soviet under Trotsky preached the doctrine of permanent revolution and constituted itself a rival government. Suppressed there on December 16, the soviet flamed into new life in Moscow, and was only ended after a week's street-fighting by regular soldiers returned from the war in the Far East. There had been other bloody episodes, such as the bombardment of Odessa by the mutinous battleship *Potemkin*, and the employment of Government artillery to clear the streets of Sebastopol. But after the close of 1905 the war against the people subsided into punitive expeditions through the provinces by Rennenkampf, and these measures restored order at the cost of about 4,000 executions. The revolution had failed. But Lenin, behind the scenes in St. Petersburg, had observed the first attempt at proletarian dictatorship.

The Dumas, the Land Reforms, and the Repression of Subject Nationalities

Meanwhile, the authorities had prudently come to terms with the constitutional middle-class reformers. In August a consultative Duma or assembly had been promised, to be chosen by indirect election. More important was the suppression of Pobiedonostzeff and other reactionary influences by Witte, who promptly issued the October Manifesto, a *ukase* or grant from the Czar promising his subjects liberty of the person and legislation in future by consent of a genuinely elected Duma. Three such Dumas were elected in two years, but constitutionally the results were disappointing. Before the first meeting Witte's success in negotiating a loan of £90,000,000 from French and British bankers enabled the Czar to feel less completely dependent upon popular support to keep his throne, and he proceeded to institute a new Upper

House, one half of whose members were to be Crown nominees. So the first Duma, in which the constitutional liberals or *Cadets* were the largest party, tried to turn the October Manifesto into a formal constitution which the Czar could not change at will, as well as to deal with the land question by partial expropriation of the large landowners. It was thereupon dissolved, and when the second Duma tried to take a rather similar line, it promptly went the way of the first. Before the election of the third Duma in the autumn of 1907, the franchise was modified so as largely to reduce the influence of the peasants, the industrial workers, and the non-Russian nationalities. The result was a parliament predominantly composed of the Russian landowning class, which co-operated quietly with the Government in moderate agrarian reform and less moderate measures against national minorities.

The economic results of the reform movement were more impressive. Count Witte, in his last short term of office (1905–6), had secured the abolition of the detested land payments under the Edict of Emancipation, thus making it easier for peasants to relieve their land hunger by purchase of the land remaining to the nobles after 1861, of which about one-half had already been sold to them piecemeal. Stolypin, the minister in power from 1906 to 1911, worked hard to increase the yield of the soil by substituting heritable consolidated holdings for the ancient strip system, by disrupting the backward village commune or Mir, and by encouraging peasants to buy or rent land in the possession of non-peasants. The result was a large increase in well-to-do peasants or *kulaks* and the removal of the incubus of the strip system from about 10 per cent. of peasant holdings within ten years. Moreover, the demand for land was being met in quite another way by the opening-up of Siberia, where about a third of a million peasants established themselves every year between 1906 and 1914. The third Duma, however, quarrelled with Stolypin in 1911 about his adoption of certain so-called emergency laws, which were submitted neither to the Duma nor to the Upper House. In September he was murdered, and it is characteristic of the intricacy and the underhand methods of Russian imperial politics that it remains uncertain whether his death was not countenanced by the Czar, because Stolypin's loss of control over the Duma had destroyed his political usefulness.

Before leaving the subject of the Russian revolution that failed, which viewed in retrospect was so obviously the prelude to the revolution that succeeded, we must note its nationalist aspect. To some extent the subject nationalities rose against alien landowners, as the Latvians and Estonians did against the Baltic barons; to some extent they rose in accordance also with international socialist doctrine, as in Stalin's native province of Georgia or in Warsaw, where a Left Wing demonstration in November, 1904, led to bloodshed. But for every people to which Russia was 'the great grave of nationalities' the failure in arms against Japan and the social upheaval which accompanied it gave a great impulse to fight for their freedom. Everywhere they failed in spite of the sympathies of European liberals. The Baltic provinces were the scene of savage punitive expeditions, the victims of which are not counted in Rennenkampf's 4,000.

Finland, whither members of the first Duma fled to issue the Viborg Manifesto, calling vainly on the people of Russia to insist upon their return to power, lost by 1910 all and more than all the concessions made in face of a Finnish general strike in 1905. The third Duma co-operated readily with Stolypin in measures against the Jews, who were now subjected to much persecution by a Russian nationalist organisation, enjoying influential support, which was popularly known as the Black Hundreds. But the most serious problem was Poland, which had thirty representatives taking the liberal side in the first Duma. The consequence was the alteration of the franchise and a reign of violence, which nationalist leaders like Pilsudski tried to combat by further violence, until the Russians, having separated Chelm from the ancient Congress Poland in 1909, proceeded three years later to deal what it was hoped would prove a mortal blow to Polish economic and cultural life, when they took away from Polish ownership and control the railway that linked Warsaw with Vienna.

The Taaffe Régime in Austria, and the Franchise Reform of 1907

The Dual Monarchy of Austria-Hungary had suffered no great social upheaval like Russia and was not liable to make

ill-considered forceful gestures such as from time to time
upset the balance of Wilhelmine Germany. Yet this was the
ramshackle empire which was not expected, and did not
itself expect, to weather further tempests. Since 1867 the

AUSTRIA-HUNGARY

German-speaking Austrians and the Magyars of Hungary
had been placed on an exactly equal constitutional footing,
but the two halves of the monarchy had developed very
differently. In Austria Count Taaffe, a boyhood friend of
the Emperor, ruled successfully for fourteen years (1879–93)
with the support of the Christian Socialists (an Austrian
counterpart to the Centre Party in Germany), the Poles and
Slovenes, and the Czechs. But he was overthrown in the
end through the opposition of the Young Czechs, a new and
strongly nationalist party which grew up under the leadership
of Thomas Masaryk, a coachman's son turned philosopher,
and was taught by him to hate the compromises on which the
Taaffe régime depended.

The downfall of Count Taaffe began a period of confusion,
marked by uproarious scenes in the imperial Reichsrat and
martial law in Prague, until the introduction of manhood suffrage

in 1907 gave the Reichsrat a closer resemblance to the parliaments of western Europe. The constituencies were made racially homogeneous (separate electorates for each of the recognised nationalities), so that the parties between which seats were contested were necessarily based on other than racial issues, the Christian Socialists and the Social Democrats being the most prominent rivals. But nationalist rivalries proved to have too firm a hold to be disposed of by any constitutional device. By 1914 the obstructiveness of the Czechs had caused the meetings of the Reichsrat to be left in abeyance; the once faithful Polish nobility had grown so troublesome that the Austrians had taken to encouraging the national aspirations of their tenants, the submerged Ukrainian peasantry; and Italian irredentists, not for the last time, were rioting in the streets of Trieste.

The Rule of the Magyar Oligarchy in Hungary

In Hungary, on the other hand, no systematic attempt was made to conciliate any of the non-Magyar racial groups, except that Croatia-Slavonia had partial home rule until the great upward surge of nationalist feeling among the Slavs after 1900, when the constitution was promptly suspended. The Hungarian parliament was active and could be stormy like the Austrian Reichsrat, but only one-fourth of the (male) population had the vote and as late as 1910 there were no more than eight non-Magyars in a lower house with over 400 members. While thus lording it over other races, many Magyars continued to agitate for a greater degree of independence from German Austria than had been given them by the Ausgleich in 1867. The chief bone of contention was the Army, where the Hungarian regiments were given separate identity, so they then began to press for the use of Magyar words of command. The ultimate goal was to make the union a dynastic union only, but the Emperor-King was able to check the extreme Magyar nationalists by threatening to introduce manhood suffrage, which would have swamped the Magyars by other nationalities. In 1910, accordingly, Tisza became Prime Minister and ruled until the war, on the basis that there was to be no further change either in the rights of the Magyars under the Ausgleich or in the general lack of rights among the other nationalities in Hungary. On an average Hungary lost 100,000 discontented subjects each year by emigration.

The Slav Peoples under the Dual Monarchy

The most important fact about the Dual Monarchy was that the constitutionally unrecognised 'minority' races formed a majority of the population. Francis Joseph had 51,000,000 subjects, of whom 30,000,000 were Slavs and perhaps another 5,000,000 of Latin origin, looking towards Italy or Rumania as their national home. But the Slavs did not form a single homogeneous group. They were divided between Austrian and Hungarian sovereignty, while the 1,500,000 mixed Serbs and Croats of Bosnia-Herzegovina formed yet a third category, since they were treated, even after their outright annexation in 1908, as the joint concern of the Dual Monarchy. It was perhaps for this very reason that, although it had taken an army of 200,000 men to establish the occupation originally in 1878, the sequel was an era of sound economic and cultural advance under the administration of an enlightened Hungarian nobleman named Kallay. It was also true of the larger groups of Slavs that some had more reason than others to be contented with their lot—the Poles, for instance, who lorded it over the Ruthenian peasantry of east Galicia and were never without influence at the Austrian court, the Czechs, whose voting power in the Reichsrat was needed to keep most Austrian governments in office, or the Croats, who may have hated the Magyars but were linked to the western provinces by their Catholic religion and culture. There was a corresponding difference in their attitude to the great Slav Empire of Russia. In 1907 a Czech started the neo-Slav movement, which aimed at meeting German and Austrian threats to their race by the creation of Czech and Jugoslav states under Russian auspices: but it found one stumbling-block in the anti-Russian feelings of the Croats and another and greater in the refusal of the Russians to countenance Ukrainian nationalism, a sentiment which was developing fast among the 3,000,000 oppressed Ruthenians of east Galicia. In 1910 the third neo-Slav congress at Sofia was boycotted by the Poles.

Since the Slavs were so disunited, and since the economic pressure making for the continuance of some form of political

unity in the Danube Valley was so strong, there was much
to be said for the solution known as Trialism, advocated by the
luckless Archduke Franz Ferdinand, heir to the dual throne.
This meant the admission to equality of some or all the
Slav peoples, beginning with the lands of the ancient Bohemian
monarchy and the Polish oligarchy of eastern Galicia, where
the development of oilfields by foreign capital was causing the
first stirrings of democracy. The project failed for three
reasons—because Tisza and the Magyars resisted every concession to the 'hordes,' because Franz Ferdinand predeceased
his aged uncle, and because the Slavs inside the monarchy could
not be pacified apart from the pacification of the Slavs of Serbia
outside it.   Franz Ferdinand's intended Triple Monarchy was
to include Serbia (which largely explains Serbian interest in
his assassination).   Serbia could only be brought in by a war,
such as the fiery Austrian Chief of Staff, Conrad von Hötzendorff, was annually proposing: but the war would either break
the Empire for ever or put the existing rulers more firmly in
the saddle, in which case there would be no further concessions
to the Slavs.

The Balkan States

After her defeat by the Bulgarians at Slivnitsa in 1885,
Serbia had remained for eighteen years under the influence
of Austria, which had saved her from the Bulgars.   Neither
the constitutional nor the dynastic history of the country was
particularly edifying. A democratic Constitution was twice
conceded and twice abolished; the first King quarrelled with
his Queen and abdicated; his son, Alexander I, made an
unsuitable and unpopular marriage and was murdered, along
with his wife and in cold blood, by terrorists belonging to his
own army. This assassination in 1903 ended the Obrenovic
dynasty. The Karageorgevic line returned, and with it the
Russian influence—which was not unconnected with the
barbarous deed. The reign of Peter I began with the so-called
Pig War against Austria, who revenged herself for the loss of
influence by closing the Austrian market to the chief export
of this backward agricultural country; but the only lesson
which the stubborn Serbs learnt from the struggle was their
urgent need of an outlet to the sea. Peter I also restored the
democratic constitution, though parliamentary forms were

never destined to command much respect in Serbia down to our own day. A far more important influence was that of the growth of Slav nationalism across the border in Bosnia-Herzegovina, bidding the warlike Serbs look northwards from their poverty-stricken mountains to plan a great kingdom of the South Slavs, or Jugoslavia.

Rumania resembled Serbia in her fundamental ambition of expansion and racial consolidation, hoping to build a greater Rumania on the ruins of the Dual Monarchy, which would provide Transylvania as her spoil. But she differed from Serbia in that she also cast covetous eyes upon Russian territory—namely, the area in southern Bessarabia which had been hers from 1856 to 1878. Hence her adhesion originally to the Triple Alliance, which was also naturally congenial to her Hohenzollern King Carol and was not deserted by her until after the King's death in 1914, when the country became convinced that Transylvania was not to be had on any other terms than war against the Austrians. The Rumanian monarchy was more powerful than the Serbian and maintained the largest army in the Balkans, which was based on the Prussian model, as was the constitution with its narrow franchise. Rumania also differed profoundly from Serbia in its internal economy. It was a land of large estates, forming one of the chief granaries of Europe, though the owners were a corrupt aristocracy who aped French culture and separated themselves as completely as possible from the ill-used peasantry. An important oil industry was growing up, but this was in the hands of foreign entrepreneurs, as was the considerable railway network; and the lack of a native middle class was one reason why the country had for long been flooded by Jewish immigrants from Russia. To these the Rumanian Government refused rights of citizenship, although this refusal was in defiance of a specific agreement undertaken at the Congress of Berlin.

The remaining states of the Balkan Peninsula looked for their aggrandisement to the break-up of the Ottoman Empire. Of the tiny principality of Montenegro, which claimed that the Black Mountain had never been surrendered to the Turk, it may be said that this was the whole basis of its existence, a nation of warriors ever ready to support their Serbian kinsmen and neighbours in the achievement of their secular

ambition, which was to win back the Old Serbia of the Middle
Ages and secure access to the western sea. Bulgaria, however,
occupied the key position, and her mediæval glories, which
rivalled those of Serbia, were supplemented by the more
recent memories of her triumph at Slivnitsa. Stambulov,
himself a peasant, had given shape and unity to a nation of
peasants, whose democratic constitution was less of a sham
than other Balkan constitutions because this was a nation of
small, independent freeholders. Their new prince Ferdinand,
who got rid of Stambulov in 1894, was perhaps the most
skilful intriguer among European rulers in the next two decades,
which makes it the less remarkable that Bulgaria, advancing
under the missionary banner of the Exarch with a plentiful
supply of bandits in support, was proving on the whole the
most effective claimant to the Turkish no-man's-land of
Macedonia. This was the area of the Vardar and Struma
valleys and their seaboard, including the port of Salonika,
which was (and is) bitterly disputed between Bulgars and
Greeks, with the Serbs intervening in its northern districts.
As if three rival claims, each with its racial and linguistic
justifications, were not enough, a further minority of Vlach
shepherds had been brought to light, whose interests were
championed by the Wallachians of Rumania. It was this
problem which had been temporarily eased by the establishment of a Macedonian gendarmerie under international supervision by the Mürzsteg Agreement of 1903.

Greece occupied a distinctive position by reason of its
traditional association with western culture, the interest
which the Powers had shared in its war of independence,
and the contacts resulting from a considerable mercantile
marine. Although it had a better start than its neighbours,
progress was disappointingly slow. The soil was barren and
communications, except by sea, were very difficult, and made
still more difficult by the brigandage for which the country
was for generations notorious. Yet the politicians, numerous,
eloquent, and quarrelsome, devoted themselves almost entirely
to foreign affairs. The main bone of contention had been
Crete, the 'great Greek island,' where the Christian part of
the population rose in revolt in 1897. They were supported by
the Greek Government at the cost of provoking a Turco-Greek
war, called the Thirty Days' War, because within that period

the Greeks were suing for peace at the cost of a cession of territory in Thessaly and a considerable war indemnity. Crete, however, came under international supervision, and within a few years the independence movement revived on the island under the most brilliant of modern Greek politicians, Venizelos. When he became Prime Minister of Greece in 1910, it could only be a matter of time before the Turks would cease to retain their nominal suzerainty over Crete. Venizelos also modernised the democratic political institutions of Greece, which dated from the 'sixties, but there seems to be an almost insuperable difficulty in re-acclimatising such institutions in the very land that first nurtured them. In 1912, at all events, the Greeks turned their attention more readily to Salonika and the Macedonian hinterland.

The Ottoman Empire

In 1912, at the outbreak of the Balkan Wars in the autumn, the Turkish or Ottoman Empire still included a considerable European territory. It stretched from the Adriatic across south-eastern Europe to the Black Sea, and it cut off Greece in the south from any land contact with the other Balkan states. The government of the sultans was monarchical in character, like that of the other three great empires which dominated central and eastern Europe. But the Sultan was more absolute and arbitrary in his authority, an oriental rather than a European ruler and governing as well as his Balkan territories the wild Anatolian uplands of Asia Minor and the Arab lands of the Middle East. Though in theory absolute, the Sultan's Government was generally capricious, inefficient and weak.

Since 1870 the other three empires had all in various ways expanded their territories and strengthened their positions: Germany had become a Great Power dominant in Europe, and even backward Russia though slow in movement was powerful by reason of size and numbers. But Turkey had continued to decline. This decline, the standing cause of the 'Eastern Question' in modern history, continued throughout the long reign of Abdul Hamid (1876–1909). It was at the expense of the Turkish Empire that the new Balkan states had come into existence, and were soon to extend their territories much further. Turkish territory was diminishing as the

Christian and European forces of Europe pushed south. But at the same time the Turks themselves were making some attempts to modernise their country and in particular to create a constitutional government. All this was the result of western ideas. Just as the western idea of nationalism had stirred the subject Balkan peoples against their Turkish rulers, so also it had had some effect on the Turks themselves. If only for military reasons, young officers had to learn foreign languages and study the military techniques of France and Germany. This brought them into contact with the ideas of nationalism and also of parliamentary government. They were led to imitate in order to attempt to keep abreast of the military advances made in neighbouring European countries. Even in the first half of the nineteenth century a prominent Turk had said: 'I am convinced that if we do not hasten to imitate Europe we must resign ourselves to return into Asia.'

On this fundamental issue a struggle developed inside Turkey. Abdul Hamid not unnaturally resisted constitutionalism. But he had an alternative policy: he would make the Ottoman Empire not more European, but more Asiatic; he would exploit the common link between the majority of his subjects, Turk and Arab. The common link was Islam. As Khalif, Abdul Hamid was the supreme head of that faith. Everything was now done to emphasise this fact. Even European modernism helped: railway and steamship were exploited to carry ever larger numbers of pilgrims to the Holy City of Mecca. At the same time the more usual weapons of autocracy—censorship of the press and the secret police—were used to check the agitation of nationalist minorities and the political organisation of constitutional reformers.

The Young Turk Revolution

The would-be constitutional reformers were known as the Young Turks. They agitated, sometimes openly and sometimes underground, for constitutional government. A parliament had actually been called by the Sultan in 1877, but was dissolved the next year. The revolution of 1908 was carried through by the Army, which threatened to march on Constantinople. Abdul Hamid gave in and called a parliament. Great rejoicing took place, both in Constantinople and elsewhere; Turks, Greeks and Bulgarians embraced in the streets.   But serious disputes broke out in the new parliament, and the Sultan staged a counter-revolution.   The troops entered the capital, the so-called Committee of Union and Progress (i.e. the Young Turks) regained control and deposed Abdul Hamid.   But the old problems remained, and the Young Turks used the weapon of force against the subject nationalities much as Abdul Hamid had done.   The new parliamentary government (with Abdul's brother as Sultan in his place) was a mere façade: behind it were the Army leaders.   The Army leaders of a backward state are not usually the best interpreters of constitutionalism.   Turkey, too, like the other Balkan countries and much of Russia, was a poor and undeveloped country.

Standards of Living in Western and Eastern Europe

Apart from the broad distinction already drawn between western and eastern Europe in the matter of more or less liberal methods of government, there was also a marked difference in the standard of life.   In this second respect, central Europe—Germany and to a lesser extent Austria— is to be grouped with the west rather than the east.   In Germany and western Europe industry had made its greatest advances, whereas in eastern and south-eastern Europe agriculture was still predominant and the peasant was the typical producer.   Industry, as we saw in an earlier chapter, had transformed western Europe during the nineteenth century.   With industrialism had come a rising standard of life.   For Great Britain it has been calculated that in 1913 aver- age incomes (measured in purchasing power) were about one- third greater than in 1880, and economic betterment was not confined to Britain.   An English worker was better fed than a German, yet German consumption of meat had more than doubled since 1860.   Wealth was increasing rapidly in western Europe, including Germany, but at a much slower rate else- where. Although great wealth was concentrated in few hands and rapid industrialisation had led to overcrowding in the slums of the cities, the general increase in wealth did bring advantages to the masses in a rising standard of life.   Popular education, the franchise, and the development of social services all helped both to improve the material lot of man and to add to his dignity.

In eastern Europe things were very different. The mass of the people were peasants; they were illiterate, and their way of life was primitive. They carried on a hard struggle for existence, their standard of life was low, and they were untrained to take part in the political enterprise of democratic Government. To a large extent, in fact, the police state and the more savage methods of government were a reflection of the social conditions of the people. It was the economic backwardness and the primitive way of life in the east and south-east which distinguished most clearly that part of Europe from the more prosperous and civilised west.

Suggestions for Further Reading

E. Ludwig: *Kaiser Wilhelm II*, c. 7.

G. P. Gooch: *Germany*, cc. 3–6.

A. J. P. Taylor: *The Hapsburg Monarchy* (1948), cc. 13–17.

Sir John Maynard: *Russia in Flux*, cc. 2 and 3.

Cambridge Modern History, Vol. XII, cc. 12 and 13 (by Sir B. Pares).

W. H. Dawson: *The German Empire*, cc. 19 and 20.

H. Wickham Steed: *The Hapsburg Monarchy*, c. 3.

R. Charques: *The Twilight of Imperial Russia*, cc. 1–9.

M. T. Florinsky: *Russia*, Vol. II, cc. 39–41.

New Cambridge Modern History, Vol. XI, c. 12 (by W. N. Medlicott).

CHAPTER 10

PRE-WAR EUROPE:
THE GROWTH OF INTERNATIONALISM

Impact of the Industrial Revolution

MODERN history, which has seen the development of the national state as the dominant political institution in Europe, has also been marked by the growth of a certain degree of European unity. There is a European tradition which is older than the national state, and which goes back through the Holy Roman Empire, when a single form of Christianity was the common faith, to a common foundation in the culture of Greece and Rome. The Reformation destroyed the mediæval unity and prepared the way for the conflict of rival national states. But while these conflicts raged and were conducted by means of both diplomacy and war, the Industrial Revolution was creating new links which stretched across national boundaries and tended to create a new unity. The development of facilities for transport and communication made possible a vast extension of foreign travel, international trade and international economic and social relations of every kind. Trade, banking, insurance, railway and steamship travel all involved international relations and made international organisation necessary.

Enduring Influence of the Church of Rome as a Centripetal Force

The Roman Catholic Church is a great international society, and as such it has frequently come into conflict with the more extreme pretensions of the modern national state. The Catholic Church is the largest of the Christian communities. It claims to be the one and only true Church of Christ. In the first decades of the twentieth century there were in the world about 270,000,000 Catholics as against 170,000,000 Protestants. The Protestants are divided into State Churches and also into various denominations. The Catholics, however, though they too are necessarily members of different states, spiritually owe allegiance to one sovereign, the Pope. The Catholic faith prevailed in France, Italy, Spain, Portugal,

Austria-Hungary, the Rhineland, Posen, and the southern states of the German Empire, in part of Switzerland, in the Polish territory of Russia, in most of Ireland, and was found elsewhere as the faith of smaller groups in other countries. It was also the faith of the states of Latin America, of the French-speaking parts of Canada, and, by reason of the large emigration from Catholic Europe, was firmly established as an important Church in the United States. Catholic missions have been established in India, Africa and in many other parts of the world. The faith of mediæval Europe, universal in character, has thus been carried from Europe to the world. But it remains representative of Europe, with its supreme direction still centred in Rome, the first city which can claim in a real sense to have been capital of Europe.

During the nineteenth century the Church was threatened on every side. With the unification of Italy the Church lost the Papal States, and after 1870 the Pope regarded himself as a prisoner in the Vatican. This created a gulf between Italian Catholics and the government of Italy. Under the Third Republic in France and in the German Empire of Bismarck the national state was claiming a degree of control over its subjects so complete that it came into violent conflict with the Church. This struggle was illustrated most clearly in the sphere of education. Who was to educate the young—Church or State? The doctrines of the Catholic Church were exposed to criticism by the discoveries of science; in an age of material-ism a conflict developed between science and religion. Political movements were also imperilling the Church. Liberalism—a term which covered democratic government and constitu-tional monarchy together with intellectual freedom—was directly opposed to the papal system which was absolutist in character. Revolutionary socialism was bidding for the allegiance of the workers of the world and aiming at a new international society on an economic basis, which would replace the older universalism of religion.

But the Roman Catholic Church remained a great inter-national organisation, centripetal in character, with its clergy and members throughout the world linked to the Pope in Rome as their centre and head. The Pope is the supreme authority at the summit of a vast and elaborate hierarchy, which includes patriarchs, archbishops, metropolitans and bishops, and, in the lower ranks, archdeacons, archpriests, deans and canons. The Church was enabled by the improvements in world communication and transport to make closer its universal contacts. Papal control was probably more effective than ever before. The Church as a centralised world system is organised on a territorial basis, the world being divided into dioceses. Though the Pope is generally an Italian prelate, Catholics of every nationality throughout the world recognise his authority—the Archbishop of New York or Philadelphia looks up to the Roman Pontiff as does the humblest Italian priest. The Papacy as a system of administration is slow to move and is staunchly conservative. It is much older than the states of Europe and their political systems. In this lies part of its strength: it has stood like a rock unchanging through many centuries of change.

To counter the threats of modernism, the Church stiffened its attitude on theological questions and turned its back resolutely on liberalism, but at the same time showed itself ready to give attention to the new social problems agitating the masses. The dogma of the Immaculate Conception promulgated in 1854 laid down that Catholics must believe that the Virgin Mary was born without original sin, as contrasted with the rest of mankind 'conceived in sin.' Faith in miracles was strengthened by visions of the Virgin seen by the child Bernadette at Lourdes. In the 'seventies a great church was erected to Notre Dame de Lourdes and a vast annual concourse of pilgrims has testified to popular belief in the special grace vested in the Virgin Mary. Pope Pius IX attacked the spirit of the age in the encyclical *Quanta Cura* of 1864. The accompanying Syllabus of Errors denounced the errors of liberty of conscience, socialism and communism, the subjection of the Church to the civil authority, and the idea that 'the Roman Pontiff can or ought to come to terms with progress, liberalism, or modern civilisation.' In 1870 the Vatican Council laid down the dogma of Papal Infallibility.

Pope Leo XIII (1878–1903), although he stood firm so far as the doctrines of the Church were concerned and asserted that the Church was in itself a 'perfect society,' was not unsympathetic to the political and social movement of the day. He favoured the creation of Catholic political parties to further the Roman Catholic interest in such countries as

Belgium, Austria and Germany.   He advised French Catholics
to accept and work with the republican constitution of their
country.   He was not blind to the good qualities of the
democratic system of government in the United States.   Above
all, the Pope gave a lead to Catholic social reformers.   In
1891 the encyclical *Rerum Novarum* took a middle position
between the extremes of economic liberalism on the one hand
and Marxian socialism on the other.   The encyclical supported
private property and the family, but it also urged the claims
of labour to fair wages and reasonable conditions.   As a
result, Leo XIII was sometimes known as 'the working man's
pope.'   His action led to the formation of Christian trade
unions in Catholic countries, and strengthened the hold of
the Church over the masses.   Under the next pope, Pius X
(1903-14), there was a further struggle with liberals and
modernists who were appearing even inside the Church.
A new Syllabus appeared in 1907 and listed the errors to be
avoided.   But any mass secession from the Church was
prevented, in spite of a considerable propaganda for *Los von
Rom* (Away from Rome) which developed in Bohemia and
Austria.   On the whole, the Church held its ground.

The international spirit of the Catholic Church was strengthened by the holding of a series of Eucharistic Congresses, the
first of which was in 1881.   These meetings brought laymen
and clergy together from many parts of the world, to centres
such as Paris, London and Jerusalem.   The Pope, as head
of an immense international community, gave his general
support to such peace movements as that for arbitration
treaties and the Hague Conferences.   Religious leaders were
to be found even outside the Catholic Church, who looked to
the Pope as possibly a decisive voice in the cause of world
peace.   To some the Papacy personified 'the greatest moral
force of the world.'

International Organisation of Protestantism

Protestants, though divided among themselves and therefore
a less potent international force than the Catholics, were also
seeking to work internationally.   There was even talk of a
World Parliament of Religions.   Modernism affected Protestants as well as Catholics, and the importance of 'good works'
came to be emphasised more than that of doctrine.   The

Y.M.C.A. (Young Men's Christian Association, founded 1844), the Y.W.C.A. (beginning in 1855), and the Salvation Army (founded 1880) all soon became international in character, and aimed at fostering peace and goodwill. An interesting and important development of international Protestant activity was that for co-operation in the missionary field. In 1910 a World Missionary Conference met in Edinburgh and set up a continuation committee to serve as a permanent international link (later, in 1921, this became the International Missionary Council). The World's Evangelical Alliance—'to associate and concentrate the strength of an enlightened Protestantism'—had been at work since 1846. It held its fourth international conference in 1861 at Geneva, its tenth in 1896 in London. The World's Student Christian Federation was meeting in Tokyo in 1907. The World Alliance for promoting International Friendship through the Churches was founded at Constance in 1914—on August 2. World organisation was in the air; if organisation and publications could have saved the world, mankind would have been safe for a thousand years.[1]

The Orthodox Church in Eastern Europe

The Orthodox Church—often spoken of as the Greek Church, but officially described as the Holy Orthodox Catholic Apostolic Eastern Church—exercised a certain unifying influence in eastern Europe. But this influence it exercised through cultural and religious tradition rather than through organisation. Its chief dignitary was the Patriarch of Constantinople, who bore the title of Œcumenical Patriarch. But as he was subject, after the Turkish conquest, to control by the Sultans, the Church gradually formed into national divisions. Thus in 1912 there were, in addition to the ancient patriarchates of Constantinople, Alexandria, Antioch, and Jerusalem, the nine national churches of Cyprus, Mount Sinai, Greece, Serbia, Rumania, Montenegro, Austria-Hungary (covering its Serb, Rumanian and Ruthenian minorities), Russia, and Bulgaria. The largest and most powerful was the Russian. But the Russian Church responded less to modern tendencies

[1] The literature on these topics is immense. Several pages of the British Museum Catalogue are given to the Evangelical Alliance alone. On the subject of Christian missionary enterprise see, to begin with, K. S. Latourette, *A History of the Expansion of Christianity*, 7 vols.

than did the Catholics or Protestants of the west. It was largely subject to the Czars; it was controlled by the Holy Synod (a council of Church dignitaries) with a lay Procurator— the 'Czar's eye,' and was used as an instrument to spread Russian influence. All Orthodox Christians had a religious faith and tradition in common, and also a certain style in art and Church architecture. In the wider field, they had a Russian archbishop in New York, and at the end of the nineteenth century were establishing friendly contacts with the Church of England.

New Cultural Links Established

Indeed, international society of all kinds was growing up. In every sphere the increased facilities for communication and travel were leading people of similar interests and aims to organise on a European and often on a world basis. Moreover, national systems of education were being organised in all the more advanced countries, so that there were more people than at any time since the Middle Ages qualified to take an interest in what was being accomplished in other countries. Trade led the way, big international exhibitions being promoted every third year, on an average, at centres which ranged from Milan to Melbourne, from St. Louis to Liége. As for the commerce of the mind, learned journals passed from country to country, lecturers and students were exchanged, international conferences or congresses were arranged by the score. Every kind of subject and interest was represented: scientists of every particular branch, doctors, engineers, historians, philosophers, librarians, liberals, socialists, anarchists, all met in their international conferences. The Rotary Clubs, which had originated in America to foster the ideal of service among business-men, formed an international association in 1912. International sports meetings were becoming common. The Olympic Games were revived in 1896 in Athens, and an International Olympic Committee formed. The Games were held quadrennially: in 1900 at Paris, 1904 St. Louis, 1908 London, and 1912 at Stockholm. In addition to conferences, occasional visits and private travel, people were more and more living for long periods of time abroad either in business or in study. Napoleon III and Eugénie had sometimes watched the cricket matches of the English colony in Paris. In Hamburg Englishmen established in business in the 'seventies used to play cricket *vor dem Lübecker Thor*. There was a large American colony in Paris before 1914; in Florence English people had long been in residence in order to study art and had their British Institute. John Stuart Mill died at Avignon in 1873 and many lesser known English people were living there at that time.[1] By travel, trade and cultural contacts, Europeans were getting to know each other and learning to share their common interests.

The Peace Movement

Apart from the work of the Christian Churches in maintaining the ideal of world peace, efforts in this direction were made by numerous individuals and also by organisations formed for the purpose. Curiously enough, the inventor of dynamite, Nobel, was prominent as a benefactor of the peace movement. This Swedish scientist and manufacturer founded a number of annual prizes for work of benefit to mankind, and one of these prizes was to be for peace work. The American steel king, Carnegie, made large financial contributions to the cause of peace. The Carnegie endowment of ten million dollars in 1910 was made with a view to 'the speedy abolition of international war between the so-called civilised nations.' Tolstoi wrote in support of international brotherhood and conciliation. In England Norman Angell, arguing that modern war would be so destructive as to place intolerable economic burdens on victor and vanquished alike, called his book on war *The Great Illusion*. The book ran through fifteen reprintings or new editions in England between 1909 and 1914, and editions were also published in France, Italy, Germany, Russia and many of the other countries of the world. The peace movement embraced many groups and societies in different countries. There were in all several hundred peace societies listed in the *Annuaire du mouvement pacifiste pour l'année 1910*, which was published at Berne by the *Bureau International de la Paix*. The movement had possessed its permanent headquarters at Berne since 1891, and a long

---

[1] A visit to the tomb of J. S. Mill in the cemetery at Avignon reveals the graves of a surprisingly large number of English people buried there during the nineteenth century.

series of international congresses had taken place. The first had met in 1843; after 1889 the meeting of international congresses of the peace movement became periodical. Organisations, speeches, publications, and pure idealism were not lacking.

The Hague Conferences

In the official and formal relations between states there appeared, before 1914, to have been a degree of improvement. The international congresses after the wars of Napoleon and the working of the Concert of Europe in the decades following 1871 all suggested a growing ability to work together and an increased realisation of a common interest in maintaining peace. There was already in existence a body of international law, so-called, which was at the least an indication of the possibility of agreement. International law has come into existence through the growth of custom generally recognised as between civilised nations, by the negotiation of treaties, and by the classic writings of great lawyers. But international law is very different in one respect from the laws of particular countries: there is no power to enforce it, and States are jealously concerned to maintain their sovereignty. To mitigate the cruelty of war, the International Red Cross came into existence. A diplomatic conference was arranged at Geneva in 1864, and as a result the Geneva Convention was widely accepted. By this Convention, States agreed that in war armies must show respect for the wounded and for medical services and hospitals and recognise the symbol of the red cross. The Convention was revised in 1906 and its principles were extended to naval warfare by the Hague Conferences.

The Hague Conferences were the most important international effort in the cause of peace; the first conference met at The Hague in 1899 and the second in 1907. The holding of the first conference was the outcome of a proposal made by the Czar Nicholas II. Russia had fallen behind in the armaments race but Nicholas may well have had a sincere wish for international peace. In a paper which his Foreign Minister sent to foreign representatives the Czar's point of view was thus expressed:

'The maintenance of universal peace and a possible reduction of the excessive armaments which weigh upon all nations represent, in the present condition of affairs all over the world, the ideal towards which the efforts of all the Governments should be directed.'

This then was the ideal to be aimed at. The paper went on to cite most of the arguments against armaments: the financial burden, the unproductive labour involved, the drag on social progress, the danger of the 'armed peace' leading inevitably to disaster. All this implies a distrust in the mind of that generation as to the ultimate effectiveness of the Concert of Europe. It has also a familiar ring to a later generation which has lived through the League of Nations period. In each case the outcome was a tragic one.

The specific aims of the first conference were to bring about a limitation of armaments and to devise methods of arbitration in international disputes. It was naturally most difficult to get the established military Powers of Europe to look with any favour on these proposals. The Kaiser, in a letter to the Czar, praised his warmness of heart but questioned the practicability of disarmament. 'Could we,' wrote the Kaiser, 'picture a Monarch dissolving his regiments sacred with a hundred years of history . . . and handing over his towns to Anarchists and Democracy.' On arbitration, Holstein, the director of the German Foreign Office, wrote: 'Little, uninterested States as subjects, little questions as objects of arbitral activity, are conceivable: great States and great questions, not.'

One may dislike the realism, but Holstein had placed his finger on the great difficulty: how to persuade Great Powers to accept arbitration which might involve them in loss, when by the use of their own strength they could achieve their full aims. But despite this difficulty most States were prepared to agree in general terms to the importance of striving to maintain peace, and the conferences duly met. To the first conference representatives came from the sovereign states of Europe and Asia and also from the United States and Mexico; in all, twenty-six countries were represented. At the second conference there were delegates from forty-four countries, including the countries of South America. To the second conference invitations were again issued by Nicholas II, and this time he was supported by the President of the United States, Theodore Roosevelt.

Neither conference resulted in any general agreement on disarmament: indeed, during the eight years between the conferences world expenditure on arms had already risen by about 25 per cent. But restrictions were accepted on the use of certain types of weapon, some regulations for the more humane conduct of war on land and sea were drawn up, and steps taken towards codification of international law. The first conference did produce one rather striking innovation: it set up a Permanent Court of Arbitration. A list of arbitrators was compiled, and in this way a standing panel was available which countries could use, if desired, when international disputes arose. The second conference recommended the calling of conferences at regular intervals in future, and this created a feeling of optimism among the workers for peace. Here, they thought, was the beginning of a new world society. The next meeting was projected for 1915.

Arbitration Treaties

Another hopeful line of development had been the arrangement of arbitration on questions in dispute by mutual arrangement between the states concerned. Thus the long-standing quarrel between Great Britain and the United States over the damage caused in the Civil War by the cruiser *Alabama*, which had been built in England and used by the Southern States, was settled in 1871 by arbitration. This method was used not infrequently: Great Britain, the United States and France had each settled some dozens of small matters in this way. Other countries used the method to a less extent. In all, between 1880 and 1900 ninety disputes were settled. Such disputes involved the ownership of territory, the delimitation of frontiers, and acts, such as arrest or seizure of property, committed by one state against subjects of another. An arbitration treaty signed in 1903 between France and Great Britain offered a model to other states. But the arbitration procedure was confined to secondary questions; 'vital interests, independence and honour' were excluded. In 1914 Mr. Bryan, President Wilson's Secretary of State, introduced another safeguard to peace. He negotiated with certain countries treaties which provided for 'cooling off,' i.e. delay and consideration of any dispute by an agreed conciliation committee before any resort to war. It is one of the ironies of history that imperial Germany rejected such a treaty, which might well have saved her in 1917-18.

Economic Interdependence of the European Powers

Many economists and other thinkers of the nineteenth century had been convinced that, quite apart from any political or diplomatic action by the states of the world, the development of the economic system would make war increasingly unlikely. The growth of international trade, the investment of capital in foreign countries (the return on which depended upon peaceful production and uninterrupted exchange), the links created and the interests involved in transport and communication, the ramifications of international banking, insurance and shipping—all these things, it had seemed, must make the outbreak of war less and less likely as the complexity of the economic interdependence of nations became steadily greater and greater. One of the arguments of the free traders was that the absence of tariffs made possible the greatest expansion of world trade: each nation engaged in trading profited thereby, and would therefore realise that its own material prosperity depended upon that of its customers.

On the other hand capitalism has often been criticised as making for war, by leading to a struggle for foreign markets to absorb the surplus product of large-scale industry, by stimulating imperialism, and by leading to interference with small or backward countries in order to compel the payment of interest on loans. It is true that international friction and war itself are caused by these things. But it is equally true that the economic interdependence of nations has given a very real reason for maintaining the peace; and it may be significant that the greatest capitalist nation of the modern world, the United States, has on the whole been the most peaceful. After 1870 there set in a tendency to more pronounced nationalism in Europe. Countries increasingly developed their industries by means of tariff protection against foreign competition, until Great Britain remained the only Great Power still maintaining free trade. But right down to 1914 the economic interdependence of the world appeared to be a strong factor on the side of peace.

The vast increase in world trade between 1870 and 1914

meant that the industrial nations—Great Britain, France, Germany, the United States—were exporting ever greater amounts of their surplus production. In this way their prosperity became dependent upon the continuation of this trade; disaster in any part of the world, any interruption of commerce by war, would have far-reaching repercussions. The interests of the European nations were closely intertwined. Germany, for example, was Great Britain's best European customer, and Germany carried on more foreign trade with Great Britain than with any other country. Another striking factor during this period was the growth of foreign lending. This naturally developed along with world trade and the lead was taken by the great industrial countries of Europe, Great Britain, Germany and France. Important groups of investors in each of these countries had interests in most countries in the world. The floating of loans enabled more backward countries to spend money on buying capital equipment in the lender country, thus creating employment there; furthermore, the use of the capital equipment after purchase helped to build up the borrower country as a continuing customer. And quite apart from long-term investments, banks kept balances abroad in order to facilitate the day-to-day process of trade.

For these reasons important commercial interests at times of international tension might well throw their influence on to the side of peace. This was thought to have been the case in Germany in 1905 and 1911. The British Consul-General reported home that the close connection between banks and industry 'must in times of international crisis result in general collapse' and during the same crisis, that of 1911, a Berlin commercial newspaper declared that the policy of the German Government by causing a war scare 'has inflicted on our commerce and our industry losses almost as great as they would have suffered from an unsuccessful war.' And when war did finally come in 1914 well-informed people still believed that it must of necessity, for economic reasons, be short. Although economic interdependence had failed to prevent war, it would surely make a long struggle impracticable. But in this also European opinion was deceived.

The growing economic interdependence of the countries of the world did, however, make necessary international agreements for the regulation of communication, transport and trade. In these matters much international organisation existed already before 1914. The Telegraph Union dates from 1864. A number of countries agreed to use the metric system, and an International Bureau of Weights and Measures was founded in Paris in 1875. In 1883 an international convention was made on the standardisation of patent rights, and in 1887 an agreement was arranged for the international protection of copyright. The management of ocean steam-ship lines, the use of harbour facilities and the running of transcontinental express trains all called for international agreement. The *Verein Mitteleuropäischer Eisenbahnverwaltungen* (Association of Central European Railway Administrations), originating as an organisation for the railways of the German states, was later widened in scope. By 1914 there were in operation about 400 international bodies of this kind; character-istic of them all was the possession of an object which was, in each case, of practical and common interest to a number of states.

The Postal Union

An outstanding example of successful international organisa-tion is the Universal Postal Union. When one reflects that by buying an English stamp with English money one can send a letter to any part of the world, one discovers that this is only possible because a high degree of international organisa-tion already exists in the field of postal communication. The Postal Union originated in a conference held at Berne in 1874; in the following year the International Postal Convention was signed. The last state to join the Union was China— in 1914. The Postal Union, with its headquarters in Berne, was characteristic of many such bodies in its constitution and machinery. It was financed by the member governments. The Union's machinery was divided into three parts: there was a conference taking place periodically which could lay down general principles, and was also of publicity value in winning the support of public opinion; there was an executive com-mittee to work out plans in detail; finally, there was a secretariat or bureau to serve as a permanent centre of action. The success of the Postal Union and many other organisations like it proved conclusively that in certain limited fields international action for the common good was practicable. This kind of international organisation had passed beyond the stage represented by the dreams of pacifists and idealists; it had passed into the stage of acceptance by governments and hard-headed men of business. It was accepted as a matter of course. The sceptic as to world peace, who was shown to be right in 1914, was nevertheless recognising the efficacy of international organisation whenever he travelled in foreign countries, changed money, bought imported goods or posted a letter abroad; and it should not be forgotten that any European country except Russia and Turkey could then be entered freely without a passport.

International Capitalism

Capitalism—the production of goods by private effort for private profit—was developing from the small to the large unit. Mergers, combines, cartels, trusts were taking the place of the independent firms of earlier days, and the logical outcome of this process was the formation of international organisations and agreements between capitalist firms. The object of such combines was to mitigate the severity—from the capitalist's point of view—of competition. Sales could be maintained at remunerative levels by agreement to control output, to fix prices, or to share markets. Internal cartels developed, particularly in Germany, between 1870 and the end of the century, and many of the international agreements were promoted by Germans, especially from 1890 onwards. The formation of these international agreements and organisations—they were of various kinds—emphasised the increasing economic interlocking of the nations. Agreements might be to divide markets or trade routes or to fix prices internationally among producers. Companies could be organised in such a way as to have their main domicile in one country but to have branches, agents or affiliated companies in neighbouring countries.

International organisation can be found in many types of industry. In 1883 was formed the International Rail Syndicate—of British, German and Belgian firms—to share orders and control prices. The dynamite cartel of Anglo-German and French producers was created in 1886. Prices for shipping were fixed by the North Atlantic Shipping Conference in 1908, and by the Mediterranean Conference in the following year. Interlocking syndicates exploited the Lorraine iron and the Ruhr coal. Oil interests merged in the combination of Royal Dutch and Shell (British) in 1907. The Turkish Petroleum Company, created in 1912, was owned, through sharing out its stock, by the Anglo-Persian Oil Company, the Royal Dutch-Shell combine, and the Deutsche Bank. Others of the newer industrial developments, in which similar large-scale measures were taken internationally, included the chemical industry (the production of synthetic dyes was a German speciality), textiles, and the manufacture of electrical apparatus. By 1914 there are estimated to have been over 100 international associations.

Socialism as an International Creed—the 'Internationals'

The organisation of working-class and socialist movements characteristic of the new industrial age was early extended from the national to the international sphere. One of the main ideas developed by Karl Marx was that the really significant division of mankind was not the political division of nationality, but the economic one of social class. The working classes in every country were linked together by common ties of economic interest. To advance that interest they must learn to work together. 'Workers of the World, Unite!' was the slogan of *The Communist Manifesto* of 1848. As the nineteenth century proceeded, the international solidarity of the working class became more and more an object of socialist activity. The 'International' has an important place in the history of the socialist movement. There have, in fact, been three Internationals of some importance, the third being the Communist International founded in 1919. It is with the first two that we are concerned here. The first, the International Working Men's Association, was founded in 1864. It was a revolutionary body, established under the leadership of Marx and Engels, and Marx himself drew up its programme.

The First International appealed to workers in many parts of Europe; in the years 1866–9 four European congresses were held, at Geneva, Lausanne, Brussels and Basle. But its powers of organisation and financial resources were slight. Marx and the central body in London approved the action of the Paris Commune in the spring of 1871, though it seems that they took no direct part in originating it. The International split up between the socialist followers of Marx and the anarchists who supported the Russian, Bakunin. Bakunin was expelled in 1872, and the International struggled on for a short time with a centre in New York. Bakunin and the anarchists formed a rival International, finding its chief support in Spain and Italy. But a rising in Spain in 1873 was suppressed by Government troops.

The brotherhood of the workers had so far been concerned in little but violence and bloodshed. In 1889, however, the Second (or Socialist) International was formed, and this devoted much time to the question of peace. It was raised in the congress at Amsterdam in 1903 and again at Stuttgart; the French socialist leader Jaurès gave special attention to the subject. A brilliant scholar and university professor at Toulouse, Jaurès was at the same time internationalist and patriot. Where *la patrie française* was in danger he was a patriot:

'Si notre patrie est menacée . . . nous serions des premiers à la frontière pour défendre la France dont le sang coule dans nos veines, et dont le fier génie est ce qu'il y a de meilleur en nous.'

But as socialist and internationalist he supported arbitration, looked for international reconciliation and hoped until the end that working-class solidarity between nation and nation would prevent war. He was assassinated on July 31, 1914.

Other socialists also hoped for peace right up to the end. The darkening of the European horizon after 1911 made them redouble their efforts. A special congress was held at Basle the following year; workers everywhere were urged to demand a peaceful foreign policy from their governments. The next congress—which would mark the fiftieth anniversary of the founding of the First International—was fixed to assemble in Vienna in August, 1914. A commemorative album actually appeared in print; but the congress did not meet.

Nationalism proved stronger by far than internationalism; the workers of the world, when war came, fought not for the figment of class solidarity, but each one for his own country. The spirit of European unity, with its long tradition, was forgotten; the solid commercial advantages of peaceful world trade went unheeded; the practical internationalism of organisations like the Postal Union was shown to be almost ludicrously insufficient.   Inspired by the fervour of patriotism, the peoples gave themselves to the slaughter.

SUGGESTIONS FOR FURTHER READING

Sir A. Zimmern: *The League of Nations and the Rule of Law*, Part I, cc. 3-6.

A. C. F. Beales: *History of Peace*, cc. 7-10.

R. B. Mowat: *The Concert of Europe*, cc. 14 and 21.

Gilbert Murray: *The Ordeal of This Generation*, c. 2.

C. Eagleton: *International Government*, c. 7.

G. T. Mangoni: *Short History of International Organization*, c. 3.

N

III

CHAPTER 11

FROM THE BALKAN WARS TO THE WORLD WAR,
1912–14

The Balkan League and First Balkan War

THE Young Turks, who had seized control of the Ottoman Empire in 1908, seemed by 1912 to be almost inviting attack by their Christian neighbours through a strange combination of evident cruelty—'a policy of extermination,' in the words of the Bulgarian Prime Minister—and apparent weakness. There were hideous massacres both of Armenians and Macedonians, and finally the Albanians, most backward of all the Balkan peoples and more than half Muslim in faith, were driven to rebel. Meanwhile, the Turkish Army was in the throes of modernisation and therefore disorganised. The Italian attack on Tripoli, begun the previous year, was indeed making little headway in the hinterland, but this was because the Turks had the support of the Arab tribesmen: the Turks had been unable to prevent either the bombardment of the Dardanelles or the occupation of the Dodecanese Islands, which the Italians kept, in defiance of Greek nationalist claims, for the ensuing thirty years. In such circumstances, the formation of a Balkan league against Turkey, to crown the hopes of many generations, could not be further postponed, even by the inveterate quarrelsomeness of the Balkan peoples. The Great Powers were in principle opposed, because they feared that a Balkan war would precipitate a general war and also because they preferred to manipulate the separate states as convenient pawns, whereas the united Balkans would seek to exclude their influence. But behind the scenes Russia helped to create a Balkan league, hoping that its success would enable her to change the regime at the Straits, which Turkey in the Tripoli War had even closed to merchant ships, with serious consequences to Russian trade. So, in February, 1912, Serbia and Bulgaria, which had virtually been enemies

Serb + Bulg alliance

since the war of 1885, made an alliance for common action against the Turks and for an eventual partition of Macedonia. In May, Venizelos, stung by a Turkish refusal formally to cede Crete, brought Greece to the side of Bulgaria and Serbia; and in August there was a verbal agreement with Montenegro. The Turks, who saw what was coming, liquidated their war with Italy by the cession of Tripoli at the Treaty of Lausanne, which was signed in the same month in which the new war opened.

In the months of October and November the Balkan peoples won a whole series of signal triumphs over their ancient oppressor. The Bulgarians, advancing southwards, forced a very strong position at Kirk Kilisse, and after a week's hard fighting at Lule Burgas drove the Turks back to their last ditch, the lines of Tchataldja defending Constantinople itself. Meanwhile, the Serbs with Montenegrin help had overrun the Sanjak and won a great victory at Kumanovo, which in their view redeemed the overthrow of their race at Kossovo in 1389 and, what was of more practical importance, opened for them the way from Old Serbia into western Macedonia and beyond into Albania. By the end of November they had reached Durazzo, and the Greeks were preparing to shell the neighbouring Albanian port of Valona. The Greek contribution had been chiefly naval—a blockade of the Turkish coastline and the seizure of the islands—but their army, after an initial check at Florina, entered Salonika a little ahead of the Bulgarians, thus putting the final end to Turkish rule in Macedonia. Turkish territory had in fact been reduced to the four great fortresses of Constantinople, Adrianople, Janina, and Scutari when a two months' armistice was concluded (December 4–February 4). But Enver Pasha staged a *coup d'état* in Constantinople: he shot the War Minister, changed the Government, and refused to give up Adrianople without a further fight. In the second campaign, which terminated in April, the Balkan League enjoyed further triumphs, as in succession Janina fell to the Greeks, Adrianople to the Bulgarians (helped by Serbian artillery), and Scutari to the Montenegrins. Only two things were needed to complete the ejection of the Turk from Europe, the goodwill of the Powers and harmony among the Balkan allies: but neither condition was fulfilled.

The Russians had at a very early stage taken alarm lest the Bulgarians should enter Constantinople, but they would gladly have seen their protégés, the Serbs, ensconced somewhere on the Adriatic coastline—that is, in one or more Albanian ports. This was anathema to the Austrians, who before the end of the first campaign had made it clear that they would fight to prevent it. Italy sided with Austria on this issue, because she too had reason to fear the creation of a strong Slav neighbour (such as Jugoslavia was later to provide). What was more important was the backing of Germany, where it seems to have been argued that, if Serbia was robbed of her expected gains on the Adriatic, she would be forced to seek compensation on the Aegean: hence a quarrel between Serbia and Bulgaria, perhaps also between Serbia and Greece, in which the Balkan League would fall to pieces and control of the Balkans by and for Germanic interests be made easier. Britain and France shared the Russian point of view, but were chiefly concerned to preserve harmony in the Concert of Europe, operating through the ambassadors in London under the chairmanship of Sir Edward Grey. Accordingly, Serbia was at an early stage warned from Berlin that she would not be allowed to retain any Adriatic port; the Powers agreed upon the establishment of a new autonomous state of Albania; and when the Montenegrins proved recalcitrant, Scutari was handed over to the new state in response to a direct Austrian threat of hostilities.

On May 30, 1913, the Treaty of London was concluded, leaving Constantinople and its environs to the Turks, reserving Albania (and the Aegean islands, where complications were caused by the Italian seizure of the Dodecanese) for disposal by the Powers, and assigning the rest of the mainland with Crete to the members of the Balkan League to distribute among themselves. Thereupon the age-old quarrel flared up over Macedonia and the Aegean ports, where Serbia demanded compensation from Bulgaria for disappointment in Albania. Greece sided against Bulgaria because Serbia offered first to guarantee her possession of Salonika. Bulgaria's only defence lay in attack, so not without Austrian connivance the warlike subjects of Czar Ferdinand on June 29 suddenly launched against Serbia the Second Balkan War, which was to ruin the fortunes of their own country for at least a generation. The Bulgarian attack has been condemned by M. Gueshoff, Bulgarian Prime Minister at the time of the Balkan League. He had resigned before the attack, the responsibility for which he laid on the Army. He has described the attack as a 'criminal act' and the campaign which followed as an 'impious fratricidal struggle.'

The Second Balkan War

The Serbs routed the Bulgars at Bregalnica. The Greeks, repaying barbarism with barbarism, followed the bloody trail of the Bulgar retreat up the Struma, until Austria intervened to forbid the destruction of Bulgaria itself, though not the laying waste of Bulgarian Macedonia. Then the Rumanians, whom the Bulgarians had vainly tried to placate by agreeing to cede part of the Dobrudja, joining in the war for the first time, marched on Sofia. Finally, the Turks saw their chance and also came in, to recover Adrianople. The Bulgarian position was so hopeless that an armistice was concluded after only one month's fighting. By the Treaty of Bucharest, signed on August 10, she surrendered her Macedonian gains for Greece and Serbia to divide between them, gave south Dobrudja to Rumania, and by subsequent negotiations with the Turks she surrendered parts of eastern Thrace, including Kirk Kilisse as well as the great prize of Adrianople. Enver Pasha returned to Adrianople like a conquering hero, and early in 1914 promoted himself Turkish Minister of War.

The Territorial Settlement and the Creation of Albania

We may now sum up the results of the Balkan wars as a whole. Turkey in Europe had shrunk from a continuous broad belt of land, 100 miles wide even in the east of the great peninsula and spreading to nearly 400 miles where it separated Serbia and Greece in the west, to a mere corner in the south-east of one-sixth the size and one-third the population, which only Constantinople redeemed from insignificance. The Ottoman Empire had virtually ceased to exist as a European Power; the three successor states, as we may call them, Serbia, Greece, and tiny Montenegro, had nearly doubled their area in each case and had enhanced their populations by 50, 65, and 90 per cent. respectively. Rumania, whose main ambitions lay elsewhere, had acquired from

THE BALKANS AFTER THE BALKAN WARS

Bulgaria at trifling cost south Dobrudja, with the important fortress of Silistria. As for Bulgaria, her net gains were insignificant—about 20 per cent. in area and 5 per cent. in population—and possession of western Thrace, without any harbour except the open roadstead of Dede Agach, was no consolation for what she had been forced to surrender in Macedonia, where about 1,000,000 Bulgars now constituted an *irredenta* under the rule of Serbs and Greeks.

Greece had come off the best. In Salonika she had acquired the chief commercial prize of the struggle, in Janina the greatest fortress; if the Italians denied her the Adriatic port of Valona, she had succeeded in grabbing a second Aegean port at Kavala; and if the annexation of Crete meant at this stage a formal rather than a practical change, the Powers ultimately allotted to her all but two of the islands remaining in Turkish hands. By comparison, Serbia still felt herself frustrated, as the German Powers had intended she should be. Though her territory now stretched far to the southwards in Old Serbia and central Macedonia, it remained completely land-locked; and her Montenegrin ally, whose frontiers now marched with hers as a result of the partitioning of the Sanjak between them, shared her feelings because of her eviction from Scutari, which, on account of its river navigation to the sea, would have made a better outlet for Montenegro than any of the tiny ports on the rock-bound shores of the Black Mountain.

It was for this purpose that the cause of Albanian independence had been taken up, if not invented, by the Powers—to keep the Montenegrins from Scutari, the Greeks from Valona, and the Serbs from anywhere. To the Austrians and Italians, as we have seen, an independent Albania was a valuable defence against the rising strength of the south Slavs; the Germans, looking a little farther, thought it might be a useful pawn to win back control of the Balkans; the English and French, more concerned to preserve peace than to foster Russian interests, looked less far and claimed it as a triumph for nationalism and liberalism. In the event, Albania did its creators small credit. The country contained a population of less than one million, wild tribesmen, having a Muslim civilisation, if any. There was no railway, roads were very few, and the sense of national unity was too undeveloped seriously to mitigate the rivalries of the two main clans of Ghegs and Tosks, which divided the mountainous interior between them. In October, 1913, Austria finally compelled the Serbs to evacuate Albania,[1] and in the following March

---

[1] The German Kaiser gave Austria his support in characteristic form. Meeting the Austro-Hungarian Foreign Minister, Count Berchtold, at Leipzig on the occasion of the centenary of the battle there, he said with reference to a possible Serbian refusal: 'If H.M. the Emperor Francis Joseph demands something, then the Serbian Government *must* yield: if it does not, then Belgrade will be bombarded, and occupied until H.M.'s will is carried out. And of this you can be sure, that I stand behind you, and am ready to draw the sword if ever your action makes it necessary.' Berchtold observed that the last words were accompanied by a movement of the Kaiser's hand towards his sword-hilt.

the last European monarchy was founded by Prince William of Wied, a German who had served in the Russian Army, who was chosen by the Powers to rule the country under the nominal suzerainty of the Porte. Six months later the outbreak of the First World War drove him from his very insecure throne. The Serbs were by this time otherwise engaged, so the Greeks and Italians seized as much of Albania as the tribesmen were unable to defend.

The Continued Struggle for Influence in the Balkans

It was not only in Albania that the two uneasy years which followed the Treaty of Bucharest figured as a mere breathing-space in a developing struggle. The result of the Balkan wars was to force Turkey to look more than ever to Germany and Austria for help against the Slavs. The Kaiser was already the friend of Abdul Hamid and he had twice visited Constantinople. Now Enver, the strongest man in the Turkish Government, was relying on Germany to rehabilitate Turkey after her losses in the Balkan wars. It is true that some German opinion regarded Turkey more as a liability than as an asset. When Enver, in 1914, declared that Turkey 'earnestly desired to connect herself with the Triple Alliance' he was at first discouraged by the German Ambassador. In fact, von Wangenheim, in telegrams to the German Foreign Office, expressed his opinion that 'Turkey is to-day without doubt still quite worthless as an ally' and that, in the event of war, 'the Turkish eastern frontier would then be the weakest point in the strategic position of the Triple Alliance and the natural place for Russia to attack.' The Kaiser's comment was, 'Nonsense.' As he put it:

> 'It is now a question of getting hold of every gun which is ready in the Balkans to go off for Austria against the Slavs, therefore a Turco-Bulgarian alliance connected with Austria is certainly to be accepted. This is opportunist politics, but must be pursued in this case.'

Von Wangenheim's doubts were set aside by higher authority, and he was instructed to do everything to encourage the Turks to work with the Triple Alliance.

Britain was perhaps alone in taking an optimistic view of the situation, based on the belief that it was the co-operation

of the Powers which had averted a general war. She therefore
negotiated conventions with Germany and with Turkey,
which only required the addition of a German-Turkish
convention to get the long-vexed question of the Baghdad
Railway finally out of the way, on the terms that the line was
to be completed to Basra, giving Germany economic control
of Mesopotamia, while Britain was to keep control of the
Persian Gulf. In the same accommodating spirit, Anglo-
German negotiations were also reopened in 1914 about the
eventual disposition of the Portuguese colonies in Africa.

Meanwhile, Russia and France joined issue with Germany
over the appointment of the German General Liman von
Sanders to reorganise the Turkish Army, a clever move by
which the Germans sought to gain the maximum advantage
from the Turkish military renaissance, of which the first signs
had been seen in the campaign against Bulgaria that won
back Adrianople. Britain gave little support to her friends
in this matter, partly perhaps because a British admiral held
a parallel appointment in the Turkish naval reorganisation.
But Russia and France, by a direct threat of war, got the
matter compromised, in appearance at least, by the denial
of any corps command to the German, though he stayed on
as Inspector-General of the Turkish Army.

More ominous was Russia's decision of February, 1914, to
reopen the question of the Straits and to work for their
occupation, even at the risk of war. Both sides angled for
support in the Balkans. Rumania, it was thought, was
shaking loose from the Triple Alliance because she could
get no promise of Transylvania from the Hungarians, so the
Russian Czar promptly visited Constanza. Bulgaria, on the
other hand, was expected to side with the Triple Alliance for
the sake of revenge on Serbia; and the German Kaiser also
paid marked attention to the Greek King, whose country
seemed balanced in the middle, since King Constantine was
strongly pro-German, though the acquisition of Salonika
had set him at loggerheads with the Austrians. Of them all,
only Serbia really knew where she stood. A victorious war
had made her more clearly than ever the predestined champion
of the south Slavs; but at the same time denial of the full fruits
of victory, in the shape of access to the sea, made her more
clearly than ever the predestined enemy of the Austro-Hungarian

Empire. Austria-Hungary, accordingly, while trying to weaken her economically by refusing access to Hungary for her exports, cast about for the right moment to wage what she could only regard as a preventive war.

Military Preparations of the Powers

Men and munitions were being made ready by each of the Great Powers, in the expectation of a short war where the element of surprise and efficiency in mobilisation might be decisive. In March, 1913, the German Reichstag was asked for a capital levy of £50,000,000, which was expended by the summer of the following year, which also witnessed the completion of the widening of the Kiel Canal, indispensable for the full employment of the new Dreadnoughts. In August, 1913, France extended the period of military training from two to three years and made the age-limits for military service twenty to forty-eight instead of twenty-one to forty-five. Russia made rather similar changes and embarked on schemes (involving new loans from France) to improve her strategic railways and the resulting system of mobilisation, so that all would be ready by 1917. Austria-Hungary, which had made ready for war in 1908 and was urged on several occasions to take preventive action against Serbia by Conrad von Hötzendorff (who had been brought back from temporary retirement to his old post as Chief of the General Staff in the fateful autumn of 1912), was always prepared—in so far as effective military preparations were possible in an empire honeycombed with nationalist rivalries. Lastly, there was pacific, liberal Britain. Not only were the Anglo-French military conversations carried a stage further in 1912, but early in 1914 the French, who knew how strained our relations with Russia had become on account of Russian activities in Persia, succeeded in arranging for naval conversations between Britain and Russia. Both sets of conversations were known to the Germans, which made it the more unfortunate that the British Foreign Secretary, when pressed in the House of Commons, virtually denied the existence of the Anglo-Russian negotiations (June 11, 1914).

But certainly among the suspicious and politically ambitious states of Europe, Great Britain was least directly concerned in the clash of interests in the Balkans and least interested in launching any military adventure on the Continent. Amid the preparations for war, as Professor Bernadotte E. Schmitt[1] has affirmed:

'There was one man, however, who had a vision of a new order—Sir Edward Grey. Although the British Foreign Secretary assumed from time to time, as in the question of Morocco or at certain stages of the Baghdad Railway question, an attitude frankly hostile to Germany; although as we have seen, he steadily strengthened the Triple Entente as a bulwark against possible German aggression—that was only one side of his policy. He was so far from pursuing a policy of encirclement that he told the Russian Ambassador in London that the isolation of Germany would be the surest road to war; for that reason he "accepted the Triple Alliance and made no attempt, however covert, to weaken it." In his mind, "the *entente* with France was not to be used against German policy or German interests." What he desired and worked for was an understanding with Germany, on the condition, as he phrased it, that it "must not put us back into the bad old relation with France and Russia." If this could be achieved, the way would be open to the creation of an effective Concert of Europe.'

Thus Grey appears as striving constantly for the maintenance of peace through international understanding. He anticipated, as Schmitt put it, 'by many years the Spirit of Locarno and the Pact of Paris.' They, in their time, unfortunately failed to prevent war just as Grey failed in 1914.

The Assassination of Franz Ferdinand and the Austrian Ultimatum to Serbia

The assassination of the Archduke Franz Ferdinand on June 28, 1914, in the course of an official visit as Austrian heir-apparent to the Bosnian capital of Serajevo is still in some respects one of the great historical mysteries. We do not know why the unfortunate prince was so badly guarded

[1] See B. E. Schmitt, *The Coming of the War* (1930). Of his two volumes, Wickham Steed, formerly Editor of *The Times*, has said that they 'are a credit to American historical scholarship and research. They foreshadow what is likely to be the considered verdict of impartial judges upon the origins of the Great War'. A fuller account is given by the Italian political journalist, L. Albertini, in *The Origins of the War* (3 vols., 1952–7).

in life that two attempts could be made in the same place the same day, or why he was so little honoured in death that foreign representation was not desired at his funeral. By his espousal of trialism, he had made many enemies inside the Empire, and also outside it among Serbs, who feared to see the great Slav kingdom of their hopes converted into one third part of an Austrian federation and also thought that trialism might provide a pretext for swallowing Serbia. Yet there is no evidence to connect either the Austro-Hungarian or the Serb authorities with the murder. After the war the Serbs erected an official statue in honour of Princep, who did the deed, but the most vigilant Austrian enquiries had never proved any point of contact higher than Dimitrievich, *alias* Apis of the Black Hand, the leader of a Serb terrorist organisation which had also butchered King Alexander Obrenovic and his Queen in 1903.

None the less whatever the deeper origins of the dark deed of June 28, it is certain that, once it was committed, the Foreign Minister of the Dual Monarchy, Count Berchtold, saw in it a heaven-sent opportunity to force an issue with the Serbs before the nationalist propaganda, with which the south Slav provinces were seething, had permeated the entire Empire and rendered it utterly ungovernable. All that Berchtold required was the support of his German allies, which was pledged within a week of the murder. The Kaiser in one of his exalted moods allowed Austria *carte blanche* to demand what satisfaction she liked from Serbia and assumed that Russia would see in it the vindication of public law against what was virtually regicide rather than any act of aggression against her small Slav ally. And this was not an altogether unreasonable assumption in view of the many attempts on the lives of Russian Czars.

A further delay of two-and-a-half weeks was due to the coincidence of a French official visit to St. Petersburg, during which Berchtold preferred to take no action, in case the presence of the French President and Prime Minister might encourage Russia to plot some counter-action. Then, on July 23, Austria sent a ten-point ultimatum to Serbia, requiring her submission within forty-eight hours, and this action launched the First World War. It was in vain that the Serbs accepted eight of the Austrian demands forthwith and offered to refer the other two to arbitration: the Austrian Ambassador left Belgrade on the 25th and Austria declared war three days later. In the meantime, the Kaiser had partly swung round, influenced by the unexpected and almost unprecedented submissiveness of the Serbians and also, it is believed, by the equally unexpected decision of the British not to disperse their fleet at the conclusion of the great naval manœuvres on the 26th. But although Germany now counselled moderation upon Austria, she refused to countenance the characteristic British proposal that the whole dispute should be settled by mediation through the good offices of the four Powers not directly concerned. Berchtold made no effort to withdraw from his original plan of a punitive expedition to crush Serbia because he knew that Germany, when it came to the point, dare not desert her only firm ally.

The Russian Mobilisation

After the Austrian war machine had been set in motion against Serbia, there was still a faint hope of localising the conflict until Russia ordered a general mobilisation (made definitive at 6 p.m. on July 30), and historians who seek to mitigate the responsibility of the Central Powers for starting the war point out that Russia was the first to take this momentous step. It is true that Russia did not consult the French Government, which thought her action precipitate, and that it was taken while Britain was still pressing for a settlement by conference. But for Russia the dominant consideration was her failure to champion the Serb (and Slav) interest in the Bosnian crisis of 1908–9. Her military strength was still not fully repaired after the disasters of the war against Japan; but to have failed Serbia a second time would have destroyed her prestige as the Slav champion for ever. There remained the alternative course of a partial mobilisation, such as Austria had ordered against Serbia. About this the Russian authorities hesitated, but came down finally on the side of general mobilisation because a partial mobilisation for a southern front only could not subsequently have been changed fast enough if Germany, with her more rapid time-table, were to begin to mobilise against Russia.

Russia's distrust was partly justified, for the German Chief of Staff, von Moltke, telegraphed to his Austrian counterpart before he learnt of the Russian decision, urging general mobilisation on him and promising that Germany's mobilisation would follow. In the event, action by Austria and Germany followed Russia, while France, after she had urged Russia to make secret military preparations instead of mobilising, and had herself made the pacific gesture of withdrawing all troops ten kilometres from the Franco-German frontier, mobilised in accordance with the terms of the Franco-Russian Military Convention of 1893, some seventy-five minutes ahead of the Germans. But from a broader point of view, once the quarrel with Serbia could not be localised, the clash of the two great alliances became inevitable and the details are largely irrelevant. Germany declared war on Russia on August 1. So began the First World War. France was bound to follow Russia, but actually Germany took the initiative by declaring war on France on August 3.

The Intervention of Britain

Less inevitable was the intervention of Britain, since the whole difference between the Triple *Entente* and an alliance lay in the fact that an 'understanding' involved no automatic obligation to act. It has already been pointed out that the decision not to disperse the fleet on July 26 made Germany pause; but unfortunately the issue of the British proposal for settlement by mediation coincided with a private report from Prince Henry of Prussia, who was on a state visit to England, that King George thought England would be neutral. The Germans then tried to get a pledge of British neutrality in return for a promise to take no territory from France in Europe. Sir Edward Grey's indignant rejection of this proposal, which was accompanied by a further suggestion of a conference of the Powers, alarmed the Germans to the extent that they warned the Austrians against starting a 'world conflagration.' It was too late for the warning to have any practical effect, but it has encouraged explorers of the might-have-been's of history to point out that war might have been avoided if the British Foreign Secretary had been in a position to state plainly a week or so earlier that Britain would intervene against Germany in a general European struggle. Actually, Grey was never in any such position, because the mass of the British public, and probably a clear majority even of Members of Parliament, saw no vital British interest involved in a sudden European complication arising out of a typical Balkan imbroglio. It must be remembered, too, that any disclosure of military or naval agreements—such as that under which the Cabinet on August 2 promised to prevent German naval action against the coasts or shipping traffic of north France—had always been accompanied by assurances to Parliament that in the event of a European war we still retained absolute freedom of choice. Hence the paramount importance of the German refusal to respect the neutrality of Belgium. It was known on the morning of August 3 that her neutrality would be violated and that she would resist and that our obligations under the guarantee of 1839 would be invoked. This, and this alone, enabled Grey to obtain almost undivided support in Parliament and in the country for the ultimatum which was dispatched to Germany the following day.

Underlying Causes of War

But, of course, both for Britain and for other countries the causes of the first of the two great catastrophes of our age lay far deeper than the immediate occasion. The formation of two great rival groups in Europe and the agglomeration of men and arms with which to promote their rival interests was a process which had been going on for many years, and the two Hague conferences had shown that no Power was resolutely determined to check it, though Germany alone was resolutely determined not to check it. Men and arms, however, were made available because each Power had vital interests which were from time to time endangered or vital claims which from time to time seemed capable of realisation. It was perhaps fitting that the final clash should arise out of the irreconcilable conflict of interest in the Balkans, between Russia and Austria, the latter backed by Germany. It was this which, in the guise of the *Drang nach Osten* versus Pan-Slavism, had produced the crises of 1878, 1885, and 1908. But even if the Serbian problem had been settled as smoothly as that of the Baghdad Railway, the war which came in the east might well have come in the west, where the British could never overlook the growth of the German Navy and the French could never forget the loss of Alsace-Lorraine. But if we go further, and ask what general issues predisposing to war lay behind the specific examples of vital interests to be protected or assured, responsibility in the last analysis seems to lie with the two ideas of economic self-reliance and nationalism. War was the accepted instrument of a policy which glorified the nation and regarded its enrichment at the expense of other nations as the highest good.

SUGGESTIONS FOR FURTHER READING

W. S. Churchill: *World Crisis* (revised and abridged edition), cc. 1–8.

J. A. Spender: *Fifty Years of Europe*, cc. 34–42.

E. Ludwig: *July 1914*.

Sir J. A. R. Marriott: *The Eastern Question* (4th edition), c. 16.

B. E. Schmitt: *The Coming of the War*.

A. J. P. Taylor: *Struggle for Mastery in Europe*, cc. 21 and 22.

New Cambridge Modern History, Vol. XII, c. 12 (by J. M. K. Vyvyan).

CHAPTER 12

THE FIRST WORLD WAR, 1914–18

The Invasion of France

THE Germans began the war in the west by the invasion of Belgium, followed up by a wide sweep through the Belgian capital and southwards into France. The French began with a large-scale offensive against Alsace and Lorraine, a target which would arouse the maximum of patriotic enthusiasm in their armies. But in it they incurred record casualties by launching repeated frontal attacks against positions which were defended by machine-gun fire—the new weapon which had proved its value in the Russo-Japanese War, but which only the German infantry formations as yet possessed in quantities sufficient to defend their front. The French failed either to penetrate the lost provinces or to divert the German armies from their aim. To the German general staff, ever since the formation of the Dual Alliance, the great problem had been how to knock out France before the Russians came seriously into action, and thus escape being crushed by the Russian numbers in a two-front war. Count Schlieffen had propounded the classic solution in 1905, which it fell to Moltke, his successor as Chief of Staff, to put into practice nine years later. There were to be three stages—a wheeling movement across Belgium by the armies of the right wing pivoting upon Lorraine as the centre of the whole German line; then the armies nearest the Channel coast, on emerging from Belgium, would drive southwards; at this point Paris would presumably fall, but what mattered was that, whether west or east of Paris, the French armies should in the third stage be forced back towards Lorraine and find themselves in a completely desperate position between the German centre and the extreme right wing (now driving eastwards), with the rest of the German forces of the right converging upon them from the north. Thus the decisive Battle of Sedan was to be re-enacted on a much larger scale. However, the plan just failed.

The Belgian resistance exceeded expectations, especially

from the forts of Liége. The British Expeditionary Force, which took up position on the left of the Allied line at Mons on August 23, though numerically unimportant, was made up of well-trained professional soldiers whose good bearing did something to encourage the French during the long retreat. At the end of the month the German Second Army was

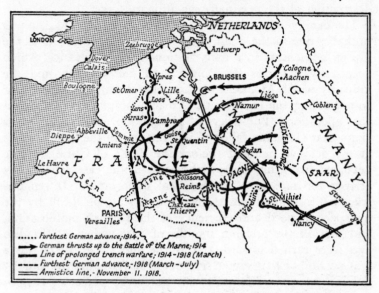

..... Furthest German advance, 1914.
➡ German thrusts up to the Battle of the Marne, 1914
▬ Line of prolonged trench warfare, 1914–1918 (March)
╌╌╌ Furthest German advance, 1918 (March–July)
═══ Armistice line, November 11, 1918.

THE FIRST WORLD WAR: THE WESTERN FRONT

seriously checked at Guise, so the First Army was asked to close in from the extreme flank, and this in turn meant that the great wheeling movement would pass about thirty miles east of Paris.   In this extreme crisis the French Government retired to Bordeaux, but their Commander-in-Chief, General Joffre, and Galliéni, the Military Governor of Paris, resolved to strike a desperate blow at the enemy's extreme right as soon as it crossed southwards over the River Marne.   Battle was joined on September 6; on the 9th the British recrossed the river and the Schlieffen Plan had failed.   The Germans having withdrawn about forty miles to the line of the River Aisne, both sides now abandoned the hope of open warfare and dug themselves in to sustain what they supposed would be one winter's campaigning, though in the north, to which the British force was transferred again, there was a race for the Channel ports. Antwerp fell into German hands early in October, but the British and the remnants of the Belgian Army fought a month-long battle at Ypres, the retention of which saved the Channel ports. This in turn made it possible that other and larger British armies could be transported and supplied, though the victory at Ypres involved the virtual destruction of the original expeditionary force.

The decisive German defeat at the Battle of the Marne was probably due in the main to such large general factors as the loss of momentum in a long-continued, rapid advance, which necessarily outstrips its supplies and ammunition, and the difficulty which Moltke and the general staff experienced in co-ordinating the movements of army commanders in such a vast operation. But lovers of picturesque detail will always claim that Germany failed to win the war in the west because at the decisive moment (before the Battle of Guise) Moltke detached two army corps for the war in the east, where they arrived too late to be of any real importance. It remains true that Germany was thrown into a state of alarm by the unexpected speed and efficiency of the Russian mobilisation, and that in the autumn months of 1914, when all English eyes were turned towards the Marne and Ypres, there was a real possibility that either side might have ended the war by a knock-out blow delivered on the great plains of eastern Europe, where large armies, lightly equipped and with few heavily fortified bases, had ample room for manœuvre.

The Eastern Front

Russian Poland, the so-called Congress Kingdom based on Warsaw and the middle Vistula, provided the Russian armies with a huge salient from which to strike northwards into East Prussia or south into Galicia. It was the blow in the north which alarmed the Germans, to whom their own soil was sacrosanct, and they brought the veteran Hindenburg from retirement, with the younger Ludendorff from France as his Chief of Staff, to meet the invasion of East Prussia. Of the two Russian armies, dependent on co-operation for success, one pressed on too fast and was destroyed before the end of August on the historic field of Tannenberg, where the Poles had once defeated the medieval order of Teutonic Knights. The other Russian Army was over-cautious and was caught and crushed in the same region a fortnight later at the Battle of the Masurian Lakes. But the Russian blow in the south was far more successful: indeed, as long as their munitions lasted, the Russians enjoyed as great an ascendancy over the multi-national forces of the Dual Monarchy as the more highly organised Germans over their own. In the course of September they overran the Austrian province of Galicia as far west as Cracow, and once Cracow was taken they would have directly threatened Silesia, the second greatest industrial area in Germany. To save the situation, Hindenburg launched two counter-attacks further north against Warsaw, which failed to capture the great fortress, but when they died away in December the pressure in Galicia had been sufficiently relieved.

At the close of the year the struggle was also more evenly balanced than might have been expected in the Balkan region where Austria had struck the first blow. The Austrian attack upon Serbia, planned originally as a punitive expedition, ended in a fiasco. It took them four months to capture Belgrade, but only three days to lose it again, which meant that the smallest of the Allies, disease-ridden and half-starved, but possessing all the recuperative powers of a primitive economy, had the rest of the winter in which to prepare for severer trials. Turkey, it is true, had thrown in her lot with the Central Powers. The secret treaty, signed on August 2, probably carried less weight than the arrival at Constantinople of two major German warships, which slipped through the watch kept by the British Navy when hostilities began: but even so it was not until the end of October that a Turkish admiral fired the first shot at the undefended Russian ports on the Black Sea. In the long run the isolation of Russia from any approach, except via the far north, proved a very grave handicap to the Allied cause, but Turkey did not at first seem likely to prove a very formidable opponent, especially if a suitable combination could be formed against her in the Balkans.

The Institution of the British Naval Blockade

So far, that is in its opening phase, the First World War had been strictly European from all points of view except the British—and Japanese, for in the Far East our Japanese

allies began immediately that conquest of the German positions
in Kiaow-Chow and the north Pacific islands which helped
so notably towards their aggrandisement in the next two
decades. The British Navy, according to plan and almost
unresisted, swept German commerce from the high seas and,
with the help of military forces formed by the Dominions, was
soon able not only to cut off but to conquer the German
colonies in Africa and the south Pacific, with the solitary exception of German East Africa (Tanganyika), where a stubborn
resistance was prolonged until the very end of the war. The
British naval blockade, which succeeded in closing the passage
between the Norwegian skerries and the north of Scotland
almost as tightly as the English Channel itself, reduced
Germany's economic as well as her political resources to
European limits. This remains true in spite of the large claims
made on behalf of neutral commerce with belligerents by the
United States, who obliged us to allow the direct importation to
Germany in neutral ships of a few articles that could not be
proved to be contraband of war, and a much larger indirect importation by Germany from the outside world of goods nominally
consigned to neutral Scandinavian and Dutch merchants. The
fact that she was at once cut off from the outside world proved
fatal to Germany in the end, but it must not disguise from us
that the war came very near to decision in her favour in the
first phase of the struggle in Europe, to which the British
military contribution was an expeditionary force of 100,000
men—about one-sixth of the numbers lost to the French army
in the first twenty days of the fighting.

Stalemate in the West—the Strategic Problem

In 1915 the war in the west entered upon a long period of
stalemate. Each year both sides planned for a break-through
in the spring or summer, partly because they could not, and
partly because they would not, recognise the inexorable laws
of the new trench warfare. The Germans, who had outnumbered the French in the first campaign, lost their preponderance as Britain for the first time drew systematically upon
her manpower to train armies of a size commensurate with
her population. But until 1918, when the Germans were
able to throw into the scales large forces released from the
eastern front, neither side had the reserves of manpower

needed to exploit an initial success. The continuous line of trenches meant that there was no free manœuvre. Their elaborate defence works (which makes the word 'trenches' something of a misnomer) largely prevented the possibility of a big surprise attack, since a prolonged artillery bombardment was required to prepare the way for the troops—not to mention the advantage given to the defence by the new use of scouting aircraft and observation balloons. And if the enemy trenches were overrun, machine-gun fire invariably levied such a heavy toll on the attackers that their opponents, with the help of even the scantiest 'defences in depth,' could re-form their line; so that all that was gained was a few barren miles of shell-torn, debris-littered earth, which often enough constituted a salient or bulge that its new owners in their turn would be hard put to it to defend. Even poison gas, to which the Germans resorted in deliberate defiance of the Hague Convention early in 1915, failed to produce a decisive breakthrough. In almost every case, casualties in attack were overwhelmingly greater than those sustained by the defence; and at no point did the most heroic efforts and sacrifices, kept up by the men of both sides throughout the three long years, achieve a total advance of more than thirty miles.

But if 1915 was the year in which the war in the west settled down to deadlock, the attempt to find a means of ending that deadlock gave rise to controversy then and to controversy ever since as to what that means should be. Briefly, there were two points of view: one, that attack should be made on the western front; the other that, while the enemy was held in the west, some way should be found of attacking in south-eastern Europe. The French and British commanders and their general staffs took the former view. The two most dynamic personalities in the British Cabinet, Lloyd George and Winston Churchill, pressed the idea of attack in the east, either by means of a knock-out blow to Turkey to be accompanied by the combination of the Balkan states for a joint invasion of Hungary, or, as Lloyd George preferred, by direct attack on Austria through Dalmatia or by way of Salonika. These were all variations on the eastern theme.

Powerful arguments could be adduced on either side. In support of the western policy was the fact that the enemy possessed the interior lines and could therefore move his forces quickly from one front to the other. If, then, the Allies were to weaken their position in the west, the Germans, by speedy concentration of their forces against the weakened front, might effect a break-through. There was the undoubted force of the maxim that you cannot be too strong at the decisive point. It would be a wild gamble to divert troops to the east if this gave the enemy the opportunity to attack with overwhelming force: a victory over the Turks in Damascus would not offset a German capture of Amiens. The Allies, therefore, in consequence of this line of thought, built up a great weight in troops and material in the west. The conviction was held that it would eventually be possible to break through: if sufficient weight of metal could be thrown against the fortress wall it must collapse.

But the analogy of the fortress wall was misleading. It is one thing to breach a wall; another to breach a system of trenches. The overrunning of one line of trenches did not admit to the fortress; it only brought the attacker up against a further line of trenches which, as we have seen, the enemy, warned by the bombardment preceding attack, would now have reinforced. The experience of the Franco-Prussian War and of the Russo-Japanese War had shown that victory was won by wide turning movements on the flanks; the deadly effect of modern fire had made the frontal attack too costly. 'But now,' as Winston Churchill puts it in his *World Crisis*, 'in France and Flanders for the first time in recorded experience there were no flanks to turn. The turning movement, the oldest manœuvre in war, became impossible.' The trenches, guarded by the millions of men and thousands of guns, stretched from the North Sea to the Swiss frontier.

It is, therefore, not surprising that some of the Allied leaders looked east for a possible way out of the deadlock. An attack in the east might be the means of discovering that the enemy had, after all, a flank which could be turned. Such a movement, at the beginning of 1915, could be supported by the argument that it would impress the Balkan neutrals and encourage them to make common cause with the Allies. Then again, the establishment of an Allied front in south-eastern Europe would enable a stream of munitions to reach Russia (in addition to the intermittent trickle at Archangel in the north). In this way the Russian effort could be co-ordinated with Allied support in a common effort against the weaker enemy Powers, Austria and Turkey. Kitchener, who was regarded as an oracle, stated his opinion in January, 1915, in the form of a cautious compromise:

'The feeling is gaining ground that although it is essential to defend the lines we hold, troops over and above what are necessary for that service could be better employed elsewhere.'

But in spite of the arguments for stronger efforts in the east, and the launching of the Gallipoli and Mesopotamian campaigns (described below), the main struggle took place in the west, involving prolonged trench warfare and heavy slaughter in massed attacks which achieved little or no result for either side.

History, therefore, can take little account of the great battles in Champagne, by which the French sought vainly to relieve the pressure on the Russians in 1915; or of the second British struggle in defence of Ypres, which succeeded; or of the Battle of Loos, where the British attack failed and probably cost three times as many men as were lost by the defence. Again, in 1916 the Germans launched an onslaught against Verdun, but after nearly six months' fighting proved unable either to master the fortress or to carry out the alternative plan of 'bleeding France to death,' though in this one exceptional instance the lives lost in the defence, being the defence of a spot made especially sacred by national tradition, were twice those lost in the attack.   No more positive result followed the mainly British attempt at a break-through on the Somme, where the flower of our new volunteer armies perished that summer in the biggest battle that the world had yet known.

The situation in 1917 was still more paradoxical, since the Germans had employed the lull during the winter to fortify along the centre part of their line a position in the rear, to which they voluntarily retired, thereby dislocating the French plans for an offensive.   General Nivelle, nevertheless, persisted in attacking at the Chemin des Dames, and failed so miserably that one result was a serious mutiny, suppressed by his successor, Pétain, at the cost of twenty-three executions, and another the necessity for a prolonged British offensive, which relieved the strain on the French, but caused us to suffer enormous casualties.   This four months' ineffectual struggle in the mud of a wet autumn to clear the Flanders coast of Germans is known as the Battle of Passchendaele. In the long run, all this slaughter, which darkened so many homes, was far less significant than the comparatively small Battle of Cambrai (October, 1917), where the British invention of the tank, which had not previously been used on any considerable scale, made the first real breach in the German line. Although the initial success was not exploited, this was a genuine victory achieved at trifling cost, and it showed, to the discerning mind at least, that there were other ways of ending the dead-lock on the western front. But, as the third year of frustration closed, the Germans were nearly ready to use once more the method of attack based upon the attempt to muster over-whelming manpower.

The War Spreads—Italy, the Dardanelles, the Balkans

For the years of frustration for both sides in the west had in the other theatres been marked by several dramatic reversals of fortune, culminating in Germany's triumph. In the early months of 1915 Russia's ascendancy over her Austrian oppon-ents was increased by Italy's entry into the war on the side of the Allies, which meant that a large number of Austrian troops were pinned down by the defence of the Alps. But it cannot be pretended that the Italians showed a military ardour at all commensurate with the size of their territorial claims upon Austrian and other territory, which were secretly endorsed by the Treaty of London (April 26, 1915) as the price for their desertion of the Triple Alliance. At the same time, an attempt was made to restore communications with Russia, upon which the regular flow of munitions to the eastern front depended, by the combined operation known as the Gallipoli campaign. If the first naval attack on the Dardanelles forts had been pushed a little more resolutely, or if the landing on the peninsula had been made a month earlier, or if the landing when it did take place had been followed more immediately by an advance to secure the heights, all might have been well. As it was, this British and Dominion effort failed narrowly but completely; and although the evacuation itself was carried through at the end of the year without loss, a quarter of a million casualties had been suffered, to say nothing of the damage to our prestige. December also witnessed the failure of another, smaller campaign against the Turk, when a minor force based on India, making its way through Mesopotamia towards Baghdad, was shut up in Kut-el-Amara, where it eventually had to surrender (April, 1916).

A by-product, as it were, of the failure in Gallipoli was the virtual bankruptcy of Allied policy in the Balkans. Already in the late autumn of 1915 the Bulgarians declined to be tempted by belated Serbian offers of a new deal in Macedonia, which Serbia, as it now appeared, might never be in a position to implement. They joined instead with the Central Powers, who sent a powerful army across the Danube and obliterated Serbia from the map. Russia could do nothing for Serbia or against Bulgaria, while Britain and France, having landed a force at Salonika, found it was all they could do to maintain their base in face of King Constantine's hostility and the desertion of large parts of the nominally neutral Greek Army to the side of the Bulgarians and Germans. There remained Rumania, where the death of King Carol I in October, 1914, gave pro-Ally influences greater play; but she waited to strike a very favourable bargain, like Italy, and came into the war too late. At the end of August, 1916, the Rumanian forces were pouring into Transylvania; by December two German armies had overrun the whole country, except Moldavia, and were in secure possession of the rich oilfield and some of the best wheat-growing areas in Europe.

Meanwhile the Russians, though not strong enough to save the Balkans, had made gallant efforts in 1915 and 1916, in spite of the cumulative effect of the shortage of munitions, from which their more heavily industrialised allies could not relieve them. In 1915 Falkenhayn, who had succeeded Moltke as German Chief of Staff, reversed the policy of the previous year and chose to make the main German offensive in the east. Warsaw fell in August, and the occupation of the huge Polish salient of which it was the base, an operation in which a million Russians were taken prisoner, relieved the pressure on the Austrians, who now had the Italians on their backs. It is the more remarkable that during the winter of 1915–16 the Russian armies won a whole series of victories over the Turks in the Caucasus, driving on towards the relief of the British in Mesopotamia, and in June, 1916,

Brussilov broke through the main Austrian line and threatened Budapest. Hindenburg, indeed, saved the situation by means of an offensive further north, but it provides the measure of Russian success (to which an Italian offensive also contributed) that before the end of the year the Austrian Government, first of all the major belligerents, was earnestly putting out peace feelers.

The War at Sea—German Submarine Campaign

This was the year of Jutland, the one great naval battle of the war, in which the British suffered the heavier losses, but, thanks to Admiral Jellicoe, were not provoked into running any risk which might have endangered their command of the sea. The naval blockade of Germany continued its inexorable course, and up to 1917 the Germans found no satisfactory counter-stroke. Neither the huge lighter-than-air dirigibles, known after their inventor as Zeppelins, nor the small aeroplanes which towards the end of the war inaugurated bombing raids, in what we must call the modern fashion, dropped bombs of sufficient magnitude or sufficiently often to have more than a nuisance value. They did, however, cause the diversion of a good deal of much-needed manpower and munitions to anti-aircraft defence.

To cut off Britain's supplies the Germans had to look elsewhere, to their submarines or U-boats, which the British Admiralty had optimistically supposed would not be used against merchant ships because it was impracticable for German submarines to take them into port as prizes, or to sink them only after due warning in accordance with the requirements of international law. Early in 1915 German submarines began to attack both Allied and neutral vessels which attempted to break their blockade of the British Isles. The Americans were highly indignant, especially when a hundred Americans were among the passengers lost through the torpedoing of the mammoth British liner *Lusitania* in April, and their remonstrances eventually induced the Germans, in fear of a breach with America, to promise to let neutral ships go free. Owing to difficulties of identification, this meant that by 1916 the German blockade had ceased to be of serious importance, whereas the British blockade was establishing a stranglehold, in spite of the skill of German industrialists such as Rathenau in producing synthetic substitutes for the missing raw materials, and the patience of the German people, who were reduced to a winter diet consisting mainly of turnips.

The year 1917, therefore, opened with the German decision which effectively turned the evenly balanced European struggle into a world war. The Germans had accumulated a fleet of 300 large submarines, and they now announced a policy of unrestricted sinkings. They had calculated that they would starve Britain into surrender before America's entry into the war could make any difference, and that this was their only prospect of victory. Both propositions proved to be wrong. The submarine blockade reached its climax in April, 1917, when one in four of ships sailing from British ports was lost; but the frantic efforts of the shipbuilding yards, the employment of such new devices as depth charges and submarine nets, and especially the concentration of all merchant shipping in heavily guarded convoys just staved off collapse. It was in the same critical month of April that Germany's action drove the United States to declare war, and although the Germans were right in thinking that a year must elapse before American soldiers could intervene on the western front, America's huge industrial potential was quickly able to produce merchant ships and its navy was at once available to protect them. Moreover, America's entry into the war, implying as it did that unlimited resources of men and materials would be made available eventually, if the Allies could only hold on, sustained the Allied morale at the darkest hour. For the Germans had been wrong in thinking that the submarine blockade was their only chance: in March, 1917, the outbreak of the Russian Revolution opened the prospect of a one-front war.

The Collapse of Russia and Its Consequences

The Russian Revolution, which broke out on March 8, 1917, is an event in the war, but not of the war: in a sense it is a larger thing than the World War which occasioned it and gave it its setting. It was not the war alone which caused a change so catastrophic in character and so pregnant in consequences for the whole future of mankind. As an event in the war, however, the important thing to notice about it is the slow stages by which it became apparent, gradually to the Germans and still more gradually to the Allies, because they were further from the scene, that it was hatred of the war which had occasioned the overthrow of the Czarist régime and that no new régime would last which did not denounce the war. Thus the formation of the first Provisional Government (March–May) was generally regarded in France and Britain as an advantage to their cause, because it would clean up the corruption and pro-German influences with which the Czarist court had been tainted; and the new Government was known to be genuinely desirous to continue the war in accordance with Russia's treaty obligations forbidding a separate peace. Its successor, in which Kerensky was Minister for War, launched on July 1 an offensive which broke through the Austrian lines, only to collapse utterly within a fortnight— the spread of the soviets had destroyed internal discipline and the peasant soldier was naturally interested in using what weapons he had to seize the land rather than to kill Austrians.

Yet even after this debacle the Allies continued to hope that some new government, perhaps that of Kornilov and his Cossacks, would rally the huge Russian armies which only slowly melted away in the vast spaces of the eastern front; and it was not until October that the Germans for their part felt sufficiently sure of the situation to force it by an advance to Ösel, where they directly threatened Petrograd. But the second revolution of November 7 achieved the object for which the Germans had allowed Lenin entry into Russia eight months before, since Lenin put peace at any price in the forefront of the Communist programme. An armistice was signed for the eastern front on December 15, although another three months passed before the Russians, under protest, accepted the punitive Treaty of Brest-Litovsk. During all this time the Allies hoped against hope for a final breakdown in the negotiations, but the Germans knew that, for the first time since 1914, they could plan their campaign on the western front on a basis of superior numbers.

In 1918, therefore, the Germans could still hope to deliver a knock-out blow in the West. Deadlock had long prevailed; now the Germans could strike before the new American armies had been trained and transported. Meanwhile, the slackening of the Russian efforts had enabled the Germans to hold the balance even on what we may call the subsidiary fronts. The

British during 1917 scored some considerable successes on the
outer periphery of the war against Turkey. Kut was recovered
in February, Baghdad occupied the following month, and the
rest of Mesopotamia brought slowly under control along the
line of the uncompleted Baghdad Railway. Other forces
based on the Suez Canal (which the Turks had several times
attacked in vain) advanced through the desert into Palestine,
and, in spite of a heavy initial defeat at Gaza, entered Jerusalem
in December.

On the other hand nearer in, on the Balkan front, there had
been no such spectacular gains. The farce of Greek neutrality,
which we had formally violated by the occupation of Salonika
as a base in 1915, came to an end when the Allies forced the
pro-German King Constantine to abdicate, so that Venizelos
and the pro-Ally republicans, long established at Salonika,
might control the whole country. In June, 1917, they duly
proclaimed a state of war against the Central Powers, but the
addition of Greek manpower did not result in any big forward
drive in the Balkans. On the contrary, the German ascendancy there was prolonged into the first half of the following
year, when, after the final Russian surrender, a similar punitive
treaty was imposed on the Rumanians at Bucharest, despite
gallant but unsupported resistance at Marasesti in August
of 1917. Lastly, the Italian front flared into sudden activity
in October, 1917, when the Germans provided the Austrian
armies with a spearhead, drawn from reserves on the western
front, which broke right through on the Piave and might have
entered Venice had not British and French reinforcements
been helped by the heavy autumn rains, which delayed the
Austro-German forces at the river crossings. But the disaster
of Caporetto, though not quite fatal to the half-hearted Italians,
further increased the prospective disparity of forces on the
depleted western front.

The Campaigns of 1918

The story of the 1918 campaign in the west is dramatic:
the Germans launched four tremendous attacks. The first,
in March, with a superiority of almost three to one, and
mainly on the British Fifth Army, won back what the British
had gained at great cost in the Battle of the Somme, but just
failed to smash the junction of the British and French forces

at Amiens. In this desperate situation, what now seems to us an obvious step was agreed upon: the appointment of the French Commander-in-Chief, Foch, to a post of supreme authority over all Allied forces in the field; also the Americans were urged to send every possible man immediately to augment those forces. But the second attack came on April 9, less than three weeks after the first, just south of Ypres. The British fought, as Haig's Order of the Day said, 'with their backs to the wall'; they fought to stave off the disaster of a break-through to the Channel ports, which would have cut off a part of our armies and ruined the communications of the rest. The third great attack, at the end of May, was against the French positions in Champagne and brought the Germans again to the Marne, but not into Paris. In this, as in the two previous crises, there was a week of agony, at the end of which the sorely pressed Allied forces held their ground, but no more. It was the more significant that, when the fourth attack was launched on July 15 and the Germans had actually crossed the fateful river, Foch not only held but repulsed them, and the attack passed into counter-attack as a second Battle of the Marne.

The Germans had shot their bolt: their reserves were at last exhausted, whereas the Americans were now reinforcing the Allies at the rate of 250,000 men landing in France every month. It was on August 8 that a colossal British attack on Villers-Bretonneux, in front of Amiens, the so-called 'black day of the German Army,' broke both the plans and spirit of Ludendorff, who, with Hindenburg as his figurehead, had been the mainspring since 1916 of every German effort in the west. From then onwards Foch's policy was to launch a series of offensives at different points on the line, which gave the Germans no time to recover. The Americans scored their first independent victory by straightening out the St. Mihiel salient near Verdun and joined with the French to press through the Argonne towards Sedan, while the Belgians attacked from Ypres, and the British moved forward against the Hindenburg and Siegfried Lines with their elaborate networks of fortifications.

Even then it was only when the Hindenburg Line itself had been pierced, at the end of September, 1918, that Ludendorff, who knew that Germany's allies were breaking up even faster than Germany herself, and who had no desire to continue a hopeless struggle until his army was completely destroyed (perhaps because he looked to it to secure the internal stability of the country), finally advised his Government to get peace at any price. It took another six weeks to negotiate an armistice, but the war in the West ceased to have much significance once the German will to fight had been broken. Suffice it to say that by November 11 the French were in the approaches of Lorraine, the Americans at Sedan, and the British, having broken through into open country in the north, were just re-entering the little Belgian town of Mons.

These last months of the war were very important on the subsidiary fronts, which collapsed in sympathy with trends evident in the West, but more rapidly and completely. In mid-September the long-postponed advance began from Salonika against the Bulgarians, who surrendered within fourteen days to the skill of a French general commanding a composite force, in which the Serbs distinguished themselves. Constantinople was now isolated. Meanwhile, the campaign against the outlying possessions of the Turks was continued. This campaign, held up by the withdrawal of forces from Palestine to meet the crisis on the western front, was completed by the British occupation of Damascus on October 1 and of Mosul on November 3—three days after the Turks had signed an armistice in Europe. The Italians, too, took the offensive against the Austrians in October and won a considerable victory at Vittorio Veneto before the Hapsburg Empire, which was rapidly dissolving into its component parts, sued for peace in the first week of November. In that last stage of the great conflict, when the Hohenzollern monarchy was likewise disappearing, to be replaced first by a constitutional monarchy, then by a middle-class republic, and then (as it seemed) by a republic of soviets, the element of comedy was still not lacking, for on November 9 the Rumanians denounced the Treaty of Bucharest and re-entered the war, thus establishing painlessly but unimpeachably their status as an Ally in the coming distribution of the spoils.

The war was over, and in the Allied countries a wild rejoicing broke out. The slaughter had ceased; men could breathe again and look to the future with hope. Subsequent events have proved that this hope was optimistic. And even then a sober reflection might have shown that there was small ground for rejoicing. A war which had begun in the Balkans over causes unknown to one in a hundred of the population of the western nations had, owing to the system of alliances, become a general European war. The European war had, in its course, become a world war. All the Great Powers of the world, and most of the small, had been involved. It had been a war on an unprecedented scale, and in it the savagery still underlying man's boasted civilisation had been revealed, a savagery now armed with scientific weapons of mass slaughter. Victor and vanquished alike had suffered enormous casualties; eight million men had been killed and twenty million wounded. The economic dislocation was to prove crippling for years to come, and was to contribute to the causes of the later, even more dreadful, world conflict. Modern war was fast developing towards total conflict: civilians as well as soldiers were involved, and the resources of the combatant nations were engaged to an extent unknown before. This latter particular was illustrated most clearly in the case of Great Britain. In the continental wars of the past she had used the weapon of sea power, subsidised her continental allies, and sent abroad small professional armies to their support. But this time, in addition to a more intensive use of her naval power, and the harnessing of her industries and financial resources to supply her allies' war needs as well as her own, Britain had also, with the help of conscription, to raise great land armies for overseas.

Suggestions for Further Reading

C. R. M. F. Cruttwell: *History of the Great War.*

W. S. Churchill: *World Crisis* (revised and abridged edition).

B. H. Liddell Hart: *The War in Outline, 1914–1918.*

J. E. Edmonds: *Short History of World War I.*

Cyril Falls: *The Great War, 1914–18.*

CHAPTER 13

THE RUSSIAN REVOLUTION, 1917-20

The Revolution in Russia a World Event

THE Russian Revolution has already been mentioned as the catastrophe which knocked Russia out of the war and thus nearly enabled Germany to win it. This was still the one aspect of the revolution uppermost in people's minds when the general war ended—Russia was thought of as being in a pitiable state of collapse, such as might be imagined of a country which had deserted its allies in their hour of need. The strange doctrines of the revolutionaries were not taken very seriously, and it was thought that, pending the success of the counter-revolution which could not be long delayed, the important thing was to isolate Russia as completely as possible. This seemed a comparatively easy task, because a broad belt of territory, stretching from the Ukraine in the south through Poland to the Baltic provinces, which had been surrendered by the Russians to the Germans at Brest-Litovsk, passed from the Germans to the Allies at the armistice. These lands could now be given independence on the understanding that their peoples could be trusted to instal counter-revolutionary governments. But for us who know how closely the whole history of Europe in the next generation was bound up with the changes which were taking place in Russia, it is natural to study them a little more carefully, before we look at the general peace settlement of 1919, which seemed so important at the time but which we now see settled practically nothing.

The First or 'February' Revolution

Communism in Russia was a minority movement which established itself in power through the breakdown of all other forms of government. The Czar and his entourage, the grand dukes and the bureaucracy, had learnt nothing from the upheaval of 1905 as regards the needs of the industrial workers, though Stolypin's agrarian legislation had helped the growth of a class of relatively prosperous, independent peasant farmers. Revolutionary outbreaks and sporadic violence had long been endemic in Russia: in 1914 there was shooting in the streets of St. Petersburg during the French official visit just before the outbreak of war. As for the liberal elements in the middle and upper classes, their hopes were centred in the fourth Duma, elected in 1912 and less conservative in tone than its predecessor. But in the autumn of 1915 the Duma was prorogued because it ventured to advocate the formation of a national coalition government; and in the following year it proved so powerless to secure reforms or a change of the Government personnel by parliamentary means that even the Right Wing leaders helped in the killing of Rasputin.

The ascendancy which this rascally ex-monk with hypnotic powers exercised over the Czar (whose afflicted only son he was able to help) and the control wielded by the Czarina, a well-meaning German princess of narrowly dynastic views, over the machine of government give some measure of the political conditions with which a few brave generals like the Grand Duke Nicholas and Brussilov had to contend, and under which millions of brave but ill-armed soldiery sustained the burden of the eastern front. Although the Russians were in the war for a shorter period than the other Great Powers, their losses were equal to those of all the other Allies put together. Nor was it to be supposed that a government which could not even distribute properly the munitions, which the concerted efforts of Russia's allies sent in on an increasing scale by the Trans-Siberian Railway, would solve the intricate problem of the food supply coupled with a further heavy strain on transport, when the armies of the Central Powers overran some of the best corn-growing areas.

What Russians, using the Old Style calendar, call the February Revolution began on March 8, 1917: the Petrograd factory workers struck for higher wages and bakers' shops were raided. On the second day the movement was swelled by students, among whom revolutionary propaganda was always rife, and groups of demonstrators penetrated to the centre of the city. On the third day, helped by the chronic food shortage, the strike became general; the police in one area were overpowered; and—what was most eloquent of the decline in governmental authority—the Cossacks for the first time sided with the strikers. Thereupon, on March 11, it was decided, too late, to take the strong measures which might have been at least temporarily effective if they had been taken three days earlier—the Duma was again prorogued, and the Military Governor of Petrograd, on the instructions of the Czar, reinforced the police from cadet formations of the Guards and shot down about 150 of the demonstrators. But other regiments of a different social origin from the Guards cadets were by this time infected with the general discontent. When they mutinied rather than serve against the popular rising, the Czar's ministers found themselves powerless, and as they went into hiding, on the night of March 12–13, the Duma committee emerged to take control. The Czar abdicated on March 15.

The Provisional Governments

The fall of the monarchy had followed almost automatically its loss of control in the capital, just as events in Paris terminated the reign and life of King Louis XVI. A provisional government under the liberal Prince Lvov, and later under the social democrat, Kerensky, followed during the next six months a traditional course in trying to maintain good order and a strong foreign policy, but at the same time tried to create a new, democratic form of society based upon the expression of the people's will. But whereas in France the National Assembly had come into existence along with the revolution, and even the organisers of the Jacobin clubs chose to work through rather than against the legislature, in Russia the fourth Duma had little following among the masses, and a powerful rival outside in the soviets.

Factory workers had spontaneously elected the earliest soviets to organise revolutionary action in St. Petersburg, Moscow, and other industrial centres during the 1905 risings. The system was revived in what was now called Petrograd with special provision for Army representatives, and from March 12 onwards its strength grew rapidly. The very first official order of the Petrograd Soviet made the popular and eminently subversive proposal that there should be a soldiers' committee affiliated to the central soviet for every military unit stationed in the city, while it soon clashed directly with the Provisional Government by making a second popular proposal, that the war (which the Government was trying desperately hard to keep going) should be abandoned except for purposes of self-defence. Similar local soviets of workers, soldiers, and peasants sprang up in Moscow and most large towns, and more sparingly in the countryside. In May the soviets were allotted five seats in Lvov's second provisional government; in June they held their first all-Russia congress; and in July, when Russia's last military offensive had just ended in disaster, they felt strong enough to attempt a *coup d'état*, which Kerensky stamped out at a cost of 400 lives with special troops brought back from the front. After this, during the short interlude of Kerensky's Government, the soviets were acquiring new adherents and, what was much more important in the long run, a new body of doctrine.

The Theoretical Basis of Communism

It was the union of communist theory with soviet machinery which made the Second or October Revolution one of the decisive events in history. The communism, of which the world was now to hear so much, was an extreme and doctrinaire form of socialism. It had been formulated by the German Jew, Karl Marx, during his long exile in England, and presented to a largely indifferent mid-nineteenth century audience in *The Communist Manifesto* of 1848, in the economic classic, *Capital*, of which the first volume was published in 1867, and through the rather obscure activities of the International Working Men's Association or First International. Communists had looked with approval on the Paris Commune of 1871, when some of the Communards were also ardent communists. But in the later years of the century the workers' movement took the strictly parliamentary form of social democracy, as in Germany and France, or that of the anarchism taught by Bakunin, which inspired most of the 'propagandas-by-deed' *alias* outrages in Spain and Italy and even Chicago.

Nevertheless communism was reinstated as a fighting creed by the decision taken at the London conference of the newly formed Russian Social Democratic Labour Party in 1903, when the majority or Bolsheviks voted in favour of the full rigours of Marxian teaching.[1] The main propositions are these: that the triumph of the workers over the middle class and

[1] See p. 155.

the transfer into their hands of the means of production (land, factories, etc.) is as historically certain as was the triumph of the middle class in an earlier age over the feudal aristocracy; that all other factors, such as religion, nationality, and culture, are of no importance as compared with the worker's obligation to his class, the triumph of which is to be secured by all means and at all costs; and that, when the revolution has triumphed, the next phase will be, not social democracy, but the dictatorship of the proletariat. This is a stage in which absolute power is exercised by a small number of resolute and well-schooled communists, to make the newly emancipated proletarians capable of living in and maintaining a society which has forsworn the familiar incentives and deterrents of competitive capitalism, and to discipline what is left of the former ruling elements. Then comes the last phase, in which 'the State will wither away'—that is, when the community life will function freely without any element of legal or economic compulsion—a communist heaven, which is not necessarily unreal because communists have not yet attained to it.

The communist teaching is most clearly set out in *The Communist Manifesto*. The main communist propositions set out above are all based on the document of 1848, although around its comparatively simple teachings a vast mass of controversial literature of comment, exposition and criticism has grown up and is still growing. The *Manifesto* puts the idea of the class struggle in the foreground:

'The history of all human society, past and present, has been the history of class struggles. . . . Our own age, the bourgeois age, is distinguished by this—that it has simplified class antagonisms. More and more, society is splitting into two great hostile camps, into two great and directly contraposed classes: bourgeoisie and proletariat.'

In other words, society is fundamentally divided between the bourgeoisie or capitalists, and the proletariat or working class. In this struggle, the 'increasing misery' of the workers would combine them in revolution against their masters: the purpose of communism is the 'forcible overthrow of the whole extant social order.' The document makes a clarion appeal to the workers everywhere:

'Let the ruling classes tremble at the prospect of a communist revolution. Proletarians have nothing to lose but their chains. They have a world to win.
Proletarians of All Lands, Unite!'

Although Marx provided a slogan, detailed examination of the class war theory shows that this simple twofold division of social class is neither so real nor, to the extent to which it does exist, so consciously felt as Marx supposed. Industrialisation has produced a great improvement in the material conditions of *all* classes in the western nations; in many ways the capitalist and worker are closer in their standard of life than the feudal baron and the serf of the Middle Ages. There is a great similarity in food, clothes, and entertainments to-day which applies to all classes. National feeling, religion, sport, all cut across the lines of social class. Standardised amusements like the cinema also help to break it down. Social services have helped to remove extremes of poverty. Another thing which Marx did not foresee was the wide appeal of order in a civilised society. This accounted, partly, for the success of Fascism later on in Italy, of the Nazis in Germany and of dictators everywhere. The 'strong man' could always count on a considerable measure of support when he promised order as against the violence and disorders proceeding from the extreme Left. Under normal peacetime conditions, no highly developed industrial nation would tolerate the dislocation of its whole way of life by revolution with probable economic ruin; only war and national disaster could produce the conditions in which communism might seize power by force. And even then it is not necessary to assume that communism— viewed as a progressive development—would follow: the result might be chaos and barbarism. History shows examples of decay as well as of progress. The early communists were too dogmatic and too optimistic. Indeed, as Bertrand Russell puts it, 'the dogmatic optimism of the communist doctrine must be regarded as a relic of Victorianism.'

The Second or 'October' Revolution

Lenin and Trotsky, veterans of 1905, returned from their respective exiles in Switzerland and America convinced that communism offered a philosophical basis for action in the

Russia of 1917. They were both brilliant writers and dialecticians, hardened by long years of adversity, sustained by a burning faith in what Marx had taught, and within a few weeks Lenin had given a handful of Bolsheviks in Petrograd the slogan which was to transform the liberal revolution— 'All power to the soviets.' As already mentioned, the first attempt, in July, 1917, to act upon the slogan was crushed by Kerensky. The Bolsheviks characteristically pretended that they had not inspired the rising on behalf of the soviets. Lenin went into hiding, Trotsky was for a time arrested, and their paper, *Pravda*, suppressed. But the leaders re-emerged in September, in which month their doctrines were beginning at last to get a firm hold on both the Petrograd and Moscow soviets; and their chance came when the German military threat to Petrograd caused Kerensky to propose to transfer the seat of government to Moscow, a reasonable precaution, but one against which it was easy to stir up factious opposition. Baulked of his first intention, Kerensky then tried to replace the Petrograd garrison by more reliable troops from the front. The rest followed almost automatically—the formation by the Petrograd soviet of a military revolutionary committee under Trotsky to assume responsibility for the capital, and the mustering of Red Guards (workers in arms) for its defence; Lenin's emergence from hiding while Kerensky made up his mind to go himself in search of loyal troops; and the surrender of the rest of the government in its leader's absence to the guns trained on government headquarters in the Winter Palace by the mutinous *Aurora* in the Neva and by the historic Peter and Paul fortress on its bank. This was on November 7, and the constitutional knot was cut the same day and with similar decisiveness.

Kerensky's main achievement as Prime Minister had been to hold a spectacular state assembly in Moscow, which fathered a so-called preliminary parliament: this had failed him in the final crisis, when he sought immediate dictatorial powers from it in vain. But the second all-Russia congress of soviets, which assembled in Petrograd one day after the soviet of the capital had seized power, proceeded to vest authority in a Council of People's Commissars, chosen mainly from the Communist Party central committee, with Lenin as its President and Trotsky as Commissar for Foreign Affairs. A minority of non-communists then withdrew and joined a committee of public defence under the auspices of the preliminary parliament, which organised the cadets of the military schools to co-operate with the Cossack general Krasnov as he advanced to recapture the city. But the sailors from the Kronstadt naval base stood firm on the side of the communists, so that in three days the military schools had been stormed and in five days Krasnov was in retreat and Kerensky on his way to final exile.

Lenin and the Bolsheviks achieved their immediate seizure of power with little difficulty and little disturbance. It was not the Communist Revolution itself, but its subsequent struggle against increased opposition, culminating in the Civil War, that brought the bloodshed and horrors which made the Russian Revolution stand out in modern history as involving most terrible calamities. The astonishing thing is that the revolution had come in a backward peasant country, and not, according to Marxist theory, in a highly industrialised state where the class struggle between capitalist employer and the factory proletariat would be most clearly marked. Another interesting feature of 1917 in Russia is that, as this chapter should already have made clear, the Russian Revolution was not one single revolution, but consisted of two separate revolutions. The first was political in character; it changed the form of government; it put an end to the monarchy, and replaced it by a form of parliamentary government. This was familiar to western Europe; it was exactly comparable to the French Revolution, it was the old style of revolution. The second revolution was something new, and unfamiliar to Europe; in fact, it was something new in history. It did not merely make a change of government; it was a social and economic revolution which took over from their old private owners all the economic resources of the state. Had the Russian Revolution stopped short with Kerensky there might have been little more to say; it was the revolution which followed so quickly that made the Russian experiment something of especial and terrifying interest.

How then was it that a revolution so novel and so profound in its consequences took place in Russia? Although Russia was not highly industrialised, there were nevertheless certain conditions present which predisposed to revolution. The social gulf between the dominant class of landlords, often with a western education, speaking French or English, and spending long periods abroad, and the mass of illiterate peasantry was a wide one; the middle class was small and inexperienced, and the monarchy by its weakness and inefficiency coupled with its absolutism had concentrated against itself most of the educated and progressive forces in the country. But above all the war gave the opportunity for revolution. It was the prolonged strain of fighting a highly industrialised and efficient modern state like Germany which finally reduced the Russian people to such a level of weakness that Bolshevism was able to take over control from the failing hands of those who otherwise would have suppressed it. The Russo-Japanese War had given an earlier chance; on that occasion revolution was put down. But in 1917 the best troops had been destroyed in the carnage at the front, and had been replaced by raw levies most interested in a redivision of the land at home in their villages. The war, then, produced the opportunity. Fate produced the leader in Lenin. His great intellectual and personal powers enabled him to dominate the situation: he saw the opportunity when others did not.

Communist Policy—the Land Seizures and the Peace of Brest-Litovsk

The story of the next three years in Russia is the story of a struggle for survival. Throughout the eight months of the provisional governments a vast empire had been steadily lapsing into anarchy, with bread riots in the towns and *jacqueries* on the manorial estates; secession movements among the suppressed nationalities, matched by gestures of independence in provincial soviets; indiscipline among the soldiers; sabotage from the despairing middle class; and the German army advancing relentlessly into the midst. It is typical of the atmosphere of chaos in which Lenin and Trotsky went to work that, when the first communist commander-in-chief was sent to the army, his predecessor was found to have been literally torn in pieces. A food supply for the towns was somehow improvised; factory soviets were in principle given control of industries and nationalisation of banks; manufactures proceeded piecemeal under the supervision of a supreme economic council.

Yet though it was the towns that had placed him in power,

Lenin well knew that in an overwhelmingly agricultural country with a peasant population the two questions of the hour were the disposal of the land and the return of the soldiers to do the disposing. It was therefore decreed that all land belonged to those who worked it, and it was made clear that, in the absence of a large landowner to be despoiled, the new government favoured the spoliation of the richer peasant by the poorer. This measure, from which the provisional governments had shrunk because confiscation without compensation was alien to the whole liberal tradition, went far to appease the Russian people. But the Treaty of Brest-Litovsk went farther.

The punitive terms of that little-remembered treaty interest us chiefly as evidence of the line the Germans would have taken, had they ever been in a position to dictate terms in western Europe; but they are also evidence that Russia had been reduced to a more desperate plight than at any other time in her history. Trotsky, though a Jew by race and an internationalist by faith, threw up the conduct of the negotiations because of the ruin they imposed on Russia. The Germans promptly renewed their almost unimpeded advance towards the heart of the country, and the supreme realist Lenin refused to remain in office unless what he called a 'breathing-space' was secured at any price. On March 3, 1918, the new communist negotiator, Chicherin, signed away one-third of the population of the Russian Empire, one-third of its laboriously acquired railways, and the territory which at that time provided three-quarters of its iron and nine-tenths of its coal production. The war indemnity was fixed at 300,000,000 gold roubles. In appearance, not everything went direct to Germany: Kars, Ardahan, and Batum were ceded to Turkey; the Ukraine was formally recognised as an independent Power, that status having been conferred upon it by the Central Powers in the previous month; and even Poland and the Baltic provinces were handed over with vague expectations of self-government under new German dynasties.

The fate of the Ukraine, where a population of 30,000,000 tilled the richest cornfields in Europe, shows what would have happened to the rest in course of time. The retention of their independence, and of certain privileges which they had secured for their co-nationals, the Ruthenians in Austrian

Galicia, was conditional upon their supplying the Central Powers with a million tons of bread corn a year; but to make their economic subservience to German and Austrian needs more certain, an army of occupation was quickly installed. Finland, of which the national history was more continuous and society on the whole more advanced, was not handed over to German tutelage but recognised by the Russian revolutionaries as independent. A civil war followed, however, to decide whether Finland should go communist like her mighty neighbour. This ended, significantly enough, in the landing of a German expeditionary force, which helped to suppress the communists. It had procured the election of a German prince as first King of Finland, when the armistice in the west intervened to annul both the legal territorial changes made by the Brest-Litovsk Treaty and the practical consequences which had hitherto flowed from the acknowledged supremacy of German arms throughout what had been the western border lands of the Russian Empire.

The Repression of the Social Revolutionary Party

It follows from what has been said that the first twelve months after the October Revolution constitute an interim period, during which Germany exploited the border lands but had no leisure to look at what was happening beyond. Much less could the western Powers, separated from Russia by the whole width of German-occupied Europe, give any serious attention to the communist revolution, apart from certain sporadic attempts to extricate Allied men and supplies which might have fallen into German hands; and these only became important as the Allies ceased to be preoccupied by the great German offensives against Amiens, the Channel ports, and Paris. Meanwhile, the communists had triumphed in the first of the bloody internal struggles by which alone a minority party could enforce the rule of its leaders—a dictatorship *over* the proletariat and a dictatorship *for* the proletariat, but not a dictatorship *of* the proletariat, which had not chosen and could not dismiss its new rulers. This was shown as early as January, 1918, when the constituent assembly, to which in a sense the events of both revolutions were preliminary, proved to have a two to one anti-communist majority and was immediately dissolved by Lenin's orders. This arbitrary action caused the middle-class groups to join forces with an organisation of much greater potential strength, namely the Social Revolutionaries, who for twenty years had preached the gospel of violence as the means, and the land for the people as the end, in campaigns which gave them the same leadership in the countryside as the communists acquired more slowly in the towns. Since Russia was still a nation of peasants, and since the peasants' enthusiasm for Lenin, because he allowed them to seize the land, was quickly overshadowed by resentment against the ruthless system of requisitioning, without which he could not have fed the towns at all, the Social Revolutionaries appeared to have the game in their hands. The territorial sacrifices involved in the Brest-Litovsk settlement had rendered Lenin and his régime intensely unpopular even among those sections of society which had clamoured for the release of the soldiers from the front, for the moment of national humiliation is not that at which the logical faculty shines brightest.

To exploit this unpopularity, on July 6, 1918, the German Ambassador was murdered by persons who hoped to provoke a complete breach between the German Government and Lenin, a situation which would have shown that humiliating sacrifices had been made in vain. This was followed by a military rising organised by the Social Revolutionaries at Yaroslav, and this in turn by a wave of terrorist activity, including an attempt on the life of Lenin. But the movement failed. The communists, though few, were better disciplined, better led, and—what was of great importance in a chaotic situation —much surer both of what they wanted and of the way to get it than any rival revolutionaries. There were about 500 executions of prominent opponents of the régime in Moscow and similar reprisals in Petrograd; it was at this time that the Cheka or secret police, founded in December, 1917, acquired a sinister importance as one of the main factors in government. Outside observers were reminded of Robespierre and the reign of terror in France in 1793-4, and looked confidently for the emergence of a general to supersede the revolution in the role of a Bonaparte. The tendency now was for the pace to quicken—commodity cards took the place of money, the co-operatives were entrusted with the whole business of retail distribution, and the system of grain requisitioning was tightened up—but the new phase of Militant Communism was judged by the Russian people as a war measure.   The period of serious foreign intervention had begun.

The Civil War of 1918–20

The struggle which raged on Russian soil from the autumn of 1918 to the autumn of 1920 has a three-fold significance. It decided the fate of Russia for the coming era.   It decided the fate of the western border-lands for twenty years.   And it gave the new Russia a suspicion of all foreign influences and fear of foreign intervention which becomes more important with every increase in Russia's strength, combining as it does so easily with the hostility which the Communist State bears to all capitalist states on grounds of theory and principle. Allied intervention had many motives.   The most funda-mental was perhaps the knowledge that communist theory required a world revolution, and that communist propaganda was doing its best to foment trouble in despairing Germany and Hungary and even among the troops of the victorious Powers, as they impatiently awaited demobilisation.   America and Japan, no less than Britain and France, had governments in 1919 which were willing to go to a good deal of trouble to keep the world safe for capitalist enterprise.   There were indeed sufficient grounds for popular indignation against a government which in twelve short months deserted its allies, repudiated its debts, murdered its royal family, and (as it was believed) erected atheism and free love into a State religion.

Intervention seemed easy because ever since March, 1917, members of the old upper classes of Russia had been escaping to organise resistance in outlying portions of the empire to which the hand of Petrograd did not reach.   Though they were really officers without an army, they made a brave showing and professed to be able to overthrow the Reds if a minimum of help was given them, chiefly in *matériel*, for a White invasion.   Moreover, in helping them the Allies had been influenced originally by the pressing need to use every means of containing the Germans in the east.   In March, 1918, a few British troops were landed at Murmansk to protect stores we had supplied and to deny the Germans a possible submarine base.   A second landing, at Archangel in August, hoped to get local Russian support, and a third British force was sent from Baghdad to occupy the Baku oil-fields. From January onwards Japanese, British, and American warships also watched over stores and tangled politics at Vladivostok.

During these events a most remarkable turn of fortune sent an army of 45,000 Czechs, recruited from Russia's prisoner-of-war camps, to make their way across Asiatic Russia to Vladivostok, in order that Russia's withdrawal from the war might not baulk them of their design to uphold the Czech national cause against the Central Powers. They set out in March, 1918, with a safe-conduct from the communist authorities; quarrelled with them about the retention of their arms, which the Czechs deemed essential for their journey; and ended up by seizing control of the Trans-Siberian Railway and establishing a White régime in Vladivostok, from which the Whites launched their first drive westwards in the summer of 1918. One result was that the local communist authorities, at Ekaterinburg, fearing that they would be overrun, brutally murdered the ex-Czar and his wife and children (July 18); another was that the British at Archangel for a moment entertained hopes of a link-up with the Czechs. But Lenin and Trotsky, who held the command-in-chief throughout the Civil War, secured a breathing-space at the end of September, when the collapse of the Central Powers and Turkey was giving the communist cause a fresh lease of life from the Baltic to the Caucasus, and it was not until November that the main war of intervention began.

On November 18, 1918, Admiral Koltchak proclaimed himself dictator of Siberia at Omsk. The Czechs were already losing interest in the White cause, but he had the support of 70,000 Japanese in his rear, 7,000 Americans, who likewise remained in the Far East, 7,000 British with him in Siberia, and 15,000 more prepared to co-operate with his advancing forces from their bases at Archangel and Murmansk. Koltchak could also rely on the help of the British and French Navies, which had taken control of the Baltic and Black Sea coasts immediately after the Armistice, and all the Allies had put at his disposal large amounts of money and equipment.

The feeling of confidence was such that, when the Allies proposed a round table conference of all Russian political parties at Prinkipo in January, it was the anti-communists who rejected it; and Koltchak's rapid advance caused the Allies to ignore overtures made by the communists in March, for a settlement on the basis of a withdrawal of foreign troops in return for the honouring of the foreign debt, the rival Russian governments to be left as they were. The converging movements organised by Koltchak twice came near to success, but the cruelties of the White terror which accompanied the advance of his armies, and their refusal to accept the land settlement, caused the peasants to regard communist rule as preferable and steeled the communist rulers to make a fanatical resistance. Trotsky's commissars had men, but no officers, Koltchak's aristocratic entourage officers, but no men. In May, Koltchak advanced up the Volga towards Moscow, but General Denikin in Georgia and the Cossack General Yudenich in Estonia had not completed their preparations for the offensive, and a British diversion in the north came too late. In October, however, there was a moment when Denikin had reached Orel, only 200 miles from Moscow, and Yudenich's tanks were within ten miles of Petrograd: but both were thrown back before Koltchak could complete the drive on Moscow. The end came quickly, once he was thrown on the defensive. In November he lost Omsk; in December he resigned his command; the Czechs betrayed him to his enemies; and, in February, 1920, he was shot.

The Russo-Polish War

The same issues were raised once more in the Russo-Polish War of May–October, 1920. Its immediate occasion lay in Trotsky's conversion of a part of the armies which he was now demobilising into a 'labour army' for work in transport and heavy industry, which the Poles regarded as a form of preparation for an attack on Poland. The availability of French war material and a big American food loan encouraged them to demand the frontiers of 1772 and an indemnity. In the first stage of the ensuing conflict the Polish armies entered Kiev, but in the second they were driven out of the coveted Ukrainian capital and the Russians in turn advanced from Smolensk through Vilna, along the German border and down to the outskirts of Warsaw. The Russians had in fact extended themselves too far and too fast, just as the Poles had done three months earlier, but there was great alarm at the

Q

prospect of a communist advance into the heart of Europe.
A British financial mission under Lord d'Abernon and a
French military mission under General Weygand hastened to
supply the Poles with moral, material, and technical support.
The Russians were routed on the Vistula and a large number
of prisoners taken. Fighting ended on October 11, and by
the Treaty of Riga, signed in 1921, Poland advanced her
eastern frontier beyond the Curzon Line (which had been
approved by the British Foreign Office as recently as
December, 1919, on the score of nationality statistics) far
into debatable districts of eighteenth-century Poland, which
were Polish only inasmuch as a small upper class of wealthy
landowners were Poles. About 4,000,000 Russians or Ukrainians passed uneasily and impermanently under Polish
sovereignty. The armistice of October 11 also cut the ground
from beneath the feet of the last of the White Russian generals,
Wrangel, who had re-formed Denikin's army in the Crimea
and advanced with the Poles into what was still virtually the
no-man's-land of the Ukraine. Russia kept what the Poles
left of the Ukraine; reannexed her long-disputed Georgian
province; and made a treaty with Turkey (February, 1921)
by which she also regained Transcaucasia, except for Kars.
Last of all, the Japanese, who had seized their chance in
1917–18, slowly and reluctantly evacuated Vladivostok and
the Maritime Provinces.

The Great Famine

Thus war, which ravaged western Europe with all its waste
and uncertainty from 1914 to 1918, ravaged Russia for nearly
three more years. In the circumstances it was not surprising
that militant communism had degenerated into something
little better than chaos. There had been countless acts of
violence, directed not only against the aristocracy and middle
class as such, but against the Church and every organisation
that could be suspected of sympathising with the reaction.
Money had been practically abolished without any efficient
substitute for it being provided. 'Committees of Village
Poor' were officially encouraged to take extreme action against
the more prosperous peasants, though they were often merely
the owners of a few humble livestock and very different from
the capitalist of propaganda. Above all, there had been a

rigorous exaction of the whole of the peasant's crop of bread grain, less household requirements, in return for which the peasant, rich or poor, received only some almost valueless commodity cards. The war period, therefore, ended with a twofold crisis. In March, 1921, the Kronstadt garrison demanded the abolition of the grain monopoly and was induced by surviving Social Revolutionary influences to mutiny. Elsewhere peasants began to refuse to submit to requisitioning, and the troops (mostly average peasants themselves) who were sent against them took their side. Next month the requisitioning was officially replaced by a food tax. But in July of the same year a failure of the crops in the black earth districts of the Volga, North Caucasus, and Ukraine drove a million peasants to take flight and threatened ten times as many with death by starvation. A situation of horror developed, in which an appeal was made for help from Hoover's American Relief Administration as well as from European sources; and in the winter of 1921–2 communism as a force in world affairs seemed to have little meaning, when about 25,000,000 persons living under the first communist administration in history were known by all the world to be starving.[1]

[1] See p. 308 for an account of American relief work in Russia.

SUGGESTIONS FOR FURTHER READING

C. Hill: *Lenin and the Russian Revolution.*
Sir B. Pares: *Russia* (Pelican Series), cc. 7–9.
J. W. Wheeler-Bennett: *Brest-Litovsk, The Forgotten Peace*, cc. 2 and 8.
Bertrand (Lord) Russell: *Freedom and Organisation, 1814–1914*, cc. 17–20.
Sir R. H. Bruce Lockhart: *Memoirs of a British Agent*, Books III and IV.
J. Reed: *Ten Days That Shook The World.*
G. Vernadsky: *History of Russia*, c. 13.
E. H. Carr: *The Bolshevik Revolution, 1917–23*, Vol. I, c. 4.
New Cambridge Modern History, Vol. XII, c. 14 (by Isaac Deutscher).
J. A. White: *The Siberian Intervention.*

CHAPTER 14

THE FIRST WORLD PEACE SETTLEMENT

The Big Four

THE Peace Conference which opened in Paris on January 18, 1919, representing as it did some twenty-six Allied and Associated Powers belonging to every continent, had without doubt an unprecedented opportunity to shape the future of the whole world for good or ill. It is now a commonplace to point out that it failed in the main object of creating a lasting peace, and that its achievement in this respect was inferior to that of the far less ambitious and much criticised European Congress which met at Vienna at the end of the Napoleonic wars. The Big Four, with whom the main decisions necessarily rested, all seemed slowly to lose in moral stature as the years passed by—the American President Wilson, so angular, doctrinaire, and self-righteous, so eager to lecture Europeans for their good, so reluctant to consider the falseness of his own position in that the American mid-term elections had already destroyed the basis, but left the façade of his power; the French Prime Minister, Clemenceau, the embodiment of cynicism, who had learnt the bitter lesson of 1870 and wished to learn no other; his British counterpart, Lloyd George, intensely susceptible to atmosphere, capable of any generosity or sometimes of real ruthlessness according to the needs of the situation as he might sense it at the moment; and the unhappy Orlando, whom the other three treated with a contempt which was inspired by their knowledge of Italy's internal weakness as well as the extravagance of her external claims.

Yet looking back to-day, it is perhaps easier than it was a few years ago to assess dispassionately the conduct of the three great figures at the Paris Conference. If Wilson had personal weaknesses he had also fundamentally the right idea; the great tragedy of post-war history was that the United States failed him and did not come into the League of Nations, the rejection of Wilson's settlement by the Senate being amply confirmed by the American people in the Presidential election

of 1920.   Of Lloyd George it can rightly be said that, in spite
of a certain opportunism, he wanted a just peace and a new
Europe.   Those who met him or listened to his electrifying oratory
will agree with the verdict of Sir Arthur Salter, who worked
with him at the Conference: 'Magnetic, eloquent, dominating,
persuasive; with gaps in his knowledge, but understanding
so much more than he knew.'   As a politician he was trying
to satisfy an electorate eager for the fruits of victory.   When
he wished to reduce the reparations to be paid by Germany,
he received a telegram from 370 M.P.s holding him strictly
to his most extreme election claims made in the excitement
of the moment.   Even 'The Tiger,' Clemenceau, was not so
unreasonable in his anti-German feeling as were the politicians
of France, who refused him the Presidency of the Republic
on account of his moderation.   Salter aptly sums up the Big
Three: 'Each was better than the prevailing majority of the
public he served.'

The Limiting Factors

In any case it is important to realise that the powers of the
Big Four and of the Conference were subject to three great
limitations.   Some diplomatic agreements had been entered
into before the Conference began; certain territorial and
other changes were coming about, in the then disordered
condition of Europe, whether they were officially approved
or not; and the peoples of the Allied countries, the Americans
excepted, had been left by the events of the war in a mood of
complicated unreason, in which their leaders would more
easily have found support for a worse than for a better settlement.

The diplomacy of the war period need not detain us long.
It had two aspects.   The most important agreement which
the Allies had made among themselves was that which
promised Constantinople at long last to the Russians, but this
promise had been cancelled by Russia's defection.   Not so
the promises made to Italy by the Treaty of London as the
price of her intervention in 1915, under which she now laid
claim, not only to *Italia irredenta* in the Trentino and the
Austrian Tyrol (where she would be engulfing 250,000
Germans), but to Istria and Dalmatia (disputed by the South
Slavs), the Albanian port of Valona, the Greek-inhabited

islands of the Dodecanese, and an area of Turkish territory in Asia Minor. There were also the armistice terms to be considered. These would have had great diplomatic significance if any of the attempts to end the war by compromise, such as had been sponsored by President Wilson in 1916 and by the Pope in 1917, and most directly and sincerely proposed by Charles, the last Hapsburg emperor, immediately after his accession, had borne fruit. As it was, the surrender of Bulgaria, Turkey, and Austria-Hungary had been unconditional.

Nevertheless the German armistice of November 11 was based specifically upon an Allied offer of terms, dated November 5, which was in answer to a Note addressed by the German Government to President Wilson a month earlier. This Allied offer indicated that the terms of peace to follow Germany's armistice surrender would correspond with the principles laid down by President Wilson in his Fourteen Points on January 8, 1918. These points had been interpreted by him in certain subsequent addresses and modified in two respects by his Allies, who indicated that there would be no discussion of the freedom of the seas (i.e. no challenge permitted to British rules of naval blockade) and a wide definition of civilian war damage, for which Germany would be made to pay.

As a matter of fact most of the peace settlement was fairly based on the Fourteen Points, except that the civilian war damage clause was interpreted to mean, not only bombed towns and torpedoed merchant ships but astronomical figures for compensation to dependants of dead soldiers and so forth. Germany never paid reparations to correspond with these figures, but it was a pity to give her any excuse, however flimsy, for decrying the treaty on the grounds of trickery. It may be noted in passing that the continuance of the economic blockade of Germany during the armistice period, which constituted another German grievance, was not due in the main to the inhumanity of the conquerors but to the refusal of interested parties among the conquered to let either the German merchant navy or the German gold reserve be used to satisfy the needs of their own people.

The other two factors which limited the work of the Conference may be taken together. A glance at almost any contemporary newspaper or diary will remind the reader of the popular passions that poisoned the atmosphere of war-sick Paris, where the Conference sat, so that wire netting was even needed to guard German delegates from the fury of the mob. More difficult to recall are the conditions of chaos in many parts of Europe that rendered it hard for statesmen to make anything at all of a situation which was all the time drifting and becoming more and more out of control. The Austro-Hungarian Empire was not carved up by the dictates of the Peace Conference,[1] it had collapsed at the shock of military defeat, and the Czechs and Poles were only the first among its subject nations to proclaim their independence in accordance with the will of the people, as indicated in tumultuous demonstrations in the streets before the Allied governments had even settled the armistice terms.

Events in the remoter parts of eastern Europe, the Baltic provinces, Bessarabia or Thrace, were not fully known to the Conference at any time, though occasional observers reported on acts of guerrilla warfare which might or might not be the work of some nation 'rightly struggling to be free.' Even accurate knowledge did not necessarily mean appropriate action, since the war-weariness of the Allied peoples, the demand for demobilisation and a return to normal at any cost, reduced the coercive power of the conference month by month, until its one effective sanction was the threat to withhold American food relief from the recalcitrant: for in the first half of 1919 all Europe except the western seaboard states was very hungry. Last but not least, the deliberations of the Peace Conference were overshadowed by the fear of communism. If the red flag waved over the Government buildings of Munich and Budapest, it seemed likely that it might triumph in Berlin, in Vienna, or in discontented Italy; and the attitude of the troops to discipline and demobilisation even caused fears about the political complexion of the British Army on the Rhine and its French counterpart. Neither the régime of Kurt Eisener in Bavaria nor that of Bela Kun in Hungary lasted long; but for the German governments with which the

---

[1] Misunderstanding is very considerable on this issue. It became very general between the two wars to blame the Treaty of Versailles for all the shortcomings, real or supposed, of the peace settlement. But the Treaty of Versailles had nothing to do with the break-up of the Austrian Empire. The other treaties gave recognition to the succession states, but did not *cause* the break-up: it was the result of popular movements in the territories concerned.

Conference had to deal a communist (or Spartacist) revolution was always just round the corner, giving point to the epigram coined at the time that a quick peace was needed even more than a good one.

'Paris was a nightmare,' wrote Professor Keynes (British Treasury Representative, afterwards Lord Keynes), 'and everyone there was morbid. A sense of impending catastrophe overhung the frivolous scene; the futility and smallness of man before the great events confronting him . . . all the elements of ancient tragedy were there. . . . One felt most strongly the impression, described by Tolstoy in *War and Peace*, or by Hardy in *The Dynasts*, of events marching on to their fated conclusion uninfluenced and unaffected by the cerebrations of statesmen in Council.' When we look back and reflect on the failure of the hopes of the time we see how right he was. H. G. Wells wrote soon afterwards of the war which 'ended nothing, began nothing and settled nothing,' and said of Wilson that 'he exaggerated in his own person our common human tragedy, he was so very great in his dreams and so incapable in his performance.' But when we consider the complications of the intricate world pattern which had to be reconstituted, when we remember the passions of the peoples, the hatreds of enemies and the jealousies, fears and rival ambitions even of Allies, we are surprised that the statesmen at Paris did even as well as they did. As Gilbert White, one of the Americans at the Conference, summed up later on the effort of the statesmen: 'It is not surprising that they made a bad peace: what is surprising is that they made peace at all.'

The Settlement with Germany

All things considered, the territorial settlement with Germany in Europe was neither impolitic nor inequitable. She lost much, but her territory remained a reasonable unity. The retrocession of Alsace-Lorraine to France, of West Prussia and Posen to the Poles, of North Schleswig to the Danes, and of the three small communes of Eupen, Moresnet, and Malmédy to Belgium, were all justifiable on grounds of national sympathies, even if the last two had not been endorsed by plebiscite. A plebiscite was also conceded in the East Prussian districts of Marienwerder and Allenstein, where the

THE PEACE SETTLEMENT: GERMANY'S WESTERN FRONTIER

vote went in Germany's favour. The compromise by which
Danzig, a German port dominating the commerce of Poland's
great river, was made into a German municipality with a
Polish foreign policy under international supervision, provided
a reasonable way out of a difficult situation; and a similar
régime was designed for Memel, on the right bank of the
Niemen.   In the case of the Saar basin complete international
control, with a military force of occupation, was imposed
for a period of fifteen years only, in order that the French, to

whom full ownership of the coal mines was given as compensation for war losses, might have a chance of acquiring sovereignty by consent.   The fact that the eventual plebiscite restored the Saar territory to Germany does not in any way detract from the reasonableness of the settlement there.   It remains to mention Upper Silesia, a great industrial district which was at first assigned outright to strengthen the new Poland; then submitted, at Lloyd George's insistence, to the test of a plebiscite, in which the Germans obtained a majority of 14 : 9; and finally partitioned by international authority in a manner which gave the Poles half the area and two-thirds of the mines.   It is often suggested that the partitioning was influenced by a rising of the Polish population with French encouragement, which preceded it in May, 1922: but actually the line of partition left rather more Poles under German, than Germans under Polish, sovereignty.

Thus the territorial settlement with Germany followed the principles of respect for nationality and self-determination, which President Wilson made the watch-word of the age and which were in the main accepted as valid by the peoples of Europe, many of whom had struggled for generations towards their fulfilment.   The same cannot be said of the important clause in the treaty with Germany which forbade any union with German-speaking Austria unless expressly sanctioned by the Powers.   This may be regarded, however, as forming an inevitable part of a settlement which was also designed to keep Germany weak.   This was the fundamental interest of France, overrun twice in half a century by a neighbouring Power whose population would soon be double what she could muster.

To emasculate Germany as a military factor was the aim of the stringent demilitarisation clauses of the treaty, which reduced her army to 100,000 volunteers enlisted for twelve years (so as to prevent the accumulation of a big trained reserve); restricted the size of the General Staff; and forbade outright the possession by Germany of any air force, any large-size capital ships, or any heavy artillery.   Coming on top of the surrender of existing equipment (including her entire Navy) under the armistice terms, and reinforced by the Peace Treaty, these demilitarisation clauses might have seemed a sufficient safeguard for the future.   But the far-sighted

THE PEACE SETTLEMENT: EASTERN EUROPE

French nevertheless asked and obtained a further guarantee against German aggression through the demilitarisation of all German territory on the left bank, or within fifty kilometres of the right bank, of the Rhine, so that the existence of this populous undefended area might constitute a sort of pledge for good behaviour.   Germany had fought out two wars in France;

the third—if there was ever to be a third—should be fought on German soil instead. An Allied military occupation was also imposed on the Rhineland, partly as a guarantee that the Germans would pay reparations.

We must pass rapidly over a series of other measures, of which in most cases the best defence is that they were intended to keep Germany too weak for aggression, even if they strengthened the will to aggress. All German colonies were confiscated, on the plea that the Germans had shown themselves unfit to govern backward native peoples, and were turned into Mandates[1] for the Allied Powers. State property in the colonies was held forfeit; the Germans lost all trading privileges in Morocco, China, and elsewhere; the Rhine was declared an international river and the Kiel Canal neutral water; and even the private property of German nationals in Allied countries was impounded to meet Germany's public obligations. A later generation looks with greater sympathy upon the provisions for the extradition of the ex-Kaiser from his place of refuge in Holland and for the surrender of other war criminals (provisions which were in substance left unexecuted), because experience has shown that what was denounced as a gratuitous humiliation of a beaten foe was needed at least as much as any other measure of demilitarisation.

Reparations

No such defence can be made of the reparations clauses. France had been compelled to pay the cost of the war of 1870, a matter of £200,000,000 to be paid within three years. The cost of the war of 1914 was beyond the capacity of any one belligerent (except possibly America) to pay: but Germany could probably have paid the lump sum of £2,000,000,000 proposed by Lord Keynes. The mischief began when their greed got the better of the judgment of certain British financiers, who suggested that twelve times Keynes' maximum figure could be extracted. Lloyd George persuaded President Wilson that the admitted German liability for civilian losses might be extended to include cost of pensions and separation allowances; and the French joined in, with less optimistic views about German resources but a shrewd belief that

[1] See below p. 250.

reparations would provide the means of making and keeping Germany bankrupt. No sum was fixed by the treaty, but unspecified Allied claims were given a legalistic justification by the insertion of a clause, more bitterly resented by the Germans than any other, which saddled the Germans and their confederates with sole responsibility for the outbreak of the war.

The reparations provisions of the Treaty of Versailles are certainly that part of the Treaty which is most open to criticism.[1] Together with the war debts of the Allies to the United States, they helped to unsettle the economy of the world and were contributory causes of the general slump in the 'thirties. They also contributed to misunderstanding between the Allies: Great Britain thought of Germany as a customer and thus did not look askance at German recovery; France viewed that recovery as a menace to her own security, and regarded reparations as a means of crippling Germany and at the same time of repaying France for her losses. Disagreement between the Allies was further accentuated by the French and Belgian military occupation, without British consent, of the Ruhr in 1923 in what proved a vain attempt to make Germany pay.[2]

The Treaty imposed upon the Germans

Such was the Treaty of Versailles, signed on June 28, 1919, in that same *Galerie des Glaces* where the German Empire had been proclaimed forty-eight years before. Though the German signatories were delegates of the new republic, not of the fallen empire, the general international usage had been abandoned and, instead of a free discussion of the Allied terms, they had been allowed only to submit observations in writing, which (except as regards a plebiscite for Upper Silesia) were almost entirely disregarded. Discussion might have softened some of the asperities of the treaty, much of which had been drafted by experts under the impression that they were to provide a basis for negotiation and possible compromise; certainly its absence assisted the Germans subsequently to claim that it was a *Diktat* which had been

[1] See the trenchant attack made at the time by J. M. (Lord) Keynes in *The Economic Consequences of the Peace.*
[2] See p. 258.

forced upon them and that it was therefore not morally binding.

The Settlement with Austria and Hungary

The ancillary treaties, which kept the experts, and to a much smaller extent the statesmen, of the Allied Powers busy in Paris for a further year or more, follow the Versailles pattern in their names (from other historic spots in the environs of the French capital), form (dictated, not negotiated) and nature. Respect for the principles of nationality and self-determination was still the watch-word, except where their application would substantially have strengthened an ex-enemy state; and the basic purpose of weakening Germany was served by a diligent regard for the interests of those smaller Powers which would help France to keep Germany encircled.

Austria and Hungary had already fallen apart into two independent republics during the military disasters which overwhelmed the Dual Monarchy. So two treaties were required to deal with situations which were broadly similar, in that the task of the Allies was to adjust and regularise the splitting-up of their possessions into national components. This splitting-up had already taken place, although in a chaotic fashion, and could not have been wholly undone, even if the Allies had wished to undo it. Thus Austria by the Treaty of St. Germain yielded the rich, industrialised provinces of Bohemia and Moravia, with a population of 10,000,000—two-thirds Czech, but one-third German-speaking Austrians—to the new state of Czechoslovakia, which was to unite them with the previously Hungarian territories inhabited by 2,000,000 backward, agricultural Slovaks and 1,000,000 Magyars and Ruthenians in the only deliberate multi-national creation of the peace settlement. As compared with Hungary, she made only a minor contribution to the other new Slav state, Jugoslavia; this contribution was in Dalmatia (though Austria and Hungary jointly forfeited Bosnia-Herzegovina to it as well). Similarly, Austria made a small addition to the aggrandisement of Rumania, which received from her the Bukovina.

Austria lost the Trentino and South Tyrol as far as the Brenner Pass, and areas along the Adriatic coast, including the

Istrian peninsula with Trieste, to satisfy Italian demands under the Treaty of London. Her Galician provinces went in their entirety to the new Poland, which had placed an army of occupation in the eastern province, where the population consisted mainly of Ruthenians with Ukrainian national sympathies living under Polish landlords. Altogether, a population of 22,000,000 was reduced to 6,500,000, with a roughly proportionate reduction in area. The new Austria included only the Austrian archduchies, Styria, and the North Tyrol, with Klagenfurt, obtained under a plebiscite, and the Burgenland, which was ceded by Hungary. From the European point of view, what was more serious was that one-third of the German-speaking population had been allotted to other states, where they would necessarily constitute disgruntled minorities; and what was most serious, Vienna had been left with a population of 2,000,000 and an agricultural hinterland which could not possibly support it—a head without a body.

The Treaty of Trianon with Hungary was not signed until June, 1920, nine months later than the Austrian treaty, a delay which was partly due to the chequered course of events in Budapest, where the communist *coup d'état* had provided a pretext for an occupation by the Rumanians in search of plunder and a reign of terror by the Hungarian Whites, who changed the infant republic into a regency for the absent Hapsburgs under the virtual dictatorship of Admiral Horthy. A democratic régime might in any case have proved impracticable in a country so ruthlessly dismembered. Apart from the cession of Slovakia to the Slavs in the north, already referred to, Hungary had to make the main contribution to the south Slav kingdom of Jugoslavia, in the shape of the highly civilised provinces of Croatia and Slovenia, and the main contribution to the new Rumania, in the corn lands of Transylvania and the Temesvar. Hungary's population fell from 21,000,000 to 7,500,000 and the reduction in area was rather greater. What made the situation even worse than that of Austria was the survival in Hungary alone of the feudal structure of society which the Magyars cherished, so that they looked out from an island of mediævalism on to the surrounding peasant states, exasperated beyond measure that their former serfs lorded it over, not merely their former lands but about one-third of the former Magyar *Herrenvolk*. Neither the Austrians nor the Hungarians were allowed to plead their case, a procedure which had worse practical results here than in the settlement with Germany, because the frontier problem was more complicated and less familiar to the Allies.

The Settlement with Bulgaria and Turkey

The first part of the Balkan settlement, the Treaty of Neuilly with Bulgaria, had been made in November, 1919. Bulgaria paid the penalty of a second defeat, the Greeks taking west Thrace, including Bulgaria's only point of access to the Ægean Sea at Dede Agach, the Serbs a smaller but strategically important area round Strumitsa, in the mountains of north Macedonia. A much more considerable series of changes, in which punitive measures were again mixed up with actions based on regard for self-determination, was propounded by the last of the peace treaties, negotiated with Turkish representatives at Sèvres in August, 1920. (This treaty was not ratified and was replaced in 1923 by the Treaty of Lausanne.) In Europe Turkey was required by the Treaty of Sèvres to cede Adrianople with most of the remaining hinterland of Constantinople to Greece; the Straits were to be internationalised and demilitarised; and Constantinople itself was only left to the Sultan, and under international supervision at that, because the United States could not be persuaded to take charge there. In Asia Turkey accepted the fact that her outlying possessions had passed by conquest into other hands: Syria, much against the wishes of its Moslem inhabitants, became a French Mandate, while Iraq, Palestine, and Transjordan were placed more or less willingly under the tutelage of Britain, who had so long held Egypt. Turkey was also required to find a 'national home' for what was left of the sorely tried Armenians—who had perished to the number of about 700,000 in the most cruel of all the Turkish massacres, perpetrated during the war, when the Turks had advanced into Russian Armenia. What was worse for Turkey than all else, she was to cede to the Greeks both Smyrna and a considerable hinterland in Asia Minor.

The dexterity of Venizelos, most successful of all the smaller Powers' envoys at the Peace Conference, had enabled the

Greeks, with Allied backing, to occupy Smyrna more than a year in advance of the treaty settlement; by the summer of 1920 they had penetrated as far as Brusa. But already, as in the case of Napoleon and Germany, nationalist aggression had provoked a nationalist reaction. Mustapha Kemal, a patriotic soldier with a brilliant record of leadership in the war, escaped from Constantinople in July, 1919, and roused the Turks of Anatolia to defend with a new nationalist fervour their ancient seat of power in Asia Minor.[1] A new capital was established in Angora (now Ankara), from which Kemal defied the Allies by refusing to accept the Treaty of Sèvres. At this juncture the young Greek King, Alexander, died suddenly; and the defeat of Venizelos in a General Election, followed by the recall to the throne of Constantine, whom the Allies had expelled only three and a half years earlier, showed conclusively that the era of apparently all-powerful peace-makers was at an end.

The Peace and the League Covenant

It is easy to criticise the peace they had made or tried to make. Germany had been injured sufficiently to render her vengeful, but not sufficiently to render her vengefulness permanently impotent. The carving-up of the empire of Austria-Hungary had been sanctioned, retrospectively at least, without any regard for the economic dislocation which was bound to follow the erection of tariff barriers throughout the Danubian area. The pretensions of the various succession states as serious democratic entities, worthy to exercise political power over large parts of Europe's ancient empires, had been accepted too readily at their face value. But to these and other similar criticisms there are two valid answers. One is that the peace had the solid merit, which can be tested statistically, that it put a larger proportion of European people than ever before under governments to which they would voluntarily pay allegiance and over which they had some direct control. In other words, the nationalism and liberalism of nineteenth-century idealists had triumphed, and all the more imposingly because no newer political ideals had yet reached the consciousness of mankind at large. The other, and perhaps more interesting, reply to the critics is

[1] See p. 259.

R

that the peace-makers of 1919, thanks largely to the persistence of President Wilson, had provided their peace treaties with the machinery of revision, which he at least hoped to see widely employed when the passions of war had begun to cool.

It was for this very reason that the American President had had himself nominated to serve on the commission to draft a League organisation; got the commission's report accepted by the Conference and the League Covenant adopted; and withstood with great firmness both Clemenceau and Lloyd George, when in March, 1919, they used the pretext of the need to speed up the Conference proceedings to try to separate the Covenant from the Treaty and have the latter completed first. Wilson's persistence got the League Covenant written into each treaty as an integral part of it, and it is from this angle that it falls to be examined now, bearing in mind that it was understood from the outset that ex-enemy states would eventually be admitted to the League on an equal footing with their conquerors.

For the League of Nations, which came into existence in 1920, the first year of the peace, had a bewildering variety of aspects. The Annual Assembly, to which all member states were to send representatives, promised a remarkable forum of world opinion, while the more frequent meetings of the Council, in which the Great Powers were to have seats automatically and a few others by process of election, would provide an embryo cabinet for all purposes of world action. The institution of Mandates—a kind of pledge taken by the Powers to which the government of what had been enemy territory outside Europe was assigned, requiring them to govern it as 'a sacred trust of civilisation' and to submit to a Mandate Commission an annual report, showing how they had discharged their trust—seemed to imply that even Great Powers were willing to let the new League trespass upon what had hitherto been jealously guarded aspects of sovereignty. Then there was a whole field of economic usefulness opened up by the International Labour Organisation, which set up a labour parliament, containing representatives of govern-ments, of employers, and of employees, to implement a labour charter of rights, included in the treaties. If this was contentious business, the League had other technical services to deal with problems of public health, international police measures, and communications, so uncontentious and so useful that it soon became difficult to understand how the world had managed without them before.

Nevertheless, the essential thing was the provision for the redress of international grievances, such as were bound to result from the peace treaties. One article gave a guarantee of territorial integrity and political independence to all member states. A second pledged members to submit any dispute for arbitration or enquiry and not to resort to war for three months after findings were published. A third obliged members to sever economic relations and to apply armed force, if necessary, where a state resorted to war in defiance of the general territorial guarantee or the findings in a particular dispute.

These three articles of the League Covenant merely legislated against aggression: but a fourth article empowered the Assembly to advise the reconsideration of out-of-date treaties. Why did this provision fail? The obvious answer is to point out that the recommendations of the Assembly were invalid unless they were unanimous, and there would always be interested parties to block unanimity. But the unanimity rule was a necessary feature of the League in 1919, if the sensitiveness of states about national sovereignty was not to hinder them from entering the League at all. The tragedy lay in the disappointment of Wilson's hopes that the very existence of the League of Nations would weaken the insistence on sovereignty sufficiently to make rational revision possible for treaties which he knew to be irrationally framed in the emotional strains of 1919. It was natural for him to suppose that co-operation learnt in other League activities would lead to co-operation in this vital matter of treaty revision. Unfortunately, the converse also held good: that a spirit of conflict, finding expression in other League functions, would render its function of treaty revision wholly unworkable—which is what actually happened.

SUGGESTIONS FOR FURTHER READING

H. Nicolson: *Peacemaking, 1919.*

Sir C. Petrie: *Diplomatic History, 1713–1933,* c. 28.

A. J. Grant and H. Temperley: *Europe in the Nineteenth and Twentieth Centuries* (5th edition), cc. 30 and 31.

T. E. Jessop: *The Treaty of Versailles: Was it Just?*

New Cambridge Modern History, Vol. XII, c. 16 (by R. Butler).

CHAPTER 15

POST-WAR EUROPE:
FROM VERSAILLES TO LOCARNO

A Period of Uncertainty

EUROPE between 1919 and 1925 bore a resemblance to the sea after the passage of a storm—the heave and swell looked so threatening and subsided so slowly that at times it required an act of faith to believe that the storm itself was really past. The situation in Russia, as we have already seen, remained at best uncertain. But it was notorious that in 1920 communism had advanced as far west as the gates of Warsaw, and the case of Italy, where fear of communism provoked a Fascist revolution in 1922, was the extreme instance of doubts and panics which were endemic in almost all the western countries. Franco-German relations provided another cause of uncertainty, since they became steadily worse until the French occupation of the Ruhr valley in 1923 fell short of a renewal of war only because it went unresisted. A few months earlier Turkey had shown how quickly a more primitive form of society could recover from defeat. The new Turkey, created by the nationalist revolution, took her revenge in a bloody campaign against the Greeks and required the peace treaty, on which the ink had scarcely had time to dry, to be redrawn to her advantage.

From what was said in the previous chapter, the reader might expect the League of Nations to have played a big part in any necessary redress of grievances. But this was not so, for two reasons. First, the League did not achieve at once a position of importance, and other means of international control were used; secondly, countries were ready on occasion to exploit the weakness of the new League organisation, by acting first and making later discussion practically pointless when the League was confronted with a *fait accompli*. Immediately after the peace settlement in Paris and before the League machinery had come into full use, there was a period of diplomacy by conference. This method of conducting international relations had been used intermittently during the nineteenth century. It had been used regularly from 1814–22 following the Congress of Vienna; it appeared again in 1856 and in 1878 with the Congress of Berlin, and in The Hague Conferences at the turn of the century.

The Great War produced frequent direct consultation between the main Allied ministers, these meetings being formalised in the Supreme Council of the Allies. During the Peace Conference in Paris, the Allied Powers acted first through the Council of Ten, later through the Council of Four. Afterwards the name 'Supreme Council' gradually disappeared, but the conference habit remained. To superintend the day-to-day work of executing the treaty provisions, the Conference of Ambassadors was employed, a body which consisted of the ambassadors of the Great Powers in Paris, together with a representative of the French Foreign Ministry. When the most important decisions were concerned there were conferences on the highest level, of prime ministers or other fully responsible ministers; a series of such conferences took place in London, at San Remo, Lympne, Spa, and Genoa. At these conferences decisions were taken and policy decided on matters of the first importance: reparations, the disarmament of Germany, the economic rehabilitation of Europe, Allied policy with regard to Turkey, and other matters.

As for the League, at least two of the most embittered disputes of these years centred round a direct defiance of the League's decisions. This resulted in a series of attempts to find a way of strengthening the League. At the same time, the Locarno Pacts of 1925, which closed this period of chronic unrest, were an attempt to exorcise war by the less ambitious method of limited regional agreements, in place of the action of a world authority such as the League had been intended to supply. Thus these were years of tension and disillusion. But they led to a short period of genuine peace, though one sustained by more prosaic and practical considerations than would have pleased the liberal idealists of 1919.

The Weimar Republic in Germany

Liberalism enjoyed one of its greatest and most evanescent triumphs in the constitution of the new Germany, which—so long at least as Russia remained beyond the pale—might be expected to give the tone to the political life of central and much of eastern Europe. The German revolution began, indeed, as a revolution imposed from outside, since the abdication of the Kaiser, which gave the signal for the automatic disappearance of the lesser dynasties, was forced upon him by the belief, which the governing class accepted, that the victorious Allies would only make peace with a republic. The majority socialists—that is to say, the majority group in the Social Democratic Party which had supported the war by its votes in the Reichstag—achieved office almost without an effort, and were duly confronted with the unenviable tasks of suppressing the attempted communist revolution and negotiating, or at least signing, a humiliating peace. The former involved two sharp bouts of street-fighting in Berlin, in the first of which the communist leaders, Liebknecht ('Spartacus') and Rosa Luxemburg were taken prisoner and murdered. In the second Gustav Noske, the strong-arm man of the trade unionists, enjoyed a complete triumph over the communists with the help of volunteer forces of ex-army officers. These, known as Free Corps, were spoiling for a fight in which to work off their feeling of disgruntlement at Germany's military collapse and to reassert their own importance by appearing as saviours of society. This was in March, 1919; the signature of the peace treaty followed, under protest and duress, in June. Meanwhile, a democratically elected constituent assembly had met at Weimar, and by August had completed and approved the constitution which is called by its name.

It was probably the most democratic constitution the world had yet seen, certainly in the case of a Great Power. The Reichstag or parliament of all Germany was to have full control over the Chancellor and other ministers, and was itself to be subjected to the control of the people. This was to be expressed on the most scientific principles by proportional representation in the elections, and by a referendum on any proposed measure whenever a third of the Reichstag or a tenth of the electorate so desired. A bill of rights ensured the fullest legal equality and liberty for every German citizen—freedom of speech, printing, and public assembly; religious freedom, based on the abolition of State Churches; economic freedom, in the sense that social services were officially recognised as desirable to give every man his chance in life. The problem of the state governments, which had done more than the Reich to hinder the growth of democracy in the past, was met by a general provision that they were to follow the democratic pattern now established in the Reich, and by a restriction of their powers.

Reich control of taxation was made complete, with partial control of education and the Churches; more important, the new Reichsrat, an upper house composed of representatives of state governments, could have its veto overridden by a two-thirds majority of the Reichstag. The states or *Länder*, as they were now to be called, were reduced to seventeen, chiefly by the amalgamation of the small Saxon duchies to constitute Thuringia; but Prussia continued to be nearly two-thirds of the whole. Lastly, a figurehead was provided for the new edifice in a President, who was required to govern through the Chancellor and ministers responsible to the Reichstag, though he had also exceptional powers to govern by decree in case of emergency. But even this last provision, of which the most sinister use was one day to be made, did not appear undemocratic when put in the hands of a President elected (for seven years) by universal suffrage, especially when the first President proved to be Ebert, a former saddler who had been the first social democratic Chancellor.

While the constitution was still under discussion, and long before the treaty was signed, the social democratic government had become a coalition with the moderates of the Democratic (doctrinaire liberals) and Centre (Catholic) parties. It was attacked from both sides—from the Left and from the Right. Of further communist outbreaks, the most serious was crushed when government troops entered Munich on May Day and the last among many more localised *émeutes* caused the government to get Allied sanction for military operations in the Ruhr nearly a year later. The extremists of the Right at no time accepted the democratic republic as a permanency. In March, 1920, matters came to a head in the so-called Kapp *Putsch*: Berlin was seized, for the purpose of installing a reactionary Chancellor of this name, by a formidable combination between disloyal elements in the new Regular Army (or Reichswehr) and the unofficial free corps. These latter the Government, having once used their help against the communists, had never dared to dissolve. The *Putsch* was defeated by a general strike, undertaken by the Berlin workers on behalf of the Government, which had prudently withdrawn from the city. But the Government on its return still did not dare to punish seditious movements of the Right, with the result that the ensuing election showed a fall in votes for the social democrats (or majority socialists) as compared with the independent socialists and communists. The socialists were no longer predominant in the coalition of parties of the middle view and middle class, from which came a succession of ministries to handle a problem which had now become more pressing than that of communism.

France and the Struggle for Reparations

In France, military victory had won increased respect for her republican institutions; and there was a new confidence in her *mission civilisatrice* both at home and abroad, which fitted in well with plans for the encirclement of Germany and the maintenance of a French military hegemony in post-war Europe. A start was made by a defensive military treaty with Belgium, signed in September, 1920, and by a more extensive alliance with Poland, the fruit of Weygand's historic intervention at the Battle of the Vistula, which resulted in French loans, French help in the construction of Gdynia (the new Polish port designed to supplant Danzig), and a direct military link evidenced in the placing of the Polish arms contracts with the great French armaments firm of Schneider-Creusot. A more sinister aspect of the same policy was the secret encouragement which the French gave to their ex-enemies, the Turks, against their former allies, the Greeks, as soon as the latter rebelled against French influence by recalling Constantine to the Greek throne. Nevertheless, the fruits of victory were in the main a disappointment for France, since Germany was left with a far larger population and a greater industrial potential than her own.

At the Peace Conference France had striven in vain to weaken her rival for ever by separating the left bank of the Rhine from the rest of Germany; the powerful industrialists of the *Comité des Forges* optimistically planned to control the Ruhr valley as well. In itself, the recovery of Alsace-Lorraine only accentuated the fear of a third German invasion, since iron and coal were concentrated so temptingly on the eastern frontier. In place of the amputation of parts of Germany, France was offered a joint Anglo-American guarantee of the new frontier. But this arrangement did not materialise owing to the repudiation of the peace settlement by the republican majority in the United States Senate and the refusal of the British Government to enter alone into any unconditional guarantee. There remained the safeguard of German disarmament and isolation. But in April, 1922, Europe was surprised by the conclusion of a Russo-German treaty at Rapallo; this in its secret clauses made provision for German officers to be trained on Russian soil in the use of forbidden weapons, such as military aircraft. It is therefore not surprising that the trend of French politics during this period was towards intransigeant ministries of the Right. The General Election of 1919 was won by the *Bloc National*, the first time that there had been an openly conservative majority in the French Chamber since the War of 1870. It was this parliament which refused the presidency of the republic to the aged Clemenceau on the ground that he had been too lenient towards Germany. He had already ceased to be Prime Minister, and in 1922 the most notable of his successors in that office was likewise ejected for his alleged leniency and replaced by the veteran Poincaré, who had already shown himself both as Prime Minister and as President to be a formidable and legalistic hater of Germans.

Hence the paramount importance attached by France during these early post-war years to the Allied claims for reparations from Germany. If paid, they would strengthen France, who it was agreed should get 58 per cent. of whatever amount was extracted; if left unpaid, they would at least weaken Germany by providing a reason for punitive action against her. The first demand was for £11,000,000,000, a fantastic total, to which the Germans returned a blank refusal; this brought them an immediate Allied occupation of Duisburg and Düsseldorf. Then in May, 1921, the Allies reduced their demand to £6,600,000,000, which was still more than thirty times as large as the war indemnity in 1871, but, what is perhaps more to the point, smaller than the sum the Germans were going to demand if they had won again in 1918.

At this point the German Government made some effort

at fulfilment, but since payment of such huge sums in gold was out of the question, they could pay only in goods or services. The French would not allow direct labour in the devastated areas of France, constituting one-tenth of the whole country, because it interfered with the employment of their own workers. Exports of commodities, such as coal, were criticised as interfering with British or French trades already established. And when the mark began to lose value under the strain, it was almost impossible to distinguish the operations of economic law from the operations of German financiers who, whatever the policy of their government, were seeking to wriggle out of their obligations. The situation was further exacerbated by the existence of inter-Allied debts, on the payment of which the United States, as chief creditor, was insisting firmly, though Britain, as the second largest creditor, offered to waive her claims both against her Allies and against the Germans if America would set the example.

In January, 1923, the Germans were again in default. The British, who saw in Germany a customer to be set on his feet again rather than a foe to be kept prostrate, refused to approve of any drastic action. The French, carrying with them the Belgians, then broke away from the British, with whom they had been keeping in step with increasing reluctance since the end of the war. French and Belgian forces entered the Ruhr valley, where they proposed to remain in occupation of the territory containing four-fifths of Germany's surviving resources in coal and iron until the Germans chose to pay up.

From January until August (1923) all the Ruhr was the scene of an undeclared war: the weapon of passive resistance— a general strike of all Ruhr workers, supported and financed by the Government in Berlin—was pitted against French military supremacy, rule by court-martial, and the importation of key workers from France. These replaced some at least of the 150,000 recalcitrants expelled from the industries of the Ruhr. In the end the French won a partial victory. Stresemann came into office to call off the passive resistance and undertake to pay what the French demanded—some reparations at once and much more later on, when conditions were normal (a Greek Kalends which never came). The strain of passive resistance had caused the mark to collapse, with or without the connivance of the German Government.

Monetary savings of all kinds (but not, of course, lands and buildings) lost their value: the thrifty German middle class as such ceased to exist. In November an Austrian ex-corporal, who was known as a demagogue in Munich, organised a *Putsch* there to make Ludendorff dictator. He failed ludicrously and expiated his offence by a few months' confinement in a fortress, where he wrote the first draft of *Mein Kampf*. From this the French, if they had cared to read it, could have learnt the unwisdom of a policy which had deprived the great German middle class of its moderating influence and desire for compromise. One further indication that France lacked the means rather than the will to maim Germany while it lay at her mercy was provided by an attempt to establish a separate Rhineland Republic. The separatist movement, supported by foreign money and the importation of hired agitators from other parts of Germany, was given a free hand in the French zone of occupation and finally, in October, 1923, recognised as an autonomous government. But when the French began to leave the Ruhr, which was about the turn of the year, the 'Republic' collapsed so ignominiously that it helped to swing the votes of Frenchmen, who hate ridicule and a fiasco above all things, against Poincaré and all his deeds at the General Election of May, 1924.

The Revival of Turkish Power and the Treaty of Lausanne

When German fortunes reached their nadir, those of their late allies, the Turks, had already revived. To British liberals, brought up to regard the final expulsion of the Turk from Europe as the consummation of progressive policy, the unexpected triumph of Turkey appeared to be 'the most humiliating incident in the history of western civilisation.' In 1921 the restored Greek King, Constantine, brought the Greek armies within fifty miles of Ankara. There they stuck for a year in a state of growing exhaustion, until in August, 1922, Kemal judged the moment was ripe to sweep them into the sea. Before the end of September the Kemalists had entered Smyrna; the Greek civil population, whose ancestors had lived in Asia Minor for centuries, was being expelled or exterminated along with the Greek Army; Constantine was in exile again, and his ministers were soon to be shot. The Greek collapse was naturally followed by a Turkish advance to the Straits, with the twofold object of ending the international régime there and crossing into Europe, where a new Balkan war might profitably have been started in alliance with Russia.

In this crisis Britain stood entirely alone. France and Italy had each already negotiated an understanding with Turkey and, in the case of France at least, provided munitions for the advance on Smyrna. They now withdrew their forces from the Straits while the British, without definite promises of help from the Dominions, remained at Chanak to face the Turks. War was narrowly averted, on the understanding that not merely Turco-Greek relations, but the whole of the provisions of the Treaty of Sèvres, should be reconsidered at a new peace conference with the Allies. The new treaty was signed at Lausanne in 1923. The Greeks surrendered, along with their vanished claims in Asia Minor, east Thrace and Adrianople and the islands of Imbros and Tenedos; the Allies abandoned the cause of the Kurds and of Armenia, which resumed its status as a Turkish province (apart from about one-third already retroceded to Russia); the Straits were still to be demilitarised and neutralised, but full recognition was given to Turkish sovereignty in Constantinople itself, where it had existed only on sufferance; and the ancient capitulations (under which foreign residents had been exempted from the jurisdiction of the Turkish law courts) were abolished. The Turks were the first of the defeated Powers to secure the abrogation of the disarmament clauses of the peace treaties, and although they made no attempt to revive the former glories of the Ottoman Empire by recovering the lost Asiatic provinces, the Treaty of Lausanne gave the new Turkish republic a firm base in Anatolia, from which Kemal, as leader or Ataturk, was able to develop one of the strongest of the new national states arising from the ruins of the old multi-national empires.[1]

The Fascist Revolution in Italy

A revival of a somewhat similar kind was taking place in Italy, fomented by the persistent Italian belief that her services to the Allied cause had been grossly underrated and even more grossly underpaid. She had been conceded the bare minimum of her Adriatic claims under the Treaty of London, but when

[1] See p. 289.

she pressed for Fiume as well as Trieste, her allies were ready to let Orlando quit the Peace Conference sooner than deprive the new Jugoslav kingdom of its commercial outlet. The lawlessness which was increasingly characteristic of Italian life was illustrated by the action of the poet-airman D'Annunzio in seizing Fiume in defiance of all authority. But this particular problem was settled in the main by a treaty at Rapallo (November, 1920), under which Fiume was erected into an independent state as part of an amicable rearrangement of disputed territories between Italy and Jugoslavia, and a few years later it was quietly partitioned between them. Unfortunately, Italy had other reasons for a sense of frustration. The war had cost her 600,000 dead and a huge Budget deficit: the former loss was perhaps offset by an addition of 1,600,000 new citizens, the latter not at all by a settlement which brought her no new industrial resources, no profitable colonial mandates, not even a protectorate over Albania.

The war policy had never gained the masses' fervent support. The reaction against it now found alarming expression in industrial strikes and localised insurrections among the peasantry, which were both the cause and the effect of steady depreciation of the currency and increases in unemployment. Communism naturally profited by such conditions, and in September, 1920, there were 600 factories with half a million employees under the control of self-constituted soviets. This particular phenomenon did not last for more than two and a half months, and in the course of the next two years conditions became on the whole less chaotic. But sporadic communist-inspired outbreaks still helped to crystallise a feeling which had been widespread in Italy for many years—that their parliamentary system, in the hands of professional politicians like Giolitti and their combinations of followers, manœuvring themselves into office and out again, had nothing in common with the English parliamentarism from which it was supposed to derive its inspiration, was a farce, and would never be anything better. This was a discovery, as we shall see, pregnant with momentous consequences for the whole development of Europe: but in 1922 the change in Italy was thought to be a mere temporary phase in the life of the body politic, and for some years later was judged chiefly by its effects on Italian foreign policy.

Mussolini

Benito Mussolini, the son of a blacksmith and a teacher, had reached the age of thirty and been imprisoned eleven times as a syndicalist agitator, when the situation in November, 1914, caused him to break with socialism through his advocacy of war against Austria. He founded his own paper *Popolo d'Italia* and was wounded in the war, facts which stood him in good stead when he afterwards started to recruit members for his *Fascio* (league or bundle) of ex-combatants. This was in March, 1919, when Mussolini was a supporter of D'Annunzio and also of many reforms of a democratic or even a socialist tendency, though from the first he was chiefly concerned to fight cosmopolitan communism by the watchwords of patriotism and order. In 1921 thirty-five fascists were elected to parliament, and what had been thought of as a strike-breaking organisation of a none-too-reputable kind, rather too handy with the castor oil and the blackjack, began to be taken seriously as a political movement with a future. The fascist squads fought groups of workmen in the streets and frequently attacked and destroyed houses and offices of labour organisations.

Whether Mussolini himself was ever anything more than a shrewd Italian peasant on the make, loud-mouthed and forceful among people who took him at his own valuation, but destitute of original ideas, is still by no means clear. What is clear is that the parliamentary system fell by its own inherent rottenness. In August, 1922, the fascists, who by this time had turned their gangs of street-fighters into the appearance of a vast, organised army, ousted a number of hostile municipalities and seized certain key points in order to defeat a general strike, which had been called to secure their suppression. Two months later they carried through a simple *coup d'état*. A fascist march on Rome was timed for the fourth anniversary of the victory at Vittorio Veneto. King Victor Emmanuel refused to allow martial law to be proclaimed in order to stop the marchers; the Prime Minister then resigned; and Mussolini, having repudiated his former republican principles, stepped into his office.

The most disconcerting thing about the triumph of Mussolini was that it illustrated the triumph of force. Italian democracy had failed; the method of discussion had proved ineffective. Both the fascists and their Left-Wing opponents were believers in violence: fascism arose to counter violence by violence. Francesco Nitti, Italian ex-premier, reminds us that Mussolini in political origin was a revolutionary, and traces the belief in violent action back to Marx's doctrine of revolution:

'That explains why not only the Red Revolution in Russia, but also the White Reaction in Italy, was the work of former revolutionary socialists, and why fascists are for the most part children of the same revolutionary socialism.'

Professor Villari, a strong defender of Mussolini's régime, naturally views the origin of fascism rather differently from the liberal ex-premier, but he too stresses the character of violent reaction:

'Fascism arose primarily as a reaction against the anti-national and anti-patriotic conduct of the Reds, aided and abetted by the ex-neutralists and by the supine attitude of the Government and of the majority of the ruling classes, who seemed ready to abdicate their power and to offer their necks to the hangman without striking a blow for themselves or their country.'

When a nation is divided and when the strongest elements on each side are committed to policies of violence, democracy can scarcely be preserved. The victory of one or the other of the extremes establishes a dictatorship. The victory of Mussolini in Italy was, unfortunately, to prove a precedent for further such victories in many parts of Europe.

Progress of the League of Nations: the Corfu Incident

It took Mussolini some years to feel his way to a complete abolition of ministerial responsibility to parliament and of the rights of a parliamentary opposition, but Europe had a foretaste almost at once of the methods of violence which were to characterise the dictators in foreign as well as in domestic affairs. The League of Nations during these years was gradually finding its feet. It had enjoyed an important economic success in the floating of an international loan for the rehabilitation of Austria, which involved a League guarantee and League surveillance of Austrian currency, banking, and taxation. One important dispute had been successfully determined between Sweden and Finland, the

strategically valuable Aaland islands being assigned to the
latter (with which they had been joined in the period of
Russian sovereignty), subject to special provision for demilitarisation and local self-government for the inhabitants, who
speak Swedish and inclined towards Sweden. Another,
involving the rival interests of victor and vanquished in the
war, had been settled with some approach to impartiality by
the line of partition which the League established to carry
out the plebiscite's verdict in the industrial area of Upper
Silesia, where both economic and national requirements
had to be taken into account. There had been only one definite
failure, and that in an obscure corner of Europe. Vilna,
the seat of the Lithuanian government, was a town with a
mainly Jewish population, inconveniently placed near the
post-war frontiers of Poland and Russia. It changed hands
several times, and was in effect allotted by the League to
Lithuania. Thereupon a Polish general seized possession and
the Lithuanian administration withdrew to Kaunas. The
League found itself unable to oust him; and, at the end of
two years, the Powers granted Poland a legal title to Vilna,
which Lithuania quite rightly refused to recognise. Rather
similar was the Lithuanian seizure of Memel, though here
the League secured certain measures of autonomy for its
inhabitants.[1] Mussolini was now about to take action even
stronger than that of the Poles; his conduct differed from that of
the Poles in that his defiance of the League was both official
and deliberate.

In August, 1923, four Italians, engaged under international
authority in delimiting the frontiers of Italy's somewhat
reluctant protégé, Albania, were murdered on the Greek
side of the frontier. Mussolini, perhaps in conscious imitation
of the Austrians after Serajevo, dispatched a thundering
ultimatum to the Greeks; and, when they replied as sub-
missively as the Serbs had done in 1914, he bombarded and
occupied the Greek island of Corfu. The Greeks appealed
to the League Council, where the Italian representative did
his best to veto any action (an ominous precedent for a later
generation!), and Mussolini defied the League point-blank
by announcing that, if the League intervened, his forces
would remain in Corfu indefinitely. The Council then

[1] See p. 241.

wriggled out of the difficulty by drawing up a plan of settlement, which was sponsored officially by the Conference of Ambassadors, a diplomatic body representing only the Allies of the war period, whose intervention Mussolini permitted—and with reason, for it promptly and peremptorily ordered the Greek Government to pay a heavy fine.

Attempts to Strengthen the League Covenant

In these circumstances, much importance attached to the efforts made about this time to strengthen the hand of the League against an aggressor. To some extent the strengthening of the League came about naturally as the war of 1914–18 receded into the background. The Conference of Ambassadors, referred to above, lost its importance as diplomatic business arising from the war was slowly wound up. Membership of the League which expanded from thirty-two original 'charter members' to well over fifty, included disinterested 'neutrals' like the small Scandinavian Powers, who set a fine example of League loyalty; and from 1924 onwards the Great Powers found it worth while for leading ministers to put in at least an appearance at the annual Assembly in Geneva. This practice might have proved to be the first step in forming a habit of deference to the collective opinion and wisdom of their smaller neighbours as expressed at Geneva. But the essential question remained: what precise obligations rested upon every member in relation to an act of aggression against any one of them? President Wilson had left the answer vague, because he argued that no one Power would be foolhardy enough to defy a combination consisting of every other Power.

However when the United States itself refused to join the League, when Soviet Russia (which was deliberately excluded) unexpectedly survived the civil war and Allied intervention, and when defeated Germany (likewise excluded) showed itself in many ways recalcitrant, the smaller Powers scented danger. There was a marked tendency to deny that a country could be automatically involved in hostilities by a League decision that a certain Power was an aggressor, against whom sanctions (punitive measures of an economic, or finally a military, character) had to be applied.

Two attempts were made to meet this point. In 1923 a Draft

S

Treaty of Mutual Assistance was circulated among members, proposing that, when the League Council declared a state to be an aggressor, the duty of taking military action against it should be restricted to states in the same continent. Some members objected to the wide judicial powers which this scheme would have conferred on the Council. But the decisive rejection came from Britain and the Commonwealth, which could not willingly accept a situation, in which the King would be at war in one part of his dominions and not in others, or alternatively in which Britain herself would have to shoulder a heavier burden than other Powers. In 1924 the problem was tackled from a different angle in the Geneva Protocol, unanimously approved by the League Assembly of that year and recommended to all member governments for their acceptance. The new proposal was to combine the three principles of compulsory arbitration, guaranteed security and a measure of disarmament. Aggression was to be made more unlikely by a simplification of the issue. Instead of the alternative forms of procedure laid down in the League Covenant, which even made it possible for a state, which had resorted without success to the prescribed machinery for settling a dispute, afterwards to go lawfully to war —instead of all this, there was to be one simple test of aggression: an aggressor was a State which refused to accept the settlement of any dispute by arbitration. In other words, whoever resorted to war would automatically put himself in the wrong. But if an aggressor, knowing that he would be convicted as such, did resort to war, then the Geneva Protocol prescribed the application of sanctions by all Powers, as laid down in Article 16 of the Covenant.

The Geneva Protocol, which had been sponsored by Ramsay MacDonald as head of the first British Labour Government, was rejected by his Conservative successor in March, 1925, not as a matter of party predilection but because the Dominions had made it clear that they could not accept an obligation to intervene if war broke out again in Europe. Since they had accepted an obligation similar in substance, as distinct from definition, when signatories of the League Covenant in 1919, this action gives a measure of the falling-away from the unity of wartime and the ideals expressed in the creation of the League. Their action was also a measure of the worsening of the European situation, which made the eventual outbreak of another war no longer an unthinkable contingency. The new realism had come to stay, so much so that the history of international relations between the wars can be summed up in a criticism of the Protocol which a French Canadian voiced at Geneva. 'In this association of mutual insurance against fire,' he said, 'the risks assumed by the different states are not equal. *We live in a fire-proof house, far from inflammable materials.*' But as regards the particular European contingency which was then to the fore in men's minds, an alternative solution was fortunately available.

The Locarno Pact

The French elections of May, 1924, had brought into office the *Cartel des Gauches*, advocates of a moderate policy at home and abroad. The fall of Poincaré was accompanied by that of Millerand, who had endeavoured as the President of the Republic to further Poincaré's aims. In the two years which intervened before the collapse of the franc caused the downfall of the government, Briand was able to give a new lead in foreign affairs. The Ruhr occupation was recognised to be a failure, though the adventure could not be finally liquidated by the evacuation of the last French troops until July, 1925. Friendly relations were established with the Russians; and France also followed the British Labour Government in supporting the Geneva Protocol. At the same time a scheme was devised to rid Europe of the nightmare of Franco-German quarrels about reparations, which had seemed likely to make economic recovery impossible.

The Dawes Plan, drafted by an American general, tried to put reparations on a business footing. This was the easier because inflation had freed German industries from their existing capital charges; a stable new currency, the *Rentenmark*, was based on the reorganisation of the bank of issue by the ingenious Dr. Schacht and survived with him the ups and downs of the next two decades; and, above all, the Americans were ready to provide a large part of the foreign loan needed to set the wheels of industry turning again. This done, it was a comparatively easy matter to collect moderate reparations payments, representing the rough equivalent of an agreed percentage of the national income, into a special fund in German currency, to be transferred by the Allied Powers into their own currency as and when the exchanges and balance of trade made it convenient. In the long run it was observed that German reparation payments were always less in amount than German borrowings abroad, so that the Allies, with America's help, were actually financing their own compensation for the war losses; but at the moment Germany's acceptance of the Dawes Plan made a genuine pacification seem possible at last.

Towards the end of 1925, therefore, the British Foreign Secretary, Austen Chamberlain, substituted for the universal guarantees proposed by the Geneva Protocol a limited, practical project, which guaranteed only the key frontiers of Europe, and guaranteed them without the participation of the Dominions. The Locarno Pact, initialled on October 15 and signed in London on December 1, provided a mutual guarantee of the Franco-German and Belgo-German frontiers by the United Kingdom, Italy and the three Powers directly concerned. At the same time a much more limited form of security was given to Germany's eastern neighbours by treaties between France and Poland and Czechoslovakia respectively, providing for mutual assistance in the event of German aggression; and arbitration treaties between Germany and her four neighbours in east and west made such aggression on either frontier more unlikely. Stresemann's Government, even at this hour of reconciliation, refused to guarantee permanent acceptance of Germany's frontiers in the east, from which the war of 1939 was actually to spring. But in the last days of 1925 the evacuation of the first zone of Allied occupied territory in the Rhineland seemed to show that the forces of the war-god were at last on the retreat.

SUGGESTIONS FOR FURTHER READING

A. Toynbee: *The World after the Peace Conference*.

J. Hampden Jackson: *The Between-War World*, Part I, cc. 2 and 3.

S. King-Hall: *Our Own Times*, cc. 9 and 10.

C. Delisle Burns: *1918-1928: A Short History of the World*, cc. 1-11.

H. C. Armstrong: *Grey Wolf* (Kemal of Turkey).

CHAPTER 16

THE LEAGUE AND THE DEMOCRACIES, 1925–30

The Improved Status of the League of Nations

THE Locarno Pact, as we saw in the last chapter, seemed to promise Europe a lasting peace because, in contrast to the Treaty of Versailles, this was an agreement into which Germany had entered voluntarily and which she could therefore be expected voluntarily to keep. The same consideration applied to her membership of the League of Nations. Briand intended it to be part and parcel of the Locarno arrangements that she should join and should occupy a permanent seat on the League Council to accord with her restored status as a Great Power. But the 'near-great' powers of Poland, Spain, and Brazil all put forward claims to a similar permanent seat on the Council, which delayed Germany's admission until September, 1926, by which time Polish opposition had been bought off by giving her a semi-permanent seat, while Spain and Brazil had resigned their League membership altogether.

In retrospect it is significant that power politics intervened even at this moment of idealist enthusiasm—the Poles, indeed, acted as they did because France had not considered Polish interests sufficiently in making the Locarno settlement—but at the time what counted was the fact that the League now included five out of the seven Great Powers. The readmission of Spain in 1928 made its European membership virtually complete, the only exceptions being Russia, which was still treated as a pariah, and Turkey, which had only a small part of its territory in Europe. Accordingly, from the European point of view, these years were a time when the triumph of democracy in the internal affairs of nation states had its counterpart in the increasingly democratic methods by which their external relations were regulated through the League. The small Powers believed that their sovereign independence was safeguarded and their right to influence world affairs beginning to be acknowledged. There was a spirit of optimism abroad in Europe—the spirit of Locarno.

EUROPE
IN 1925

272 THE EUROPEAN WORLD 1870-1945

Although to-day the League is judged chiefly by its failure to discharge its primary function, the pacific settlement of international disputes, it must not be forgotten that it had many other activities which were in full swing at this time. Annual reports from Powers which had been entrusted with colonial mandates were being examined by a commission of colonial experts drawn from states members of the League, though it was the Council which actually discussed their criticisms with the mandatory Power. Minority populations, for whose protection (except in Germany) provision had been made in the peace treaties, had their (usually ineffective) hearing before a committee of the Council. There was the administration of the Saar and that of Danzig, for both of which the League had final responsibility. Financial co-operation had resulted in the organisation of loans for the reconstruction of Austria, Hungary, Greece and Bulgaria, all countries which had been ruined by the war or the peace and were set on their feet again by League intervention. In 1927 a League economic conference launched a still more ambitious general project for reducing tariffs and other trade barriers.

Greater success attended the League's humanitarian work, since there was—on the surface at least—a unanimous wish to deal effectively with what remained of slavery and slave trading in backward areas of the world, the illicit drug traffic, the dissemination of disease, and the unregulated migration of refugees. This was work in which the representatives of small Powers with high ethical standards often took the lead, and this is also true of the International Labour Organisation. From 1934 its membership included the United States. Its excellent conventions constituted a veritable charter for labour, but each convention was accepted on an average by less than one in six of the governments concerned, and the most important of them all, the Washington Hours Convention of 1919, by no industrial state of greater magnitude than Czechoslovakia and Belgium.

The Settlement of International Disputes

As regards the settlement of disputes, the League registered progress along two separate lines. One was the growth in the practice of referring disputes of a legal character, such as those which turned upon the interpretation of a treaty, to the Permanent Court of International Justice at the Hague, with its panel of fifteen judges, which always included nationals of some smaller states. Its first important case had been to determine whether the treaty of Dorpat entitled the Finns to demand autonomy for the Finns of the Russian province of East Karelia, a matter over which the court decided that it had no jurisdiction. By 1926 there was a prospect of American adhesion to the court; and, although this did not materialise, the so-called Optional Clause, the signing of which pledged a state to submit all its international legal disputes, was accepted by the British Commonwealth (in 1929) and by some fifty other states, both large and small. Altogether, the Permanent Court settled about fifty disputes in fifteen years, but these were mostly semi-technical questions and not those in which the national honour or vital interests were held to be at stake. But in this more dangerous field the League also scored two small successes during these years, which at least entitled the world to look more hopefully to the future.

The first of these concerned Mosul on the frontier between Turkey and Iraq, the allocation of which was referred to the League under a special clause of the Treaty of Lausanne. The area had been in British occupation since the armistice in 1918 and Britain held the main interest in its oil wells, so that she naturally favoured its inclusion in Iraq, which had been assigned as a British mandated territory. The Turks on the other hand pointed out that its population was mainly Kurdish, not Arab. The League Council sent a strictly neutral commission to study the boundary question on the spot, but while its work was still in progress the Turks prejudiced their case by the savagery with which they suppressed a general revolt among their Kurdish subjects, many of whom took refuge in Iraqi territory. An Estonian general was appointed by the League to report on the Turkish atrocities, the upshot being that nearly the whole of the disputed area was allocated to Iraq. The Turks protested, but the Permanent Court ruled that under the Treaty of Lausanne they had bound themselves to accept the decision of the League Council, and in 1926 they finally gave in.

A much sharper vindication of the League's authority occurred in 1925, when the Greek Army crossed the Bulgarian frontier with the intention of avenging the murder of two Greek soldiers by Bulgarians. Bulgaria's appeal to the League resulted in a successful demand by the League Council for the immediate withdrawal of Greek troops, and Greece was subsequently required to pay an indemnity for their intrusion. This was in itself a perfect illustration of the efficient working of the League machine, spoilt only by the inevitable contrast between it and the Corfu episode only two years before.[1] Thus the League showed sufficient strength to prevent a war between two small Powers, neither of which had important friends on the Council. In the Mosul question also the League had had enough authority to enquire dispassionately into all relevant facts, when those facts happened to favour the cause of the stronger side in the main. By so doing it rendered the weaker side the service of enabling it to submit to the stronger, as it would have been forced to do eventually in any case, without an acute feeling of humiliation. The Concert of Europe, much less formal than the League and without permanent machinery, had achieved similar successes in the nineteenth century. To us, who know the sequel, the achievement may appear relatively small: but in the years 1925-30 it was quite reasonable to argue, as people did, that the League's present achievement, using only the technique of conciliation, meant that at a later date, when more firmly established, it might be able to apply the Covenant wholeheartedly, so as to judge and punish an aggressor in accordance with the famous Article 16, which provided for sanctions.

The Kellogg Pact

At all events, membership of the League was still expanding from the original thirty-two 'charter members' towards the maximum of sixty, though this figure was not actually reached until 1934. In December, 1925, the Council appointed a Preparatory Commission to pave the way for a final Disarmament Conference, which was to solve the problem of security by direct action. Although the Commission was delayed for years by unexpected difficulties, such as the realisation that a country's capacity for waging modern war depends upon the whole of its economic potential and not merely upon the

[1] See p. 264.

ownership of certain weapons, the League continued to throw up annually new projects for strengthening security by less direct means. The 1928 Assembly, for example, approved a General Act for the Pacific Settlement of International Disputes, which specified appropriate machinery for settling every kind of dispute: states might adhere to a part of the Act or to the whole, it being believed that the example of those who would promise to let arbitrators settle even non-legal disputes and disputes in which vital interests and national honour were at stake, would encourage other states to do likewise. Four small Powers alone adhered to the entire Act by 1930. In 1931 the British Commonwealth (except the Union of South Africa) followed suit, but by this time the general situation was deteriorating and promises were not enough to produce the sense of security. The same criticism holds for the most famous security project of these years, which grew out of a Polish resolution, to prohibit all wars of aggression, adopted by the League Assembly in 1927. The idea was unexpectedly taken up by the U.S. Secretary of State, Kellogg, to whom the French Minister, Briand, had made a separate proposal that France and America should explicitly renounce war as an instrument of policy in their mutual relations. The idea took the form not of a separate but of a general agreement, known as the Pact of Paris or Kellogg Pact, pledging signatories to the renunciation of war. The Great Powers, including Russia, signed in 1928, and the Pact was accepted eventually by sixty-five states, the only exceptions being three south American countries. Unfortunately, the exceptions allowed to the apparent meaning and intention of the Pact were more important—war was still to be allowed in self-defence, and the term self-defence covered action by the United States to uphold the Monroe Doctrine, or by Britain to defend non-British territory in which she claimed a 'special and vital interest.' Yet the outlawry of war, as it was rather illogically called, was in itself a step forward. No agreement had been accepted by so many sovereign states in the whole of the world's history; and the Kellogg Pact survived to give a legal basis to the charges brought against the German leaders after the next launching of an aggressive war in Europe.

Pacific Trend in Franco-German Relations and Elsewhere

In the narrower field of Franco-German relations, however, Locarno seemed to have borne real fruit. After long negotiations Briand and Stresemann arranged for the complete evacuation of the Rhineland in June, 1930, five years before the date fixed in the Treaty of Versailles. The evacuation was conveniently forgotten later on when Hitler argued that Germany had gained nothing from the Allies except by a threat of force. There was also a revision of the reparations payments, known as the Young Plan. This fixed the total amount for Germany to pay, limited the payments to fifty-nine years, threw on Germany the onus of arranging their transfer into foreign currency, and—though this passed largely unnoticed during this short era of prosperity—allowed Germany no escape-clause if world prices fell. The completion of the Plan was complicated by a quarrel between Britain and France about the demand of the latter for an increased percentage of the total immediate payments. The French demand was believed to be encouraged by Sir Austen Chamberlain's francophil tendencies but was firmly rebutted after the general election by the representatives of the new Labour Government at the Hague Conferences of 1929 and 1930. Stresemann's death in October, 1929, left Briand alone among the men of Locarno, but in the autumn of 1930 he still looked on events with the old optimism and offered the League his proposals for a United States of Europe. The League regarded them coldly, being engrossed by this time in the prospects for the assembly at long last of the disarmament conference. The preparatory commission had achieved nothing beyond a dummy scheme for limitation, with the actual figures left out, and even in the field of naval armaments, where the issues were simpler, the London Conference of 1930 could do little more than limit cruisers for three Powers (two of which had not reached the limit) where the Washington Conference[1] of 1922 had produced a genuine limitation of capital ships for five Powers. The shadows were lengthening in the east as well as in the west.

[1] The Japanese never made a full legal ratification of the provisions prescribing a maximum tonnage for individual battleships, which they secretly exceeded.

Internal Politics of France

As we have seen, the Locarno agreements between France and Germany were what produced a general atmosphere of pacification, conducive to the growth of democracy in Europe. This was further encouraged by the fact that democratic principles appeared to be firmly established in the internal affairs of these two dominant Powers—France dominant by reason of her military alliances with Belgium, Poland, and the so-called Little Entente (Czechoslovakia, Rumania, Jugoslavia), Germany by reason of her past greatness, present population, and prospective industrial leadership. In France the Left lost power in 1926 owing to its inability or unwillingness to impose drastic taxation to stop the inflation, which by this time had reduced the franc to one-sixth of its pre-war value. But its successor was a government of National Union, in which the stronger economic policy of Poincaré (who resumed office as Prime Minister) and his Right Wing supporters, including the big industrialists, was combined with the conciliatory foreign policy of the Left.

Thus the Maginot Line, with Poincaré's minister for war as its eponymous founder, was designed as a strictly defensive measure to make up for a reduction in the period of military service and the evacuation of the Rhineland. The Government came under heavy fire from the communists on the one hand and a resurrected royalist party, small but influential, on the other. It also fell foul of the people of Alsace, who, when the first raptures of reunion to the mother-country had had time to subside, showed themselves ungratefully critical of the centralisation which set strict limits to Alsatian self-government and the anticlerical principles which secularised their schools. Nevertheless, the stabilising of the franc, though at one-fifth its pre-war value, and the general prosperity of the country, helped by such realistic measures as direct collaboration between the French and German steel firms, made democracy seem as secure as at any time in the chequered history of the Third Republic: and in 1928 it scored a definite success when the Pope excommunicated the main royalist group. It may be noted, however, that the country from which Europe derived its conception of democracy still refused to carry it to its logical conclusion by conceding the vote to women. Though this had been approved by the Chamber of Deputies as early as 1923 it never became law, because the influence of the priesthood on women's opinions was still feared by the anti-clericals, who predominated in all the main political parties. It was also sometimes maintained that the vote was unnecessary because Frenchwomen, by the use of feminine wiles, had already complete control over their menfolk.

The Centre Coalition Governments in Germany

In Germany Stresemann as Foreign Minister was the dominant influence in a series of coalition governments, the heads of which ranged from Centre (Catholics and moderates) to moderate socialist. As in France, there was opposition both from the extreme Left and from the extreme Right, but it was opposition of a more sinister and more determined character. The ardent nationalists, who had organised the reactionary free corps in the troubled years of the peace settlement, now made full use of public meetings and of propaganda; so also did the communists, under the protection which German democracy allowed to all parties. But beneath the surface of party politics was the threat of armed violence to destroy the democratic machinery of the Republic. The extremists of both sides, Right and Left, were waiting for favourable circumstances.

On the whole, however, during the years 1925–30 circumstances were less favourable to extreme measures by Right or Left than they had been during the confusion immediately following the German defeat and than they were to be again in the 'thirties. Stresemann exercised a modifying influence at home and abroad. He, perhaps, realised that the weakness of Germany made a policy of partial co-operation with England and France imperative if Germany was ever again to achieve a position of strength and influence. At the same time Germany had not fulfilled completely the disarmament clauses of the Treaty of Versailles. The Allied Commission for carrying out the clauses had found secret stores of arms and reported opposition from the Ministry of Defence and Commander-in-Chief downwards. The army chiefs maintained contact with the free corps; secret arrangements were also made for building aeroplanes and for training in Russia.

In addition to the evacuation of foreign troops and the scaling-down of reparation payments, Stresemann's policy brought real advance at home. German industry was largely unharmed by the war, in marked contrast to that of France; heavy armaments were forbidden and this burden the German taxpayer therefore escaped; the inflation helped big business and wiped out debt besides enabling the exporter to sell cheaply abroad. Rationalisation and standardisation, together with the aid of foreign loans, placed German industry once more in a position near the front. The election in 1925 of the hero of the war, Field-Marshal Hindenburg, to be President of the Republic, against the candidature of a leader of the Catholic Party, for whom loyal republicans might be expected to vote, momentarily shook confidence abroad, but in the outcome did not alter the immediately favourable position.

Post-war Conditions in the Smaller Western Democracies

With France and Germany more tranquil than they had been since before the Great War, Europe as a whole enjoyed a period of comparative rest. Certain smaller countries of western and northern Europe continued to be centres of a really civilised life to which a high standard of living, a considerable degree of social equality and firmly founded democratic principles all contributed. If the position of the League of Nations and of European democracy depended in the first place, as it did, on the traditional democracy of the two Great Powers, Great Britain and France, these smaller countries of the north-west gave enthusiastic support. In these countries democracy was firmly rooted in the past constitutional development and the present social character of the peoples; it was not something new and experimental as in the states of eastern and south-eastern Europe.

Belgium had been most affected by the war. The greater part of her territory had been occupied throughout by the Germans. There was considerable unemployment in 1919 and the Government had to organise relief work. But the moral position of Belgium was strengthened by her gallant resistance to invasion in 1914; her territory was less devastated than that of France, and the peace settlement brought her the territorial additions of Eupen and Malmédy. In addition to her already existing colonies in the Congo, Belgium received a League mandate for the African territories of Urundi and Ruanda. In 1921 she completed her system of democratic government by abolishing plural voting, but to some extent Belgian political life was troubled by the Flemish question.[1] The term 'Belgian' covered both the French-speaking Walloons and the Flemish-speaking Flemings; and during the occupation the Germans had done their best to exacerbate this difference. To pacify the Flemings an act was passed in 1921 making Flemish the official language of administration in the Flemish districts of the country.   But the Flemish question still offered a weapon to trouble-makers, and, after the rise of Hitler, a pro-Fascist party in Belgium—the Rexists—tried to make use of it to gain support from Flemish nationalists.   But these efforts had little result.

Holland, Sweden and Switzerland were least affected by the war. All three states are stable, bourgeois democracies, with a prosperous and contented people. They were able to maintain their neutrality, and continue their industrious way of life, although the Allied blockade and German submarine warfare had interfered with their imports and exports. The general tendency after the war was towards a completion of the democratic system of government by making the franchise universal, though women did not get the vote in Switzerland.   In Sweden in particular great attention has been given to social reform, to housing, co-operation, aid to the aged and measures to prevent unemployment.   The people of Switzerland, of German, French and Italian stock, speaking their own languages and practising different religions, have preserved their democracy which is firmly based on local self-government, and combined it with a long tradition of neutrality. With the League of Nations headquarters in Geneva, Switzerland was, even more than in pre-war days, a centre of internationalism.   As a famous tourist resort in summer and winter, Switzerland impresses every visitor not only by its natural beauty but also by its busy industries, its wide use of hydro-electric power, its fine railways surmounting immense natural obstacles, and the clean and ordered life of cities like Berne and Zürich.

Norway with her important mercantile marine had been affected in two ways by the war.   High prices and increased

[1] See p. 141.

shipping charges caused a financial boom and shipowners became wealthy; on the other hand, 2,000 sailors lost their lives and many ships were sunk. During the ten years following the war Norway achieved a considerable effort of reconstruction in the rebuilding of her merchant fleet. With progressive governments at home, Norwegians also took an interest in the problems of the wider world. Represented by the famous explorer, Nansen, who was the head of the relief work during the Russian famine, Norway was active in the work of the League of Nations.

In Denmark democracy rests upon a highly successful system of agriculture. The great majority of farmers are owners of their land, and have thus every incentive to put their whole heart into their work. The Folk High Schools— schools for adult workers, mainly the farmers—saw their greatest days in the 'eighties and 'nineties, but were still an important educational feature. In 1933, the Minister for Social Affairs, Steincke, passed a series of acts collectively termed 'The Social Reform.' They completed the existing system of social services and covered medical aid, child welfare and poor relief; they also obliged everyone to join a sickness benefit society. These measures put Denmark among the most advanced states: few really poor people are to be found, for there is a remarkably high degree of social, and even of economic, equality.

The New States of the Baltic

Along the Baltic coast there was also a strip of territory where democracy appeared to have prospects of success. Estonia, Latvia, Lithuania, and also Finland were peasant countries in the main, though Finland has important wood working industries and both Tallinn and Riga have a strong commercial tradition as natural entrepôt markets for Russian trade. They were new countries, having gained or regained their independence as a result of the collapse of the Russian Empire in 1917 and the German Empire in 1918. They had been harassed and ravaged during the world war and still more during the revolutionary conflict which followed.[1] Moreover, in common with most of eastern Europe, they experienced a tremendous economic upheaval in the land

[1] Their independence was not finally determined until 1920, when four peace treaties were signed between the U.S.S.R. and the respective states.

T

reform of the post-war years, which broke up the great estates and replaced large landowners by a mass of peasant proprietors. Sometimes there was confiscation, sometimes compensation, but in either event much immediate economic dislocation and decline in the productivity of the soil. Nevertheless, in each of these countries there was a brief flowering of the institutions and culture which we associate with western democracy before the Second World War intervened to extinguish again the independence of the Baltic States, and imperil and impair the independence of Finland.

Western influences were particularly strong in Finland because of its past history, for centuries of Swedish rule had superimposed a small but active upper class of Swedish origin and culture upon the more primitive Finnish population of Asiatic antecedents, probably related to the Magyars and the Turks. What is still more important, those centuries had bequeathed a parliamentary form of government, the Diet of the Grand Duchy, which had never wholly disappeared under the Russian Czars: indeed, Finland in 1907 was the first country in Europe to establish women's suffrage. The three Baltic States now followed Finland's example in choosing a republican form of government based on universal suffrage, with severe limitations upon the powers of the President. In Lithuania, which had the poorest and most backward population of the three states, and was in addition the victim of the steadfast hostility of her Polish neighbours,[1] democracy received a check as early as 1926, when a military *coup d'état* gave dictatorial powers to the President and the Prime Minister. Elsewhere a general growth of loyalty to the new state, a rising standard of life (helped by new agricultural exports to the west), and the rapid decline of illiteracy all boded well for the future of these small but characteristically enthusiastic members of the League of Nations. But in the 'thirties they were to find no protection in the League, when Germany had become aggressively nationalistic once more and Russia reacted to the German threat. Latvia renounced parliamentary government for dictatorship in 1934, and in the same significant year—the year after Hitler seized power in Germany—the Estonian President assumed plenary powers in order to forestall a projected fascist coup. In Finland the

[1] See p. 264.

democratic régime remained outwardly intact, but an ugly scar was left on the national life by the Lapua movement in 1930, which repressed the Finnish communists (who had been numerous enough to fight a civil war in 1918) by methods of violence with the connivance of the 'democratic' authorities.

Poland and Its Problems

In Poland, now a near-great Power, political life was more disturbed. Poland by reason of its large population, its economic potentialities, its strong national feeling and living tradition of struggle for independence was a country stronger than any of the other new states which emerged from the collapse of the Central Powers and the Russian Empire. But otherwise the situation in Poland was in many ways unsatisfactory. Poland proved a source of trouble from the start. Not unnaturally in view of her previous history Poland was involved in quarrels with Germany and Russia, but she was also involved in disputes with Czechoslovakia and Lithuania. Polish troubles soon became European troubles, until the final catastrophe in 1939 when the German attack on Poland precipitated the Second World War. 'La Pologne, c'est le rheumatisme de l'Europe,' Briand had once said, aptly enough. Poland had started off optimistically with her new-found independence and a democratic intention not unnatural in the enthusiasm which followed 'the war to make the world safe for democracy.' Poland was proud of her connections with the west; she looked to France for political and military support, and her new democratic constitution was based on that of France. But Poland had problems almost insoluble in their complexity. The mass of the people—primitive peasants—was unprepared for democracy. The agrarian problem was severe: social life in the countryside was still marked by an almost feudal character, with Polish landlords living on a backward peasantry.

Most serious of all was the minority problem. In eastern Poland there were several million Ukrainians, and also white Russians, subjected to a police régime; of these minoritie some looked to Russia, and lived uneasily under Polish rul the Ukrainians had dreams of an independent state, a several attempts to establish one took place at the end of war.[1] There were, too, large German and Jewish minorities, the Germans in the 'Polish Corridor' and the Jews more widely scattered in towns and villages. In their traditional costume, the Jews were conspicuous in the Warsaw streets. Anti-semitism was strong. In a poor country, the Jews could not easily be absorbed into the community as has happened in richer countries like England and America. In Poland the Jews were clearly distinguished from the Roman Catholic Poles, and material success on the part of the Jews was bitterly resented. The Jews, as later in Germany, were easily made a scapegoat for national difficulties. As for the Germans, Polish-German friction was severe. 'Der Riss im Osten'—the rent in the east, by which East Prussia was cut off from the rest of Germany—was a subject of continuous nationalist propaganda; every visitor to Germany at this time was compelled to listen to German stories of Polish ill-treatment of the German minority. A common story was that of the German fire-engine refused permission by officious Polish frontier-officials to cross to the aid of a German whose house on Polish territory had caught fire. The Polish fire-engine failed to appear and the house burnt down, while the German firemen had to watch from the other side of the frontier. Doubtless some of these complaints were justified, but in a new country like Poland, where the Poles themselves had long suffered bitterly as a subject people, there was bound to be some trouble until things settled down. But things did not settle down.

To the western liberal, indeed, the years between the two world wars are a melancholy period marked by the successive collapse of many of the democratic experiments which originated in the nationalist enthusiasm of 1918. Even during this comparatively quiet period of 1925–30 there were already forbidding signs of what was to happen. It is not surprising that in Poland the democratic optimism of the time suffered a severe blow. In 1926, the popular hero, Marshal Pilsudski, determined to set up a stronger government than was possible under the existing party system. He ejected the Peasant Party Prime Minister, Witos, and also the President of the

[1] The racial character of Poland's eastern provinces was exceedingly complicated, and the territories have been disputed for centuries between Russians and [Po]les.

Republic. Pilsudski put in his own nominee, Moscicki, as President. Becoming War Minister and with an army of 250,000 men behind him, Pilsudski greatly strengthened the presidential executive power at the expense of parliament and himself exercised virtually the authority of a dictator. He remained thus, an 'unofficial dictator,' until he died in 1935.

Minority and Other Problems in the Succession States

In another Slav state, Jugoslavia, there were also disquieting signs. Here the basis of the problem lay in the uneasy union in this new composite state of the Serbs (of the former country of Serbia) with the Croats and Slovenes. The Croats and Slovenes who had previously been under Austrian rule were Roman Catholic and also more advanced than the primitive and Orthodox peasants of Serbia. There was also a minority problem: there were numerous Moslems whose religion was the result of the earlier Turkish conquest. A struggle therefore developed inside Jugoslavia between the demands made for local autonomy by the non-Serb provinces, which wanted to make the South Slav kingdom into a federal union of Serbs, Croats, and Slovenes, and the centralising tendencies of the government in Belgrade. The unrestrained violence of this conflict of social and political interest was illustrated by the murder, in the parliament building itself, of Raditch, the Croat peasant leader who opposed the centralised state. This happened in 1928. Parliaments exist for talking, not for shooting. When shooting takes the place of talking, democracy is at an end. The outcome was the establishment of a royal form of dictatorship under King Alexander. He was, as might be expected, an exponent of a strong central government in Belgrade.

Rumania had greatly increased in size as a result of the Allied victory, adding to her territory Transylvania from Hungary, Bukovina from Austria, and Bessarabia which had joined her after the collapse of Russia. She now found that she was faced with a lasting difficulty in that the new province of Transylvania contained a large minority of Hungarians. The peasants of Rumania were better off on the whole than peasants elsewhere in the Balkans because of the fertility of the land; the country also possessed natural wealth in its oil, although the oil wells were largely exploited by foreign interests. Government and administration were marked by general corruption and inefficiency, and the country seemed in that respect most unsuited to democratic methods of government. However, just as Bucharest claimed to be the 'Paris of the Balkans,' so Rumanians looked west for their system of government. Universal male suffrage was adopted at the end of the war. But parliamentary government worked very uneasily; there was pressure exercised at elections and the legislature was sometimes, as a result, boycotted by opposition parties. In the 'thirties a very violent form of Fascism grew up under the name of the Iron Guard. This led to a wave of violence and successive disorders, until its leaders were seized and killed and the King established a royal dictatorship. The underlying violence of Balkan politics was vividly illustrated in 1940 and 1941 by a new wave of terror let loose by the Iron Guard, after Rumania had come under German control. Order was at length restored by the army with German backing.

Another country which, although not a succession state, well illustrates the turbulence of Balkan politics, is Greece. In the post-war years Greece was first monarchy and then republic; then, after a plebiscite in 1935, a monarchy again. Periods of republican government were intermixed with periods when some strong-handed general set up a dictatorship. Political power alternated with exile.[1] The leading statesman Venizelos, several times Prime Minister, died an exile in Paris in 1936. In the same year, General Metaxas, called upon to become head of the government by the King, established a dictatorship which lasted until the war.

In Czechoslovakia, however, another of the new states, democracy did appear to be secure. Czechoslovakia was in most senses a western state. Material standards of life were more advanced, for this was the most heavily industrialised part of the Austrian Empire; she had an old-established educational system, and this was extended after 1918. Adult education was given special attention. Public libraries were set up, and lectures on citizenship organised throughout the country. The *Sokols* (gymnastic societies) also devoted some

---

[1] The outlook of the Greek on politics is admirably illustrated by the story of the Greek peasant who, told of the defeat of Mr. Churchill's government in 1945, commented: 'I suppose Mr. Churchill has now taken to the hills.'

of their time to lectures. Her national leaders, Masaryk (President, 1918-35) and Beneš, were good Europeans in that they thought of their country as part of the European states system and worked hard for the success of the League of Nations. The breaking up of large estates by purchase in 1920 had gone far to solve the land problem. There were minority problems—particularly that of the three million Austrians in the Sudetenland; there were also the Magyars in the south, and the Slovaks were not altogether content. But the minorities in Czechoslovakia were probably the most fortunate in Europe, and these problems could have been overcome in time. During this period they did not seriously complicate the affairs of the country itself or of Europe. Until 1938 Czechoslovakia was a bulwark of democracy in central Europe.

The Lot of the Defeated—Austria, Hungary, Bulgaria, Turkey

If the lot of the new states which had emerged triumphant and enthusiastic from the Allied victory was one marked by problems and internal rivalries which forced their governments, even in the heyday of democracy, along the road towards dictatorship, it can well be imagined that the position of the defeated nations was even worse. Indeed the fate of Austria and Hungary was deplorable. Austrian economy was completely disrupted: in place of a great Austro-Hungarian Empire there was now a province; Vienna was a capital city without a country; and the high tariffs maintained by the succession states made industrial recovery impossible. But the Allies were determined to maintain the separate existence of the Austrian Republic. Any union (*Anschluss*) with Germany, although economically it would have benefited both Germany and Austria, would have destroyed the political security of Czechoslovakia and offered a potential threat both to Italy and to the Balkans. Austrian independence was therefore maintained by Allied loans. The form of government was democratic. The Christian Socialists (Conservatives) usually controlled the government of Austria, but the city government of Vienna was in the hands of the Social Democrats. Vienna socialists carried out a policy of social reform; Vienna's social services and her large municipal blocks of flats, a challenging feature of a bankrupt city, were renowned all over Europe.

But the poverty of many people, particularly in the case of the old and those who remembered the pre-war splendours, was pitiable. In Vienna, men went down on their knees to beg from the passing foreigner.

Hungary, perhaps, suffered most of all the defeated countries. Here again poverty was extreme, and gloom hung over the once brilliant capital of Budapest. The Hungarians agitated vigorously for a revision of the peace treaties, and considerable propaganda was carried on with some support in a section of the British Press. The country remained in theory a monarchy. King Charles—the last Hapsburg Emperor— attempted to regain his throne, and made two appearances in Hungary in 1921. But he did not receive much support, and the Allies secured his ejection. The Hungarians were forced to agree to make no choice of a new monarch without Allied consent, but Hungary remained a monarchical state calling the head of its government the Regent. A White terror—as opposed to the Red terror—followed the brief period of communist rule in 1919, and Hungary reverted to its conservative tradition. The parliamentary system was of a restricted form; the ballot was open, not secret, except in the towns. Economically Hungary remained a country of large estates and aristocratic landlords. But for the decade after 1920 under Horthy as Regent and Bethlen as Prime Minister order was maintained and with it a degree of moderation. In the early 'thirties under the influence of economic depression and powerful fascist countries elsewhere in Europe, Hungary became openly fascist in character.

Bulgaria had, like so many of the countries of south-eastern Europe, its succession of parliamentary experiments, *coups d'état* and outbreaks of violence, leading almost inevitably to the re-establishment of a dictatorial form of government. In 1923 the peasant leader Stambolisky, whose Agrarian Party had triumphed at the elections of 1920, was overthrown and shot, and his parliament dissolved. The new government, representing the bourgeoisie and the military, had now to face a communist rising. A communist bomb outrage in 1925 killed over a hundred people in the Cathedral at Sofia. A dangerous growth of communism showed itself in the municipal elections of 1932. The threat from the Left provoked a reaction from the Right, and a *coup d'état* in 1934 led to a military dictatorship. The Government now devoted itself to preventing all forms of political party activity and to suppressing the Macedonian terrorists in Bulgaria. These were agitating for an autonomous Macedonia at the expense of the other Balkan states, and the agitation and frontier clashes led to international complications.[1] The Macedonian terrorists quarrelled among themselves, assassinated each other and even fought out one of their feuds in a street battle in Sofia. They were now suppressed. In 1935 the King asserted himself, and maintained henceforth what amounted to a royal dictatorship.

It was indeed strange that the one country in south-eastern Europe to show marked stability and powers of recovery at this time was the one whose decadence had given rise during the nineteenth century to the 'eastern question.' But the old Ottoman Empire was transformed into the Republic of Turkey. The national leader, Mustafa Kemal, put an end to the Ottoman sultanate (one of the oldest dynasties of Europe) in 1922, and followed it by abolishing the caliphate, the religious headship of Islam, in 1924. Kemal became President of the new republic, which showed itself intensely proud of its national independence, based upon its victory over the Greeks which had resulted in the Treaty of Lausanne.[2] Although the new state had been created by a Turkish national-ist reaction against the first peace settlement of the western Allies and their support of the Greeks, Kemal looked to the democratic west for the ideas which inspired his actions. Nationalist, republican, democratic ideas—these he took from the west. The language of the Turkish constitution recalled that of the French Revolution and the American Declaration of Independence of 1776. Internally, Turkey was transformed. Women were emancipated and unveiled, monogamy was enforced, harems disappeared, Turks were compelled by law (1925) to wear hats in order to demonstrate their equality with Europeans. For the fez, which the Turk now ceased to wear, had been a mark of racial and religious difference. The Latin alphabet was introduced in place of the complicated Arabic to make it easier for Turks to learn to write, and the

---

[1] See p. 273 for the frontier clash of 1925 with Greece which brought League of Nations action. There was a frontier dispute with Jugoslavia in the following year.

[2] See p. 260.

whole educational system was reorganised. Agriculture, banking and industry were developed by state initiative; a five-year plan began in 1933.

Turkey joined the League in 1932, and her policy of conciliation soon made her a pillar of stability in the stormy Balkans. As far as its constitution goes Turkey is a democratic state—every citizen has the right to vote. But Kemal exercised, in effect, the powers of a dictator. He realised that the Turks needed a strong leader while all these reforms were being pushed through. He was head of the one party, the People's Party, and so retained control of the parliamentary machinery of the state. But his dictatorship was educative: he aimed at developing the capacity of his people in the direction of democracy. This process takes time. Under Kemal, however, the Turks probably enjoyed a longer period of peace and ordered government than at any earlier time in their history.

A Period of Optimism

It was not only in the Balkans that government often showed a dictatorial character. Spain and Portugal were both under dictators, and more will be said of them in a later chapter. Here we must simply remark that even in the heyday of democracy in Europe dictatorship was by no means uncommon. But the direction in which the troubles and difficulties of 1925–30 were leading Europe was not fully understood at the time. These are seen more clearly for what they were by us who look back to-day and can see also the dire events which followed. At the time these years were on the whole a period of optimism in Europe. The great states were more tranquil; the troubles in some of the smaller states were either ignored or regarded as the growing pains of democracy rather than as serious flaws in the political life of the countries concerned. And, after all, disturbances in the Balkans were nothing new. But it is regrettable that no more interest and sympathy were shown for the new states of Europe. Sir Harold Butler, formerly Director of the International Labour Office, has well remarked that 'they were plunged into a struggle for survival before the mortar binding their national edifices had firmly set.' Neither Britain nor France worked systematically to help them. In Whitehall it was fashionable

to ignore them, and it was not until they were already weakened and threatened by the rise of Nazi Germany that their
plight was recognised. No British statesman made an official
visit in the earlier years. It was only in 1935 that Mr. Eden
went as a cabinet minister to Warsaw and Prague.

Men's hopes were centred on the new League of Nations.
Those who were young at the time grew up to assume that
the War of 1914–18 had really been 'the war to end war.'
War came to be regarded as a thing of the past. In the
League men saw the machine provided by human enlightenment to solve all the international disputes of the future.
To the soldier and statesman, General Smuts, as to the
scientist and writer, H. G. Wells, the League appeared as the
culmination of a process of social evolution. Man's struggle
towards political unity, it seemed, was reaching a final stage
in the creation of a new world system of co-operation. A new
era of peace, disarmament, and scientifically directed social
progress was to follow the out-moded past of ignorance, folly
and war. From this dream men were to be rudely awakened
by the events of the next decade, and the Americans, most
prosperous, most secure and most optimistic, were to be
forced to turn their eyes again to the spectacle of storm in
Europe.

Suggestions for Further Reading

Sir A. Zimmern: *The League of Nations and the Rule of Law*, Part III, c. 2.

Sir H. Butler: *The Lost Peace*, c. 6.

H. G. Wanklyn: *The Eastern Marchlands of Europe*, chapters on the various
    countries.

E. D. (Lord) Simon: *The Smaller Democracies*.

H. Seton-Watson: *Eastern Europe, 1918–1941*, c. 6.

T. L. Jarman: *Turkey* (Modern States Series), cc. 11 and 12.

D. Thomson: *Democracy in France*, Section 5.

J. P. T. Bury: *France, 1814–1940*, c. 15.

CHAPTER 17

THE AMERICAN INFLUENCE ON EUROPE

American Influence a New Factor

IN the period 1870–1914 the United States, hitherto indifferent to world affairs, had become another of the Great Powers of the world. When the campaigns of the Franco-Prussian War were being fought no one would have supposed that on the occasion of the next great struggle in Europe an American intervention would be decisive. In 1870 Americans were still recovering from their own bitter and destructive conflict, but the Civil War had decided that the States were to remain united and democratic in character: unity meant strength, political and economic, and America was thereby enabled to become in due course a powerful reinforcement to the democracies of Europe. 'Not by aggression but by the naked fact of existence,' wrote Oliver Wendell Holmes of the Americans, 'we are an eternal danger and an unsleeping threat to every government that founds itself on anything but the will of the governed.'

America, like France and Germany, was a latecomer in the field of industrial development. But by 1914 the United States had passed Britain as a producer of iron and steel, the basis of heavy industry, and was far on the way to becoming the paramount industrial country in the world. This economic strength, the final arbiter in modern war, has made America a force in world politics. Three thousand miles of ocean separate Europe from the United States, but as American economic resources developed so isolation gave way to contact, and contact grew into influence and policy.

Underlying Principles of American Foreign Policy

It has been said, indeed, that 'the traditional American foreign policy is to have no foreign policy.' The difficulties of communication and the different character of American life were real obstacles to close contacts between America and Europe. It was thus possible for the United States in

the early days to confine its attentions largely to its own problems and avoid entanglement in foreign policy. This was its
avowed intention; this, too, naturally resulted from the fact
that Americans had freed themselves from Europe, and
wished to build up their own way of life in the new world.
When once they had escaped from the wars and revolutions
in Europe, the people in America set to work to develop
the great lands and resources they found as they moved
westwards, and they had little need to worry over
the reports which reached them from the other side of the
Atlantic.

But in the end increasing wealth brought both the means
and the urge to expansion. From about 1890 onwards
Americans passed through a phase of rather aggressive
nationalism and imperialism. The growing surplus of wealth
at home which marked the development of American capitalism
increased the pressure for foreign markets and opportunities
of investment overseas. This tendency towards an American
expansion overseas brought contacts with various European
Powers, leading at times to clashes of interest and, in one
case, to war—with Spain.

Until the last decade of the nineteenth century American
expansion had been mainly internal: the frontier had been
pushed westwards at the expense of the Red Indians, and war
with Mexico had brought a vast accession of territory, including
Texas, New Mexico, Arizona and California (1848). The
geographical implications of such expansion included the
development of the United States as a Pacific Power, just as
her position on the Atlantic gave her interests in the Caribbean
and Latin America besides involving relationships with the
European Powers on the other side of the Atlantic. But
early American contacts with Europe were directed towards
establishing a complete political independence of Europe.
The United States had simplified the political pattern at
home by purchase (Louisiana from France in 1803, Florida
from Spain in 1819, and Alaska from Russia in 1867), and
thus removed from the countries concerned the pretext and
the necessary foothold for any intervention in the affairs of
the North American continent.

The Monroe Doctrine, asserted in 1823, became a fundamental principle of American foreign policy. It had been

evoked by the fear that certain states of Europe might send over troops to compel the republics of Latin America to return to their allegiance to the mother-country of Spain. In his Message to Congress of 1823, President Monroe included two declarations: that the American continents 'are henceforth not to be considered as subjects for future colonisation by any European Power'; and, that any European action 'for the purpose of oppressing' the states of Latin America or 'controlling in any manner their destiny' would be regarded as an unfriendly act by the United States. These declarations set the direction of future American policy: American independence of Europe and an interest in the independence of the neighbouring states of Latin America.

Isolationism, like the Monroe Doctrine, originated in the early days of the United States, and springs from the same basic desire for freedom and security as against Europe. Washington in 1796 had warned his fellow Americans against holding 'inveterate antipathies or passionate attachments' for other nations; Europe and America had divergent interests, and Europe was better left alone. In 1801 Jefferson added to this his view that the United States should strive after friendship with all nations but 'entangling alliances with none.' These warnings of the founders of the United States had great and lasting influence on American public opinion in regard to foreign affairs. Isolation remained until the Second World War a characteristic of the American outlook; Americans wished to avoid the danger of being drawn into European controversies which might lead to war. It was, indeed, not unnatural that the Americans should try to isolate themselves from the troubles of Europe: many of them had left Europe to escape those very troubles. Fresh opportunities offered in a new world. The Americans had the immense task of opening up their own continent and they wished to do so without being hampered by any entanglement in what must have seemed the remote and foolish quarrels of the continent they had left behind.

In effect, however, the American policy of the Monroe Doctrine and of isolation was made possible not so much by American as by British power. Walter Lippmann, a contemporary American publicist and student of international affairs, has summed up the position:

'During the nineteenth century British sea power had unchallenged command of the approaches to the Americas. In that era it was, therefore, possible for the United States to assume that Britain would provide the primary strategic defence by restraining the transoceanic powers, and that ours [i.e. the American] was the secondary obligation of defending the territories of the two Americas.'

After 1900, with the development of the German and Japanese Navies, British naval power became an insufficient safeguard of the American position. More and more the United States was forced to take an interest in the affairs of Europe and the world.

The Operation of the Monroe Doctrine

The operation of the Monroe Doctrine was seen in its most dramatic form in 1867, when the refusal of the U.S.A. to recognise the Emperor Maximilian, whom the French had installed upon the throne of Mexico, encouraged the Mexican resistance movement which overthrew him and had him shot at Queretaro. Manet's famous painting, based on careful study of the reported details of the execution, shows us the final scene. But Mexico was a border state and a state where European control had been established by very dubious means. Some twenty years later the meeting of the first Pan-American Congress at Washington may be held to mark the moment at which the Monroe Doctrine was extended to imply a 'natural protectorate' over Central and South America, on which Europe might well have set covetous eyes before the era of imperialism reached its climax. In 1895, during the Venezuela boundary dispute with Britain, the then American Secretary of State, Olney, put forward the twin propositions that 'any permanent political union between a European and an American state is unnatural and inexpedient' and that 'the United States is practically sovereign on this continent, and its fiat is law upon the subjects to which it confines its interposition.' As we have already seen, the dispute was settled in the end without testing the validity of either of these extreme assertions.[1] But when Venezuela again aroused international attention in 1901–3, this time

[1] See p. 99.

because she would not pay her debts, not only did Britain abandon the project of joint naval pressure with Germany in deference to President Theodore Roosevelt's remonstrances, but European financiers were left to draw the inference that the Monroe Doctrine covered a ban on European investment at any point in America where it might conflict with the interests of the United States. At about the same time the Alaskan boundary dispute showed the United States as determined to assert her wishes against Canada if the British Boundary Commissioner failed to yield to them, as he fortunately did. Since then it may be said that the Monroe Doctrine has been accepted by Europe to mean that in practice the United States is to be treated as paramount in the American continent, except in so far as other American Powers may be able to assert their independence without European aid.

Hawaii and Samoa

The use made of the Monroe Doctrine was not wholly imperialist, since it was used to safeguard the independence of small American Powers as well as to extend United States influence among them. Outside the American continent, too, United States imperialism was of slow growth, and it never challenged European rivals except in those Caribbean and Pacific waters where the intervention of the United States could be at least excused by the needs of defence. Her interests in the Sandwich Islands (Hawaii) dated back to visits by traders and whalers, and grew with missionary enterprise and the settlement of immigrants, American, Chinese and Japanese. A form of control was actually established in 1887, and yet it was not until July, 1898, at the end of the Spanish-American War, that they were definitely constituted as United States territory. Much the same is true of Samoa, where German activities forced the issue and the United States for the first time used her Pacific naval squadron to assert a position of equality. In 1889 British, American, and German naval forces assembled in a Samoan harbour all suffered by a disastrous hurricane; the fact of the assembly showed that the United States, with British support, was determined not to be jostled out of its remaining rights in the Pacific Islands. The result was the establishment of a three-power condominium, which did not work smoothly and was replaced during the Boer War by a straightforward division of the islands between America and Germany.

The Spanish War and the Roosevelt Era

Other minor American acquisitions of the same period were due to the desire to occupy key points in Polynesia in advance of the Japanese, whom they early regarded with suspicion because of the difficulties created by Japanese immigration in California. But in relation to Europe America figured as a non-imperialist Power, splendidly isolated, until at the turn of the century events altered her course. The pioneer stage of internal development was now completed, and she was ready to look abroad. The outbreak of the short war between the United States and Spain in April, 1898, had for its occasion the mysterious destruction of the cruiser *Maine* by a mine at Havana the previous February. Behind this there was a long story of misgovernment and insurrection in Cuba. Disturbances in this Spanish colony had always been a nuisance to its neighbours on the mainland. They became an increasingly serious impediment to increasingly profitable business relations, and finally caught the imagination of the newspaper-reading public because of the cruelty with which the latest rebellion among the colonists was being suppressed by a certain General Weyler. The fighting involved two naval actions, off Manila, in the Philippines, and in Santiago Bay, Cuba, in both of which well-found American fleets destroyed their opponents completely with negligible losses. Rather less easy were the military operations, in which volunteers played a large part, for the occupation of Cuba and the Philippine Islands.

Peace was signed at Paris in December, but the Filipinos then raised the flag of independence in a revolt which took the Americans a further two and a half years to suppress. America's permanent acquisitions by the war were limited to Porto Rico in the Caribbean and Guam as an outpost in the north Pacific. Cuba received conditional independence: that is to say, its foreign relations and attitude on internal questions of law and order had to conform to American wishes, failing which an American governor was installed on a temporary basis. The same goal of independence was kept in view for the Philippine Islands, where parliamentary government was

U

established at once, with generous representation for the uncivilised and rebellious native population.

The biggest results lay in the impetus the war gave to the emergence of the United States as a major factor in world affairs. The Kaiser reacted by trying to work up a European combination to defend Spain. Austria and the Pope were approached. But these efforts did not stop the United States. The war foreshadowed the alignment with Britain against Germany, when in Manila Bay the British naval squadron interposed itself between the Americans and the Germans, who took up a threatening attitude when they saw the chance of acquiring the Philippines slipping from their grasp. Joseph Chamberlain, apostle of British imperialism, welcomed the possibility that 'the Stars and Stripes and the Union Jack should wave together over an Anglo-Saxon alliance.' More immediately, the conquest of the Philippines confirmed the American interest in the fate of China. The war as a whole quickened interest in naval matters, underlining the lessons which Admiral Mahan was teaching at this time about the influence of seapower on history and rendering the upkeep of a large navy not uncongenial to a people to whom military conscription or even the formation of a large professional army was quite abhorrent. By 1900 the United States was the third naval power in the world: the Germans liked to think of it as a new rival for Britain, but it was a truer appreciation of the position which led the British to set aside America in assessing the two-power standard, that is, in making sure that the Royal Navy was stronger than its two largest potential enemies.

Then the assassination in 1901 of President McKinley unexpectedly brought into power the Vice-President, Theodore Roosevelt, the hero of the campaign in Cuba, the idol of the imperialists, and more of a man of action than any president had been since the civil war. He was confirmed in office at the presidential election of 1904, making 1901-8 the Roosevelt era. In it the Panama Canal negotiations exhibited the strength of the United States on the American continent and the Treaty of Portsmouth (New Hampshire) its emergence on the world stage and admission to full membership of what had been the Concert of Europe. In the time of the Frenchman de Lesseps' attempt to build the canal the need for it was purely commercial; now Roosevelt wanted also to be able to move warships for the easier protection of his country's growing interests in either ocean. He was greatly helped by the new willingness of Britain to cancel an agreement dating from 1850, by which the canal was expressly forbidden to be placed under the control of any single Power, and the new Hay-Pauncefote Treaty was quickly followed by the buying-up of the French Panama Canal company's concessions. But the State of Colombia still refused to cede the strip of territory through which the canal was to be cut. Whereupon Roosevelt, in 1903, taking a leaf out of the book of the British chartered companies in Africa, arranged an independence movement in the appropriate area, whereby a new State of Panama was carved out of Colombia, which at once received United States recognition, and immediately transferred the canal zone. Formidable natural obstacles had still to be overcome, and it was not until 1914 that the canal was opened. The negotiations in 1905 at Portsmouth, New Hampshire, had no such dramatic quality, but they were a complete success.[1] The negotiations also prepared the way for the less public, but hardly less important, intervention by Roosevelt, based on his personal friendship with the German Emperor, to get the Moroccan question brought before the Algeciras Conference of 1906.

America as a Pacifying Influence in World Affairs

The cruder and more boisterous form of imperialism, associated with the easy triumphs of the Spanish War, did not outlast Theodore Roosevelt's presidency, though Wilson's intervention in Mexico a few years later showed the influence on American foreign policy of powerful business interests, which to an increasing extent sought to make alien fields of investment safe for exploitation. In the main, however, the United States figured in the Concert as a pacifying influence. Thus in 1899 it was the American Secretary of State, Hay, who formulated the so-called 'Open Door' policy for China— the principle that foreign intervention should be limited to securing the same trade facilities for all the Powers, instead of trying to carve China up into areas of exclusive privilege for particular Powers. This policy, which was backed up

[1] See p. 111.

by Britain, was obviously advantageous to the two Powers
which had the best developed commerce; but it was also a
bold attempt to stop the drift towards a partition. At the
Algeciras Conference, again, American influence was exerted
to prevent a partitioning of Morocco, much to the surprise
and chagrin of the Kaiser. Peaceful inclinations are also
indicated by the participation of the United States in the
Hague Conferences of 1899 and 1907.[1] The Carnegie
endowment, founded the year before the second conference
met at The Hague, is only one of a number of important projects started by wealthy Americans to conduct propaganda, based on accurate information, for the cause of world
peace.

At the second conference she was joined by other American
states; they made one specific addition to the general programme—an agreement, sponsored by Argentina with obvious
reference to the recent Venezuela episode, that the use of force
to collect international debts was contrary to international
law except in a case where payment of a claim approved by
international arbitration had been refused.   At this conference which chiefly elaborated the laws of war, America
championed the doctrine of the freedom of the seas, that is,
free passage for neutral shipping in time of war, which Britain,
who regarded an unrestricted blockade as her most effective
method of warfare, steadily refused to accept.

A Rival to the European Powers in World Trade

The freedom of the seas was an old issue, one of the prime
causes of the war of 1812 with Britain, but its enhanced
importance during the period of American neutrality in the
war of 1914–18 may serve to remind us that America's
influence on Europe was economic as well as political. Between
1850 and 1900 agricultural products and raw materials
(grain, meat, cotton) formed about four-fifths of American
exports and effected a social transformation in Europe,
wherever the tariff was insufficient to exclude them.   The
decline of high farming in England, the resort to co-operative
marketing of dairy produce in Denmark, the keeping down of
the peasant standard of life in less enterprising arable regions,
the growing importance of agricultural science in France and

1 See pp. 176–8.

Germany—all have their roots in the transformation of the American Middle West. But in the new century there was a turn-over to semi-finished and finished exports, such as rails and machinery. The proportion of the total American output which went abroad was not more than 8 or 9 per cent., but the Homeric battles for markets fought by gigantic combinations like Standard Oil, the American Tobacco Company, and the U.S. Steel Corporation had much to do with the growth of trade cartels in Europe, which in many cases became world-wide in 1919. It was also significant of the coming change in the balance of power that by 1913 the United States was taking over the position which Britain had held throughout the preceding century as the dominant commercial influence in Latin America, especially in Central America and Brazil. The total British investment in South America was still twenty times that of the United States, which was also exceeded to a much smaller extent by France and Germany. But the tide was beginning to turn: the United States could now supply the current requirements of her neighbours, while superfluous U.S. capital invested in Europe rose from $10,000,000 to $200,000,000 between 1900 and 1912.

Impact of Emigration to America on European Life

But this huge exploitation of America's natural resources, which provided the raw materials, the manufactures, and ultimately the capital for export, was itself the result of an importation of human material, the social importance of which can hardly be exaggerated. Between 1865 and 1900, 13,250,000 immigrants entered the United States from Europe, to which the following decade added a veritable tidal wave of 8,200,000 persons. That final decade was likewise the period of most rapid immigration into Canada, where the creation of the new provinces of Alberta and Saskatchewan proclaimed the great northward extension of the cultivable area for wheat; and it was in the two decades after 1890 that South America began to attract her two main streams of modern European immigrants—the Italians of Argentina and the Germans in the San Paulo state of the federal republic of Brazil. The United States, however, remained the great attraction because of the political freedom associated with

the very name of the great republic, because of the almost
infinite variety of opportunity which its development offered,
and because immigrant tended to follow immigrant, long
after the exhaustion of the supply of free land along the
westward-moving frontier of cultivation had destroyed what
was originally the great incentive. In 1906 the exclusion
of further Japanese settlers from the Pacific coast, and the
introduction of a language test for naturalisation, showed that
the American public had awoken to a change in the national
origins of immigrants—the British Isles, for instance, contributed 18 per cent., Russia and south Europe 50 per cent.,
where the corresponding percentages a generation earlier
had been 45 and 1·1. Restriction of entry was in the air,
but it did not take effect seriously until after the interruption caused by the First World War. Meanwhile, what
had been the effects on Europe of this, America's greatest
influence?

The economic life of Europe profited by the remittances
which passed from emigrants to dependants and connections
left behind and by the introduction of small sums of capital by
the homesick, who saved to return and die in the familiar
surroundings of Italy or Greece or the stony Balkan mountain-
side. It also profited more regularly and substantially from
the fact that emigration provided an automatic safeguard
for overpopulated territory. Politically, Europe gained a
safety-valve for political persecution: Russian anti-Semitism
sent the Jews to New York, German liberals and socialists
founded a more congenial fatherland by the Great Lakes,
and the Irish brought the tale of their wrongs to enliven the
local politics of all the larger cities. The grievances of oppressed nations and classes acquired, moreover, a new dignity
and importance from the fact that meetings could be held
and subscription lists filled in security overseas: from Sinn
Fein to Bolshevism each European movement was helped
by its exiles. Americans of the older stocks often deplored,
and did what they could to discourage, this diversion of
interest in the minds of newcomers most of whom had taken
American citizenship. But in the long run it meant the acquisition by the people of the United States as a whole of at
least a nodding acquaintance with those Polish, Italian,
Baltic, and above all Balkan problems, to the solution of which

they were within a few years to be compelled willy-nilly to contribute.

Beginnings of American Cultural and Social Influence

With the political development of the United States and the vast expansion of her economic resources during the period well called 'the gilded age,' Americans began to exercise a certain cultural influence on Europe. An increasing give-and-take between American and European culture grew up. During the nineteenth century and the early years of the twentieth, the United States was a great 'melting pot' into which the immigrants from the many races of Europe were poured and from which has been created the American people. But Americans are in the main 'transplanted Europeans,' and it was in a sense an English culture which flowered during the nineteenth century in New England. The common language and to a large extent the common literature of the Americans, as well as their democratic system of government, have brought the United States into cultural contact with western Europe. The American-born writer, Henry James, in a letter to his philosopher brother, William James, in 1888, complained of any implication that the British and Americans had separate cultures. One, he maintained, was a continuation of the other, both being rooted in the culture of western Europe.

Contacts were becoming closer. Europeans were visiting America, and Americans were visiting Europe. In the year 1888, there appeared James Bryce's book *The American Commonwealth*. In this a great English scholar, with the old culture of Europe behind him, turned his mind to the study of the new American democracy. In 1907 Bryce went as ambassador to the United States and worked with marked success. The United States had already sent one of its outstanding literary figures as an ambassador to Europe. James Russell Lowell was minister to Spain from 1877–80 and minister to England from 1880–5. He was a poet and man of letters who had followed Longfellow as professor of modern languages at Harvard. Lowell proved popular in European society and helped to interpret America to Europe both through his personal relationships and also by such formal addresses as that of 1884, 'On Democracy.' During the century the famous men of letters in America had close contacts with Europe.[1] Longfellow had studied in France, Spain, and Germany. He toured Europe in 1868-9, received honorary degrees at Oxford and Cambridge and had a private audience with Queen Victoria. He was, on his death, honoured with a bust in Poets' Corner in Westminster Abbey. His work was popular, was translated into European languages and helped to bring some knowledge of American culture to Europe. Emerson visited England and France early in life and was in Europe again in 1872. Mark Twain carried the humour and the anecdotes of American pioneering days to a wide audience on his world lecture tours. More unconventional in the heyday of American capitalism was *Progress and Poverty*, by Henry George, which put forward as a solution of the social problem the idea of a single tax on land values. This was in 1879. In 1908 Jack London in *The Iron Heel* foreshadowed the rise of fascist dictatorship, and also forecast a war between Germany and America—though he was far from the mark in describing the calling-off of the war by a general strike of workers in the United States and Germany. Both these critics of existing society had a large following of readers in Europe as well as in America.

But in spite of the black spots—for America had its poverty even in those gilded days of rapid expansion—industrial development had created a fabulously wealthy plutocracy, which formed influential links with the older aristocracies of Europe. In 1874 Jennie Jerome, daughter of a Wall Street broker, married Lord Randolph Churchill; the stately Lord Curzon maintained his state by marrying two American heiresses in succession; and one of the New York plutocrats, William Waldorf Astor, came himself to England and received an English peerage.

The First World War:
Turning Point in American Relations with Europe

American intervention in the First World War marked a real turning point in the relations of the United States with Europe. Previously Europe had influenced America more

---

[1] See for examples of such relationships, *The Correspondence of Thomas Carlyle and Ralph Waldo Emerson* and *Letters of John Ruskin to Charles Eliot Norton*, both edited by Charles Eliot Norton.

than America had influenced Europe; Americans had in the main sprung from Europe, and they looked back to Europe as the source of their cultural life. To some extent Americans depended on Europe, economically as well as culturally; before 1914 America was a debtor nation, but by the end of the war she had paid off her debts and become a creditor. The part taken by the United States in the war and the vast economic strength of the nation henceforth made American influence in Europe considerable. Potentially American influence was much greater still; there was no doubt after 1918 that the United States had emerged as a great world Power and that American reactions must be taken into account in dealing with European problems. But Americans themselves were divided: some were for playing a part in the world scene, others were for isolation. American policy vacillated in the post-war years.

When the United States entered the war in 1917 she cut adrift temporarily from her traditional policy of isolation. But she declared war because Germany was infringing upon two other principles of her foreign policy: unrestricted submarine warfare destroyed her freedom of the seas; the German proposal to Mexico of an alliance against the United States in the event of war was a blow at the Monroe Doctrine. The Americans, however, also entered upon war in the spirit of a crusade. When President Wilson spoke to Congress on April 2, 1917, he said:

'. . . The world must be made safe for democracy . . . the right is more precious than peace, and we shall fight for the things which we have always carried nearest our hearts, for democracy, for the right of those who submit to authority to have a voice in their own Governments, for the rights and liberties of small nations, for a universal dominion of right by such a concert of free peoples as shall bring peace and safety to all nations and make the world itself at last free. To such a task we can dedicate our lives and our fortunes, everything that we are and everything that we have. . . .'

This was the voice of a great American calling upon his countrymen to redress the wrongs of Europe. Wilson said again and again that the war was a crusade of the democracies against the autocracies. He was enabled to take this view by the overthrow of the Czardom in Russia.[1] The United States' intervention was decisive for the Allied cause. The great economic resources and the fresh American troops put new heart into the Allies.

Wilson also hoped to make a just and lasting peace and to create a League of Nations which would ensure world order in future. He came to the Peace Conference almost like a messiah. The League of Nations was largely his idea; he struggled for it, and insisted on making its constitution an integral part of the peace treaties.[2] But he failed—partly for reasons of failing health and of personal obstinacy—to carry the day at home. Large numbers of the American people felt that their country had done well to repudiate the Paris settlement: repudiation seemed to free them from responsibility for Europe's pressing problems. For Europe it was a tragedy that the most powerful and disinterested of nations had retired into isolation. In spite of the failure over the peace, however, America's share in the victory had finally established her place among the Powers, and her influence remained a strong force in the background to make itself felt whenever the Americans chose. Never again could the United States live in anything like real isolation in spite of all the vacillations of official policy. Her seat at the council table might often be empty but it could never be ignored.

Relief Work in Europe

During the war and the immediate post-war years America exercised a direct and invaluable influence in Europe through the organisation of large-scale relief work. The work, carried out with the backing of the government while still neutral, was organised by an energetic and able engineer of Quaker stock, Herbert Hoover, afterwards to become President of the United States (1929–33). The first task was to provide for the people of occupied Belgium and northern France. What was achieved was remarkable; the Allies were persuaded to open their blockade, the Germans to give guarantees against

[1] See Morison and Commager, *The Growth of the American Republic*: '. . . When Russia went republican, just as we were about to enter the war, Wilson found it easy to identify the cause of the Allies with that of democracy and of civilisation itself . . . the last taint of autocracy in the Allied cause disappeared.'

[2] See p. 250.

interference, and food supplies were safely brought through mine-sown waters and along obstructed canals and passed through the German lines. The organisation was given special diplomatic rights and obligations; an appeal was made to the charity of all the world and a committee of Americans, Belgians and Germans supervised distribution, while communal committees were set up in Belgium and northern France. For purpose of liaison with governments, offices were established in Washington, London, Paris and Brussels. After America's entry into the war, the work went on except that Americans could not now operate behind the German lines, and that part of the common task was undertaken by a neutral, Spanish-Dutch, committee. During the whole period of hostilities, until the Belgian and French Governments took over their own food responsibility in May, 1919, the Commission brought in food and helped to preserve the lives of the people. Of the total funds made available more than half came from the United States.[1]

In November, 1918, new tasks awaited Hoover. Millions of people needed feeding in central and eastern Europe. Agricultural production had been dislocated by war and revolution, and famine was imminent. Hoover organised the American Relief Administration, and took temporary control in parts of Europe of railways, and of telegraph and telephone lines. Food was brought in great quantities to Europe from overseas—two-thirds of it from the United States to a value of $870,000,000. It had to be distributed in twenty-one countries. It was paid for in cash in the case of the ex-enemy countries (except Austria); credit arrangements were made for delivery to the Allied countries; and the newly-created states received help in the shape of long-term loan or outright gift.

The official American and other Allied relief organisations came to an end in 1919 with the signing of peace. But Hoover carried on with a new private organisation, also called the American Relief Administration, and mass-feeding of children was continued in eastern Europe and in Germany. It is calculated that about 8,000,000 children benefited.

But the greatest task for American relief lay in Russia.

[1] See G. I. Gay, *Statistical Review* (Commission for Relief in Belgium: Herbert Hoover, Chairman).

Hoover was aware of the menace of widespread famine there and had made efforts to organise relief in 1919 and 1920. It proved impossible to arrange an agreement between the Russian and the western governments. By 1921 famine was actually prevalent in south Russia, especially in the Volga valley. The newspaper, *Pravda*, admitted famine among a population 'of about 25,000,000.' At last the communists overcame their scruples about asking for help from capitalist governments, and the internationally-known writer Maxim Gorki was allowed to issue an appeal in the Press (July 13, 1921):

> 'I ask all honest European and American people for prompt aid to the Russian people. Give bread and medicine.'

This time agreement was reached and Hoover brought relief on a vast scale. A small body of Americans supervised the Russian relief workers; food, seed grains, and medical supplies were hurried in under conditions of hardship, danger and every kind of difficulty. The total value of American relief to Russia came to about $60,000,000. The U.S. Government made a large contribution to this amount, and many voluntary organisations assisted, especially the Society of Friends. Between 1921 and 1923 millions of Russian peasants had cause to thank the goodwill of Americans.[1]

Restriction of Immigration

But if in the sphere of relief work American energy and generosity were of great assistance to Europe, in another sphere American action was harmful. The years 1921 and 1924 saw the passing of legislation to limit the number of immigrants: quotas were fixed. During the nineteenth century the movement of people from Europe to America had stimulated the development of America, but had also provided a safety-valve for the pressure of population in Europe. After the war Americans felt that too many aliens were coming in, that they could not be Americanised fast

---

[1] The full story of American relief in Russia is told in H. H. Fisher, *The Famine in Soviet Russia, 1919–23*. Michael Asquith, *Famine (Quaker Work in Russia, 1921–23)*, describes the work of the Quaker teams, British as well as American. The International Red Cross assisted in forming an International Russian Relief Committee, but the American effort was by far the biggest.

enough, that they might have the effect of lowering wages and the standard of life, and also that the larger number of aliens was coming from the more backward parts of Europe. The following table shows the total immigration (from all parts of the world) in certain decades, the parts of Europe from which immigrants came, the effects of the law in reducing immigration and also the selective operation of the reduction:

	Total immigrants into U.S.	From northern and western Europe	From southern and eastern Europe
1871–80 ..	2,812,191	2,080,266	181,638
1901–10 ..	8,795,386	2,007,119	6,128,897
1921–30 ..	4,107,209	1,281,650	1,196,203

Thus immigration was radically cut down; it was cut still further during the depression years of the 'thirties. This fell particularly hardly on some of the poorer European countries. From Italy, for example, immigrants drop from 265,542 in 1913 to 4,245 in 1931. Restriction meant not only the closing of the safety-valve for over-population but also limitation to further growth in the volume of remittances which Italians in the U.S. sent home. Thus legislation in America could add to the difficulties of Europe.

Allied War Debts to the U.S.

In the Allied war debts to the United States there was an outstanding subject of contention between Europe and America. The war left behind it a vast legacy of debt. Great Britain had loaned large sums to Russia, France, Italy and the other Allied countries. While America was still neutral Great Britain had been faced with exchange difficulties in purchasing from the United States, but managed to finance her greatly expanded needs by payment in gold, loans from American nationals, and the sale of British-held American securities through Morgans of New York. After the United States entered the war the American Government arranged loans to the Allies, including Great Britain, totalling about $10,338,000,000. Were these great debts to be paid and, if so, how? Not unnaturally Allied answers to these questions diverged sharply. Great Britain proposed a general cancellation of the inter-Allied war debts; she would give up her claim to payment from the European debtors, if the United States would do the same with the debts due to her from those countries and from Britain.

Many Europeans and some Americans thought that the United States, having entered the war late and suffered relatively few casualties, should wipe off the debts and regard such action as a contribution to the common cause. Economically, too, the United States had benefited during the period of her neutrality by being able to pay off her debts when Great Britain realised securities, by the increase of prices caused by enlarged Allied demands for her goods, and by entering markets lost to Europeans as a result of the war. But most Americans took a different view: the Allies had 'hired the money,' as President Coolidge put it, and they must repay with interest. It was also thought salutary that the European countries should learn the lesson that they must pay for their wars. The mass of American taxpayers felt that it would be unfair to shift the burden of the debts on to their shoulders.

Eventually the debts were funded: agreements were made by which capital and interest were to be paid over a period of sixty-two years. The American Government demanded payment of the full capital sum lent in each case, but reduced the rate of interest in accordance with the special circumstances of each country. Thus the Italian rate was reduced by three-quarters, that of the British (who had been the first to settle up) by only one-quarter.

The European Allies had argued that they could only repay America in so far as they themselves received reparations from Germany. But this connection between the inter-Allied debts and reparations the United States would not admit. The U.S. did not take part in the Reparations Commission because of her refusal to ratify the Treaty of Versailles. Later, however, individual Americans, like Dawes and Young, were allowed to assist on expert committees engaged on the problem of reparations. During the middle 'twenties the Germans were paying reparations to the Allies; the Allies were making debt payments to America; and America, through its bankers, was lending to Germany the money which made it possible for her to pay the reparations. Meanwhile America was rendering international payments to her

very difficult by high tariffs; foreign countries were prevented from selling their goods in the United States and so
acquiring dollars with which to pay their debts. All this led
to a certain amount of friction and bad feeling; it was also
a factor contributing to the economic slump of the 'thirties.

American Prosperity and the Americanisation of Europe

Perhaps the strongest American influence in Europe during
the first post-war decade was the sheer fact of American
economic prosperity. Nothing succeeds like success. Just
as democracy and self-determination became powerful political
ideas in Europe because they were backed by the obvious
example of success in America and the west European
countries, so the creation of a high standard of life for the
masses made America appear like paradise to the poverty-
stricken peasants of south-eastern Europe and even attracted
admiration in the more advanced countries of western Europe.
The dominant characteristic of American industry is mass
production and this has had two important effects: it has
raised the standard of life and also standardised the way of
living. This new American way of life—which provides high
wages and a vast output of material goods to buy with them—
has an enormous attraction for the masses; for they relish
material plenty and do not notice the absence of some of the
spiritual and intellectual values of which a highly standardised
way of life deprives them. Sophisticated Europeans may
find it hard to appreciate this. As an American writer
has put it, they have 'no adequate conception of the drawing power of Americanism. It constitutes the strongest
apostolic force in the modern world, and perhaps the only
one that can successfully dispute the future with Russian
communism. . . . Add to military prestige our visible triumphs
in the scarcely less esteemed realms of machinery and organised
economics—our mechanics and our money—and it is clear
why the United States to-day are coming to impose their
style of life on both Europe and Asia—and are loved and
hated accordingly.'[1]
But American material triumphs appealed also to European
business men. Although capitalism, industrial technique,
and the ideas of modern democracy were all imported from

[1] Edgar A. Mowrer, *This American World*, pp. 101 and 131.

Europe into America, the resulting American industrialism reached such an advanced stage that it reacted on the industrial system in the countries of Europe.   In the 'twenties much was heard, in Great Britain for example, of the need for a policy of high wages, rationalisation of business, mechanisation, and so on, in order to imitate the success of American capitalism.

American material success and the desire to imitate it have led to a considerable (if, sometimes, unconscious) Americanisation of Europe and other parts of the world.   Modern bathrooms and plumbing, safety razors, vacuum cleaners, sewing machines, refrigerators, cash registers from Dayton, Ohio, the ubiquitous Ford car, department stores, buying on the instalment plan—the use of all these has been widely spread by American influence.   More and more entertainment for the masses—amusement parks, jazz bands, the passion for motors and radios, newspapers ever more colourful and sensational—all this is part of Americanisation.   The American way of life has been popularised by the American film.   Certain styles, fashions and patterns of living have been carried in this way throughout the world.   After Jean Harlow's success in *Hell's Angels* (1930), women clamoured to imitate that shimmering head, and the phrase 'platinum blonde' passed into the English language.   The American film appeals everywhere because it fits the measure of the average human heart: it portrays 'life according to the heart's desire.'   The film, even though it often exaggerates, has made America better known abroad than any country has ever been before. The film has set up the American standard of life for universal admiration; it has also imposed a standardised form of entertainment characteristic of an industrial society.

In the post-war years American literature, too, developed a prestige of its own.   The novels of Theodore Dreiser, Sinclair Lewis, Upton Sinclair, John Dos Passos, Thornton Wilder, and Ernest Hemingway were read and respected in Europe, and the American-born T. S. Eliot became an international name in the sphere of poetry.   But on the whole America's influence on the inner life and deeper beliefs of Europe is small; the culture of Europe is still something looked upon with respect by the educated American.   It was on the economic side that, in the 'twenties, America's appeal to Europe was supreme: the United States offered a land where all could prosper, was symbolic of a luxurious and expanding material existence, and appeared as a dispenser of well-being to all through the medium of its foreign loans.

The Slump

The era of unparalleled American prosperity ended in a slump, also of unparalleled dimensions. In October, 1929, the crash came in Wall Street: the values of stocks, which had been pushed up to dizzy heights by a wave of confident speculation, sagged, and then collapsed. Thousands of investors lost their savings and were ruined, purchases declined, factories reduced production, wages and salaries were ruthlessly axed, and unemployment mounted. A long period of depression followed. But the effects were not limited to America: they were felt all over the world. Economic depression spread and became world-wide, and its results will be described in later chapters. It was soon apparent that there was an acute crisis in the capitalist system; things had gone wrong even in America. Everywhere confidence in the whole social order was profoundly shaken; Russia began to appear as a possible rival to America for the soul of the European masses. It could not at the time be clearly foreseen that the crisis would pass, that losses though great would be written off, that the industrial system would readjust itself, and that the United States would emerge once more as a country to be wondered at in Europe for its industrial might and its prosperity. The slump showed, more clearly than anything before it, how close were the links between America and Europe.

SUGGESTIONS FOR FURTHER READING

A. Nevins: *America in World Affairs.*

Sir C. Petrie: *Diplomatic History, 1713–1933,* c. 24.

E. M. Hugh-Jones: *Woodrow Wilson and American Liberalism.*

New Cambridge Modern History, Vol. XI, c. 24 (by A. E. Campbell).

H. Koht: *The American Spirit in Europe,* cc. 9–14.

H. C. Allen and C. P. Hill (editors): *British Essays in American History,* pp. 297–315.

R. Heindel (editor): *American Influences Abroad.*

CHAPTER 18

SOVIET RUSSIA, 1920–39

Increased Interest in the Russian Experiment

THE death of Stresemann in 1929 marked the end of a period of comparative calm in Europe because it removed a stabilising element from Germany and a restraining influence from Franco-German relations. Another event in 1929 can now be seen to be of even greater significance as a dividing line. This event was the big stock market crash in Wall Street, New York, the immediate occasion of the unparalleled economic slump which spread across the world during the next three years. The slump had its most severe effects in Germany, where it created economic conditions which gave Hitler his opportunity; its effects on Japanese trade had a similar result in encouraging the policy of military aggression among the nationalist leaders of Japan. The rise of the fascist dictators will be described in the next chapter. But the world slump also had an important effect on the relations between Soviet Russia and the outside world, and this is therefore a suitable place to consider the history of Russia since the end of the civil war in 1920.

The world slump which shook men's confidence in the so-called capitalist system made them look to Russia as offering a planned economy as an alternative. This brought Russia right into the foreground of interest. At the end of the Civil War the country was devastated, weak and helpless, and during the quiet years of 1925–30 the countries of Europe could afford to ignore the new Soviet state. If people in western Europe thought of Russia at all, they remembered that she had made a separate peace with Germany in 1918 and cut herself loose thereby from the Allied peace settlement; people remembered, too, the horrors of the Revolution. Russia was regarded as a violent, treacherous but distant outsider; when not ignored, she was feared and disliked.

In 1919 the Russian leaders took the principal part in forming the Third, or Communist, International, often known as the Comintern. The arrangements for holding a conference to create the new organisation were made by the foreign affairs ministry in Moscow. From the start the new movement was dominated by Russia in spite of its allegedly international character. The Russians expected world revolution to follow the revolution they had already achieved in one country, so the object was to accelerate this course of events by forming Communist Parties in each country and co-ordinating their efforts through the central bureau in Moscow. Thus the International, closely supervised by the Soviet leaders, carried on an energetic propaganda in many parts of the world and tried to take advantage of the economic dislocation, the hardship and widespread unrest following the war. But such propaganda, though it produced temporary results here and there, brought about no successful revolutions (up to the Second World War), and in many places it tended to have the opposite effect—reaction against Russia and the suppression of communism as unpatriotic.

Anti-Russian feeling helped considerably to decide the British general election of 1924 which turned out the first Labour Government. But after 1929 the collapse of world prices and the great volume of unemployment in the industrial countries forced men to reconsider many of their basic economic beliefs, and this had the effect of largely altering the popular view of Russia. Men were looking for a new economic system in place of the western structure which appeared to be breaking down under their eyes; Russia was therefore idealised. Instead of remembering that Russia had been the most backward of the Great Powers of Europe and was desperately trying to industrialise—to do in a few years what had taken a hundred in western Europe and America—people thought of the problems of Russia as comparable with those of the western industrial nations; the Soviet planned economy was pictured as already a working alternative to capitalism. It was a misleading comparison.

From the end of the Civil War and intervention to the years of the world slump Russia developed largely in isolation. She had secured her national independence, she was not a member of the League of Nations, and some of the exponents of the new socialist economic system claimed that one of its merits was that it worked independently of the capitalist economy of the outside world. During this period the political and economic development of Russia may be studied for its own intrinsic interest and because of its later importance; from about 1930 onwards the story of Russia comes once more to be linked with that of the rest of Europe, and Russian foreign policy becomes an important part of European history as a whole.

Recovery under the 'New Economic Policy'

The Civil War was followed by famine and disease on a large scale in 1921-2. The period of 'war communism'—a direct system of military control, barter and forced requisition of foodstuffs from the peasants—reduced the economic life of the country to a low ebb. The peasants often resisted requisitions and even sowed less grain. The ravages of civil war added to the causes of the famine. Privation encouraged the spread of disease, as did also the wide movement of refugees. At the end of the Russo-Polish War in 1921, people driven into the interior of Russia during the Great War returned to the west. Typhus, cholera, smallpox, typhoid, and relapsing fever were rampant. Refugees from the Volga famine travelled into Turkestan in search of food; they brought back a malignant malaria which caused a great epidemic. The League of Nations health service, the Quakers' and other foreign relief organisations were called in. A sanitary cordon was drawn from north to south across Poland; no one could pass without being quarantined and disinfected. In this way the typhus-carrying lice were destroyed and the spread of disease into Europe checked. In Russia itself political opposition to the full communist economic policy developed. Lenin was forced to call a temporary halt or 'breathing space.' The new policy he now introduced was known as N.E.P.—New Economic Policy.

The new policy introduced in 1921 made important concessions to the peasants. In place of the forced requisitions, a regular tax on grain was organised, payable at first in kind and later in money. The Russian economy became a mixed one, partly State, partly private, conducted in general on a money basis (with which war communism had seen fit to dispense). Peasants and small middlemen were allowed to carry on private trade, and a certain amount of small-scale industry was allowed. With the stimulus of private gain production and distribution increased; peasants gained by being able to sell part at least of their foodstuffs in a free market; and they were encouraged to sow more wheat, when they found private traders bringing to the villages some of the manufactured goods which the peasants had been unable to obtain during the previous troubled years.

Gradually order began to take the place of chaos. Economic recovery began. And, in spite of N.E.P., the State still retained control over the essentials of economic production. The State held 'the commanding heights'—the nationalised banks, heavy industry, transport, and foreign trade (such as it was). By about 1927 production had made some headway and the country had reached once more something like the level of 1914. This, of course, was a low level when compared with that reached by the industrial countries of western Europe and America. The quality of goods produced in Russia was poor although quantity was increasing, but after the dreadful privations of the preceding years it meant a lot that the processes of production were moving steadily once more.

The reasons for recovery were several. Perhaps the most important was the toughness of the Russian people. They had always been accustomed to a wretched standard of life, and their powers of endurance were sufficient to overcome the many obstacles which they had found in their way. A certain oriental fatalism enabled them to accept calamity as in the nature of things, but this fatalism did not prevent occasional enthusiasm for a new cause and the putting out of great efforts to support it. This natural toughness of the people was to stand them in good stead twenty years later when they were again called upon to face prolonged horror and hardship during the Nazi invasion. The enthusiasm of the communist leadership—an enthusiasm comparable to that of a religious faith—was sufficient to direct the toughness of the masses to the essential task of economic recovery. Russian territory is immense, natural resources are great, and, given direction, the necessary labour power, mostly unskilled, was waiting to be trained and harnessed to the task of production.

The Death of Lenin and Rise of Stalin

Lenin died after a long illness in January, 1924, at a moment when his party was in the midst of the struggle for recovery, and while the successful outcome of that immediate struggle was still uncertain. Mr. Churchill once declared that the greatest disaster for Russia was the birth of Lenin, and the second greatest his death. Certainly at the time his guiding genius was still badly needed, but in spite of its removal the next few years saw Russia make up the ground that had been lost since 1914.

The death of Lenin was followed by a struggle inside the Communist Party between Trotsky and Stalin. Stalin was successful in taking the lead, as Secretary of the Party, and the economic developments brought about under his direction are sometimes known as the Second, or Stalinist, Revolution. He was convinced that Russia must concentrate on developing her own resources on a national basis. For the time being, at least, plans for world revolution and the spread of socialism abroad would have to be put aside and every effort devoted to the most rapid possible expansion of industrial and agricultural production. Socialist policy was expressed in a programme of State-planned economic advance on a wide front. Stalin's Five Year Plan—a thing which aroused controversy and interest everywhere, and was imitated with modifications in some foreign countries, such as Turkey—began in 1928, and was followed by a second, and then by a third, five year plan. The aims of the plans included the collectivisation of farming and the utmost possible expansion of industry.

The First Five Year Plan in Agriculture and Industry

The policy of collectivisation in agriculture was pushed forward most rapidly in the years 1928–34. This policy had a double aim: it had to increase agricultural production in order to feed the industrial workers in the new factories and to raise the standard of life, but it had also to reassert the socialist character of Russia by 'the liquidation of the *kulaks.*' These *kulaks* were the richer and, one supposes, often the most skilled and hardest working of the peasants. They had grown more prosperous by private trading under N.E.P. and the communist rulers of Russia recognised in a prosperous peasantry a potential bourgeois enemy. Thus, under the twofold urge of the need for increasing production and of communising the peasantry, the policy of collectivisation

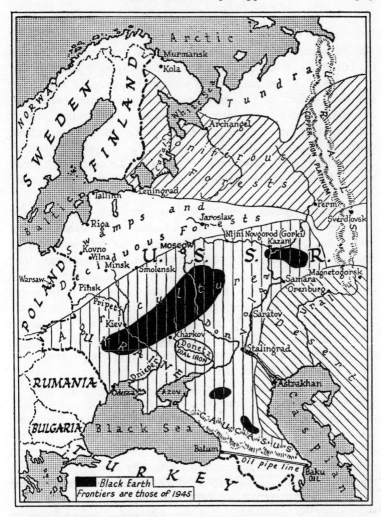

RUSSIA IN EUROPE: ECONOMIC RESOURCES AND DEVELOPMENT

was carried out. Stalin's policy made it necessary to
persuade the peasants to give up the concentration of their
efforts on individual holdings and, instead, to farm large
areas on collective, that is, on co-operative, lines. But
persuasion and propaganda were not enough. The policy
provoked resistance, especially in the Ukraine and the North
Caucasus; it also led to the slaughtering of livestock by the

recalcitrant peasants. Once more famine was caused by interference with the peasants, although this time the famine was less severe than that of 1921–2 and less extensive. Punitive expeditions and deportations followed.[1] By applying a policy of coercion the peasants were ultimately forced to submit to the new order, and with its establishment came eventually acceptance and increasing production. The policy was a ruthless one; no account was taken of the individual human suffering caused. But the policy was largely successful. Agriculture was collectivised, the *kulak* threat to socialism was removed, and output was in the long run enormously increased.

The collectivisation of agriculture certainly involved the carrying out of an immense technical and administrative revolution. By 1940 there were 240,000 collective farms instead of the 25,000,000 separate peasant holdings that existed in 1928. These holdings were often scattered strips in the open fields; now they were consolidated in large farms which were brought under centralised control and technical direction as part of the plan. On these farms lived 75,000,000 people, mostly in villages. Each farm would consist, on the average (actually size varied considerably), of a village of 70 to 80 households farming 1,200 acres under crops. Apart from the consolidation of holdings the most essential feature was mechanisation. Tractors were used as widely as possible in ploughing, and machines were introduced extensively for sowing, reaping and threshing. This involved the setting up of service stations for maintaining the new agricultural machinery—a task of especial difficulty among a simple country folk quite unused to machinery. Of the total produce of each farm a certain amount went at a low fixed price to the State; the remainder could be sold either to the State or in the open market at higher prices. The return on this sale was divided among the peasants on the basis of the labour-days contributed by each. Dwelling-houses and garden-plots, together with implements and some animals, could be held individually.

In industry, the first Five Year Plan and the later plans

---

[1] At Samara on the Volga in the summer of 1932 a large gang of miserable-looking men was to be seen marching under armed guard. Russian friends affirmed that they were peasant resisters being punished by forced labour.

called for a vast expansion of production in almost every direction. The outstanding feature of the Russian economy was scarcity. Whatever was done it was virtually impossible to produce too much of anything. In this respect the problem of production was simpler than in the capitalist countries. It was claimed that there was no unemployment in Russia —this is doubtful in any case in the strict sense because at least until well into the 'thirties beggars and destitute were to be seen in the streets and churches, and the many changes in industry and agriculture caused frequent dislocation which meant temporary loss of employment for some people—but there was certainly always a steady demand for skilled artisans and also for able-bodied men and women who could put their physical strength into the struggle for output. In the 1930's during the world slump unemployment of the able-bodied was the most marked social feature of the capitalist countries; this was in strong contrast with Soviet Russia where the workers were needed in every kind of industry. During the slump some trained men left the western industrial countries to find work in Russia. In this way the slump in the western world actually helped Russia in its production drive by bringing to the country the badly needed mechanics, experts and skilled workers—especially from America. These foreign workers were offered considerable inducement in the way of high pay; their standard of life was much superior to that of the Russian workers.

The industrial expansion of the three plans showed rather different characteristics. In the period 1928-32 a maximum effort was made; this was Russia's 'iron age' and, as in the case of the struggle with the *kulaks*, policy was ruthless in demanding industrialisation at whatever human cost might be involved. Living standards were ignored: the essential object was the creation of capital equipment. 'Guns not butter' was Göring's slogan in Nazi Germany a few years later; in Russia during the first Five Year Plan the slogan might well have been: 'heavy industry not butter'. Everything was subordinate to the plan; foreign trade was controlled by the State to meet its needs. The export corporations mobilised goods for export—in spite of low prices prevailing during the world depression—in order that Russia might import what was necessary for the plan. As the Soviet paper

Izvestia put it: 'Goods have been exported which would be very useful on the home market, but this has been done because we are in need of foreign raw materials and industrial equipment.'[1] Engineering and agricultural machinery and machine tools were imported, but control remained in Russian hands.

The essential aim was to equip the backward, peasant land of Russia with the modern heavy industry which the Industrial Revolution of the nineteenth century had given to western Europe and America. An American worker at Magnitogorsk, in 1933, described the scene: 'A quarter of a million souls—communists, *kulaks*, foreigners, Tartars, convicted saboteurs and a mass of blue-eyed Russian peasants—building the biggest steel combinat in Europe in the middle of the barren Ural steppe.' Here as in the inevitable development of some natural process 'men froze, hungered and suffered, but the construction work went on with a disregard for individuals and a mass heroism seldom paralleled in history.' The feverish pace of the industrial development was demonstrated in the excited enthusiasm of communist youth, the tension and grim determination of the workers and the pressure and drive to be felt everywhere. Occasional open opposition or sabotage was encountered; great factories like the motor plant at Nijni Novgorod were protected by fortified towers, concrete walls and guards with rifles and fixed bayonets. The atmosphere was the atmosphere of war, and war it was: war against the forces of nature and human inertia, and propaganda war against the capitalist enemies ceaselessly denounced by radio, newspaper and poster to stimulate that hatred on which war is most successfully based. But the immediate difficulties were overcome.

The Second and Third Five Year Plans

During the period of the next plan, 1933-7, conditions were less severe. The creation of the capital equipment by the first plan was now resulting in greater production of consumer goods: in other words there was more to eat and wear. In 1936 the people of Moscow were told by poster: 'Now, comrades, life is better, life is brighter.' The food position in the towns had improved sufficiently by 1935 to

[1] Quoted in A. Baykov, *The Development of the Soviet Economic System.*

allow the rationing system to be brought to an end. It was estimated that peasant families in 1937 were eating 50 per cent. more bread and milk and several times as much meat as in 1914. Houses had increased in number, although building materials were still scarce. But urban population had increased faster than accommodation, so that over-crowding was still considerable as the rapid growth of industry attracted workers from the countryside. But even in the second plan the expansion of heavy industry took first place; steel output made a big advance. And after the plan was in operation the resources devoted to the consumption goods industries had to be reduced. Fascism with its threat of war was the cause of this. As Molotov stated later (in 1939): 'The international situation . . . made it imperative to accelerate considerably the expansion of heavy industry at the cost of reducing to a certain extent the growth of light industry.' The third plan which commenced in 1938 was more definitely marked by the fear of war, and creature comforts had to be sacrificed. The main emphasis was put on transport, steel and the non-ferrous metals, and on the chemical industry. Every effort had to be made, for production per head in Russia was still low. This was urged by Molotov himself: 'People have begun to forget that we are still behind some capitalist countries economically, that is in industrial production per head of the population . . . we cannot rest content.'[1]

The Industrialisation of Russia Achieved

By the carrying out of the plans, Russia was equipped with gigantic steel plants, huge factories for producing tractors and agricultural machinery, new hydro-electric works, new railways and mines. This development of industry made Russia a great industrial country, although it must be remembered that the population is very large and total production was not commensurate with it. The standard of living was still low. A comparison of output with that of the older industrial nations shows that, in spite of the considerable advances made, Russia, when size of population is taken into account, was still behind. On the eve of the Second World War approximate annual figures were as follows:

[1] Quotations of Molotov's economic report in 1939 are taken from M. Dobb, *Soviet Economic Development since 1917* (1948).

	Population (millions)	Pig Iron	Steel (millions of tons)	Coal	Electric Power (millions of kilowatts)
Russia	170	14·9	18·4	164·6	39,600
U.S.A.	131	31·9	47·2	395	115,900
Germany	73	18·3	22·7	{ 186 198 (Lignite)	55,200
Great Britain	47	6·7	10·3	227	30,700

Nevertheless, when the state of Russia under the Czars and its reduction to absolute chaos at the end of the Civil War are remembered, it is clear that stupendous efforts had been made and considerable results achieved. The industrial expansion was brought about by the large-scale planning of the State Planning Commission, working subject to the Communist Party and the Russian Government. In carrying it out a mixture of ruthless coercion and planned incentives was used. To talk of equality became tantamount to counter-revolutionary activity. Money incentives were resorted to; workers were graded according to skill, and high output was rewarded with high pay. The name Stakhanovite—derived from Stakhanov, a pioneer of high output—was used of workers who could step up their production to a sensational extent, thereby setting a much-needed example and, incidentally, earning extra pay. Increased production all along the line was the overriding object of the plan. The whole country was affected. There was a growing self-sufficiency; indeed, the country was producing its own food, its own coal, iron, steel and agricultural machinery. Although Russia was exporting again, she could be self-sufficing economically though at a low standard of life. Industry under the plan was geographically dispersed in many parts of the country. The old industrial regions around Leningrad and Moscow and in the Ukraine have continued to expand, as have also the oil-producing districts of the Caucasus; mining in the Urals and the Altai has been developed; and new industrial zones have grown up in Central Asia and the Far East. With this industrial expansion went the creation of a great system of social services—free medical attention and complete social insurance—although in a country still poor many of these existed on paper rather than in fact. Education, too, especially technical education, was extended on the widest possible scale; it was compulsory and free. Results were shown in the increasing productivity of labour. By 1936 the communist leaders claimed to have reached an important objective— the almost complete socialisation of the productive means of the country. To run this system thousands of trained scientists, engineers and doctors were being turned out, and the schools were enabling the younger generation to grow up literate—an indisputable transformation from the old Russia.

How much was lost, however, in the transition from the old to the new Russia and the strain which the transition involved for the individual is illustrated by the tragedy of the young poet, Sergei Essenin (1895–1925). 'The last poet of the village,' he called himself, but he welcomed the revolution with his poem *Inonia*, in 1919. He looked forward to a new world, an Arcadia of freedom ruled not by machines or proletarians but by peasants. How different was the frantic drive of the industrial State growing up around him. In his *Return Home* (1924) he is a stranger in the Soviet village, and finds his sister, a blooming peasant girl, poring over Marx's *Capital* 'as if it were a Bible.' Bitterly he felt the contrast between the rural Russia of his boyhood and the new urban society of the Soviets:

> '*No hope have I now of returning*
> *To the fields where I played*
>
> . . . . .
>
> *The little thatched hut I was born in*
> *Lies bare to the sky,*
> *And in these crooked alleys of Moscow*
> *I am fated to die.*'

From the new way of life he found escape by suicide.[1]

Russia a Federal Dictatorship in Form

During the years between the end of the Civil War and the Nazi invasion of Russia, while the country was being industrially transformed, certain political and constitutional changes were also taking place. Throughout, however, a strong control had been maintained by the central organs of government; to a large extent that power had been exercised by one man,

[1] See Janko Lavrin, *Aspects of Modernism*. Translation of the verse by R. M. Hewitt.

Stalin, as Secretary of the dominant and only political organisation, the Communist Party. The system of government is, therefore, rightly regarded as a dictatorship.

The constitutional pattern of Russia, however, is extremely complicated, as the country is not only vast in size but is also, at least in theory, federal in character rather than centralised. The federal organisation of government springs from the fact that Russia is multi-national; many different races, languages and religions exist. Thus Russia is a federation of state members, and is officially termed the Soviet Union or U.S.S.R.—Union of Soviet Socialist Republics. The largest of the state members is the R.S.F.S.R.—Russian Soviet Federated Socialist Republic (it is so described because it is itself a union of autonomous territories); it includes most of European Russia and stretches right across Asia to the Pacific; it has a population of over 100,000,000. The other member states of the U.S.S.R. in 1939 were the Ukraine, White Russia, the Transcaucasian republics of Georgia, Armenia, and Azerbaijan, and the republics of central Asia.

A large number of soviets or councils were created ranging from city and village soviets up to the soviets of the republics and the Union Congress of Soviets. Election was by an indirect system, and clergy, aristocratic and bourgeois elements were excluded from the franchise. The people, either in factory communities or in a village meeting, elected their representatives to the lowest soviets, city or village; after that the soviet itself selected those to represent it in the next highest soviet. A feature of the system was the differentiation between town and country. The village soviet was very humble; there were several stages between it and the provincial congress which selected representatives both to the soviet of the republic and to the Union Congress. The city soviet, however, filled by politically-conscious industrial workers, sent forward representatives directly to both the soviet of its republic and to the Union Congress. Voting in local elections was by show of hands. Another important feature was the giving of greater representation to the towns than the country. The effect of this was to ensure that the point of view of the many peasant individualists was overshadowed by that of the communist proletariat of the urban areas.

The Constitution of 1936

In 1936 a new Constitution was created. It was eventually adopted by the Union Congress after its drafting by a special constitutional commission presided over by Stalin himself. It was issued as a democratic constitution; it was hailed as such by communists and their sympathisers all over the world.[1] It did, in fact, make some changes both in procedure and in terminology. Direct voting by secret ballot was introduced and takes place in single-member constituencies; all citizens, whether peasants or industrial workers, have electoral equality. The Union Congress of Soviets was replaced by the Supreme Soviet or Council of the U.S.S.R. This has two chambers of equal rights, the Council or Soviet of the Union and the Council of Nationalities. It is the former which is directly elected, as described above, and is in form comparable to a western lower house. The Council of Nationalities is also elected directly, but it represents the constituent republics of the Union and also the autonomous republics and lesser national territorial divisions. The Supreme Council elects a Presidium, a smaller body which acts on its behalf when the larger body is not in session. Chosen by the Supreme Council is the Union Council of Commissars, of which Stalin is chairman; supreme legislative power is vested in the Supreme Council and the Council of Commissars is its executive or Cabinet. On paper, the rights of the individual are guaranteed. It would appear to anyone simply reading the Constitution of 1936 that here was the constitution of a democratic state.

Yet knowledge of the constitutions and practice of many modern states reveals that theoretical form and actual practice are often different. The democratic form of the Russian constitution is apparent rather than real. In fact, the whole vast constitutional system is controlled by the Communist Party. No other party is allowed—although non-party candidates are possible. There is only one candidate for each constituency, and nomination comes from the Communist Party or other approved agencies (such as trade unions) so

[1] See *Constitution* (*Basic Law of the U.S.S.R.*), published in 1936 in England, with forewords by a number of eminent English liberals who acclaimed what appeared to be a Russian movement towards democracy. Curiously it was one of the strongest admirers of the Russian system, Mr. D. N. Pritt, K.C., M.P., who struck a note of warning: 'The critic, friendly or unfriendly, will guard against assuming that theory is followed automatically by practice.'

that communist direction is assured. The provision of one candidate only for each constituency was made by a supplementary article added after the making of the constitution but before the elections! A partial explanation of this apparently meaningless performance of voting with only one candidate is to be found in the fact that *several* persons would be considered previously and their claims discussed in the local Press. Another point made by defenders of the system is that the choice between voting for the one candidate and not voting at all enables the elector to express confidence or lack of confidence in general. In other words the election is used by the government as a kind of sounding-board. In the Supreme Council the great majority of members are Communist Party men. Nor has the boasted freedom of the federal republics much reality. The demands of economic development and the needs of defence have led to ever greater control from the centre through the Party, the Supreme Council, the Council of Commissars and the high command of the Red Army. The organisation in the open of any opposition bodies or the making of political criticism are impossible: the fate of all those who have disagreed is a standing warning to those who might be tempted to disagree in future.

Struggles for Power inside the Communist Party

The full truth about the struggles within the Communist Party will probably never be known. The official record is that of the triumphant section of the Party; most of those who might have given the other side have been silenced. Throughout, however, the Communist Party—the carefully selected and trained élite or ideological aristocracy—has been the dominant force. Stalin's power has lain in the fact that he has long held the position of Secretary of the Party, and is a member of the Politbureau, or Political Bureau of the Central Committee of the Party. The Politbureau with its all-pervading influence in Russian politics is really more powerful than the State Cabinet, the Council of People's Commissars, which is officially the executive instrument of the Supreme Council of the Union. Inside the Party a struggle developed between Stalin and Trotsky. This has been the great personal drama inside the Party, which claimed to be scientific and impersonal in its theory and in the application of that theory in society.

Stalin had been appointed as Party Secretary by Lenin, and after his climb to leadership everything was done so as to magnify his part in the Revolution. At the time, however, the names of Lenin and Trotsky were often coupled; Stalin was hardly heard of. Trotsky, in exile, wrote a life of Stalin which hints that Stalin may have poisoned Lenin and describes the Russian Government in the Kremlin as the greatest lie-factory in history. Whatever may be the exact truth, it is known that Trotsky and Stalin disagreed also on policy. Trotsky held the view of 'permanent revolution.' He regarded the Russian revolution as only the first in a chain of revolutions; he did not think that one socialist state could survive in a capitalist world. He therefore urged the policy of stirring up revolution all over the world. Stalin on the other hand decided for 'socialism in a single country.' He argued that the immediate task should be the full development of socialism in Russia whereby Russia would become an example for imitation elsewhere. Stalin's view triumphed. Trotsky was expelled from the Party's Central Committee in 1927 and exiled in 1929. In 1940 he was assassinated in Mexico.

A series of purges and spectacular public trials (in 1936, 1937 and 1938) removed the opposition to Stalin; most of the 'Old Bolsheviks' and the higher Army chiefs were executed. The casualty list reads like a communist *Who's Who*. The very men who carried through the Revolution of 1917— men with famous names in Russia, Zinoviev, Kamenev, Bukharin—were liquidated, as were seven of the leading generals, including Marshal Tukhachevsky. These men were accused of every sort of political crime, treachery, fascism, counter-revolution, working with foreign Powers. If they were innocent, their removal illustrates the ruthless nature of the Stalin dictatorship; if they were guilty, the fact that such men had occupied for years high positions shows how extra-ordinary was the character of a State in which such a thing was possible.

The Development of Russian Foreign Policy

The internal struggle in the Communist Party was connected with Russian foreign policy. It centred on the attitude the

x

Soviet Union was to take in its relations to the other states of the world. By definition, Soviet Russia regarded all capitalist states as enemies. The horrors of the Revolution alienated the west; foreign intervention against the Communist Government had antagonised the Russians. Together these things kept Russia isolated from the rest of Europe. Broadly speaking, down to about 1933 Russia stood aloof, but was gradually coming closer to the other nations. From 1934 onwards she worked with them in the League of Nations. Then in the summer of 1939 the Russo-German Pact, which immediately preceded the outbreak of the Second World War, began a second and even more dangerous period of estrangement, which lasted until the German invasion of June, 1941. All the various changes in her foreign policy—all ultimately subordinate to the principal object of maintaining the independence of the one communist State and of extending its influence as widely as possible throughout the world—can be traced in detail in the long series of agreements and treaties negotiated between Russia and foreign nations. At first a number of commercial agreements took place; then, during the Genoa Conference, came in 1922 the Treaty of Rapallo with Germany. The two outsiders of Europe agreed, and their agreement caused general consternation. Mutual recognition, trade relations, and a secret military pact were arranged between Germany and Russia.[1] In the following years, Russia was gradually recognised by other states and diplomatic relations were established. Russia signed the Kellogg Pact for the renunciation of war in 1928. But Russia was still virtually an outsider, and the Communist International was active in its propaganda against capitalist states.

Then, in 1933, came a change. Hitler obtained power in Germany as the avowed enemy of communism, and had already pointed to eastern Europe as the main field for German expansion. At home, Russia resurrected nationalist patriotism, with the conquering Czars figuring once more as heroes in films and schoolbooks, and a new military oath to the 'Soviet Fatherland' replacing allegiance to the 'Workers of the World.' Abroad, Russian policy turned westwards in search of support at the very time when France looked east. Negotiations began in 1933, and in the same year a common

[1] See p. 257.

fear of another potential aggressor, Japan, drove the United States at long last to accord the Soviet Union official recognition. In 1934 Russia became a member of the League of Nations. In 1935 the Franco-Soviet Pact was signed: each party promised support to the other if attacked, while a supplementary treaty made special provision for Russian help to Czechoslovakia if France became involved in the defence of the latter. Thus the threat from Germany appeared to bring Russia into line with the nations of western Europe, though, as we shall see in due course, in the crisis of 1938 her assistance would probably have been forthcoming but was not asked, and in that of 1939 it was asked and was certainly not forthcoming.

Russia in 1939

To point a few conclusions after tracing the complicated and exacting story of Russia from 1920–39 we may try to answer the question: What are the most significant features of Soviet Russia? First, is the industrialisation of Russia; this had given her heavy industry and made her a Great Power in the modern world. But increased output was thinly spread in so large a country. The standard of life was still very low. To those who knew both Russia and India, Russia was more like India in the poverty of the masses than like the older industrial nations of western Europe and North America. Industrialisation has been carried out by centralised planning, and so Russia is considered a socialist State. The communist theory has, however, been considerably modified in practice. There is no equality of incomes. Secondly, there are the great natural resources and the large and growing population. This gives a kind of biological supremacy: the Russians have been outfought but never outbred. Thirdly, there is the increasing nationalism of Russia which suggests a revival of the old Russian imperialism—this will be more apparent when Russian policy during the Second World War and afterwards has been studied. Fourthly, there is the absence of freedom and democracy in Russia. None of the ordinary personal freedoms exist; Russians are deliberately isolated from the outside world and are virtually prisoners in their own country. Soviet people and Soviet Union were dominated by Stalin, who was the controlling power in the Communist Party. As

President Roosevelt put it in 1940: 'The Soviet Union is run by a dictatorship as absolute as any other in the world.' This, after all, is not really surprising. Russia has never known anything but dictatorship: formerly that of the Czars, now that of the Communist Party.

SUGGESTIONS FOR FURTHER READING

B. H. Sumner: *Survey of Russian History*, cc. 3 and 7.

Sir B. Pares: *Russia* (Pelican Series), cc. 12–18.

M. Lovell: *The Soviet Way of Life* (Home Study Books).

M. Oakeshott: *The Social and Political Doctrines of Contemporary Europe*, Section 3.

M. Dobb: *Soviet Economic Development since 1917*.

M. Beloff: *Foreign Policy of Soviet Russia, 1929–41*.

IV

CHAPTER 19

THE RISE OF THE FASCIST DICTATORS

The Decline of Democracy and the League of Nations

FOR many years after 1917 Russia, as we have seen, remained isolated from the rest of Europe: the 'dictatorship of the proletariat' stood aloof from the democratic states of the west and from the international democracy of the League of Nations. But Soviet Russia was at that time an outsider. It is more strange to have to record that even during the years 1925–30, which seemed to be the heyday of democracy crowned by the acceptance of the League and League principles, there were other states of importance in Europe where parliamentary government worked uneasily and dictatorship found an opening. After 1930 the position rapidly deteriorated: democracy suffered a decline, and in many states people began to look for a strong man to lead them out of their economic and political difficulties. There was a fundamental difference of spirit and method between the new dictatorships and the League of Nations; the rise of the fascist dictatorships marked the decline of the League. From the international point of view the history of the years between the two World Wars falls into three phases: first, the making of a peace settlement after the world conflict; second, the building up of the new international order represented by the League of Nations which was to take the place of the 'international anarchy,' so called, of the years before 1914; third, the decline of the new international order leading to the outbreak of the second great world struggle in 1939. The decline of the international order coincides with the rise of the fascist dictators.

Mussolini's establishment in power as dictator of Italy had been a warning to the democratic states that European democracy rested on weak foundations; still more the Italian retaliation against Greece by the shelling of Corfu was an indication that dictators might, when it suited them, ignore the new international order. These warnings were unheeded

at the time. But a great change was coming. Even during
the optimistic period the exiled Italian Premier, Francisco
Nitti, writing on *Bolshevism, Fascism and Democracy*, looked
back nostalgically to the liberalism of his youth which already
in Italy was a thing of the past. In 1927 he wrote:

'Thirty years ago certain principles of political, economic
and religious freedom seemed definitely to have become the
property of the more civilised section of mankind.

'In the universities and parliaments, and especially on
political questions, we were all disciples of the English
liberal philosophers.

'John Stuart Mill's book, *On Liberty*, moulded the liberal
thought of two generations before the war. We regarded
it not only as a monument of English wisdom, but also as a
synthesis of the practical British spirit. We were certain
that all unjustified coercion was an evil. We regarded
freedom as an absolute good, and human personality as
inviolable in the harmonious development of its moral and
spiritual qualities. We believed that freedom should be
considered not merely as necessary to civil life, but as the
common aim, on which depend all other aims, spiritual,
civil, and political.'

Liberty of this kind had never really been known in eastern
Europe; it had now been set aside in Italy. And Signor
Nitti lived to see at least its temporary disappearance in most of
Europe with the triumph of the Nazi dictatorship in Germany
and the subsequent extension of its power over the Continent.
The rise of the fascist dictatorships to a position of dominance
is the characteristic feature of the Europe of the 'thirties.

The Consolidation of Fascism in Italy

Mussolini's revolution had not taken place all at once.
He was called upon in 1922 by the King to become Prime
Minister. This was a constitutional procedure, although by
the 'march on Rome' Mussolini had used the threat of force.
As Prime Minister, Mussolini had to feel his way; he governed
with a coalition at first, and found the support of a majority
in parliament. It was only by degrees that he was able to
complete his revolution by ridding himself of all opposition.
In 1924 his position was shaken by the scandal caused by

the murder of Matteotti. This socialist deputy was kidnapped by fascists and found dead; the Fascist Government was openly accused of complicity, and a large part of the Opposition withdrew from parliament. Certain fascists were tried for the murder and punished with imprisonment. Mussolini, however, survived the crisis, and on January 3, 1925, he announced that opposition would be crushed by force. The fascist squads had already been turned into a militia or special police. Anti-fascist newspapers were suppressed and organisations dissolved; there were further affrays and killings, especially in Pisa and Florence; Nitti, Orlando and others fled from the country; and many political prisoners were banished to the Lipari Islands. All this was a foretaste of what fascism was to bring elsewhere in the future, but in Italy the oppression was not so severe and far-reaching as later on in Germany. There was not, for example, an anti-Semitic drive until much later when the Germans urged Italian fascists in this direction. By passing new laws through parliament in 1926 and 1928 Mussolini took advantage of the absence of so many opposition deputies to change fundamentally the constitution of Italy; now at last he was able to complete his revolution and transform Italy into a fascist State.

The State remained in form a monarchy and retained a parliamentary chamber and a nominated senate. But all real power was vested in the hands of Mussolini, as Prime Minister and chairman of the Grand Council of the Fascist Party. Italy became a one-party state, and the Fascist Party in its rigid discipline and its character of a trained élite was comparable to the Communist Party in Russia. The law of 1926 laid the foundations of what was known as the 'Corporative State.' The old trade unions and the right to strike disappeared. Economic life was organised into thirteen corporations: in the six divisions of industry, agriculture, commerce, banking, land and inland water transport, and sea and air transport there were separate corporations for capital and labour; the thirteenth corporation was an organisation of the professions. Strikes and lock-outs were declared illegal, and machinery was created to decide all labour disputes. In the new economic and social organisation of Italy, the fascists were attempting to create an alternative to both capitalism and communism.

In theory the new corporations were linked up constitutionally with the political system in the law of 1928. The choice
of candidates for parliament was now to be made through the
corporations, each of which was to be represented in a fixed
proportion, thus making the basis of parliamentary representation functional rather than geographical. Each corporation had to submit a list of its own candidates to the
Fascist Grand Council. This body, combining and modifying
the lists submitted, drew up a final list. The electorate then
voted on the list as a whole, for or against. Thus Italian
elections ceased to compare with democratic elections in the
ordinary sense: they became largely a demonstration of
popular approval of the Government. Local self-government
was also superseded by strengthening the provincial prefects
and setting up government-nominated *podestas* over the local
administrations or communes. To guard against the breakdown of the system in the event of the sudden death of Mussolini, power was given to the Fascist Grand Council to prepare
a list of persons suitable for succession to the premiership.

In 1929 Mussolini strengthened his position by coming to
an agreement with the Papacy which ended a long estrangement between Church and State dating back to 1870. The
agreement was regarded as a great diplomatic triumph for
the Fascist Government because it regularised the relations
of the régime with the Church, although in fact a *modus
vivendi* between Church and State had long ago been arrived
at and the papal contention that the popes were 'prisoners of
a usurping power' was little more than a pretence. By means
of a treaty, a concordat and a financial convention the position
was now regularised. The Vatican City was recognised as a
state under the sovereignty of the Pope, and with the right to
send and receive ambassadors. The Government confirmed
the Church's faith as the State religion and recognised marriages
carried out by the Church, but the State could still object,
on political grounds, to the appointment of a bishop or archbishop. Religious instruction was to be given in secondary
as well as elementary schools. The Church received, in cash
and securities, a large sum to settle its claims against the Italian
State. The new agreements did not prevent the Fascist Party
dominating the whole educational system of the country.
Religious instruction might be permitted, but it was over-

shadowed by the general character of fascist schools and youth movements which were aggressive and warlike. In this respect the Pope suffered misgivings, and friction between Church and State did not entirely cease.

Positive Results

The great concentration and consolidation of power in Italy was not without its positive results. Internal order was secured, and both industry and agriculture were encouraged and sustained by that in itself. There was a marked improvement in administration; Mussolini was determined that the State should be strong and for that efficiency was essential. The notorious Sicilian secret society called the Mafia, which had defied many governments, was at last put down, city streets were cleaned, beggars disappeared, trains ran to time as never before. The currency was stabilised; the banning of strikes encouraged production, and the workers themselves were assisted by rent and price control. And although the economic depression of the 'thirties hit Italy hard and brought unemployment, a great effort was made to maintain the balance of economy. 'The battle for wheat' had as its object to make Italy as far as possible self-supporting in basic foodstuffs. To relieve unemployment, public works were undertaken, like the draining of the Pontine Marshes. To add to the prestige of the régime, everything possible was done to associate with it the memories of ancient Rome. Archæological research was encouraged, and classical sites and monuments were carefully preserved and opened to public inspection. Outwardly at least, Rome in the 'thirties was an admirable place: a modern and orderly city where the remains of antiquity were respected and contributed to the amenities of the present.

There is little doubt that so far as Italian internal stability and the use of the economic resources of a rather poor country were concerned much was achieved. What was disconcerting was the aggressive spirit of fascism; its imperialist claims were likely in time to lead to trouble abroad. The inspiration of ancient Rome was good in so far as it found expression in archæological research and a desire for political stability; it was evil when it led to dreams of imperialist expansion. The glorification of war was a constant theme of fascist exhortation and Italians began to look south and east. Italy held the

Dodecanese in the eastern Mediterranean; she finally acquired
Fiume in 1924, which gave her an outpost on the Dalmatian
shores; she gradually extended her influence in Albania by
the making of loans. She antagonised France over the
questions of Italian labourers working in France and of
Italian settlers in Tunis; she maintained close relations with
Austria and Hungary which gave her a hand in central
European affairs. And she was beginning to look overseas
for possible colonies.

The Appeal of Fascism

The term 'fascism' is Italian in origin but it soon came to
be applied more generally to the new dictatorships in Europe.
The word *fascio* means a bundle, group or league; the term
fasces was used in ancient Rome for the axe and rods, carried
in a bundle as the symbols of authority. As a movement
the outstanding characteristic of fascism is its assertion of
authority and leadership; it is anti-democratic; it asserts the
authority of the State and its greatness as against the weakness
of the individual; it condemns the dissipation of power
caused by party strife. It was perhaps no accident that
fascism established itself so strongly in the two great countries
of Europe where nationhood was of recent date: Italy, and
later Germany. In each case, national unity and democracy
were both new; a special effort seemed necessary to develop
unity and to overcome the divisions in national life brought
about by the exploitation of democracy by the rival extremist
factions. Fascism firmly rejected the old liberal ideal of the
individual, and of the State as simply consisting of and for
individuals; it rejected the idea of equality and the doctrine
of socialism to which that idea gave rise. Instead it regarded the State almost as a mystic entity. The State, wrote
Villari,

> 'is not merely the aggregate of all the individuals comprising
> it, but comprises the infinite series of generations which
> have contributed to form it in the past, constitutes it to-day,
> and will continue to constitute it in the future.'

The highest political virtue was, therefore, fanatical devotion
to the State and its leaders. This was expressed in various
rules issued to members of the fascist organisations: 'Mussolini

is always right,'   'He who is not ready to sacrifice body and soul to Italy and to serve Mussolini without question is unworthy to wear the black shirt, symbol of fascism,' 'Thank God every day that he has made you an Italian fascist.'

Though these extremist slogans had a strange ring in the democratic 'twenties, the kind of government they implied was really nothing new in Europe; it was democracy which was new and was now to face a stern struggle with its own internal weaknesses, which events were revealing, and also with the age-old tendency of government to turn towards discipline and even to tyranny. The fascist State had its parallel in the national state of the Renaissance: in the self-conscious nationalism of Tudor England, in the Spain of Ferdinand and Isabella, in the city-states of Italy with their petty tyrants. We see the common features of autocracy: suppression of liberty; elevation of the State power as against the Church, the individual or any liberal tendency; the struggle for racial purity in Spain, repeated in Nazi Germany; economic state control, whether mercantilist or corporative; and everywhere methods of violence. These things were unfortunately not new; it was the optimism of the liberals which had relegated them to the past.

The Dictatorships in Spain and Portugal

After a study of fascist Italy, it is not, therefore, surprising to find dictators established in the Latin countries of Spain and Portugal. In both cases the disorders of parliamentary government and the dangers of revolution had produced the exasperation which led men to prefer order to liberty. A Portuguese historian has quoted de Tocqueville's words which are particularly apt in application to the Iberian Peninsula: 'A great revolution may sometimes lay the foundation of a country's freedom, yet a succession of revolutions makes it ... an impossibility.' Indeed it is not too much to say that in Italy, Spain and Portugal, dictatorship sprang from the weakness and incompetence of parliamentary régimes: a succession of political disturbances or revolutions must almost inevitably lead to dictatorship of some kind.

In Spain, parliamentary government had brought the old order of King, Church, nobility and Army face to face with hostile forces both old and new: there were the regional nationalisms of the Basques and Catalans; the disruptive, modernising theories of the intellectuals; the revolutionary ideas and violent activities of socialists, syndicalists, anarchists and communists. Liberal politicians were too inexperienced to maintain order and secure a balance between the forces of Right and Left. In Spain, too, there was a tradition of interference in politics by soldiers. Dissatisfaction was brought to a head when the Moorish chieftain, Abd-el-Krim, inflicted a severe defeat at Anoual in 1921 upon the forces which at great expense had been trying to subdue Spanish Morocco ever since 1909.

General Primo de Rivera made an armed seizure of power by a *coup* in Barcelona and was promptly invited by the King to form a government. He did so, dismissed the Cortes or Parliament, and ruled Spain as a dictator from 1923 until 1930. Spanish wits coined the phrase: *Primo de Rivera, ma secondo di Mussolini*. But a Spanish general regarded himself as second to no foreigner: he was simply in the Spanish tradition. He ruled by instinct and inspiration; as a soldier he believed in discipline, as a man he was a Spaniard and a patriot. His principles were summed up in the words: 'Country, Religion, Monarchy.' Though his policy might be called fascist, there was nothing surprising about a military dictatorship of this kind in Spain. But by 1930 King and Parliament had tired of the dictator; the dictator himself was tired. The King asked him to resign, and he resigned. General Berenguer followed as Premier, and ruled with difficulty until he also resigned early in 1931. But just as revolutions lead to dictatorships, so do dictatorships often end with revolutions. People blamed the King for the régime of Primo. Municipal elections in April produced a republican majority. There was strong popular feeling for a republic and a demand for abdication. The King 'to avoid bloodshed' left Spain. How easy it had all been! Spain was now a democratic republic, and without bloodshed. *La Niña Bonita*, the pretty girl, as nineteenth-century conspirators had called the republic to which they looked forward, had come at last and come smiling. But the republican period was to be marked by new disorders, and the bitter Civil War of 1936–9 brought dictatorship once more with the victory of General Franco. These events will be considered in the next chapter—they became of concern to the whole of Europe.

Portugal had been a republic since King Manoel lost his throne in 1910, but her political history was marked by great instability and by many disturbances of a revolutionary nature. It is estimated that between 1910 and 1926 there were twenty revolutions and forty ministries. At last, in 1926, General Carmona established a military dictatorship and suspended the parliamentary system. In 1927 he suppressed a violent outbreak of revolution caused by communists, and in 1928 had himself proclaimed President. A new constitution was created in 1933 in which the ministers were responsible to the President and not to Parliament; a single-chamber legislative assembly, half elective, half nominated by economic bodies, was set up. The economic bodies were similar to the corporations created in fascist Italy, and strikes and lock-outs were forbidden. One rather unusual feature of the Portuguese dictatorship was that General Carmona found an able, highly trained and conscientious man to run the State for him. This was Dr. Salazar. He became Minister of Finance in 1928, and Prime Minister in 1932. He had been a professor of economics, and was associated with a group of Catholics who based their social policy on the encyclical *Rerum Novarum*. His administration in Portugal has shown the possibilities of a moderate fascism: a dictatorship, but one which was not to be allowed to run to the extremes of imperialism and war.

The Attack on Parliamentary Institutions spreads

We have already observed (in Chapter 16) how, even while democracy was at its zenith in western Europe, dictatorships were being established one by one in the small countries of eastern and central Europe. The optimism of the late 'twenties, which Locarno had encouraged and which the progress of the new international society at Geneva maintained, concealed the hard realities of the situation. Even reputable historians could support the League of Nations by pointing out that it embraced in one organisation states of all kinds; they did not at first perceive that this all-embracing character of the League covered a fatal division of principle between the methods of democracy and those of dictatorship.

While the interminable discussions were going on at Geneva in the 'thirties and it was fondly supposed that such proceedings were indicative of a new democratic way of life growing up in the international sphere, the actual area of democratic government was ominously shrinking.

Italy and Portugal had dictatorships of long standing; Spain had just had eight years of dictatorship and her republic was only to endure for a few years before being smashed in civil war by renascent military autocracy. In both Poland and Lithuania there were dictatorships; in 1934 there were suspensions of parliamentary government in Estonia and Latvia. Between 1928 and 1934 there were moves towards a strengthening of the executive power at the expense of parliament in Yugoslavia, Rumania, Greece and Bulgaria.[1] There were local variations on the main theme, but the backward social conditions and the violent histories of most of these countries reveal a general unreadiness for democracy. An older, stronger form of government backed by force was reasserting itself to restore order when inexperienced or corrupt politicians failed to maintain it. This was not surprising. And where a dictator promised order and security he would find support from the propertied classes, the richer peasants, the Church and the military. By nationalist propaganda and State-sponsored programmes of economic development he could build up also a considerable volume of support in the mass of the people.

What was surprising—although it need not be if one examines past history—was the establishment of the most powerful dictatorship of all in Germany, a country materially advanced, highly educated, and with the constitution of Weimar which had given her a complete democratic system. It was the establishment of dictatorship here, in the heart of Europe, which destroyed the hopes of the democrats and internationalists and which eventually plunged Europe and the world into another cataclysm. This new and very menacing dictatorship was set up by the Austrian ex-corporal of whom we have already heard as organiser of a *Putsch* that failed in Munich in 1923. To account for the catastrophic change of 1933 which Adolf Hitler accomplished in Germany we must examine certain characteristics and events of German history

[1] For some details as to the general tendency in these countries see Chapter 16.

and also some external factors. Let us look first at the external factors.

Causes and Effects of the World Economic Crisis

It was above all else the world economic slump commencing in 1929 which swung so many peoples from democracy to dictatorship. World-wide depression weakened public confidence in the economic system and so led directly to public criticism of the political system of democracy which was so closely associated in Great Britain and the United States with industrial capitalism. The slump, then, was a challenge at once to the economic system and to democratic government, and democratic government only survived where it was based on firm foundations; where it was new and weak, as in Germany, it was swept away.

A cycle of boom and slump, of prosperity and depression, was familiar to economists. But this slump was more severe and far-reaching in its effects than any before. To some extent, it caught business men and economists by surprise, because in 1929 the production of the United States had reached a level previously unknown. It seemed as though unbroken prosperity lay ahead; President Hoover had himself used words to that effect. Then in October, 1929, occurred the crash in security prices in Wall Street; the prices of goods fell because stocks had piled up in excess of demand for them; farmers could not dispose of their crops profitably; industrial producers found surpluses on their hands; profits fell; men were paid off. The mounting unemployment was the most dire effect of the depression; it was a staggering sight in America to see men down and out, sleeping in the noonday sun in the parks of Chicago or New York—this in a land which had been humming with productive enterprise and where everyone had eagerly sought and easily found employment. The slump started in America, but it spread to Europe and ultimately affected the uttermost parts of the earth.

Economists are not altogether agreed on the causes and exact nature of the world depression. But it is possible to find agreement on a number of factors in the situation, though economists may differ as to their relative importance. The Great War had caused destruction, economic dislocation and the unnatural speeding up of industrialisation. So far as the standard of life goes, however, the world had recovered by 1925: production and consumption per head were higher than in 1913. By 1929 the world as a whole was above all earlier standards. The payment of reparations and war debts had made the United States a great creditor country, and had concentrated there the major part of the world's gold. The gold was kept unused, which reduced the world's money supply, thereby reducing prices. Tariffs, and the widespread effort of countries to export without importing, led to further dislocation of world trade.

Technical advances in production had brought about over-production in both agriculture and industry. Machinery was now available to produce on so vast a scale that the products could not be sold profitably, because of the falling prices which plenty always brings. This does not mean that everyone in the world had enough; there were still hundreds of millions of miserably poor people in the world, but these people had little or nothing to give in exchange for the products of the highly-capitalised countries. Short of giving away their surplus of production, these countries could not dispose of it. The ultimate solution—which took several years to achieve— came about through cuts in production, unemployment, and a reduction in the amount of goods to be sold which adjusted prices once more to the advantage of the producer. The paradox of the slump appeared in the fact of poverty in the midst of plenty: while people were starving in the Far East and the unemployed were reducing their standard of life in America and Europe, the great producing countries were destroying stocks to try to raise prices: coffee was burnt and wheat ploughed in.

The American slump soon became a world depression. American lending had for years been keeping Europe going; these loans had helped Germany to reconstruct her industrial system and to pay reparations. During the boom years Americans had looked eagerly to Europe as a place where they could employ their surplus in the form of loans. In 1929 with the slump this lending suddenly stopped. Sir Arthur Salter, who as General Secretary of the Allied Repara-tions Commission and later Director of the Economic and Finance Section of the League of Nations, had unrivalled experience and was in a position to judge, has underlined this cause of the slump: 'It was ill-directed, and often excessive, foreign lending that undermined the financial structure; it was the change in the form of foreign lending from investments to short-term advances that laid the train; it was the sudden arrest of this lending that fired the mine.'

The slump produced a cataclysm: in May, 1931, the *Kreditanstalt*, the largest private bank in Austria, was on the verge of collapse and had to be assisted by the government. The scheme for an Austrian-German customs union, which might have done something to help Austria, had been blocked by the other Powers and was, after the failure of the bank, eventually abandoned. The Austrian crisis shook financial confidence at the very time that American bankers were recalling their short-term loans. Financial crisis followed in Germany where in July the *Darmstädter und National-Bank* closed its doors. The German Government temporarily shut all banks and stock exchanges. This was in spite of the initiative of President Hoover which had brought about a moratorium on reparations and international debts.

Thereafter further international action followed to fix or freeze all the existing short-term credits to Germany. This helped to precipitate financial crisis in Great Britain where bankers, unable to withdraw their credits to Germany, were in difficulty in meeting obligations elsewhere. Britain already had her own troubles: falling exports, unemployment, the cost of social services and the consequent problem of balancing the budget. The new crisis resulted in the formation of a National Government, followed by suspension of the gold standard and, a little later, of the war debt payments to America. A general election at the end of 1931 smashed the Labour Party and returned a huge Conservative majority, although the new government was still termed National and led by Ramsay MacDonald, the former Labour Prime Minister. The United States reacted the other way: in 1932 the conservative, Hoover, was defeated and Roosevelt elected as President, with the New Deal programme of public works to alleviate unemployment. For this was the principal social menace: it reached at its peak about 12,000,000 in the United States, 6,000,000 in Germany, and 3,000,000 in Great Britain.

Y

Japanese Aggression in Manchuria

While the depression was shaking Europe and even America to their foundations, it also gravely worsened the general situation in the Far East. Japan was by long tradition an autocratic and a militarist state; but in the early years of the League of Nations her position as an original member encouraged the native peace movement, and liberal politicians in the Japanese parliament contrived, though with difficulty, to get a moderate policy adopted. The urge towards aggression was, however, powerfully stimulated by the hard facts of her economic position—a rapidly growing population, which in relation to cultivable area had become the densest in the world; hence the absolute necessity to the national life of secure export markets; hence the ascendancy of the soldiers, who alone could make them secure. The depression caused a big drop in the export of raw silk to the United States, which adversely affected employment in Japan, so the war lords seized their chance. In the autumn of 1931 they launched a campaign of conquest in the outlying Chinese territory of Manchuria, and in the face of world opinion and the wholly adverse Report of the Lytton Commission, which the League of Nations sent to investigate Japanese claims and pretexts on the spot, they were eventually successful. This was a heavy blow to the prestige of the League. It also had much to do with the atmosphere of discouragement in which the long-awaited World Disarmament Conference opened in February, 1932, though the prevalence in France of the view that only her retention of superior armaments could offset Germany's superior numbers, would in any case have made agreement very hard to reach, even in a world that was less distraught than that of 1932.

Causes of the Rise of Hitler

Everywhere there was fundamental criticism of an economic system which had broken down so disastrously; everywhere belief in democracy and international co-operation was weakened; peoples began to look to new men and new methods. Writing in 1932, Sir Arthur Salter well summed up the character and the social and political tendencies of the slump:

'The defects of the capitalist system have been increasingly robbing it of its benefits. They are now threatening its existence. A period of depression and crisis is one in which its great merit, the expansion of productive capacity under the stimulus of competitive gain, seems wasted; and its main defect, an increasing inability to utilise productive capacity fully and to distribute what it produces tolerably, is seen at its worst. And, to the mood of desperation caused by impoverishment and unemployment, the challenge of another system becomes formidable. No one can expect that even if we now get through without disaster, we can long avoid social disintegration and revolution on the widest scale if we have only a prospect of recurring depressions, perhaps of increasing violence.

'We have indeed before us only the alternatives of collective leadership, collective control, or chaos. . . . We must do our best to eliminate the third, and make the best mixture we can of the first two.'

It was the 'mood of desperation' in Germany which gave Hitler his opportunity; in that mood men were looking to leadership for salvation, and in their despair they were not inclined to examine too carefully the credentials of the leader. There had been many critics of the Treaty of Versailles who had blamed it for all the difficulties of Europe during the post-war years; there were some who blamed it for the rise of Hitler to power in Germany. Hitler, it is true, made much play with the treaty in his propaganda, but Hitler himself made little headway until the 'thirties. In the preceding years of optimism it was permissible to think that Germany had forgotten the humiliation of defeat. The troops of occupation were withdrawn; Germany was a member of the League; Stresemann worked well with Briand and Austen Chamberlain for European pacification. But then came the slump; economic depression produced the mood of desperation. The growth of Hitler's National Socialist Party in Germany coincides exactly with the years of economic depression. At first Hitler's party was only one among many parties in the Reichstag. The figures for successive elections during the depression period show how it climbed towards a position of dominance:

			Seats	Votes
1928	..	..	13	810,000
1930	..	..	107	6,409,000
1932 (July)		..	230	13,779,000

(out of a Reichstag of 609)[1]

There had been since the war a struggle in Germany, between the new forces of democracy and peace and the old forces of autocracy and militarism, for the soul of the German people. The decision had long been in doubt: the depression decided it. Germany passed under the dictatorship of Hitler. We must now turn to the characteristics of Germany and the events in its history which helped to bring this about.

The democracy of Weimar was something new; Bismarck had all too successfully destroyed German liberalism, and established a respect for force. Weimar democracy had no deep roots in German history and tradition. On the contrary, it was associated in the German mind with the acceptance of the Versailles *Diktat*, against which all classes of Germans rebelled, not chiefly on account of its form or content, however galling these may have been, but because it was the symbol of defeat. A defeated Germany was in German eyes a paradox—there must be a mistake somewhere. Thus they had little to attach them to the new political system, and when that system came to involve widespread unemployment, economic stagnation and the growth of social disorder, with extremists of both sides brawling almost daily in the streets, men looked back once more to an older Germany and to the tradition of military leadership.

Militarism, because of its successes, became deeply ingrained in the German character during the nineteenth century. It is misleading simply to say that Germans have always been warlike; this is perhaps true, but all peoples have been warlike and savage in their early periods. The Germans, however, did not grow out of their aggressiveness. With the Germans their belief in force was strengthened by victory in the wars of 1864, 1866 and 1870: war had paid. Still more, it was victory in war that had created the German Empire and made it dominant in Europe. Teaching in schools and universities, compulsory military training, the writings of philosophers all

[1] See note on p. 353.

supported the view that the national state was the highest good and that it was rightly supported by war. Thus there was, in fact, a military tradition which was potent for evil. The Germans as a result of their history were not unprepared to accept a strong military lead. There was widespread unemployment in the United States and also in Great Britain, where the slump led to deep political changes, but not to fascist dictatorship. In Germany, depression swept into power a militaristic dictator who used his position to destroy democracy altogether, and to do it with all possible contumely and derision.

Hitler, in spite of the ridicule which his humble origin and lack of education evoked in some quarters, was a great popular orator with a real power of personal magnetism over the masses. He promised everything to everybody. He played up the German race as a pure race, a *Herrenvolk* or master race, destined to rule other inferior races; he harped on the theme of an overcrowded Germany and the need for *Lebensraum* (living-space) which could be won by the sword in Russia or taken in colonial territory from the feeble hands of the pluto-democracies. He attacked pacificism, internationalism, Versailles and the League of Nations; he thus won the support of those who hoped for jobs as officers in a new German Army. He attacked communists and socialists; this brought him the support and (even more important) the funds of the great capitalists. He attacked monopolies, trusts and combines, and plutocrats and profiteers; this won him the support of some socialists, and of many of the middle classes who had lost their savings in the inflation. He attacked the vice of the streets and decadence in art and literature, which brought him some support from the churches. He attacked the Jews—as communists and also as capitalists, for inconsistency did not worry Hitler—and he promised their jobs to the professional classes. Lastly, not only did he attack in theory, he attacked in practice. He organised a vast private army— the brownshirts or S.A. (*Sturmabteilung*)—which went into the slums and working-class quarters, challenged the communists on their own ground and broke up their meetings.

Germany was dividing into two armed camps: Communist and Nazi (National Socialist). Moderate or liberal Germans were being forced by the march of events to consider which was the lesser of the two evils. The tension was acute.

Hitler probably exaggerated the danger from the communists, but there was a marked dislike on the part of moderate Germans for attending political meetings because of the danger of violent outbreaks between communists and Nazis. The atmosphere of violence was just what the Nazis needed: it gave scope to their own thugs and by fear of communism terrorised the moderate Germans. All the time the Nazi propaganda went on: marches and torchlight processions, great mass meetings, and the ceaseless, diabolical appeal to the lowest instincts of the mob. Hitler found a scapegoat for their desperation and an excuse for their hatred in the 'stab in the back' theory: Germany had never been defeated in battle, she had been stabbed in the back by the Jews, communists and pacificists.

Brüning and the Struggle for the German Chancellorship, 1930–3

During these years of frantic Nazi propaganda the German Government had to contend with an almost impossible situation. Already in June, 1930, Brüning, who was Chancellor but had not a secure position in the Reichstag, had to govern by presidential decree which was provided for in the constitution in case of emergency. In September the Nazis became the second largest party in the Reichstag. Brüning was trying desperately to cope with the financial necessity for economies, the social menace of unemployment and the danger of revolution. But it was becoming rapidly evident that Hitler and the Nazis now had a real chance of gaining power. In April, 1932, Hitler stood as a candidate in the presidential election and gained 13,000,000 votes, although Hindenburg was re-elected with 19,000,000. The elections for the Reichstag in July revealed the great numerical strength of the Nazis and made them the largest party. The position was: out of 609 seats—Nazis 230 seats, Social Democrats 133 seats, Communists 89 seats.[1] In another election held in November, the Nazis received a check and the communists increased their representation—which led certain optimists outside Germany to conclude that Nazism had reached its zenith and might now be expected to decline.

Yet in Germany Hindenburg had to resort to every kind of shift to keep Hitler out. In June, 1932, Brüning was replaced

[1] See note on p. 353.

by the Conservative, von Papen; it was hoped that he would be able to maintain a Right Wing government in power without Hitler. In July the President himself broke the constitution, in spirit if not in letter, when he invoked its emergency clauses to justify the forcible ejection of the State Government in Prussia, which had been social democratic as a result of every election since 1918. A Reich Commissioner replaced the social democrats, who offered no resistance. Meanwhile von Papen as Chancellor was the go-between in further negotiations with Hitler, who still demanded full dictatorial powers which Hindenburg would not concede. General von Schleicher then succeeded von Papen, but neither of these makeshift premiers had any real backing in the Reichstag. Once again approach was made to Hitler. This time he agreed to a coalition. On January 30, 1933, Hitler became Chancellor. Astute and experienced politicians like von Papen, who was a member of the new Cabinet, thought that they would be able to keep the fire-eater under control, but they proved completely wrong in their calculations. Hitler was now master, as events were soon to show. January 30 marked a turning-point in European history. The success of National Socialism in Germany was, as Professor Toynbee described it in his survey of the year 1933:

'the outstanding and dominating political event of the year in the whole field of international affairs. It signified in Europe what had been signified in the Far East and the Pacific by the Japanese *coup*. . . . Taken together, these two outbreaks of violence brought the post-war chapter of history to a close and opened a new chapter which was manifestly fraught with the most momentous issues of good or evil.'

Democracy and internationalism were now on the defensive: the immediate future lay with the dictators.

SUGGESTIONS FOR FURTHER READING

H. W. Schneider: *Making the Fascist State*, c. 3.

T. L. Jarman: *The Rise and Fall of Nazi Germany*, cc. 4–7.

W. L. Shirer: *The Rise and Fall of the Third Reich*, cc. 1–6.

S. King-Hall: *Our Own Times*, cc. 7, 25–7.

M. Oakeshott: *The Social and Political Doctrines of Contemporary Europe*, Sections 4 and 5.

CHAPTER 20

FASCISM IN THE ASCENDANT, 1933–9

The Nazi Revolution

THE National Socialist Revolution in Germany came after and not before Hitler's accession to power in January, 1933. He was called upon to become Chancellor in a constitutional way; Mussolini in 1922 had also been summoned in a more-or-less constitutional manner to become Prime Minister by the King of Italy. For this reason the fascist revolutions differed from that of the Russian Bolsheviks in 1917, where power had actually been seized from the previous government by a revolutionary *coup*. In both Italy and Germany the revolutionary change was made after the accession of the leader to power, although in Germany it was accomplished much more rapidly than in Italy. But for the moment the new German Government was a coalition; it included von Papen, and also members of the Nationalist Party, which though similar to the Nazis was distinct in organisation and had its own private army, the *Stahlhelm*. The social democrats still hoped they could continue to play the party game as an opposition in the Reichstag. But Hitler had other ideas.

Preparations were quickly made for holding new elections. Göring, a minister in the Central Government and also Minister of the Interior in Prussia and thus in charge of the Prussian police, enrolled as auxiliaries members of the S.A. and the *Stahlhelm*, supplied arms and ordered the police to use them 'without regard to the effect of their shots.' 'The bullets they fire are my bullets,' he declared. A fire broke out in the Reichstag building: this was announced as the work of the communists (strong suspicion attaches to the Nazis themselves) and made the excuse for a decree suspending the clauses of the constitution which guaranteed personal liberty. Göring was thus free to arrest all communist deputies; and many other arrests were made. The Nazis were adepts at violence and terror; they controlled the radio, broke up the meetings of their political opponents, and openly threatened all those who did not support them. In this atmosphere of violent suppression the elections took place on March 5. They resulted in giving a majority to the Nazi-Nationalist Coalition—but a small one: 341 seats out of a total Reichstag of 647.[1] The communists suffered, but the Social Democratic Party and the Catholic Centre Party retained approximately the same number of seats as before. It is noteworthy that at this election many millions of Germans voted against Hitler and still supported the parties of moderation. The election result indeed caused much dissatisfaction among the Nazis and incited them to violent anti-Semitism and a wider use of terror; it also made advisable the taking over by the government of dictatorial powers.

These moves gave Hitler complete control of the Reichstag: he therefore was free to proceed to the measures necessary to destroy the remaining opposition. First, as Germany was a federal state, the elected parliaments of the states were dealt with. This had already happened in Prussia; in each case a *Reichskommissar* or regent was put in charge, with power to nominate and dismiss members of the local Cabinet. An enabling bill was passed through the Reichstag conferring what were virtually dictatorial powers on the Coalition Government. Shortly afterwards the Nationalists merged their organisation with the Nazis, and the German Government became completely Nazi. Next the Social Democratic Party was forcibly dissolved and its private army, the *Reichsbanner*, liquidated; the trade unions were broken up, the socialist offices and newspapers seized and the funds confiscated. The Catholic Centre Party was persuaded to liquidate itself. On July 11, an official order proclaimed the Nazi Party the sole party and declared the revolution at an end. In November, a plebiscite on Germany's leaving the League of Nations approved such action by 39,000,000 out of a total vote of 42,000,000.

None the less during the first eighteen months of power a divergence began to be marked between the nationalist and the socialist elements in the Nazi Party. On June 30, 1934, Hitler struck hard at those whom he suspected of hostility,

[1] The Reichstag membership varied in number according to the total votes cast at each election. A useful table of the elections from 1919–33 is given in G. Scheele, *The Weimar Republic*. Numbers of seats attributed to parties differ slightly in different accounts. German parties were many and exact classification difficult.

that is, mainly at the socialist element: a massacre took place with the seizure and immediate shooting of those thought dangerous. These included, besides the socialist element represented by Hitler's early Nazi followers like Gregor Strasser and the S.A. leaders Röhm and Ernst, several Catholics, several Bavarian politicians, two of von Papen's secretaries, and the preceding Chancellor, General von Schleicher. 'In those twenty-four hours,' Hitler declared in the Reichstag, 'the Supreme Court of the German People was I.' Hitler was virtually a law unto himself, and when Hindenburg died in August there was no election of a new president. The presidential office was merged with the chancellorship and Hitler became *Führer und Reichskanzler*.

The German Government was now in the hands of a fanatic who believed that he had a divine mission to make the Germans the dominant Power in the world. He was, he claimed, the true representative of the German people. In his mission he had complete confidence. 'I go my way,' he said in a speech a few years later, 'with the assurance of a somnambulist, the way which Providence has sent me . . . if I have done wrongly, then I shall ask God Almighty to strike me down.' The triumph of the Nazi Party marked a German reaction after the political and psychological prostration into which Germans had fallen as a result of their defeat in 1918; it also signified a new deification of the German State and a further stage in the old struggle between the tribal, local or nationalist interests of one race or group and the Christian idea of universal brotherhood. In raising this issue anew and destroying the basis of the League of Nations Hitlerism was a symptom of a crisis in western history. Anti-Semitism revived in an acute form. The Jews were cruelly persecuted; those who were able left the country. Jews were condemned as an inferior race, and their synagogues attacked and burned. Mankind was to be classified afresh on the basis of race, with the Nordic race (of which the Germans were held to be the leading representatives) at the top; bloodshed, intolerance, war, were glorified as splendid demonstrations of Nordic heroism. And all this came from a nation at the heart of Europe, a nation supposedly advanced and supposedly Christian, and a nation which could back its theories and aims with all the apparatus of propaganda and, when rearmed, with all the scientific destructiveness of modern war. The new Germany at once became a threat to her neighbours.

Grouping of Powers against Hitler—the Defence of Austria

International reactions were immediate. The menace of a renascent Germany alarmed France; it also alarmed Russia. In 1934 Russia was admitted into the League of Nations. It was a singular event. In early years the Soviet leaders had denounced the League as a robber band of capitalist states; now Russia found it expedient to join with these same capitalist states. Russia also made pacts in 1935 with France and Czechoslovakia. In spite of great differences of internal policy France and Russia came together again; just as the danger of the old imperial Germany had made allies of Czarist Russia and republican France, so again Nazi Germany forced Soviet Russia and capitalist France to make a pact for mutual defence against attack by any European Power. In July, 1934, the British Government, too, embarked on an air programme which was designed to restore the R.A.F.'s supremacy in Europe—a programme which was to have a long and chequered history; but it produced radiolocation and the Spitfire fighter. An understanding was hastily concluded between France and Italy, minor colonial concessions being made by the French in order to release troops from her Alpine frontier for possible service elsewhere.

What had happened in Germany had its direst immediate effects in troubled Austria. The Chancellor, Dollfuss, found his position increasingly difficult between the communists on the Left and the Austrian Nazis on the Right, who looked for union with Germany. Dollfuss and his Christian Socialist Party tried to maintain Austrian independence, but were forced to rely increasingly on support from Prince Stahremberg and his semi-fascist organisation, the *Heimwehr*. This organisation looked to Italy. Mussolini still regarded Germany as a danger to his own position and was therefore anxious to maintain an independent Austria. In February, 1934, there was a short, sharp struggle in Vienna between the government of the Republic and the socialist provincial government of Vienna, before the working-class quarters—the great, new municipal blocks, the *Karl Marxhof* and the *Goethehof*—were bombarded into submission. This action alienated the workers, and in the summer the government was challenged by the Austrian Nazis. Dollfuss was murdered. But the attempted *coup* failed: Mussolini mobilised Italian troops on the Brenner, Hitler held back and Dr. Schuschnigg took up the chancellorship from Dollfuss. Schuschnigg clung on uneasily until 1938.

Mussolini's determined action in 1934 is an illustration of how, in the three years immediately following Hitler's accession to power, fascist Italy could be regarded as a useful balance to Nazi Germany. Indeed, Mussolini's policy of a strong Italy won support outside during these years wherever the wish to check Germany was a factor in the situation. At the Stresa Conference in 1935, France, Italy and Britain reached agreement on a common front against German rearmament and the threat of Nazi aggression. Laval, the French Foreign Minister, was particularly anxious to ensure the continued friendship of Italy. He depended upon Russia on Germany's eastern flank, but the position of Italy was also basic to his policy: 'as long as Italy was France's ally we had a bridge leading to all those countries . . . of eastern Europe which were then our allies. We could, therefore, not only benefit by whatever military strength Italy represented, but also by the added strength of Jugoslavia, Czechoslovakia, Poland and Rumania.' This coloured his attitude to Italy's imperial claims and weakened the position of France as a supporter of League policy during the Italo-Abyssinian conflict. But the effect of that conflict was, in spite of the efforts of Laval, to estrange France and Italy and drive the latter into the German camp.

Failure of the Disarmament and World Economic Conferences

The Stresa Conference resulted in the demonstration of an apparent unity in face of the Nazi menace, but it ignored the indications of the coming Italo-Abyssinian conflict. Meanwhile, too, the various efforts to achieve some lasting agreement and reconciliation in the world were breaking down. Nothing had come of the plea in 1925 that the League of Nations should be 'a first rough draft of a United States of Europe.' Indeed the prestige of the League itself was much lowered by the Japanese success in Manchuria. Japan refused all compromise and left the League, and the League Powers were unable or unwilling to coerce her. The League failure signified the return of 'power politics' in the Far East. The Disarmament Conference opened at Geneva in February 1932. Preparations for it went back to the first meeting of the Preparatory Commission in 1926; now at last it met while the Japanese were overrunning Manchuria and the world economic depression was at its worst. Several plans were put forward and discussed but no agreement could be reached. During the years that disarmament had been considered all kinds of suggestions were put forward varying from a Russian plea for complete disarmament to the German claim for equality in armaments; suggestions included abolition of offensive weapons and retention only of weapons of defence and also a plea for a League armed force. They all came to nothing: the Conference was not formally dissolved but just petered out. It ceased to meet after the end of 1934.

Yet another failure of a rather different kind was the World Economic Conference of sixty-six Powers, the largest muster of sovereign states known to history, which met in London in June, 1933. The payment of reparations and inter-allied war debts had already virtually ceased: in 1932 Germany made one final payment in the form of 5 per cent. redeemable bonds; France defaulted on her debt to the United States, and Great Britain made only token payments in 1933. After that nothing more was paid. It was hoped that the World Economic Conference would agree to a reduction in tariffs and quotas with a view to stimulating a revival in world trade. But France demanded currency stabilisation as a condition. This the American Government refused, as it had just abandoned the gold standard and discovered the advantage of a flexible currency. Nothing of real importance was achieved. Thus world co-operation failed in every sphere: the political, that of disarmament, and in the field of economics.

The Italian Conquest of Abyssinia

The most serious event of all was still to come: this was the Italo-Abyssinian conflict. The Italian attack on Abyssinia in 1935 demonstrated that the worst could happen: a clear act of aggression against a fellow member by a European foundation member of the League of Nations. No mention was made of the dispute, then in an early stage, at the Stresa

Conference, and Mussolini may well have been encouraged by this to push on with his preparations for war. Mussolini felt an urgent desire for imperial expansion and Italy had an old interest in Abyssinia and also an old score to settle. Italy had attempted its conquest forty years earlier and her troops had suffered complete defeat at Adowa in 1896. This time trouble started late in December, 1934, with an affray at Walwal, near the border of Italian Somaliland. Abyssinia appealed to the League in January. But soon the original dispute was almost lost sight of in the alarm caused by Italian preparations for war. In February, 1935, Italy was already sending fresh troops to East Africa. General de Bono has since described how for three years he had been making careful preparations in Eritrea. In Italy itself threatening speeches were being made and militaristic demonstrations were taking place. Abyssinia brought Italy's preparations to the notice of the League, but the League several times postponed consideration of the problem in the vain hope that it might be settled by the two parties concerned in direct negotiation. The British Government put forward a scheme of settlement, a conference of British, French and Italian representatives met in Paris and made suggestions, the League Council appointed a committee to seek a peaceful settlement: all failed. Mussolini was adamant. Then, in September at the League Assembly, the British Foreign Secretary made a bold speech. It sounded like a call to action, not a call for further committees. Sir Samuel Hoare, later Lord Templewood, said:

'The League stands, and my country stands with it, for the collective maintenance of the Covenant in its entirety, and particularly for steady and collective resistance to all acts of unprovoked aggression.'

But, despite all this, it had already been agreed to rule out all action 'that might lead to war.' There would be no resort to military sanctions, no naval blockade, no closure of the Suez Canal. Worst of all, Mussolini knew of this. He realised that he was safe in proceeding with his plans for the conquest of Abyssinia.[1]

---

[1] For a full account of these proceedings see R. W. Seton-Watson, *Britain and the Dictators*, c. 10.

Mussolini's own attitude was clearly illustrated in his speeches. When he deigned to excuse himself he declared that he was simply acting as British empire-builders had acted in the past, and that the Abyssinian affair was a purely colonial matter which need not affect Europe. At other times he was more frank, and gave full vent to his militaristic and imperial aims. Thus, in 1934, he said:

'It is . . . necessary to be prepared for war, not to-morrow, but to-day. We are becoming, and shall become so increasingly because this is our desire, a military nation. A militaristic nation, I will add, since we are not afraid of words.'

Sometimes he spoke of a 'mission of colonisation'—'Italy could above all civilise Africa.' Fundamentally he appealed to Italian self-interest and to force as the means of furthering it. In 1935, he declared:

'The essential arguments, absolutely unanswerable, are two: the vital needs of the Italian people and their security in East Africa. Put in military terms, the Italo-Abyssinian problem is simple and logical. It admits—with Geneva, without Geneva, against Geneva—but one solution.'

It was to be 'against Geneva.' On October 2, 1935, the Italian invasion of Abyssinia began.

This time, however, the League did take some action, even though the action proved ineffective. The League Council found that Italy had resorted to war in disregard of the Covenant. The Assembly met, and fifty nations out of fifty-four accepted the Council's findings and set up a committee to take action under Article 16 of the Covenant, the famous sanctions article. Economic sanctions were in fact applied on November 18: they included an embargo on supply to Italy of arms and war material, a prohibition of loans to Italy, and an embargo on imports from Italy. It was a notable step in the right direction, but it was not enough. For, in spite of the natural obstacles of the country which made guerrilla resistance fairly effective at first, the well-armed Italian troops were pressing on into Abyssinia. England and France, meanwhile, made one further attempt at settlement. After consultation in Paris, a plan for dividing

Abyssinia was put forward, with a large part going to Italy. There was a storm of popular indignation in England, and Hoare resigned, to be succeeded by Mr. Anthony Eden. In January, 1936, the practicability of an oil sanction against Italy was discussed by a League committee, but in March the whole scene was transformed by the German military re-occupation of the demilitarised Rhineland. This brought Nazi forces right up to the French frontier: French and British attention turned away from Abyssinia to central Europe. Mussolini's troops in Abyssinia were now reaching the final stage of the conquest, which they expedited by the use of poison gas sprayed from the air. They entered the capital, Addis Ababa, on May 5. Abyssinia was soon afterwards formally annexed and the King of Italy took the additional title of Emperor. In July sanctions ceased, and in October Germany recognised the Italian annexation of Abyssinia.

The triumph of Italy was a victory for violence and unscrupulous nationalism over the democratic ideals of internationalists. Italy's success was a grave blow, almost a fatal blow, to the League. It revealed the weakness of the democracies. It encouraged Germany; Hitler knew that what Mussolini could do he could do. If Italy could get away with it, Germany might get away with it too. The League had missed its opportunity of teaching one dictator a lesson. As a result of the missed opportunity, the two dictators came together in what was known as the 'Rome-Berlin axis.' The forces of aggression were thus strengthened. Clearly and finally Mussolini's action had demonstrated the menace which fascist dictatorship constituted to peace and democracy. But even now, as the following years were to show, the democracies of the world were still unprepared to unite to prevent further aggression.

The Spanish Civil War

In 1936 as the Italo-Abyssinian conflict came to an end a new conflict—the Spanish Civil War—was beginning. It threatened to plunge Europe into an ideological struggle. For what was essentially a Spanish affair—one in a long series of disturbances—brought to each side the support of foreign backers, on the one side fascist Italy and Nazi Germany, and on the other communist Russia. The democracies made a desperate attempt, by following a policy of non-intervention, to avoid being drawn in. The outstanding feature of the Spanish struggle as an international problem was that its origin lay outside the general course of European events and was largely unconnected with the First World War and the peace settlement. If it had not been for the fascist and communist interference the war in Spain would have had little direct concern for Europe. The causes of the Civil War in Spain were essentially internal, Spanish ones. The Republic had had an uneasy existence since 1931: the machinery of democratic government existed, but the balance was precarious between royalists and reactionaries on the Right and communists and anarchists on the Left. Violence was common; for example, a rising of socialists in 1934 at Oviedo and waves of church burning in 1931 and 1936. The finances were chaotic. Elections in 1936 gave a majority of seats in parliament to the Left Wing Popular Front. But in votes the country was nearly equally divided. The Right Wing, supported by most of the landed, Army, Church and business elements, was ready to resist. In July, General Franco, commander of the troops in Spanish Morocco, launched a rebellion. He crossed into Spain with his army, largely composed of Moorish troops, and overran the south and west of Spain. By November his troops were in the Madrid suburbs and the government withdrew to Valencia. But at this point a desperate Republican stand in Madrid, stiffened by the determination of the communists, held up Franco's advance; the government resistance was maintained, and the struggle settled down into what was to prove a prolonged war.

From the start Franco received Italian help; Italian aeroplanes assisted in transporting his troops from Morocco. A few months later Germany as well as Italy was more or less openly sending arms to the insurgents; Russia was assisting the government. Although the government was not a communist one, Russia doubtless hoped that eventually the communist element would dominate it. Russia had long had its eye on backward Spain with its illiterate peasant population as a country which, given circumstances comparable to those of Russia in 1917, might be a favourable ground for a communist revolution. A Spanish member of the Communist International, Joaquin Maurin, wrote in 1935:

'In Spain, as in Russia, there will be civil war. It is inevitable and necessary.'

The Spanish Civil War, as it went on, took more and more the complexion of a European ideological conflict. Italian and German troops fought with Franco. Russians, anti-fascist Italians and anti-Nazi Germans, and the International Brigade of volunteers from many countries fought on the side of the government. When the fall of Madrid appeared likely, in November, Italy and Germany officially recognised the rival government set up by Franco. They hoped for a Franco victory because this would be a blow to communism, would help to give Italy control of the western Mediterranean, and would weaken France by giving Germany an ally beyond the Pyrenees. Britain and France, on the other hand, aimed at maintaining their neutrality and at the same time preventing Germany or Italy from gaining any permanent foothold in Spanish territory. Almost at once Britain and France imposed a ban on export of arms to Spain; in September a non-intervention committee (including, ironically enough, Germany, Italy and Russia) met in London, and in April, 1937, a system of naval control and frontier supervision was set up. It was farcical. In May the German battleship *Deutschland* was attacked by Spanish Republican planes and shelled Almeria as a reprisal; Germany and Italy then withdrew from the non-intervention committee. Submarine attacks now became frequent—on British, French and Russian ships—and it soon became clear that Italian submarines were responsible in their efforts to blockade the coasts of government Spain. The Nyon Conference in September arranged concerted measures against submarine activity, and it ceased.

But the large supply of arms getting through to Franco from Italy and Germany was beginning to turn the scale, although the struggle dragged on. In the spring of 1938 Franco severed the territory which linked Barcelona with Valencia, and so divided the government forces. In the following winter his troops conquered republican Catalonia and in January, 1939, Barcelona fell. General Franco's troops soon afterwards entered Madrid and hostilities came, almost unnoticed, to an end. Britain and France formally recognised the Franco government: it was a victory for fascism, but attention had meanwhile moved to events in central Europe where the expansion of Nazi Germany was fast leading to the final crisis.

The Principles of German Expansion

At this point it is convenient to go back to 1933 and to trace the events of German expansion in one continuous sequence. Germany was by far the most powerful of the fascist dictatorships, and it was the rapid growth of Nazi Germany into the dominant force in Europe which character-ised the years between 1933 and 1939. German expansion went on almost without a check and continued with the outbreak of war in 1939. As von Clausewitz, the German military writer, had said years before: 'War was the continua-tion of policy by other means.' It was not, in fact, until 1942 that German expansion was checked.

Hitler's determination to advance the German race, to find it new living space in the wide, fertile plains of Russia and to dominate Europe by force was expressed in *Mein Kampf*, but western statesmen showed themselves remarkably heedless of this book. Hitler's immediate foreign policy after getting into power in Germany was to throw dust in the eyes of the leaders of foreign nations by talking of peace and to cover up his ultimate objects until Germany was rearmed. 'The German nation wishes to live in peace with the rest of the world,' Hitler declared in the Reichstag almost immediately after he became Chancellor. He spoke to journalists from abroad in similar words, assuring Ward Price of the *Daily Mail* that the Nazi leaders were old soldiers who knew the horrors of war and wished for no repetition. But the British Ambassa-dor, Sir Horace Rumbold, reported that the new German government's only programme was 'the revival of militarism and the stamping out of pacifism.' Hitler, he wrote—

'declares that he is anxious that peace should be maintained for a ten-year period. What he probably means can be more accurately expressed by the formula: Germany needs peace until she has recovered such strength that no country can challenge her without serious and irksome preparations. . . .'

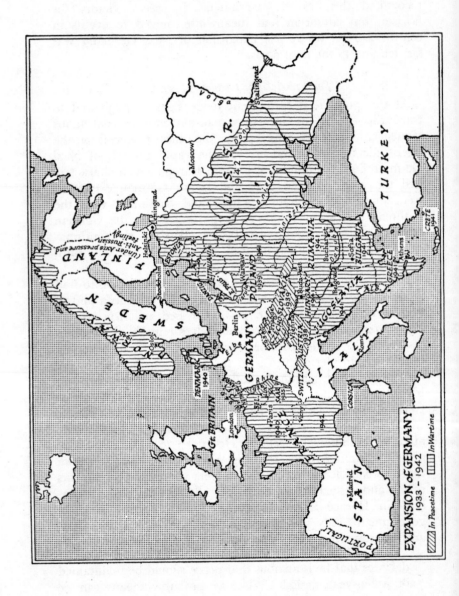

EXPANSION of GERMANY
1933 – 1942

In Peacetime   In Wartime

Britain and France were indeed materially and psychologically unready to make those preparations. Hitler, in the long game of power-politics, was always a move or two ahead. He gained, too, no little sympathy from conservative elements in the west for his claim that a strong Germany would be a bulwark for Europe against the advance of Russian Communism. Thus the controlled German Press with its repeated sensational headings on 'The Menace of the Red Army' had the twofold object of uniting patriotic Germans and winning support abroad. Hitler aimed always at an immediate and limited objective; he avoided uniting against him all foreign interests opposed to his policy. 'A clever conqueror,' he had written in *Mein Kampf*, 'will always impose his demands on the conquered by instalments.' And in his policy of expansion he took care to show a certain amount of reason in his immediate and limited claim: he disclaimed any intention of absorbing foreign elements, like the Czechs and Poles, by force. He aimed only, he maintained, at uniting with the fatherland people of German race—a policy which could be justified even by appeal to the Wilsonian principle of self-determination.

Hitler's initial success was achieved by a piece of deception which effected a sensational change in German relations with Poland. Friction had been continuous since Versailles—over the Polish Corridor and the Germans in Danzig. Now a ten-years non-aggression pact with Poland was signed, in 1934. This was possible partly because Poland was then offended with her old ally France. France had signed the Four-Power Pact of 1933 with Great Britain, Germany and Italy, a pact which Poland was not invited to join. This pact was an attempt at agreement between the Great Powers, but in the outcome was not ratified and had little importance. Poland now felt a false sense of security as a result of her pact with Germany, and cooled off still further as regards France —the Poles indeed showed themselves to be the worst possible psychologists. Hitler had secured his eastern frontier by placing a barrier between Germany and Russia. He could now safely turn his attention westwards and southwards: he could leave the settlement of his final account with Poland until later.

The Saar Plebiscite

Early next year, on January 13, 1935, took place the plebiscite in the Saar. This territory with its many coal-mines had, since the peace settlement, been governed under the auspices of the League. The plebiscite had been fixed to decide, after fifteen years, whether the Saar should remain as it was, or become German or French; these were the three choices on the voting papers. An international force under British command maintained order and guaranteed a free vote,[1] although the Saarlanders may have felt that, whatever the result, Hitler would seize the Saar and that those who had shown anti-Nazi feelings might then be victimised. The Saarlanders voted with their eyes open; for months past Max Braun and the social democrats had been holding meetings and warning the inhabitants of the Saar of the fate of the socialists and liberals in Nazi Germany. It had little or no effect. The result of the plebiscite was—

	Votes
For return to Germany . . .	477,119
For *status quo*	46,513
For joining France	2,124

It was the clearest possible demonstration that the masses would freely accept a Nazi lead. The people of the Saar were, of course, overwhelmingly German. But, notwithstanding, the result was a singular demonstration of the strength of nationalism in spite of the evil character of the Nazi government of Germany. It showed how much stronger nationalism was than internationalism and common sense. Hitler now quietened fears abroad by declaring that he had no further territorial claims on France.

The Build-up of Germany in Arms, Alliances and Economic Resources

It soon became clear that Germany was rearming. A German air force was being created, Germany was building submarines, and in March, 1935, conscription for military service was announced. This was, of course, contrary to the

[1] This has sometimes been doubted. One of the authors was in the Saar during the plebiscite and saw no sign of disorder. The whole proceedings were carried out under impartial, international control. A full account with the official documents by one of the members of the Saar Plebiscite Commission is in S. Wambaugh, *The Saar Plebiscite* (Harvard University Press, 1940).

Treaty of Versailles. Negotiations were going on meanwhile—in particular Britain was trying to exercise some measure of control by attempting to reach an agreement on armaments with Germany. The British Foreign Secretary, Sir John (later Lord) Simon, and the Minister for League of Nations Affairs, Mr. Eden, visited Hitler in Berlin. In June an Anglo-German naval agreement was reached. It allowed Germany one-third of British naval strength, and permitted the building of submarines. This, although to the British it looked like common sense to agree on what Germany intended to do in any case, meant allowing Germany to repudiate in part the military clauses of the Versailles Treaty. It caused consternation in France, and generally bewildered those who, menaced by German aggression, looked to Britain for support. British policy was vacillating: at Stresa and at Geneva Britain supported a stand against Nazi rearmament in repudiation of Versailles; by the Berlin visit and the naval agreement Britain was making concessions to Nazi demands.

In March, 1936, Hitler seized his chance, when Europe was distracted by the Abyssinian conflict: his forces reoccupied the demilitarised Rhineland. This was not only contrary to Versailles; it was also contrary to Locarno which Germany had freely accepted. Hitler made the Franco-Russian Pact his excuse. Although France was gravely alarmed, no action was taken. British opinion was little moved; to many people it seemed that Hitler was only doing what any strong German government must eventually do. Belgium now backed out of the Locarno arrangements and declared her neutrality for the future, although Britain and France undertook to defend Belgium if necessary. The move in the Rhineland was a remarkable triumph for Nazi Germany: it was, too, the last occasion on which Germany might have been checked without a major war. Just as Hitler had safeguarded his eastern frontier by the pact with Poland so now he was able to protect his western border by building a formidable system of defences along the Rhine and the Saar. The Siegfried Line soon confronted the French Maginot Line, and these opposed systems of static defence promised a stalemate in the west in the event of an outbreak of war.

While Germany was fast becoming a dominant military power, Hitler also devoted attention to strengthening his position by diplomatic and economic means. A common interest in aggression and the need for precautions against the hostility it aroused were forcing the aggressor nations together. The world was dividing into two main groups, sometimes called the 'haves' and the 'have-nots'; the latter were profoundly dissatisfied with the distribution of the world's territories which the peace settlement had fixed or confirmed, the former were in the main satisfied. The so-called 'have-nots' were now concerting their actions. In October, 1936, Germany recognised the new Empire of Ethiopia (Abyssinia), and on November 1 Mussolini announced the creation of the 'Rome-Berlin axis.' At the end of the same month Germany and Japan signed the Anti-Comintern Pact, in which Italy also joined a year later. This pact for consultation and collaboration was nominally directed against the Communist International and thus appealed to all those, inside and outside the three states concerned, who regarded Soviet Russia with anxiety. In fact, it marked a *rapprochement* of the aggressor nations which was a common threat to all other states: in 1937 Japan renewed her aggression in China—and this invasion was war although there was no formal declaration.

Inside Germany, Hitler was pursuing his policy of stifling all opposition, whether from pacifists, the Churches, the socialists, liberals or communists. The persecution of the Jews continued. The means of suppression were the secret police, the concentration camps, torture, and execution. Meanwhile Germany was making every effort to develop her economic resources as the essential backing for modern war. Unemployment was very greatly reduced by the rearmament programme. Scientists turned their skill to the production of synthetic raw materials and of oil from coal, so as to make Germany largely independent of imports. The term *Autobahn* was used, not altogether accurately, for the fine, broad roads which would serve to speed the movement of troops and supplies. In 1936 a Four Year Plan was announced, by which heavy industry was expanded for the purpose of producing munitions for the new mechanised army.

No Sense of Urgency among Other Powers

But in spite of all these things the nations opposed to Germany remained deluded and impotent: in France the *Front Populaire*

(a coalition of Radicals, Socialists and Communists) led by
Léon Blum was carrying through socialistic changes which
distracted attention and emphasised class antagonisms; Soviet
Russia was immobilised by the treason trials and the execution
of suspected generals weakened the Red Army by removing its
trained leaders; in Great Britain opinion was slow-moving
and complacent, and people thought more of the test matches
than of politics. In spite of the repeated warnings by Mr.
Churchill and Mr. Eden no real effort was made to stop the on-
ward march of the dictators. In 1935 and 1937 America passed
Neutrality Acts; one forbade the export to a belligerent of
arms and ammunition, the other restricted the export of
certain accessory goods like scrap-iron and cotton, unless
fetched and paid for by the belligerent. So this time
the New World did not intend to be called in to redress the
balance of the Old. And what was worse: however great the
loathing decent people everywhere felt for the aims and
methods of Hitler, when they were aware of them, there was no
doubt that Hitler's actions were decisive, resolute and successful.
Germany was pulsating with new life and energy from end to
end of the country: in comparison France and Britain appeared
not to know what they wanted. A fatal malaise seemed to have
descended upon them. The Nazis openly regarded the
democracies as decadent: and Hitler was now nearly ready
for stronger and even more sensational deeds.

The Annexation of Austria

In February, 1938, Hitler declared:

'Over ten million Germans live in two states adjoining
our frontiers. It is in the interest of the German Reich to
protect them.'

These 'Germans' were Austrians who lived in Austria and
Czechoslovakia. Hitler now proceeded to take action against
each of these states in turn. Hitler had failed against Austria
in 1934, but this time he counted on the inaction of Mussolini.
This time there was to be no mobilisation of Italian troops
on the Brenner, although, in spite of the Rome-Berlin axis,
Mussolini could scarcely have liked the advance of the Nazis
to the Italian frontier. Hitler brought heavy pressure to
bear on Dr. Schuschnigg. The Austrian Chancellor was

summoned to meet Hitler at Berchtesgaden after public demonstrations organised by the Austrian Nazis. Schuschnigg accepted Hitler's terms and admitted certain Nazis into the Austrian Cabinet, making Seyss-Inquart Minister of the Interior.

Nevertheless, on his return to Vienna, Schuschnigg announced his intention to hold a plebiscite on Austrian independence. Had this plebiscite resulted in a vote for independence it would have been a severe blow to Nazi prestige. Frantic telephone calls now went on between Göring and Seyss-Inquart: Schuschnigg was compelled to abandon the plebiscite and ordered to resign. In his last speech broadcast to the Austrian people on March 11, Schuschnigg announced that Nazi reports that his government had lost control of the situation were 'lies from A to Z' and declared 'we have yielded to force.' 'God protect Austria,' he concluded. German troops crossed the frontier, and on March 12 entered Vienna. There was no resistance by Austria where ties of race and language predisposed large numbers of people to favour the *Anschluss* or union. It caused horrified amazement in England and France—though neither was prepared to act—as a new and yet bolder repudiation of the peace treaties. It added nearly seven million people to Germany, it brought new economic resources and military potential, and by creating so powerful a central European bloc it enabled Germany to dominate the economic life of the Balkan countries. Most significant of all, it put Germany in a position to make Czechoslovakia her next victim.

Czechoslovakia: the Munich Crisis and Settlement

Czechoslovakia, as a glance at a map shows, was between German jaws to north and south. She was the most democratic and advanced of the new states of 1918, but under Nazi pressure she was now threatened with internal disruption. Out of her total population of under fifteen millions, three and one-eighth millions were German-speaking inhabitants of the Sudetenland, where they lived in compact groups along the northern and western frontiers adjoining south-east Germany; to the south were about three-quarters of a million Magyars now encouraged to look for reunion with Hungary; and on the east Poland had a claim to the mining district of

Teschen. There was also some discontent among the backward Slovaks of the eastern half of the State, who resented the predominance of the more progressive urbanised Czechs. Hitler found his excuse for threatening Czechoslovakia in the existence of the large German-speaking minority (though these people had never been inhabitants of Germany; they were Austrian subjects in 1914). He accused the Czechs of persecuting and torturing the Sudetens; he made violent personal attacks on President Beneš. This was almost entirely an artificial agitation. The Sudeten 'Germans,' like all minorities, had some grievances, but they were probably the best treated minority in Europe. There was a more real reason for the Nazi pressure: Czechoslovakia was a democratic state, she had alliances with Hitler's enemies, France and Russia, which made her position a strategical danger to Germany, and for a small Power she was well prepared, possessing, in addition to a well-trained army, the important Skoda armament factories and also a line of prepared defences in mountainous country along her northern frontier. Therefore, before Hitler could act with impunity in the east or the west Czechoslovakia must be disposed of.

German pressure on Czechoslovakia was applied during the spring and summer of 1938. In May there was a crisis, with a partial mobilisation of the Czech Army, but for the moment the trouble passed. European opinion was, however, seriously disturbed and the British government sent Lord Runciman to Czechoslovakia to attempt to bring about some settlement between the government and the 'German' minority. Excitement in Germany was whipped up by Hitler's furious speeches at the Nuremberg *Parteitag*, the Nazi Party rally, in early September. A German attack on Czechoslovakia might have precipitated a general war. At this point the British Prime Minister, Neville Chamberlain, took the unprecedented step of arranging a personal meeting with Hitler; he flew to Munich and was then conducted to Berchtesgaden on September 15. He hastened back to consult the Cabinet. A second meeting took place at Godesberg on September 23; Hitler increased his demands and Chamberlain returned to London. In a last effort at peace, Chamberlain appealed to Mussolini, and a conference met at Munich on September 29. Chamberlain, Hitler, Mussolini and, as an ineffective fourth, Daladier, the weak French Premier, were present; no representative of Czechoslovakia or of Russia was invited. Onerous terms were forced on the Czech government by its own allies, and President Beneš resigned and left the country. Czechoslovakia handed over the Sudetenland, and on October 1 German troops began their occupation of the territory. Poland and Hungary also satisfied their claims. Czechoslovakia was now helpless: her fortress frontier was gone, her internal unity disrupted by the virtual autonomy of Slovakia, and her foreign alliances now clearly worthless. Russia had not been consulted by England and France, and was thus alienated from the west.[1] England and France had suffered a major diplomatic defeat: Hitler was triumphant.

Nevertheless on their return Chamberlain and Daladier were welcomed as saviours by their respective countries. There was hysterical rejoicing because war had been averted. But relief was short-lived and the scene changed. In the following year—March, 1939—German troops overran the remainder of Czechoslovakia. The President, Hacha, summoned to Berchtesgaden, had been bullied into asking for protection. Hitler himself entered Prague as a conqueror. Czechoslovakia had disappeared as an independent state. It was now clear that Hitler had fooled and deceived Chamberlain; the British Prime Minister himself reacted in a speech at Birmingham with a strong condemnation of Hitler's action. But new aggressions were imminent. Almost at once Chamberlain demonstrated his change of policy by guaranteeing Poland against attack. In this guarantee France joined. On Good Friday, Mussolini occupied Albania, and to check a possible expansion south-eastwards by the Axis British and French guarantees were given to Greece and Rumania. Turkey was brought into this defensive system a little later by agreements with Britain and France for mutual assistance in the Mediterranean area. On April 27, for the first time in British history, the principle of peacetime conscription was accepted by the House of Commons. At long last the democracies were beginning to take action to check the menace to their security, but it was now too late to avoid a major struggle.

---

[1] The treaty of mutual assistance between Russian and Czechoslovakia (May 16, 1935) came into effect only in the event of active intervention by France. Chamberlain, it is now known, deprecated any recourse to Russia.

The German Aggression against Poland

Germany had already turned east and stepped up her claims. After an ultimatum to Lithuania, Memel was occupied on March 21. Next, Ribbentrop, the German Foreign Minister, made demands to Poland that Danzig should become part of Germany and that Poland should hand over a part of her Corridor to the sea so as to link East Prussia with the rest of Germany. Danzig was a port inhabited by Germans which the peace settlement had made a free city. This meant that it was under League of Nations supervision, while Poland controlled its customs and its harbour facilities. Leading Nazis were now at work in Danzig, inflaming the people against the Poles. The Polish government now realised that German demands were only a cover for a further campaign against Poland, and the demands were refused. Demands and negotiations were accompanied by the usual propaganda attacks: all the old allegations against the Poles of ill-treatment of German minorities were raked up and the racial superiority of the Germans, the master race, over their Polish oppressors was asserted. To the German public the alleged persecution was made to appear intolerable, and German national feeling was excited in preparation for war. At the end of April Germany repudiated her pact of 1934 with Poland and also the Anglo-German Naval Agreement. Hitler complained that Chamberlain was forgetting their friendship formed at Munich and that Britain was adopting a policy of encirclement of Germany. Repeated warnings were given to Germany that if she sought to settle her claims to Polish territory by force then Britain and France would intervene to assist Poland. During the summer of 1939 there were frequent incidents in Danzig where the local Nazis had a majority in the senate and looked to Hitler for support.

Britain and France made an attempt to reach an understanding with Soviet Russia, for only from Russia could active support be given to Poland in the event of war. It seemed only natural to suppose that Russia—so frequently denounced by Hitler—must join with the western Powers against the common danger. But there were long delays in the Moscow negotiations, to which Britain and France were

content to send diplomatists of the second rank. Russia wished
to include in any agreement a Soviet guarantee to the Baltic
states, Lithuania, Latvia, Estonia and Finland. These states,
however, regarded such a guarantee from Russia as a threat
to their independence; Poland, too, refused to agree to any
protective measures, which might involve entry of Soviet
troops into her territory. The delays in negotiation were
followed by breakdown: reports current in diplomatic circles
for some time that Russia might make a *volte-face* had unfortunately been disregarded. Suddenly came the news that
Ribbentrop was actually in Moscow. On August 23 a non-
aggression pact was signed between Germany and Russia.[1]
The whole situation was changed. Poland was isolated; her
western allies were impotent to help her. Germany had once
more safeguarded her eastern flank and avoided the danger
of a major war on two fronts.

Renewed demands were made on Poland, and made in a
most high-handed manner. Sir Nevile Henderson, the
British Ambassador in Berlin, who was trying to arrange a
way out by working as an intermediary between the German
government and the Polish Ambassador, well summed up the
situation in his final report:

'There was, in fact, for Herr Hitler only one conceivable
alternative to brute force, and that was that a Polish
Plenipotentiary should humbly come to him, after the
manner of Dr. Schuschnigg or President Hacha, and sign
on the dotted line to the greater glory of Adolf Hitler.
And even that must happen at once. The Army was
asking "Yes" or "No."'

The last Polish attempts to negotiate were brushed aside, and
on September 1 the German invasion of Poland began.
On September 3 Great Britain, in fulfilment of her
guarantee to Poland, declared war on Germany, and after
significant last-minute delays was joined later in the day by
France.

[1] The secret archives of the German Foreign Office subsequently captured
by the American and British armies have been published officially in America.
The pact had secret protocols whereby Germany and Russia agreed to divide
Poland between them and Russia was given a free hand to deal with the Baltic
states. See Appendix N in J. W. Wheeler-Bennett, *Munich*.

Hitler's Conquest of Europe, 1938-42

Although the outbreak of war at last would seem to make a clear dividing line in the sequence of events, in effect the course of German aggrandisement went on for some years still unchecked. Nazi Germany continued to extend her hold over Europe until 1942. So carefully laid were Hitler's plans, so powerful the military machine he had created, so weak in comparison the military forces which his original enemies could put against him, that his initial advantages gave him sufficient momentum to continue his advance for some time, even after Russia and the United States had been added to his opponents. In September, 1939, the Germans occupied western Poland, including Warsaw. The spring and summer of 1940 added Denmark, Norway, Holland, Belgium and the greater part of France. In the winter of 1940 German influence permeated the Balkans, and in the spring of 1941 Yugoslavia and Greece were attacked and overrun. At the end of this campaign the only part of south-eastern Europe which remained independent was the Turkish territory adjoining Istanbul (Constantinople). In the south-west the Spain of General Franco was under strong German influence, and the German and Italian forces in north Africa and in Crete gave the Germans a degree of control over the Mediterranean. Further north the precarious neutrality of Switzerland, Sweden and Eire, did not seriously limit German power and influence, which halted only at the English Channel and the North Sea. In June, 1941, the German invasion of Russia led to a further great advance, which brought their forces to the outskirts of Leningrad and Moscow, carried them to Stalingrad on the Volga, and brought them far into the Caucasus. It was not until late in 1942, with the British victory at El Alamein and the Russian defence of Stalingrad, that the tide of Nazi advance was stayed.

Occupied Europe: Hitler's 'New Order'

The occupation of the greater part of Europe, including a large area of Russia, called for the creation of new administrative machinery by the Nazis, but added great economic resources to German war potential and largely freed her from the danger of blockade which had been employed effectively in the First World War. From an administrative and economic point of view a certain unity was imposed upon the many states and races which the Nazi war-machine had overrun. Indeed, in the early years of the war the Nazis made great play with the conception of a 'new order' for Europe, which was to unify and develop European economic life under German direction. But this was little more than a trick of propaganda. German economic control of Europe meant simply the co-ordination of European economic resources to feed Germany's war-machine and bring about her domination of the world. It is the tragedy of Europe that, although Germany is qualified by her central position and highly developed industrial resources to co-operate with the agricultural and raw material producing countries of the Balkans and Russia, the Germans have proved themselves unsuited for leadership in this rôle because of their lust for domination and their lack of the capacity for conciliation and compromise.

German control of occupied Europe was strict and ruthless, but it varied in different parts of Europe; in some countries control was exercised directly by German administrators, in others puppet governments of native pro-Germans were maintained in power. German treatment of subject peoples was less severe in western Europe; their full barbarity and ruthlessness were reserved for the Slavs and the Jews. Reprisals, executions, extermination centres and concentration camps accounted for victims whose total ran into a figure of millions. One of the worst camps was the Jewish extermination centre of Auschwitz in Poland. But men of all races suffered, and women suffered as well as men.

The Germans, of course, made every possible use of the industrial and agricultural resources of the occupied territories. One heavy demand was for labour—'slave labour' as it was termed by Allied propaganda during the war. Many of those who worked for the Germans were, however, volunteers or even willing collaborators—they were paid and conditions of life were sometimes quite good. But when the Germans could not obtain sufficient labour heavy pressure was applied, and German demands were insistent.[1] The real slave labour was that supplied by the concentration

[1] See *The Unpublished Diary of Pierre Laval.*

camp prisoners. Those from Camp *Dora*,[1] for example, worked on the making of the secret weapons—flying-bombs and rockets. These men, largely Russians, French and Poles, lived and worked in hidden tunnels in the Hartz Mountains, to which German research plants were removed after the Allied bombing of Peenemünde in 1943. These prisoners were driven to work; beatings and hangings were part of the daily round. Such was the German organisation of Europe to meet the demands of total war.

SUGGESTIONS FOR FURTHER READING

G. M. Gathorne Hardy: *Short History of International Affairs* (3rd edition), cc. 21-6.

E. H. Carr: *International Relations between the two World Wars*, cc. 10-13.

Sir H. Butler: *The Lost Peace*, cc. 4 and 7.

J. W. Wheeler-Bennett: *Munich*, especially Part II.

R. W. Seton-Watson: *Britain and the Dictators*, cc. 7-13.

Winston S. Churchill: *The Second World War*, Vol. I, Book I, 'From War to War, 1919-1939.'

E. Monroe: *The Mediterranean in Politics*, cc. 4 and 6.

E. L. Hasluck: *The Second World War*, cc. 22 and 23.

T. L. Jarman: *The Rise and Fall of Nazi Germany*, cc. 8-13.

[1] *Dora* was at first a branch camp of the better-known Buchenwald. See the reports of the American War Crimes Case, *Nordhausen*.

CHAPTER 21

THE SECOND WORLD WAR, 1939-45

The Campaign in Poland

POLAND felt the first blow of the new Nazi Army, and the campaign was fought to a conclusion without any serious interference from outside. The German attacks were launched from Pomerania in the north-west and Silesia in the south-west, and also from East Prussia in the north and from the newly-acquired position of Slovakia in the south. The Poles fought with the highest courage, but a fighting spirit and an army of infantry and cavalry were quite insufficient to meet the mechanised forces which Hitler moved with lightning rapidity into their country. This was the first *Blitzkrieg* or lightning war:[1] the *Luftwaffe* (air force) opened the attack by bombing Polish towns and knocking out the small Polish Air Force on its airfields; by disrupting communications and smashing means of transport it pinned the land forces to the ground they occupied. Thus whole units could be surrounded and destroyed by the German tanks. England and France dared not risk overwhelming reprisals by launching a war in the air over Germany. Otherwise they were powerless to help Poland except by patrol activities on Germany's western frontier, no fleet could reach the Baltic, and it was not long before the German armies encircled Warsaw. The Polish Government was forced to take refuge in Rumania. On September 17 Russia invaded and began the occupation of eastern Poland. The Polish forces found themselves surrounded —General Anders was wounded by the Germans in the morning and by the Russians in the afternoon. Warsaw, after a desperate and heroic siege, surrendered on September 30 and a few days later all organised resistance ceased. The Poles continued throughout the war to resist by such means as sabotage, but the campaign was over. Poland was divided, by agreement, between Germany and Russia.

The 'Phoney' War

Throughout the winter the west remained quiet. The British Expeditionary Force crossed the Channel and took

[1] For further explanation of *Blitzkreig*, see pp. 382 and 392.

up its position under the French Supreme Command along the Franco-Belgian frontier. The bombing of London, half expected at the outset of war, did not come; Italy did not enter the war; the Maginot and Siegfried Lines on the frontiers of France and Germany appeared to have produced stalemate on land. This first winter was the period of the 'phoney war' or *Sitzkrieg*. It was a strange period of bewilderment and rumour, and in view of Germany's swift, crushing victory in Poland it may be asked why Germany did not at once proceed to attack the west. There were, however, a number of considerations which made it not unreasonable for the Germans to halt temporarily. They had achieved their immediate objective and might well feel that Britain and France would realise the impossibility of altering the fate of Poland and would therefore come to terms; or, it might be possible to divide Britain and France on this issue. The hope of embroiling the western Allies with Russia may not have been beyond German calculation.   In any case the Germans would scarcely wish to make their main offensive in winter, and their lead in armaments was so great that they would lose nothing by postponing activity until the spring. Britain and France, for their part, believed that time was on their side and that they would gradually reduce the disparity in trained men and modern equipment. The French trusted in their Maginot Line, the system of defences on their frontier facing Germany. The line—with its great underground fortifications—was 'in itself strong, but the "Maginot mentality" of passive defence was disastrous.'[1] They were not eager to follow an active and aggressive policy in case they should provoke strong retaliation by the Germans; Allied planes dropped, not bombs, but leaflets optimistically urging the Germans to rise against Hitler.

At sea, however, there was some activity. The British Navy, with French help, applied a blockade against Germany as in 1914-18, to cut her off from supplies from overseas; this blockade (by mine-laying, naval patrol and aircraft) was directed to preventing the passage of the Dover Straits and barring access across the North Sea between Scotland and Norway. German U-boats were a menace from the start: they sank the liner *Athenia* on September 3, one of our few

[1] Cyril Falls, *The Second World War*.

aircraft-carriers, the *Courageous*, later in the month, and the battleship *Royal Oak* while at Scapa Flow in October. In the south Atlantic, the British scored one notable success in December. Three British cruisers, though much inferior in gun-power, fought, damaged and finally cornered at the mouth of the River Plate, the pocket-battleship *Graf Spee*. There she scuttled herself rather than face three British cruisers a second time.

Russia attacks Finland

Russia caused one considerable diversion during the winter. It was clear that Germany had given her virtually a free hand in the Baltic: not only did Russia secure half of Poland, she also brought under control the states of Estonia, Latvia and Lithuania, provision being made for the movement of the German minorities to Germany. The Baltic states were compelled at first to admit Russian garrisons, and were finally incorporated in the Soviet Union during the following summer (August, 1940). Only Finland dared to resist the Soviet colossus, and on November 30 the Russians attacked with air bombing and invasion. This act of aggression was accompanied on the radio by a war of words against Finland which in its militaristic and imperialist note rivalled the propaganda of the Nazis. The Finns resisted bravely behind their Mannerheim Line, and were at first successful in holding off the Red forces. Britain and France sympathised with Finland—Finland had appealed to the League of Nations and Russia was formally expelled from it—and prepared to send a small force to Finland's assistance. But Norway and Sweden were unwilling to allow the force to pass through their territory, and the plan was abandoned. Eventually Finland was compelled to give way and to come to terms with Russia; military bases and territory of strategic value were conceded.

What was behind these events? In the first place, Russia's action is to be explained by a policy of creating buffers between herself and Germany. In Poland and the Baltic states she secured outposts and thereby increased the space through which German armies would have to fight their way if they attacked Russia; by defeating Finland she pushed back the frontier from its dangerous proximity to Leningrad and secured naval bases in the Gulf of Finland. From the Allied point of view there was an incentive to extend their front against Germany by gaining a foothold in the north: a force sent to Finland would have had to maintain a line of communications across Scandinavia. They could then have enabled Norway to repel a German attack, for there was always the possibility of Germany occupying the Norwegian coast. Germany, too, had strong reasons for taking an interest in Norway. The long coastline would provide bases for U-boats and warships, and would greatly extend the range of German air power. Most important of all, Germany obtained high quality iron ore from the north of Sweden. While the Swedish east coast port of Lulea was frozen up in winter, the iron ore was carried by train to the Norwegian port of Narvik and shipped south, mainly through Norwegian territorial waters, to Germany. Thus control of that coast was something which Germany would not lightly see pass into Allied hands. Allied economic policy reposed at this time on the belief that the German war machine could not function without the Swedish iron ore. The British announcement on April 8 of the laying of mines in Norwegian waters near Narvik indicated British determination to interfere with the iron ore traffic—it could be defended by arguing that Norwegian neutrality was already being abused by the Germans.

The Norwegian Campaign

Hitler attacked on April 9, 1940. The Germans occupied the neutral states of Denmark and Norway by means which were ruthless and unscrupulous in conception and ingenious and brilliant in execution. The attack had been carefully prepared. Denmark was overwhelmed; Norway resisted, but she was unprepared and the Germans made rapid headway. The Germans operated by landings from the sea and some use of transport aircraft. They were helped by 'Quislings'—a term which was derived from the name of Quisling, the pro-German Norwegian politician, and later it came into general use to describe all collaborators. Almost at once the Germans succeeded in seizing the ports and airfields; Oslo, Stavanger, Bergen, Trondheim, Narvik, fell the first day. The Germans had to cross the sea to reach Norway, but this their air superiority enabled them to do. The British Fleet could not be risked in the Skagerrak. As a result, German reinforcements poured into Norway. The Allied forces

landed on the west coast at Namsos and Aandalsnes were
intended to envelop and take the port of Trondheim. But
they were not strong enough for this and were heavily attacked
from the air: after a fortnight they were taken off. At Narvik,
in the north, the navy destroyed the German ships which
had seized the port, and an Allied force after much delay
captured the town. This, however, was a solitary success,
and the Allied troops were eventually withdrawn due to events
elsewhere in Europe. The King of Norway and his government escaped to Britain and retained control of Norway's invaluable merchant marine. Both Norway and (later) Denmark
had important underground Resistance Movements.

The Germans overwhelm the Low Countries and France

On May 10, eight days after the evacuation of Namsos,
the real war in Europe began. On the same day, as a result
of the failure in Norway, Mr. Winston Churchill took the
place of Mr. Neville Chamberlain and formed a coalition
government in Great Britain. This time Germany attacked
the neutral countries of Belgium, Holland, and Luxembourg,
without warning, and with overwhelming force by land and
air. This was the prelude to attack on France itself. The
threat to the whole Allied position was soon revealed, and
three days after the first attacks Mr. Churchill warned the
British people that he could offer it only 'blood, toil, tears,
and sweat.' The Allies were now to learn that the German
blow in the east against Poland was only the precursor of a
still heavier blow against the principal Allied forces in the
west. The new method of *Blitzkrieg* was to be tested with
complete success. This method depended upon speed and
mechanised forces. The air arm was used as an initial striking
force, and also carried attack far into the enemy's rear, disrupting communications, blocking roads with refugees, and
causing widespread panic and dislocation. Dive bombers and
tanks broke through the defence and opened the way for the
swift advance of tank columns to be followed by mechanised infantry. Thus an initial break-through might lead with appalling
rapidity to the complete disruption of the opposing forces.

Although the French troops in the north and the B.E.F.
moved forward into Belgium to meet the advancing Germans,
it was not long before Holland and Belgium itself were overrun.

Holland was disabled by the capture of Rotterdam airfield on the first day, the ruthless low-level bombing of the city, and the advance of German tanks to Moerdijk, which cut the country in half. The Queen and government escaped with some ships, but by May 14 Dutch resistance was virtually over. Belgium lost its advance defences along the Albert Canal at once for the Germans landed glider-troops behind them. And events elsewhere were making Belgium one vast trap for the Allied armies. The Germans had penetrated the main Allied defences at their weakest spot near Sedan. The Maginot Line only defended France's frontier against Germany; along the Belgian frontier the B.E.F. had erected some superficial defence works during the winter. Between Namur and Sedan on May 14 the main German attack was launched with the full force of armoured divisions and dive-bombers. The armoured force advanced at incredible speed; it reached Amiens on May 18 and two days later the sea. The Allied forces were cut into two: the B.E.F. and the French northern army were separated from their supplies and reserves. The Germans now turned north along the French coast to effect a vast encircling movement. Not only were the Allied forces split but they had neither the necessary tanks nor guns nor air support to withstand the German armour.

The Belgian King and Army surrendered on May 27. The trapped northern armies withdrew to Dunkirk. Here followed what seemed a miracle: the German army failed to press home its advantage; good weather, naval supremacy and the support of the home-based R.A.F. made possible the evacuation of 335,000 British and Allied (mostly French) troops, although their equipment was abandoned. More than 200 naval vessels and over 600 other ships were assembled to get the troops away from the beaches. A realisation of the extent of the disaster in France was brought to the folk at home when capless, ragged and unarmed British soldiers appeared in the streets of British cities: the survivors of Dunkirk had arrived. The evacuation was completed on June 4.

There was an uneasy pause: General Weygand tried to form a new line along the rivers Somme and Aisne. But the German armour could not be stopped: on June 7 the tanks advanced across the Somme; on June 10 they crossed the Seine near Rouen. Italy declared war on the same day, and on June

14 the Germans entered Paris which the French had decided to save from destruction by not defending it. France was fast falling into chaos: refugees and soldiers struggled along the roads and the German bombers attacked them from the air. The democratic government gave way to a dictatorship, and on June 22 France signed an armistice.[1] France was out of the war: the north and west of France were occupied. Hitler proclaimed that Germany had founded a new order in Europe which would last a thousand years. To the French and to many people all over the world it seemed that Britain must also come to terms and recognise the German hegemony in Europe.

The Battle of Britain

But Great Britain did not hesitate. Although the troops in the beleaguered island were almost without arms, Mr. Churchill proved himself at once an indomitable war leader and the whole nation prepared for resistance. The Home Guard grew up (often armed with pikes while rifles were lacking); all the Allied ships and men which could be got out of France were brought back to Britain; and General de Gaulle formed his Free French movement in England. The British Navy, meanwhile, had to fight actions at Oran and Dakar against the French (those supporting the Pétain dictatorship) to prevent French warships falling into German hands; four out of five capital ships were put out of action. However the Germans now controlled the long coastline of western Europe from the north of Norway to the Franco-Spanish frontier. Britain waited for the expected attack.

The Battle of Britain began in July. If Hitler could destroy the Royal Air Force he could bomb British ports and cities by day and with impunity; he could also deprive the Navy of air cover: a crossing of the Channel by his armies might then prove to be little more than a follow-up operation. The Germans had a fleet of barges ready. The daylight air attacks on Britain were the first step to invasion, but the move was never completed, though the issue remained in doubt all through August and September, with their tremendous

---

[1] M. Reynaud, the French Prime Minister, wished to continue the struggle. But he was outnumbered in his cabinet; he announced his resignation. The French President called on Pétain who supported the making of an armistice. M. Reynaud tells his own story in *La France a sauvé l'Europe* (the title refers to France's decision to fight in 1939).

aerial battles fought daily over south-east England. Of the achievements of our fighter pilots at this time Mr. Churchill has said that 'Never in the field of human conflict was so much owed by so many to so few.' But it is important to note also the technical superiority of the R.A.F. Spitfire aircraft, which were just coming into mass production that fateful midsummer (about one-fifth of the fighter squadrons were so equipped), and the farsightedness of the government's refusal to expend these limited resources, as it was urged to do, in trying to stem the tide of disaster in France before the Dunkirk evacuation.

Furthermore a considerable advantage was now being derived from the development of radar, which made possible the detection in advance of approaching enemy aircraft. By 1939 twenty radar stations existed between Portsmouth and Scapa Flow. Radar made possible the most economical use of the all-too-few fighter pilots and planes available by enabling them to avoid continuous patrolling and to be sent directly to points where they could intercept the approaching enemy bombers. Radar was further developed in the next phase of the war—the hideous night bombing when the Germans switched their attack from airfields to cities on the night of September 7. But the change indicated that the Germans had failed to win the Battle of Britain. A long ordeal followed for London and the great provincial cities, especially the ports. Nearly 44,000 civilians were killed (to the end of 1941) but the people were not demoralised: the war went on. Meanwhile factories in the U.S.A. and Canada were backing up the factories in Britain: American policy was modified in stages to give support. Americans were sympathetic to the Allies but did not wish to be involved in war. Prohibition of sale of weapons to belligerents gave way to 'cash and carry' even for munitions.[1] 'Cash and carry' meant that the U.S. would sell munitions if they were paid for and could be carried away. This helped Britain as she controlled the sea. Late in 1940 President Roosevelt had provided Britain with fifty destroyers in exchange for bases on British territory in the Caribbean. Thus Britain was assisted and American shores protected. When Britain ran short of dollars, 'Lend-Lease' was introduced early in 1941. 'Lend-Lease' allowed the actual lending of vast supplies of war material and its

[1] See p. 369 for American neutrality legislation passed in 1935 and 1937.

sending over in U.S. ships. Britain survived: but she was alone, apart from the distant nations of the Commonwealth and the refugee troops in British territory. The future was uncertain.

Further Aims of Germany

Hitler had failed to win a quick war against Britain; he must now settle down and prepare for a long struggle. Was there, perhaps, some alternative to the attack on Britain? Hitler believed in the superiority of land power over sea power and thought control of a vast European-Asiatic land block would give him control of the world. If he could conquer Russia and acquire her vast resources, which could be developed rapidly with the aid of German technical skill; if he could, with Italian aid, extend his conquests over the Mediterranean to Africa and the Middle East—then he would indeed be master of the world. He would be in a position either to subdue or ignore the democratic nations of Britain and the U.S.A.[1] Expansion eastwards was also in line with the policy of *Mein Kampf*: Hitler pictured a vast colonisation of south Russia by Nordic heroes which would support political control by racial domination. Rapid moves followed in the autumn and winter of 1940 and the spring of 1941.

The Area of War widens: North Africa and the Mediterranean; the Balkans and Crete; the Italian Colonies, 1940–1

The first of the new moves was made by the Italians. The collapse of France freed the Italian north African colony of Libya from any danger of attack from the French territory of Tunis in conjunction with pressure from the British forces in Egypt. The Italians, thus able to turn against the British, invaded Egypt on September 12, and at first made some headway. But Churchill had boldly decided to send out tanks from Britain (at a time when she was threatened with invasion) via the Cape, and an imperial force had been built up in Egypt: there were contingents from India, South Africa, Australia and New Zealand as well as from Britain. In

---

[1] The theory that world domination would pass into the hands of the Power controlling a central European-Asiatic land mass had long been developed by Karl Haushofer and his school of Geopolitics. The ideas strongly influenced Hitler and the Nazi leaders. See, for example, Haushofer's *Der Kontinentalblok: Mitteleuropa—Eurasien—Japan*, published by the Nazi Party, Munich, 1941. He says: 'Without doubt the weightiest world-political conception of our time is that of a mighty continental bloc embracing Europe and north and east Asia.'

December, General Wavell struck back. He drove the Italians out of Egypt and advanced far into Libya, to Benghazi (February 6, 1941). In the course of this brilliant advance he destroyed the Italian army. Meanwhile, in November, British naval aircraft crippled three of the six Italian capital ships at Taranto. British power was, temporarily, re-established in the eastern Mediterranean.

But elsewhere preparations had been going on which were shortly to extend German control throughout the Balkans and to result in striking a heavy blow at the British in Libya. Germany first built up by diplomatic means and economic pressure a strong position in those countries where she could find some measure of support.[1] Then, on October 7, 1940, German forces were allowed to enter Rumania on the plea of reorganising the Rumanian army; Rumania, Hungary, and Bulgaria were brought into close relations with Germany and increasing pressure was applied to Jugoslavia. Germany continued her military preparation for further moves south-eastward in the spring, and for this purpose created airfields in Rumania and Bulgaria.

Meanwhile, Italy, hoping to score an easy triumph by advancing from her Albanian bases, attacked Greece on October 28. But the Greeks under their dictator, General Metaxas, showed heroic powers of resistance, and pushed back the Italian invaders. The German attack came the following spring, after a revolution in Jugoslavia had overthrown the government which had just signed a pact of friendship with Germany and Italy. On April 6, 1941, the Germans with their wonted force struck both Jugoslavia and Greece. The Jugoslav army of tough and fierce fighters was broken up in ten days. A small British force had already been sent to support the Greeks, but the German victory in the Balkans was soon completed. The British troops were evacuated with considerable loss. The Germans followed up their success by attacking Crete from the air; the island was captured in May and heavy British losses were incurred. The capture

[1] With the collapse of France, Germany had almost a free hand in the Balkans. She was able to override Balkan territorial claims and counter-claims, and impose arrangements most convenient to herself. In August and September a territorial rearrangement was forced upon Rumania to the advantage of Bulgaria and Hungary. Russia, however, had already taken advantage of the situation to extend her frontiers at the expense of Rumania, in June, thus putting yet another buffer between herself and Germany.

of a defended island like Crete by invasion from the air was a shock to the Allied authorities and suggested several lessons. Allied naval power had prevented invasion from the sea; two attempts had been broken up. But in the air the British were almost powerless: the German planes could fly in from airfields in Greece and the Dodecanese Islands, but the remaining R.A.F. fighters had to be withdrawn from their Cretan bases after heavy enemy bombing. There were no other bases for fighters within reach. Bombing, together with the landing of parachutists and glider-borne troops, overwhelmed the British and half-armed Greek troops. The lesson—the importance of air superiority—was clear. Nevertheless German losses were considerable, and it is still arguable that a longer time for preparation inside the island might have made possible a successful resistance. The Germans took a risk: had they failed to secure a foothold their force would have been destroyed. They too may have learned a lesson of caution for the future.

The Italians, defeated alike by the British and the Greeks, suffered further losses in the spring and early summer of 1941. British and Indian troops were successful in overrunning the Italian colonies of Eritrea, Somaliland and Abyssinia. On May 5 the Abyssinian Emperor, Haile Selassie, reached his capital and was restored to his throne.

In north Africa, meanwhile, the Germans had come to the rescue of the Italians. The Germans with the help of a strong air force in Sicily had transported to Africa the well-equipped and armoured *Afrikakorps* under a bold commander, Rommel. Wavell's army, depleted by the sending of forces to Greece, was pushed back to Egypt by the end of April, although a garrison held out in Tobruk and was supplied by sea. The British position in the eastern Mediterranean thus became difficult. In spite of the naval victory of Cape Matapan (March 28), Britain's control of Mediterranean waters was incomplete, for the German air power in Sicily made precarious the passage of convoys to Malta. On land, British forces had to put down a military rising in Iraq at the beginning of May—a rising which was assisted by the Germans and by the French in Syria. The British were forced to make certain that the oilfields and pipe-lines of the Middle East were secure. British and Free French forces therefore entered Syria on

June 8, and—after some stiff fighting against the Pétain French—occupied the territory. Thus Britain clung uneasily to her positions in the Middle East. Europe, except Russia, was in German hands. Where would the next German move come—through Spain to Gibraltar and north-west Africa; through Turkey to wrest the whole Middle East from Britain and cut the Suez route to India; or against Soviet Russia?

The Invasion of Russia

On June 22, 1941, the German armies attacked Russia on a vast front of over 1,000 miles. Mr. Churchill immediately broadcast an announcement of British co-operation with Russia. Britain was no longer alone. A powerful ally at last was in the struggle, a fact which altered the whole trend of the war. So far, except for the loss of the Channel Islands, Britain had just held her own—a beleaguered island on the outskirts of Hitler's Europe. The outlook was dark. Now suddenly there was a chance of eventual victory. Russia, relatively to her size, seemed weak, and invasion might even precipitate a revolution—but whatever happened Germany had undertaken a colossal task in attempting to conquer a people of nearly 200 millions, and the occupation of the main German armies in Russia would afford a needed breathing-space elsewhere.[1]

The advance of the German armies was rapid at first, and the border territories that Russian aggression had earlier secured as buffers against Germany—eastern Poland and the Baltic states—were occupied by the invading troops. The Germans, by the onset of winter, were encircling Leningrad, though they never captured it; threatening Moscow, after having taken the great cities of Kiev and Kharkov; and, in the south, had pushed as far east as Rostov-on-Don. German superiority in tanks and aircraft had told, but the Russians had avoided large-scale encirclement and still possessed great armies intact. Though the loss of many important industrial regions affected supplies, some of their factories had been dismantled and carried into Siberia; their new Ural industrial zone now showed its value; also supplies were coming in from Great Britain and America. To guarantee their passage through Persia British and Russian troops made a joint occupation of that country.

[1] Professor Cyril Falls points out that all through the remaining years of the war Russia never engaged less than two-thirds of the German army.

The American Entry into the War and the Disasters in the Far East

But the year in which the war had spread from the western and southern fringes of Europe to a front a thousand miles long in the east ended with its extension from Europe to the world. In August the signing of the Atlantic Charter, in which President Roosevelt joined with Mr. Churchill to proclaim his belief in the principle of freedom for the individual and for the nation, showed that America was uncompromisingly opposed to the Nazi New Order, which rested on the principle of subjugation to a 'master race': but American support continued to be economic, not military. On December 7, however, Japanese carrier-borne aircraft surprised the American Pacific Fleet at Pearl Harbour, Hawaii, and put it completely out of action in a matter of minutes. Japan's action proved as successful as it was perfidious: the American islands of Wake and Guam fell rapidly into her hands, and her naval supremacy in Pacific waters was confirmed within three days when her shore-based aircraft sank *H.M.S. Prince of Wales* and *Repulse* off eastern Malaya.

For the moment the fact that Germany and Italy declared war on America, just as Britain automatically did on Japan, seemed less important than the collapse of power of the white man throughout the Far East. Japanese land forces advanced through Indo-China, where the French had previously been compelled to admit them to 'joint defence,' and through Siam. They overran Malaya at incredible speed and in February captured the great modern naval base of Singapore although our forces there outnumbered them. When Hong Kong, the Philippines, the Dutch East Indies, and Burma all lay in Japanese hands; with China isolated by the cutting of the Burma road;[1] with the extremities of Japanese power reaching the Andaman Islands to the west and New Guinea to the south-east—it was hard to foresee that this was only a passing phase in the titanic struggle in both hemispheres.

The intervention of Japan changed the whole character of the war: it was transformed from a European into a global conflict. Japan had long been a cause of suspicion—ever since her invasion of Manchuria in 1931. Since 1937 she had been at war with China. Now China, the United States

[1] This supply route had been closed for three months (July–October, 1940) by Britain under strong Japanese pressure.

and Great Britain found themselves together as allies against Japan; Russia and Japan, however, remained neutral as regards each other. Japan's sudden moves in the Far East enabled her to extend rapidly her control over vast areas of territory and ocean. But she might have done better still had she moved first against the Dutch colonies and the British possessions in the Far East; some of these she might have acquired without involving America in the struggle. By the attack on Pearl Harbour she shocked the United States into a huge and rapid organisation of her vast resources; she also involved America with Germany and Italy. Thus as a result of Japanese action the United States were plunged fully into the global conflict, in the Far East and in Europe. American resources were so great that eventually she must triumph if the immediate Japanese onslaught could be checked. And it was checked. In May and June, 1942, the Americans won two great naval victories—the Battle of the Coral Sea and the Battle of Midway Island. These battles, fought entirely by carrier-borne aircraft, without a shot being fired by the fleets, which never came in sight of each other, mark a new era in naval warfare. They also made the danger of an invasion of Australia, which Japanese landings in New Guinea appeared to portend, much less imminent. Meanwhile American troops had been stationed in Australia.

The General Position in the Summer of 1942

During the summer of 1942 events were still moving on the whole in favour of the aggressors. Sinkings by German and Japanese submarines had stretched Allied shipping resources to their absolute limit and the danger to Atlantic communications was great. On the other hand, British bombing attacks on Germany, which had begun in 1940, were being stepped-up in intensity; May 30 saw the first 1,000-bomber raid on Cologne.

The Russian winter had proved to be the first real setback to the Germans. This time the *Blitzkreig* had been checked, and the Germans were caught without adequate clothing and equipment to endure the intense cold. Frost-bite as well as battle caused heavy loss of men, and in Germany there was acute anxiety about the position on the Russian front. The German armies were now waging war under very different circumstances from those they had met in western Europe.

The strategy of *Blitzkrieg* depended upon building up a thrusting force of tanks and aircraft so strong as to be able to break through any line of defence. In western Europe the area to be overrun was, comparatively, small; once through the defences there was nothing left to hold up the Germans. Eventually even an army of attack like the German would run up against difficulties of supply when its lines of communication were drawn out. In Russia the German army was involved in this difficulty: it had to contend with vast spaces as well as winter cold. The Germans had to reconstruct some 16,000 miles of Russian railways and build huge supply depots behind their Moscow front. Even for a superb fighting machine like the German army the effort was a heavy strain. In the spring, however, the Germans rallied and moved forward in the south, clearing the Crimea and sending one force into the Caucasus towards the oil wells and another east to the Volga (where it would cut the oil route from the Caucasus). This Volga force laid siege to Stalingrad.

In North Africa the position was still in doubt. The rival armies had ranged several times back and forth along the coastal stretch. But in June, 1942, Rommel made his most formidable attack: this time the British lost Tobruk and were chased right back to El Alamein. If they failed here, Alexandria and the whole position in Egypt lay open.

The Turn of the Tide—Stalingrad and El Alamein

But now the whole tide of war changed. General Alexander and General Montgomery had during the summer built up a great attacking force in Egypt. On October 23 Montgomery's Eighth Army attacked and the famous Battle of El Alamein began. This time the Germans were heavily defeated: the new American-built Sherman tanks went forward and the long pursuit through North Africa began again, for the last time. A few days later (November 8) big British and American forces under the command of General Eisenhower landed in the French colonial territory of Morocco and Algeria. However, some of the Americans would have preferred, even as early as this, to risk a landing in France.

In Russia on November 19 a counter-offensive began which saved the ruins of Stalingrad and eventually (January–February, 1943) destroyed the German army besieging it.

So far the Russians had excelled in defence: now they were
launching a major offensive. The Allies had at last gained
the upper hand: planes, tanks, equipment of all kinds were
pouring in, Hitler had lost the long start which his carefully
prepared aggression had given him, and the Allies were at
the beginning of the road to final victory. In January, 1943,
Mr. Roosevelt and Mr. Churchill met at Casablanca; plans
were worked out with the ultimate aim of achieving the
unconditional surrender of the enemy.

But the road to victory was still a long one, and Allied
progress was checked from time to time during 1943. It took
some time for the interlocked Russian and German armies
in south Russia to disentangle themselves. The numbers
engaged were, of course, far larger than those in North
Africa. The great victory at Stalingrad accounted for 22
German divisions either destroyed or captured. It also brought
in as a prisoner Field-Marshal von Paulus himself—the first
surrender of a field-marshal in the history of modern Germany.
The large Russian forces now free to advance moved forward
towards Rostov. The Germans had lost their chance to seize
the Caucasus oil-wells, and had to withdraw.[1] Their army in
the Caucasus, its rear threatened, extricated itself in orderly
fashion, part retreating through Rostov, part crossing the Kerch
Strait into the Crimea. Meanwhile the Russians relieved the
pressure on Leningrad, and in March captured Rzhev and
Vyazma, two great German fortress positions west of Moscow. But
with the thaw, the Germans managed to strike hard once more in
the Ukraine and in March recaptured Kharkov which they had
lost to the Russians in February. On the whole, however, the
winter of 1942-3 was disastrous for Germany on the Russian front.

In North Africa, after the complete success of the Anglo-
American landings all along the coasts of Morocco and
Algeria, the Germans had reacted strongly and effectively and
Allied progress had been stayed. A large German force
got into Tunisia by air and sea. It seized the principal ports
of Bizerta and Tunis just ahead of an Allied advance from the
west which was repulsed. This was a skilful operation
carried out almost in the old German style. The Germans
now built up a powerful position in Tunisia: the new army

[1] Oil was regarded throughout the war as the Achilles heel of the German
military power.

faced west. It was joined by Rommel who had raced across Libya after his defeat at El Alamein. He took up position in the old French Mareth Line, facing east against the advancing Eighth Army. By the end of January, 1943, the Germans were well established. Eventually, however, the German armies were pressed together by the Allies to west and east. The Germans were defeated, Bizerta and Tunis captured on May 7, and by the 13th the German-Italian force was taken prisoner—more than 250,000 men. Thus the whole North African coast was brought under Allied control, and the Mediterranean re-opened to Allied shipping.

The War at Sea and in the Air

While the titanic struggle was going on in Russia and the long backwards and forwards coastal conflict in North Africa was being waged, there was a ceaseless warfare at sea and in the air. The main German effort at sea was made by submarines, but occasionally a surface ship also intervened. The German policy was to strike at Allied ships by every possible means; the Allied objective was to prevent, if possible, the departure of German warships and submarines from German-occupied ports and to destroy them when they did escape. Thus in May, 1941, the *Bismarck* broke out into the north Atlantic and sank the battle-cruiser *Hood*. A great air and naval chase developed and the *Bismarck*, probably the strongest battleship in the world, was at last destroyed. The disappearance of the *Bismarck*—a ship which might have sunk a whole convoy in a single action—removed one severe threat to British shipping and lightened the task of its protection by the Navy.

The German submarines were a grave peril to the Allies, because the sinkings of Allied shipping were numerous enough to endanger the whole supply position. The Battle of the Atlantic might have won the war for Germany by cutting the vital supply lines to America. The position was more difficult than in 1914: now there was an independent Eire. Eire was neutral and Britain could not use the Irish naval bases. The German submarines were larger too, and had radio contact with aircraft which spotted for them. The worst period for the Allies was 1942 and the first part of 1943. But by the middle of 1943 Allied anti-submarine devices, including radio-location, were developed sufficiently to give victory over the submarine.

In the air R.A.F. bombers were smashing away at industrial areas in Germany and Italy and to a less extent at specific targets elsewhere in German-occupied Europe. This, for the greater part of the war, was Britain's only means of striking directly at Germany. But the air offensive called for a great concentration of industrial output and of R.A.F. effort on one object. Great damage was done. Yet German industry was not completely crippled; to protect it against attack it was dispersed and some of it was operated underground. The air offensive involved heavy British losses in planes and men. It has been suggested that some of the effort expended on the bombing policy might have been better directed to other ends, either by using air power to help the Navy more effectively in the anti-submarine campaign and for close support of military operations, such as the defence of Crete, or by giving the Navy and Army a larger share of our total resources for their own direct requirements. The bombing policy was, however, carried through: the scale of raids and the weight of the bombs being vastly increased as the war went on. From the late summer of 1942 American bombers joined in, mainly specialising in day bombing while the R.A.F. carried out night operations. By 1943 the joint air offensive had developed into a heavy and continuous striking at Germany which helped to hamper the war effort inside the country while the Allies were carrying out their preparatory moves for the destruction of the German armies in the field. It also served the needs of the Russians, who were at first outnumbered in the air, by tying down large quantities of German fighters to home defence.

Resistance in Occupied Europe

In the later stages of the war less was heard from the Nazis of the 'New Order' (see Chapter 20) and more of 'Fortress Europe.' The Nazis pictured Europe in their propaganda as a stronghold threatened by the Russian hordes, and to the last hoped to divide the Allies on the issue of a menace to the west from Communist Russia. But the German fortress of Europe had its fifth column. Throughout the war 'underground' resistance movements were active in occupied countries, and there was from time to time open insurgent warfare, particularly in Jugoslavia, where large German forces had to be stationed to deal with it, and also in parts of Poland.

Governments in exile had their headquarters in London and maintained contact with their countries through an 'underground' courier service. Leaders were parachuted into occupied Europe, and supplies of arms from Britain were dropped. The broadcasts of the B.B.C. helped to encourage and inform all those who awaited liberation.

France had a great variety of resistance movements made up of very mixed elements, some of them disciplined but some 'more like an organisation of gangsters.'[1] British Intelligence used its own French agents in France, the Free French in London had their representatives in the country, there was the O.R.A. (*organisation de la résistance armée*), the Communists had their own set-up, and there were numerous other groups representing the many political parties and publishing clandestine newspapers. When the Allies at last landed in France they received the assistance of organised forces—the F.F.I. (French Forces of the Interior) under General Koenig— in every kind of sabotage and, where possible, the liberation of villages and towns.

The Invasion of Italy, 1943

In 1943 the Allies were ready to strike back in Europe. Hitler's 'Fortress Europe' this time awaited attack. But where? And what considerations influenced the Allies? The United States had agreed with some little hesitation that, though the war with Japan must be vigorously carried on, the war against Germany must take first place. If Germany were once defeated Japan could never win. But it was not so easy to decide where to make the attack upon Germany. Russia demanded a 'second front' in Europe, and her supporters and sympathisers in Britain had been vociferous in calling for it even when the country was quite unprepared to take the offensive. Lord Beaverbrook had been sent to Moscow in September, 1941, to arrange with Stalin for the sending in of supplies, and when he returned he urged the need for helping Russia with an early second front in the west. But high military opinion was against it; also heavy Canadian casualties in a big raid on Dieppe (1942) showed how hard invasion would be. Besides there was some disagreement between the British and the Americans. Agreement was reached on

[1] So described to the authors by a member of the French movement.

invasion of Sicily—that followed naturally upon the conquest of North Africa and would give the Allies control of the Mediterranean. But after that, what? The Americans inclined to the idea of immediate invasion of France. The British wished to cross from Sicily into Italy, and knock Italy out of the war first. This seemed timid to the Americans, and even if it succeeded it would eventually bring the Allies up against the barrier of the Alps. At length, however, the British plan was adopted: it was felt that there was not time to make the necessary preparations for the French undertaking. Italy first; the invasion of western France must wait until 1944.

On July 10, 1943, our invasion of Europe began: British and Canadian and American troops entered Sicily. This was a big Allied landing, for which valuable experience had been gained from North Africa, the Dieppe raid and other British coastal raids, as well as from the attacks made by the Americans on Pacific islands. The new landing technique required large numbers of special landing-craft which could put tanks and guns ready for action ashore upon open beaches. It is evident that during the second main phase of the war, while Allied power was increasing and enemy strength relatively declining, the production of landing-craft for invasion was an important factor in fixing the Allied time-table. The Sicilian landing was a success: air-cover was provided from Malta and Pantelleria (captured in June), and airfields in Sicily were seized on the first day; on the second the port of Syracuse was occupied. But the Germans—and some of the Italians— fought hard and the conquest of the island was not completed until the middle of August. With great skill the Germans got two-thirds of their men over to the mainland and had time to prepare for the coming invasion of Italy. The Germans, however, had also to improvise means of meeting the, for them, forbidding facts of the Italian political situation.

The Allied success in Sicily caused Mussolini's downfall. The Fascist Grand Council appealed to the King: Mussolini was arrested, and Marshal Badoglio formed a non-Fascist government. He entered into negotiations, which led to an armistice in September. On the 3rd the British Eighth Army landed on the Italian mainland, north of Reggio in Calabria. On the 9th the Fifth Army, partly Americans, partly British, were landed further north in the Bay of Salerno. But the

Germans reacted quickly and resolutely to events; they disarmed the Italian forces, and took over in Rome; only the
Italian fleet escaped. The Fifth Army on the west was
pinned to a narrow strip of coast, but it was saved by Montgomery's Eighth Army which captured Taranto, Brindisi and
Bari, and advanced northwards to its assistance. The Fifth
Army then occupied Naples on October 1. A little further
north, however, the Germans, after fierce and bloody Allied
attacks, established a strong defence line across the peninsula
from sea to sea. Thus they stabilised their position on a
short line with remarkable success, and the defection of
Italy—Badoglio declared war against Germany on October
13—hurt them much less than had been expected. The
Germans even rescued Mussolini from the clutches of the new
Italian Government. In January, 1944, the Allies tried to
turn the German lines by a big landing behind them at
Anzio. But, perhaps, too long was spent in consolidating
instead of breaking out to seize a strong position in the Alban
Hills. The Germans managed to seal off the Allied pocket,
and the whole position in Italy stagnated until the summer.

Russian Recovery on the Eastern Front, 1943–4

Meanwhile, the Russians in July had defeated an attack
on the Kursk salient, and then went over to the offensive.
A big push developed. The Russians struck blow after blow:
they captured Orel on August 4, Kharkov on August 23.
In the centre they took Bryansk, and Smolensk on September
25. The Germans in the south were falling back to the River
Dnieper, but the Russians advanced fast along the Black Sea
coast and by November cut off the considerable German
forces in the Crimea. Further north again the Russians
reached the Dnieper at Kiev and retook the city on November
6. The Germans counter-attacked later in the month and
checked the advance, but by the end of December and in
January, 1944, the Russians were moving forward again.

There was no pause that winter for the Germans; Russian
pressure continued. In January the Russians staged an
offensive on the Leningrad sector; since the autumn of 1941
the city had been ringed round, but now at last it was freed
from direct danger. The main line to Moscow was reopened,
Novgorod was taken. The Russians were advancing all

along the front and over immense distances. By March the Russians were back on the borders of Poland and Rumania.

Vast battles on a vast front—that was the general picture. The numbers engaged in the eastern front ran into millions. The Soviet Information Bureau announced in 1944 that during the first three years of war the Germans had lost 7,800,000 killed and captured, while the Russians had lost some 5,300,000. These figures may, indeed, be exaggerated but at least they indicate the really huge scale of the conflict. The Russian advance is one of the marvels of military history. It was made possible by the doggedness of their troops despite deficiency in transport. For their railway system up till the war was perhaps the most inefficient in the world. With much of it destroyed they were partly dependent on horse transport. The Americans sent in motor vehicles by the hundred thousand. From the U.S.A., Britain and Canada, supplies poured in. Their movement to Russia through submarine-infested seas was another miracle of the war: the convoys sailing round the north of Norway had the Arctic Ocean to face as well as U-boats, bombers and surface ships like the *Tirpitz* and the *Scharnhorst*.

In the west air attacks on Germany went on all the while. From the spring of 1943 onwards the Allies steadily increased them in intensity: the German cities were reduced to rubble; industries were sought out and bombed in every corner of Germany. By early 1944 American bombers were surpassing the R.A.F. in the total weight of bombs dropped; they operated from Italy as well as from their bases in Britain. The air attack on central Europe was developed as one of the Allies' most formidable weapons.

The First Stages of Recovery in the Pacific Area

At the same time that she was sending her squadrons of 'flying fortresses' into the European skies, the U.S.A. was extending the war in the Pacific with a growing deployment of air and naval strength. Great battles were fought on sea and in the air, and gradually the Americans and Australians established themselves in various Pacific islands—in New Georgia and New Guinea (to part of which the Australians had hung on grimly all the time) in the summer of 1943, in New Britain in December. During the same winter the Americans gained footholds in the Gilbert and Marshall Islands. In the summer of 1944 they captured Saipan in the Mariana Islands, which gave a base within bombing range of the Philippines and of Japan itself. The recovery of Burma proved to be an even slower undertaking, the British Fourteenth Army being handicapped by the lack of shipping resources for a landing from the sea and forced to fight its way through some of the most difficult country in the world, though with ever-increasing support from air transport. In February, 1944, the last Japanese offensive was broken and the first victory won: by the end of the year the Fourteenth Army was pressing on towards central Burma.

The Grand Strategy of the Allies

In a global war in which vast forces, military, naval and aerial, were operating at the same time in different parts of the world and over immense distances, close co-operation between the Allies was essential. Great questions of strategy—which also involved questions of international politics and national psychology—had to be considered and decided. What proportion of the Allied effort should go to the war in the Far East and what proportion to the war in Europe? How much could be sent to Russia? Where should Allied landings be made, and what should be the time-table? What political arrangements should be made with regard to the administration of territories occupied by Allied action? These were all questions of difficulty and questions involving the national interests, often conflicting interests, of the several allies. President Roosevelt and Mr. Churchill were in day-to-day contact by telephone and telegram, but with Marshal Stalin communication was more difficult by reason of geographical position and difference of language. There was also the obstacle of ingrained Russian suspicion of the capitalist west. A series of conferences between Roosevelt and Churchill were held during the years 1941–1943 in Washington, Casablanca, Quebec and Cairo. Churchill went to Moscow to meet Stalin in 1942, and all three met at Teheran in 1943, and at Yalta in 1945. The Teheran Conference was particularly important: here plans were made for 1944 when Germany could be attacked on three fronts, and attacked with hope of final victory. The Allies were in position on two fronts, on the Russian and the Italian. But where would come the great landing in the west? The secret was kept, while plans and preparations went ahead. The American General Eisenhower was to be supreme commander, and Britain's most famous general, Montgomery, was brought back from Italy to lead the land forces in the first phase. Eventually, of course, the American would vastly outnumber the British troops taking part in the campaign.

Italy: the Capture of Rome

The first big attack came in Italy on May 12. General Alexander, with his mixed Allied Army, formidable concentration of artillery, including support from naval guns at the coast, and with complete domination of the air, after a three-day battle broke through the German lines. The much-shelled and bombed German position in Monte Cassino was at last captured, the Germans were pushed slowly northwards and contact was established with the Anzio beachhead. The Germans now made a general retreat, and Rome was liberated by the Allies on June 4.

France: 'D' Day

All through the spring and early summer of 1944 the air over southern England and northern France was hardly silent by day or night: a vast air offensive was going on in preparation for 'D' Day (the designation of the day of invasion). This offensive was to make certain of air superiority and to destroy German radiolocation, which was intended to warn of coming invasion; it also systematically disrupted rail and road transport, knocking out vital bridges at the last moment so as to make it impossible for the Germans to achieve their 'build-up' (i.e. gathering of their forces at the invasion point) faster than we could get our forces landed and consolidated. On June 6 the invasion took place, in the bay of the Seine between Caen and the Cherbourg peninsula on a frontage of five divisions *plus* three air-borne divisions, these being the smallest initial numbers on which Montgomery was prepared to base the operation. The earlier years of the war had taught many stern lessons about the conduct of combined operations, and this time all worked smoothly. Over 4,000 ships took part, with a huge 'umbrella' of aircraft;

the airborne divisions were towed over by glider; special prefabricated harbours were put into position and used for unloading. A large measure of surprise was obtained; the Germans thought the invasion force would make for ports, so they had them heavily defended. The coastal batteries were disabled and many of the defences destroyed by air attack immediately before the landings. The outcome was that powerful British and American armies were disembarked with slight loss, and did consolidate their positions before the Germans could concentrate against them. The Allies did not capture Caen at once as they had planned, but they built up their strength along the coast, and the Americans moved across the peninsula of Cherbourg and took the port itself on June 25. Operation 'Pluto' (pipe line under the ocean) soon made possible the pumping of oil direct to the Allied armies, at first from the Isle of Wight to the tip of the Cherbourg peninsula, later from Dungeness to Boulogne, and, in the final stages, even across the Rhine.

Russia: the Advance into Poland

Next came the Russian attack on June 23; the advance was spectacular. The Germans were overwhelmed, losing nearly twenty-five divisions out of fifty on the central part of the front in killed, wounded and prisoners. The Russians pushed on towards Latvia and Lithuania, threatening to isolate the German divisions further north in Estonia. The Red Army attacked also south of the Pripet Marshes. The Russian advance menaced the whole German position in eastern Europe, and at this very time, on July 20, some of the German generals tried to kill Hitler by a bomb explosion at his headquarters. But he survived and the German forces stood their ground in front of East Prussia and Warsaw. Inside the city the Polish underground movement launched a rising against the Germans. Street fighting followed for some weeks. The Poles, who looked to London rather than to Moscow, were crushed; an attempt to help them was made by the R.A.F., but its planes were refused landing grounds by Russia.

The Liberation of France and the Last Stand of the Germans in the West

In France, meanwhile, after hard fighting, the Allies had trapped a large part of the German troops and armour. The

Americans on July 25 broke through westwards to Avranches; they then pushed on to the Loire, cutting off Brittany (one American force went on to Brest). They then wheeled round, catching the Germans in the Falaise 'pocket' pressed against the British and Canadians to the north; here immense destruction was effected by Allied planes and artillery as the Germans retreated eastwards. Free French Forces of the Interior (F.F.I.) operated in many parts of France to assist the Allies, and on August 15 a new Allied army landed in the south of France and commenced a successful advance up the Rhone Valley. Everywhere the Germans were moving back towards Germany: on August 22 in Italy the Allies reached Florence, on the 23rd Paris and Marseilles were liberated, and, on the same day, Rumania surrendered to the Russian advance.

The Germans were going back but they were prepared for a fight to the finish; it remained for the Allies to move forward to the last desperate battles for the conquest of Germany itself. The British and Canadians crossed the Seine and advanced through north France and Belgium; the Americans moved to the east of them, through Belgium and Luxemburg. By September 14 the German city of Aachen was under shellfire. But the Germans had plenty of fight left, with many natural obstacles and the Siegfried Line to help them. The Allied attempt to turn the whole German position by crossing the Rhine in the north failed, in the heroic and spectacular dropping of airborne divisions at Arnhem. As a result the Germans stabilised their front in spite of the fall of Aachen on October 21. In December the Germans made their last offensive in the west, striking in the direction of Liége, with even a hope of further exploitation towards Antwerp and the division of the Allied forces. Von Runstedt struck hard through the Ardennes; attacking in fog he scored by surprise. But he was checked, held and at last turned back.

The End of Hitler's Germany: Invasion from East and West

During the winter the Russian advance continued through Rumania, Bulgaria and Jugoslavia and was assisted by insurgent movements in those countries. In Hungary the Red Army met stubborn resistance; Budapest stood a long siege and was not taken until February, 1945. The Germans everywhere showed great power of resistance in spite of the overwhelming blows being struck against them on all sides.

Nor was the last year of the war without its surprises. Soon after D-Day the Germans had commenced the bombardment of southern England with new weapons. First came the flying-bombs (V1).[1] These caused considerable loss of life, but the destruction would have been much greater had not the invading troops cleared, when they did, the coasts from which these projectiles were launched. Next came the rockets (V2). These could be fired to a great height and fell without warning; there was no real defence against them. If the Germans had had longer to develop these weapons—if the invasion had been postponed—their effect would have been very serious.

But the Germans were not given the time to develop their new weapons. The Russians poured into Poland after three great attacks in January. One of these the Germans described as the 'greatest of all time.' Russian forces, estimated at 3,000,000 men, moved forward irresistibly. Warsaw was captured and the Russians entered Germany itself. The Germans stood their ground again along the River Oder to defend Berlin. They made a supreme effort against the Russians. But by April 23 the Russians were attacking the capital. Vienna had fallen into Russian hands a day or two before, so Berlin was the scene of the last of the sieges, marked by long, bloody and destructive street battles, which were a conspicuous feature of the Second World War.

At the same time the Americans and the British were advancing into Germany from the west. Their armies breached the defences of the Siegfried Line or *Westwall*, once declared impregnable by the Germans, and crossed the Rhine in March. The first crossing was at Remagen, where the Americans found a railway bridge that had not been blown up. On April 12 American forces reached the Elbe; on the 26th Russians and Americans met. The war in Europe was almost over. In Italy Mussolini had been disposed of by partisans, and on the 29th all German forces there capitulated. In Berlin the death of Hitler was announced by radio on May 1, and the city surrendered the following day. Hitler had died, it seems, by suicide, but his body was never found.

[1] V for *Vergeltungswaffe*. It is remarkable that this pilotless aircraft, the approach of which was both visible and audible, so that some degree of defence was gradually established against it, had worse psychological effects than the irresistible rocket.

The final unconditional surrender of the German forces was made on May 7, 1945. The Third Reich and its Führer perished together.

The Last Phases of the War against Japan

But Japan remained to be defeated, and when the war ended in Europe there was little to indicate to the public a rapid ending in the Far East. Although the secret preparation of a new weapon—the atomic bomb—was far developed, the American and British leaders could not yet be certain what its effect would be. The planning and organisation of a series of moves, to culminate in an all-out invasion of Japan itself, had therefore to be undertaken. With the defeat of Germany, the full weight of Allied war effort was transferred to the Pacific theatre; even before Germany's surrender the Allied effort in this theatre had greatly increased. The main lines of Far Eastern strategy had been laid down in 1943, and the brunt of the struggle was borne by the Americans and, within the limit of their comparatively small population, the Australians. The general direction of advance was to be from bases in New Guinea towards the Philippines; and a second advance across the Central Pacific was to be made by way of the Gilberts, Marshalls and Marianas to reach the Ryukus in comparative proximity to Japan itself. These advances were made by a series of gigantic hops from island to island with the combined operation of sea, air and land forces. Each had its vital part to play.

By mid-1944 the Americans were encroaching on the Philippines. In October two big assault forces went ashore on Leyte Island. Several large Japanese naval formations approached to deal with the Americans but were defeated (October 25) in the greatest naval engagement of history—ships being in action this time as well as carrier-borne aircraft. Next landings were carried out in the other islands, and after much fierce fighting the Philippine capital, Manila, was taken in February, 1945. Meanwhile the Americans were pushing ahead with their island-hopping across the Central Pacific, and reached the Ryukus: on April 1 they landed on Okinawa. The fierce and bloody battle for this island lasted nearly three months, but the Americans were now established only 320 miles from the Japanese mainland.

The American operations in the Pacific were on a colossal scale; their bombers ranged the Pacific air, and their battle-fleets the ocean. Japan was brought under direct bombardment, both by air and from the sea. Tokyo and Yokohama were largely burnt by incendiary bombs. The British fleet— Britain's greatest battleships were all in Far Eastern waters for the closing phase—joined in shelling the Japanese coast. The British Fourteenth Army was advancing in Burma, and fighting disease, jungle and rain as well as the enemy; it captured Mandalay on March 19 and Rangoon on May 3. British troops were pouring into India for a projected invasion of Malaya. During July terrific American air-raids on the Japanese naval bases destroyed most of their remaining ships. By the beginning of August the Americans were ready, and five thousand planes were waiting. 'The most powerful armada in air history is being mounted to strike the final death-blow to Japan,' said the American General MacArthur.

Yet Japanese fanaticism and desperate courage might still have inflicted heavy loss on the American forces had landings in Japan been necessary. By this time, however, the secret weapon was ready. On August 6, under a decision taken at the Potsdam Conference[1] a few days earlier, the first atomic bomb was dropped on Hiroshima. This one bomb killed about 78,000 people. On the 8th the Russians, hitherto neutral with regard to Japan, declared war and sent their armies into Manchuria. On the 9th a second atomic bomb was dropped, this time on Nagasaki. By August 14 the Japanese had surrendered. They were allowed to retain their emperor as a nominal sovereign, but their country was occupied. The main part in this occupation was undertaken by America. After six years of war, the great aggressors had all been vanquished—but only after the most destructive catastrophe in history.

SUGGESTIONS FOR FURTHER READING

R. C. K. Ensor: *A Miniature History of the War.*
Winston S. Churchill: *The Second World War.*
Cyril Falls: *The Second World War.*
Chester Wilmot: *The Struggle for Europe.*

[1] See p. 408.

CHAPTER 22

ATTEMPTED SETTLEMENT

The Aftermath of War

THE Allied victory solved one problem, but raised others in its place almost more formidable than the one it had solved. The war had often been pictured in the West as a struggle between democracy and dictatorship; victory assured that the particular dictators responsible for the war were not thereby to possess the world, but it did not assure the triumph of democracy. The democratic nations were indeed triumphant, but their position was shared by one great ally whose tradition and system of government appeared to be the antithesis of democracy.[1] And victors as they were, the democratic nations of Europe were gravely weakened by the war. France had been occupied and exploited for over four years by the Germans, and turned into a battlefield at the beginning and end of that period; she was still weakened internally by social and political division. Great Britain, which had faced the enemy for six long years, was soon revealed as a country seriously overstrained and facing economic problems of great magnitude.

As for the vanquished, devastation and ruin were general. Bombing had reduced many German cities to masses of rubble. The policy of unconditional surrender had led to a fight to a finish, and the Allies had therefore to take over and administer the territory of the stunned and leaderless German people. In Japan devastation in the cities was also great. All over the East, too, there was unrest: civil war in China, and national independence movements in India, Burma, and Indonesia. In the Middle East there was trouble in Syria and Palestine. And as time went on the most menacing problem of all became more evident: there was revealed the fundamental clash of outlook and policy between Soviet Russia and the democracies. The optimism of victory gave way to a realisation that the world was facing renewed perils:

[1] See p. 425 for definition of democracy.

the old conflict between capitalism and communism was accentuated.

The Occupation of Germany and Austria

German surrender to the Allies on May 7, 1945, was unconditional. Admiral Dönitz, before the surrender, had announced the death of Hitler and that he was to take the Führer's place as head of the state and supreme commander. Broadcasting to the German people on May 8, Dönitz said—

'The foundation on which the German Reich was built is a thing of the past. The unity of state and party no longer exists. The party has disappeared from the scene of its former activity. With the occupation of Germany power has passed into the hands of the occupation forces.'

The Allies had foreseen the need which would arise for military occupation of Germany. A provisional scheme was worked out at the Yalta Conference in February, 1945, and at Potsdam on August 2 the final arrangements were made and an agreement signed by the American President, Marshal Stalin and the British Prime Minister. This time new men were acting for America and Britain: Roosevelt had died on April 12, and had been followed as President by Truman; Churchill's Conservative Party was defeated at the General Election in July and C. R. Attlee became head of a Labour Government. The Potsdam Agreement meant that supreme power in Germany was transferred to the governments of the four principal Allies—the U.S.A., Russia, Great Britain and France. This power was to be exercised by the four commanders-in-chief in a Control Council, meeting in Berlin. At the same time Germany was divided into four zones of occupation, and each commander-in-chief was to be the governing authority inside his own zone. The city of Berlin was also divided into four sectors of occupation, and to control its administration a four-power *Kommandatura* (commandants' council) was to be set up.

The four zones of occupation in Germany covered territory lying adjacent to that of the occupying Powers or territory in which their armies had operated. Thus Russia occupied an eastern zone between the new provisional western frontier of Poland (fixed to compensate Poland for the incorporation of

GERMANY AFTER THE SECOND WORLD WAR

her eastern territories in Russia) and a line passing roughly
north and south through the centre of Germany. Berlin lay
as a four-power island in the middle of the Russian Zone.
The British Zone was based on the North Sea coastline
between the Russian Zone and Holland; it included Hamburg,
Lübeck and the devastated Rhineland. The Americans
held the south, including Bavaria, and a small enclave at
Bremen. The French Zone, shaped like an hour-glass, lay
along the Rhine from a point north of Coblenz to Basle, with
the neck near Karlsruhe. Germany had ceased to exist as a

unified state with a central government: and although in theory the Allied Control Council was supposed to function in matters affecting Germany as a whole, the country was in fact divided among the four occupying Powers.

Certain principles were, it is true, laid down and agreed to at Potsdam. The purposes of the occupation were stated to be—

'(i) The complete disarmament and demilitarisation of Germany and the elimination or control of all German industry that could be used for military production. . . .

'(ii) To convince the German people that they have suffered a total military defeat and that they cannot escape responsibility for what they have brought upon themselves, since their own ruthless warfare and the fanatical Nazi resistance have destroyed Germany's economy and made chaos and suffering inevitable.

'(iii) To destroy the National Socialist Party and its affiliated and supervised organisations, to dissolve all Nazi institutions, to ensure that they are not revived in any form, and to prevent all Nazi and militarist activity or propaganda.

'(iv) To prepare for the eventual reconstruction of German political life on a democratic basis and for eventual peaceful co-operation in international life by Germany.'

Although it was essential to aim at each of these objects, the first three were negative. The last was a positive aim, but one of a long-term character. Meanwhile the situation of Germany was desperate. Every city of any size was in ruins; industries were destroyed and communications disrupted. It is doubtful if anyone who did not see it can picture the utter desolation of large urban areas in post-war Germany. And this devastated country had to maintain at least temporarily about 12,000,000 displaced persons—mostly imported foreign workers, the great majority of whom were back home by 1947.[1] In addition German refugees poured in from the Sudetenland, from which the German-speaking population

[1] Many Russians, Poles and Jugoslavs were massacred on their return, declared the Earl of Selborne in the House of Lords, June 23, 1948. It was reliably reported to one of the authors by British officers in Berlin that a number of Russians repatriated were shot out of hand, as soon as they got out of the lorries in which British drivers delivered them to the Russian authorities. These lorries did not take a second load.

was expelled by the Czechs, and also from the eastern part of Germany which was now brought under Polish government. In the British Zone the social problems were particularly acute. In this area Germany's largest industries were situated and, therefore, bombing had been most severe and destruction most widespread. This industrial region was very densely populated—by about 22,000,000 people. To this large population were added about 2,500,000 refugees. A serious housing shortage and also a real menace of starvation were pressing problems with which the British authorities had to deal. The Russian area would normally have had a food surplus available to Germans elsewhere but much of this was consumed by the occupying troops. The Americans and the French had similar problems with which to contend, although they were not, perhaps, as serious as those in the British Zone. But cities were everywhere in ruins, and on the railways one could see the long refugee trains—men, women and children crowded into cattle-trucks and moved, whither they knew not, out of the Sudeten areas of Czechoslovakia. Money had become of little value; for one thing shops with their stocks had largely disappeared in the bombing. Food was very scarce and the only really prosperous people were the farmers, who could exchange their products for personal or household goods brought out as a means of barter by the townspeople. Strangely enough a perishable commodity, cigarettes, became a general form of currency, presumably because they are easy to handle and in universal demand among a people starved of all luxuries.

De-militarisation, de-Nazification and a certain degree of de-industrialisation were then carried out. The de-industrialisation went on as a part of Allied reparations policy. The principle was accepted among the Allies that Germany should compensate them to the greatest possible extent for their losses. In order to effect this compensation, the Powers were to remove from their zones German industrial equipment, and for this purpose factories were dismantled and their machinery carried away. In addition to what she recovered from her zone, Russia was to receive a certain quantity of industrial material from the western zones. Germany was very completely disarmed and all Nazi organisations were also dissolved. A large number of war criminals, too, were tried by Allied courts, sentenced and punished—many with death. The major war criminals—including Göring, Hess, von Ribbentrop, and leading generals and admirals—were tried at Nuremberg by a specially constituted four-power court. Most of these were hanged or sentenced to long terms of imprisonment (November, 1946). Göring escaped execution by suicide. And suicide saved from trial Göbbels, Himmler and, as we have seen, Hitler himself.

While the Allies were destroying the Germany of the Nazis they were also trying gradually to build up a new democratic Germany. The zones were divided into autonomous *Länder* or states following traditional regional boundaries, and each *Land* had its *Landtag*, a freely elected German assembly, with prime minister and cabinet. The Allies, however, retained the final control, and considerable powers of direction. But subject to this over-riding control the German people were encouraged to create political parties and to form democratic governments of their own. What was lacking was any real central government, and the Allies proved unable to agree among themselves. Increasing difficulties with Russia led to joint action by Britain and the United States. From January 1, 1947, they agreed that the British and American Zones should be treated for economic purposes as a single entity, and a joint Economic Council (composed of members elected by the various *Land* governments) was set up. America also agreed to shoulder part of the financial responsibility for the British Zone. This effort towards greater economic integration appeared a step in the right direction, but France as well as Russia held aloof. France feared any steps which might lead to a reunification and eventual strengthening of Germany. But early in 1949 the French were able to agree with the British and Americans on the principles of a West German Federal Republic, which was intended to take the place of military government in the near future. To create a democratic and peaceful Germany, however, demands the remaking of the German character, and this is a formidable task of re-education. It means, as a great German democrat put it—

'. . . the transformation of the German mass-man from a patient and obedient beast into an integrated type of man, independent in character, upright, sure of himself, and jealous of his right to freedom.'[1]

A four-power occupation was also imposed upon Austria, but the Allied attitude to Austria was different from that towards Germany. It was recognised at the Moscow Conference of 1943 that Germany had annexed Austria by force in 1938, and the Allies stated that they wished 'to see re-established a free and independent Austria.' In accordance with this declaration, as they said, the Russians at once, in April, 1945, recognised an Austrian provisional government under Dr. Renner, a social democrat, as Chancellor, but with a number of communists in Cabinet posts including the Ministry of the Interior. The Russians were in occupation of Vienna, and the western Allies were not willing at first to recognise the new Austrian Government. But in the following months the four-power occupation of Austria followed, by agreement, and a Control Council for Austria and a *Kommandatura* for Vienna were set up, similar to those created for Germany. The Austrian Government was reorganised to give wider representation to the peasantry and was then recognised by all the Allies in October. Military occupation continued. At the end of 1945 free elections were held in Austria; the People's Party (Roman Catholic Right) won, and Dr. Figl, who had spent sixty-two months in Dachau concentration camp under the Nazis, formed a government, with members of other parties included, in order to do the utmost to achieve a new Austrian unity. Economic conditions and social hardships in Austria were severe, as in Germany, but Austria had now its own government recognised by the Allies, and was given a fairly free hand by the Control Council and its forces of occupation. Russia, however, did not make it any easier for Austria by taking over all property in the Soviet Zone formerly owned by Germans.

The Peace Treaties with Italy and the Lesser Enemy States

No peace treaty could be signed with a divided Germany, and peace with Austria was delayed until 1955, but treaties of peace were made with Italy and the lesser enemy states. Provision was made at the Potsdam Conference in 1945 for

[1] Alfred Weber, quoted with approval by Mr. Robert Birley, when Educational Adviser in the British Zone.

a means of preparing a peace settlement. The Council of Foreign Ministers (of the U.S.A., Russia, France, China, and Great Britain) was constituted for this purpose, and its first task was to draft treaties of peace with Italy, Rumania, Bulgaria, Hungary and Finland. It was intended that the Council should then go on to prepare a settlement with Germany, which would be ready when a German government might at last be established. Fundamental disagreement between Russia and the western Powers prevented this, and, though peace treaties with Italy and the lesser enemy states were signed, it was only after hard bargaining between East and West, and also because military occupation or military control by one side or the other induced the other side in each case to make the best of a bad job. In the case of Italy, Russian troops had played no part in the campaigns and the fact of British and American troops in occupation gave the western Allies the advantage in bargaining; in the case of the Balkans and Finland Russian armies dominated the scene, and there Russia had the upper hand. A full Peace Conference of twenty-one Allied nations met on July 29, 1946, in the Luxembourg Palace in Paris, and treaties were eventually signed on February 10, 1947. It was something, at least, that nominal agreement was reached. But no one was really satisfied: all the ex-enemy states, except Finland, presented notes of protest; Jugoslavia criticised the Italian treaty as 'damaging to Jugoslavia's national interests.'

The Italian treaty had indeed almost come to grief over the old clash of interests (which had caused so much friction after 1918) between Italy and Jugoslavia in the Istrian peninsula. The port of Trieste and the territory of Istria had been 'liberated' from Austria in 1918. Trieste was largely an Italian city, but the inhabitants of the Istrian hinterland are Slovenes, and over this whole area there was a direct clash of aim between Italy and Jugoslavia. A compromise was reached in the new treaty: Trieste and the Istrian Peninsula were made into a Free Territory under the protection of the United Nations.[1] But the matter was not yet settled, as Italy and Jugoslavia could not agree on a Governor (as required by the treaty), and Allied troops therefore remained in occupation until 1954, when the city was handed over to

---

[1] For description of U.N. and its machinery, see pp. 421–4.

Italian administration and the rest became Jugoslav. Failing any settlement among the four powers the question of the former Italian colonies was likewise to be passed to the United Nations; the upshot was that they each in turn achieved complete independence. Italy also ceded the Dodecanese Islands (seized from Turkey in 1912) in the eastern Mediterranean to Greece, and three small strategic areas on the Alpine frontier to France. With regard to reparations, the United States and Great Britain renounced their claims in order to ease Italy's economic difficulties. But reparation payments fixed at a total of £90,000,000 were to be paid to Russia, Jugoslavia, Greece, Albania and Abyssinia, partly in the form of dismantled factory plant and partly out of current industrial production. At the same time Italy was disarmed: her army reduced to 250,000 men, and her navy and air force reduced. Submarines and bombers were prohibited, and long sections of her coast demilitarised.

Italy and the smaller ex-enemy states had all broken off relations with Germany and given active support to the Allies before the end of the war. This fact was mentioned in the preamble to each treaty, and accounts for the rather lenient handling of these states in the peace settlement. The remaining territorial provisions can now be briefly stated, country by country.

Rumania both lost and gained territory. She abandoned Bessarabia and Bukovina to Russia, and the South Dobrudja to Bulgaria. Russia had occupied Bessarabia and Bukovina in 1940 after compelling Rumania to accept an ultimatum. This was part of the Russian policy of putting screens between herself and possible Nazi aggression. Rumania regained Transylvania from Hungary, and thus in that quarter the pre-Nazi frontier was restored.

Bulgaria was confirmed in the possession of the South Dobrudja, as has been stated above. Thus she retained a territory long in dispute: it had been occupied by Rumania after the Balkan Wars and held by her until 1940. But in that year Rumania had been virtually dismembered by her neighbours, when the fall of France had led to a scramble for territory in the Balkans. To prevent the outbreak of what might have been embarrassing new wars in that area, Hitler had coerced Rumania into territorial surrenders and one of these was the handing over of the South Dobrudja to Bulgaria.

Hungary went back to her frontiers of January, 1938, except for the Bratislava bridgehead which she ceded to Czechoslovakia. This bridgehead was an area of only a few square miles on the south bank of the Danube opposite Bratislava. Thus Hungary lost her gains of the Nazi period: Transylvania, which she had been allowed to take from Rumania in 1940; and Ruthenia which Hungary had annexed from Czechoslovakia at the time of Munich in 1938. Ruthenia had already been ceded, at the end of the war, by Czechoslovakia to Russia. Thus Russia obtained a common frontier, which she did not have before the war, with Hungary.

In the case of Finland, frontiers were fixed very much as they had been left by the terms imposed on her in March, 1940, after the Russian war of aggression. The Karelian Isthmus remained Russian. In addition the Russians now leased an area south-west of Helsinki for a naval base, and took over the territory of Petsamo in the far north, thus cutting off Finland from access to the Arctic Ocean and giving Russia a common frontier with Norway.

Each treaty included provision for limited payments of reparations, for the restriction of armed forces, and for the dissolution of 'all organisations of a fascist type.' Lastly, they promised to the inhabitants of the respective states—

> 'the enjoyment of human rights and the fundamental freedoms, including freedom of expression, Press and publication, religious worship, political opinion, and public meeting.'

How hollow these expressions of pious hope in many cases were, was quickly revealed. It was a programme of benefits which the Hungarian and Balkan peoples had not been able to secure under the constitutional régimes of the past, when western influence was strong. That influence was now reduced almost to vanishing point, leaving power in the hands of statesmen whose inspiration came from communist Russia. The result was an economic and social revolution, ruthlessly carried out, which may have conferred many benefits on these peoples but not the benefits of the treaty programme. What went on behind the 'Iron Curtain' gave rise to much speculation—even the extent to which Russia dictated the foreign policy was not clear—but what was quite clear was that individual liberty had perished.

The European States after the War

A casual glance at a map of the new Europe would suggest that it had changed but little since the war and the familiar names of most of the old states would still be found, and many national frontiers would have a not unfamiliar look. Indeed the map would be very much closer to that at the beginning of 1938 than to the map of 1942 when Nazi Germany's territorial expansion was at its greatest. It might seem that the defeat of Nazi Germany had simply restored to national independence the states which had been its victims. But the map concealed the reality of the picture: France was a weakened France, the Germany which had dominated central Europe and separated East and West no longer existed as a Power, and the new and preponderating force in Europe was that of Russia.

Although Soviet Russia suffered invasion and devastating losses, she emerged relatively much stronger from a war which also shattered the rest of Europe. Russian sources reported casualties for the first three years of war at 5,300,000, killed, captured and missing. An American estimate put total Russian casualties (military and civilian) between 12,000,000 and 15,000,000. The Russians say that 25,000,000 people were rendered homeless and 6,000,000 buildings destroyed. Russia, however, gained greatly in territory. Quite apart from acquisitions in the Far East, Russia had added to her territories in the West nearly half of the former Poland, the Baltic states of Estonia, Latvia and Lithuania (independent states in 1939 which have now disappeared), parts of Finland, Ruthenia from Czechoslovakia, Bessarabia and Bukovina from Rumania, Königsberg and part of East Prussia from Germany, and through the Russian Zone had extended her power west of Berlin to the Elbe. These territories, except the German and Czech portions and Bukovina, were held by Russia in 1914, and were lost as a result of the revolution and temporary weakness. Now Russia, with her added control over eastern Germany and the Balkans, was stronger than ever. Always strong in numbers and large in area, with these accessions Russia as a Power quite outweighed any other of the continental nations and, at least for years to come, any combination of them. Were it not for the presence of American forces in Germany, Russia would be dominant in Europe and would be in a position to establish the continental land bloc of which Hitler dreamed.

The nations of central Europe and the Balkans had reappeared on the map in name, but had in effect passed completely under Russian influence. The fact that these countries were 'liberated' by Russian armies brought them at once under Russian control to the almost complete exclusion of any democratic influence from the West. The only exception was Greece where British troops got in first from the sea, but even there a civil war was still going on against communist partisan forces four years later. In most cases, free elections had proved impossible, and all opposition to communist or communist-dominated governments was ruthlessly suppressed. General Mihailovitch, who led the first Jugoslav resistance to the Nazis, was executed (July, 1946) in Jugoslavia; there Marshal Tito had emerged as communist leader during the war, had liberated and largely united the country, and had established a government. Mikolajczyk, the Polish democratic leader fled for his life (October, 1947);[1] Petkov, staunch opponent of the Nazis, was executed in Bulgaria, an execution which was officially termed 'judicial murder' by the British government (September, 1947). The Smallholder Party Prime Minister was forced to flee from Hungary (May, 1947); in Czechoslovakia, in March, 1948, the communists seized control of the government.

Yet in these last two countries, which held free elections, the communists were not in a majority. But they were strong enough to overawe their opponents and, relying on Russian backing, to establish communist governments. Once in power they suppressed all the organisations of the opposition: democracy disappeared; a totalitarian régime took its place. The suicide—if it was a suicide—on March 10, 1948, of Jan Masaryk, son of the founder of the Czech Republic, was a sign to the world of his desperation at the disappearance in

[1] Many of the Poles who had fought abroad were unwilling to return to Poland. A Polish Resettlement Corps was formed in Great Britain and by June, 1948, 67,000 Poles had been found jobs. (Answer to Question in the House of Commons by Parliamentary Secretary, Ministry of Labour, June 22, 1948.)

his native land of the western liberalism which he and his
father had represented.[1]

Democracy, based on representative government, as in the
West, had now no place in eastern and central Europe: it never
had any deep roots in these parts, and the Nazis and communists had destroyed between them all that there was of promise.
At the same time, Left Wing governments appeared to lead a
considerable popular movement with a determination to
rebuild in eastern Europe; miracles of reconstruction are said
to have been worked in Warsaw and Belgrade. The desire
to build and progress is a strong one with the young. Popular
excitement and enthusiasm is whipped up by every means,
including verbal attacks on capitalists and fascists. Industrialisation is the key point of policy as it was in the Russian
five-year plans. Thus Jugoslavia aimed at immense increases
in the output of hydro-electric power, coal and steel. Land
reform was also being pushed ahead—big estates were broken
up in order to provide land for the peasants. Some sympathisers with communism suggest that political democracy is
well sacrificed for economic and social progress. But of this
western liberals are profoundly sceptical. And in countries
where no opposition is allowed, where no independent
investigation or criticism is tolerated, it is difficult to find the
truth about anything, even as to whether social and economic
progress has in fact been made. What is certain is that in
the whole sphere of politics a new tyranny had been imposed,
more ruthless, more efficient and more far-reaching than that
of the Czars.

Among the nations of western Europe, amid great economic
dislocation and considerable social austerities, life was probably
closer to what it was before the war than was the case in central
and eastern Europe. The full independence of Iceland added
to the list of the small, stable democracies. Belgium, however,
was suffering from prolonged constitutional deadlock over what
was called the 'king question.' King Leopold, when released
from German captivity wished to return, but considerable
political opposition to this had developed in the country, and

[1] Jan Masaryk may have been murdered. It might well be to the interest
of the communists to have out of the way a man who was so clearly opposed
to totalitarianism, and who was not only popular at home but known the world
over. There was a bomb plot to kill him five months before the communist
coup.

prevented it. His brother had been made Regent at the liberation, and in 1951 Leopold finally agreed to abdicate in favour of his son Baudouin. In Portugal and Spain the same dictators maintained their positions as in 1939; General Franco, who crushed the Spanish Republic with the help of Hitler and Mussolini, avoided being drawn into their war and escaped their fall.

In both France and Italy—and also in both Germany and Austria—a big feature of post-war politics was the revival or formation of powerful moderate parties representing Roman Catholic opinion—the M.R.P. (Popular Republican Movement) in France, the Christian Democrats in Italy, the People's Party in Austria, and so on. At the same time in Italy and also in France the Communist Party went ahead fast, to become in each case a powerful party and a possible government party. Uneasy coalitions functioned for short periods, but in both countries the situation was unstable. Italy became a republic—Umberto succeeded his father, but in 1946 a plebiscite went against him, so he left the country. In France, the internal position was further complicated by the overshadowing figure of General de Gaulle, who condemned the existing parties as making for weakness and attacked in particular the communists, whom he termed 'separatists,' for their subservience to Moscow; he appeared to aim at some kind of national leadership centred in himself. But in 1946 the Fourth Republic was approved, by a small majority of voters; it resembled the Third. France and Italy were both beset with serious economic problems of disruption and poverty. But France had the advantage that she is largely self-supporting in foodstuffs, and thus, though there may be shortages and high prices in Paris, in the countryside the people do not go short. But French industry was undeveloped as compared with British or American, and she was dependent on imports of coal; her position had been still further weakened by widespread strikes. The political future of both Italy and France—and indeed of western Europe generally—depends on the economic situation. If economic recovery could be brought about in a measurable period of time then there was reason to hope that internal political stability could be assured.

The United Nations Organisation

Great efforts were made, as in 1918—efforts which began even before the fighting ended—to create a united world out of the chaos of war. Plans were prepared to bring a new world order into existence, and the United Nations Organisation was fashioned to replace the old League of Nations. Although the League had failed—or, perhaps, more correctly, the member states had failed to use it—its principles were held to be sound. In spite of the victories of aggression in Manchuria and Abyssinia, Mr. Churchill had declared in 1938 that the League remained 'the wisest, the most noble, the most sane, and the most practical path' towards the prevention of war. 'Arm, and stand by the Covenant' was the expressed policy of the most clear-sighted of British statesmen in that fatal year. 'If the League of Nations has been mishandled and broken, we must rebuild it.'[1] The experience of Allied co-operation in the conduct of the war aroused hopes of success for a renewed effort at world co-operation afterwards. These hopes strengthened as the war went on; the idea was implicit in the Atlantic Charter of 1941, and in the declaration of 1942 in which twenty-six Allied nations adhered to that Charter; it was formally discussed at the Moscow Conference in 1943. In the summer of the following year Mr. Churchill declared—

'We must undoubtedly in our world structure embody a great part of all that was gained to the world by the structure and formation of the League of Nations. But we must arm our world organisation and make sure that, within the limits assigned to it, it has overwhelming military power.'[2]

A preliminary scheme was worked out at Dumbarton Oaks, Washington, in 1944, by representatives of the greater Allies, and a general conference of the United Nations met at San Francisco from April to June, 1945. The Charter of the United Nations was there drawn up, fifty-one nations being foundation members. Arrangements were made whereby the assets and functions of the old League of Nations could be transferred to the new organisation. The General Assembly

[1] Mr. Churchill, speech at Manchester, May 9, 1938.
[2] Mr. Churchill, speech in the House of Commons, May 24, 1944.

of the United Nations met for the first time in January, 1946, in London. Eventually New York became the new international headquarters.

U.N., as the United Nations Organisation is known for short, replaced the League and has six principal organs:

> The Security Council.
> The General Assembly.
> The Secretariat.
> The International Court of Justice.
> The Trusteeship Council.
> The Economic and Social Council.

Much of this structure is similar to that of the old League. A Council, Assembly, and Secretariat were the main organs of the League. They are roughly comparable to cabinet, parliament and civil service in a national system of government. The International Court is composed of judges elected by a special procedure in the Assembly and Security Council voting separately, and has jurisdiction in legal disputes, such as the interpretation of a treaty or any question of international law. But states are not forced to submit cases to it. The Trusteeship Council takes up the work of the former mandate system of the League; it supervises the administration of certain territories previously held under League mandate and also certain territories detached from enemy states after the Second World War. The United States are trustees for the strategic area of the Pacific islands previously mandated to Japan (by decision of the Security Council, April 2, 1947). The Economic and Social Council aims at promoting international co-operation in its own important sphere.

In addition to these, there exist a number of specialised agencies which are linked up with the United Nations. The old International Labour Organisation continues, and there are the Food and Agriculture Organisation, the Educational, Scientific and Cultural Organisation (U.N.E.S.C.O., which has many grandiose schemes in the ill-defined fields of 'educational reconstruction, international understanding and fundamental education'), the International Civil Aviation Organisation, the International Monetary Fund, the International Bank for Reconstruction and Development and there was a Trade

Organisation intended. There is also the World Health Organisation, and a High Commissioner for Refugees whose office has inherited the refugee work of U.N.R.R.A.—United Nations Relief and Rehabilitation Administration—which had previously handled not only refugees or displaced persons, but also assistance to the many lands ravaged by Axis aggression. U.N.R.R.A. relief amounted to over £900,000,000.

This immense administrative creation, with its budgets running into many millions of dollars, its huge staffs and headquarters, its large actual and potentially even larger output of documents, resolutions and reports on every conceivable subject, all has as its prime object the maintenance of peace. But has it, one may ask bluntly, any better chance of achieving its object than had the League of Nations twenty-five years earlier? The U.N. has one great advantage which the League never had: for it includes the United States. It is a fact of great importance, and at the start gave to U.N. what real power and authority it possessed. Unfortunately, indeed tragically, the other great nation which had been outside the League almost as long, namely, the Soviet Union, although a member of U.N., proved to be an obstacle to international co-operation and frequently reduced the proceedings of U.N. to a farce. By means of its veto in the Security Council (referred to below) Russia could block any important action except for matters of procedure. This fact, and jealous regard for national sovereignty, caused frustration—as under the League of Nations.

The General Assembly has been called by the Americans the 'town-meeting of the world'; it meets in regular, annual sessions (though special sessions can be called) and to it all member-states send representatives. It is an organ of deliberation and criticism. The Security Council, however, functions continuously, and has the primary task of maintaining peace. Of its eleven members, the U.S.A., Russia, France, China, and Great Britain are permanent members. These five must concur on important issues: if one of them disagrees, or exercises the veto, a proposal cannot go through. This provision, intended as an ultimate protection of the national sovereignty which, it is assumed, a Great Power will not surrender, for use occasionally and on major issues only, has been used by Russia both frequently and almost frivolously. Thus this supreme international council is reduced almost to impotence. The Security Council has a number of subsidiary organs. A Military Staff Committee in theory assists on all questions of the Council's military requirements for maintaining peace—this is the rather weakly offspring of Mr. Churchill's demand to 'arm our world organisation.' There was a Disarmament Commission—to give effect to an Assembly resolution for reduction of armaments. Most important of all—but equally inconclusive in achieving any result—was the Atomic Energy Commission (with its Working Committee, Committee 2, Sub-Committee on Definitions, Scientific and Technical Committee, and Legal Advisory Committee).

The result was failure to agree on international control of atomic energy. Russia would not accept outside inspection of her factories, and without that any control of atomic energy or indeed of armaments in general would be farcical. In May, 1948, failure was officially admitted in its report to the Security Council: 'The Atomic Energy Commission reports it has reached an impasse.' The formation of all these committees and commissions with high-sounding names and ambitious objects, the passing of resolutions full of good intentions but carefully worded to involve no decisive action, are both features only too reminiscent of the League. Until there is goodwill and mutual understanding between Russia and the democracies, international machinery may help to conceal but will not remove the menace of war. Nevertheless, U.N. represents the best mankind can do so far in the international sphere; the experiment must be persevered with. With all its limitations the United Nations Organisation, in the words of a French statesman, *reste la conscience du monde.*

SUGGESTIONS FOR FURTHER READING

M. Balfour and J. Mair: *Four-Power Control in Germany and Austria 1945-6*, pp. 253-265 and 367-376.

N. Mansergh: *Survey of British Commonwealth Affairs 1939-1952*, cc. 4, 5, and 7.

Everyman's United Nations.

G. D. H. Cole: *Intelligent Man's Guide to the Post-War World.*

Barbara Ward: *The West at Bay.*

CHAPTER 23

A NEW WORLD IN THE MAKING

The Ferment of the 1950's

THE years which immediately followed the Second World War were undeniably disturbed, but for a time most people expected the period of acute disturbance to pass. The great conflict seemed to have settled some great issues; the United Nations had been successfully established; self-government without separation should satisfy the European empires; the main problems were those of economic rehabilitation; the world would slowly settle down. Only very gradually was it realised that on the contrary we stood on the threshold of a period of continuing and fundamental upheaval. Before the new decade opened, events occurred which presaged a long and bitter conflict in Europe and a decisive change in the rôle of its neighbour continents. Ten years later, the Iron Curtain still dominated the politics of Europe, and war over Berlin had so far been postponed rather than avoided. Meanwhile Communist China had emerged—not recognised by the American government and excluded from the United Nations in favour of a residual anti-communist regime based on Taiwan (Formosa). But China was indisputably a third world power, with its population of 700,000,000,[1] and might even prove to be a *tertius gaudens* in the existing disputes of east and west. Still more unexpected was the rapid emergence of Africa from European tutelage to piecemeal independence, with results that at once modified the balance of power both in the U.N. Assembly and in the counsels of the Commonwealth. In the same short period man had also learnt both how he might visit other worlds and how he might destroy his own. Clearly, this final chapter can do no more than point to a few of the main events in an epoch as progressive as the Renaissance, as divisive as the Wars of Religion.

East and West: the Cold War

The growth of a Cold War between east and west proved to be a dominant feature of the post-war world—in Europe and also

[1] The Chinese government's estimated figure for 1961.

in the Far East. In spite of every endeavour on the part of Great Britain to play a mediating rôle, Europe has split ever more sharply into two: the eastern areas are dominated by Russia and its agents, the communist parties; the countries of western Europe whose way of life is democratic look to the United States as their champion. Some people speak of there being two forms of democracy, a western and an eastern form. The communists themselves call their states People's Democracies, and claim their method of government to be truly democratic. If it is indeed legitimate to distinguish two kinds of democracy, they might be described briefly in the following words. Western democracy is based on the right of the people to hold free elections and make an orderly change of government. Eastern democracy presents the people with a government list of candidates and there is no organised opposition. A small poll for the government list might, however, be an indication to those in control that public feeling was hostile or indifferent. The eastern type of government also says it is democratic because it claims to act in the true interests of the people with their tacit support. This may or may not be true. But it is significant that a similar claim—to represent the true interests of a nation—has been made by many of the despots of history, including not only a mild one like James I, but also the most ruthless, such as Mussolini and Hitler. The attempt to distinguish two kinds of democracy was described by the philosopher Bertrand Russell as political humbug. It would, he argued, be just as reasonable to maintain that there were two kinds of happiness—one kind being that which everyone recognised as happiness, the other being unhappiness.

But apart from theoretical differences as to the meaning of democracy the division of the world was clearly a tragedy in the sphere of concrete reality: it was a profoundly disappointing outcome to the Allied co-operation which brought about the defeat of Hitler. The courageous, prolonged and mighty war effort of Russia won her a great fund of admiration and goodwill in the west; this was steadily dissipated by her continued refusal to make any genuine effort at understanding, and cooperation with, the west. It may be that Russia was embittered by America's possession of the secret of the atom bomb. Early in 1945 Russia had asked the United States for a long-term reconstruction loan totalling $6,000,000,000: consideration was postponed. Lend-Lease arrangements, too, were ended promptly with the war, and out of the total expenditure of U.N.R.R.A. no more than 7 per cent was allocated to reconstruction of the very heavily devastated areas of Byelorussia and the Ukraine. These things may also have caused bad feeling. But the impression remained that the Russians, or at any rate their government, had a deeper and a fundamental suspicion of, and hostility to, the west. The Americans as well as the British were everywhere trying hard to work with them: in the Security Council, in the Atomic Energy Commission, in the Control Council for Germany, in the Council of Foreign Ministers, and at the Paris Peace Conference. Again and again Russia's attitude was negative and obstructive, and not only that; she added to it accusation and insult.

In these years Britain was led by a Labour Government with a large majority. Many of these men had habitually looked in a friendly, socialist spirit towards Russia. If they could not work with the Russians, if they could not win Russian understanding and co-operation, no one else could. Whatever one may feel about Russia or communism in theory, the hard fact remains that no western, democratic party or government had succeeded in working with the Russians. An impenetrable barrier of suspicion and mistrust grew up. In Russia, nearly 200,000,000 people were deliberately kept in isolation and ignorance of the outside world. This people had at its disposal a huge army; and there was an old tradition of imperialist expansion, especially in the Balkans, in Turkey and in central Asia. Under communism Russia has in addition to the old imperialist incentive a new ideological urge: the urge of world revolution. It now appears that the apparent parting of the ways between Stalin and Trotsky over world revolution was merely a tactical manœuvre on the part of Stalin: he seems just to have concealed, but not given up, the idea of a struggle with the capitalist west to be followed by world revolution. In his study of 'Leninism' Stalin made clear that the communist aim is revolution which will be world-wide, using Russia as a base, and with Russian forces ready to cross the frontiers in order to 'liberate' other states. This suggests that no permanent peace is possible between the communist and non-communist worlds, since Russia is regarded as 'a powerful base whence the world revolution can continue to develop.'[1]

It was a matter of deeds as well as words. In 1947 the Communist International, which had been abandoned as a gesture of good will in 1943, was to some extent revived under the new style of the Cominform or Communist Information Bureau. This was followed by a direct attempt to drive the western allies out of Berlin as a reprisal for the economic measures which, as we have seen, were restoring prosperity and strength to western Germany. From 24 June 1948 to 11 May 1949 the Russians blocked access to West Berlin by road, rail, and canal, and were defeated only by a protracted and costly mobilisation of air strength, which by the spring was flying in an average load of 8,000 tons a day.

Antecedents of N.A.T.O.

To the Russian determination to regard the west as hostile and to expand communist domination everywhere by persuasion, by fraud or by force, the west itself at first reacted slowly and somewhat uncertainly. It is difficult for western governments to deal with communist parties for, as long as they are in opposition, they claim the democratic freedoms of speech, association and organisation. Yet it can be powerfully argued that a democracy 'should tolerate everything except intolerance.'[2] The Americans, for their part, in contrast to their attitude in 1919, realised that they could no longer follow a policy of isolation: American administration of Japan and of their zones in Germany and Austria demonstrated the determination of the United States to shoulder a new responsibility in world affairs. Still more: the American leaders realised that a positive policy was necessary, both to assist European economic recovery and to help the European nations to maintain a bulwark of defence against the communist-dominated east. For the United States was beginning itself to fear encirclement as communism advanced westwards across Europe and south-eastwards through China.

By the early months of 1947 it had become apparent that a general world peace settlement was not in immediate sight,

---

[1] See J. Stalin, *Leninism*, section entitled 'The October Revolution as Prelude to World Revolution.'

[2] J. Middleton Murry, *The Free Society*.

while Germany and western Europe were in the grip of economic paralysis. It seemed that Russia even desired such a condition to continue and develop: economic deterioration leading to widespread hardship and discontent would create conditions in which world revolution might become a possibility. In March President Truman agreed that America should replace Britain in providing military support for Greece, where the civil war had flared up again, and for Turkey. Then in June General Marshall, wartime American Chief of Staff and now Secretary of State, made a speech saying that, if the European states would join in putting forward plans for economic reconstruction, the United States would be prepared to give assistance. Mr. Bevin, the British Foreign Secretary, at once welcomed the plan; he 'seized it with both hands,' as he said himself.

On the other hand, the U.S.S.R. denounced the Marshall Plan as an instrument of American imperialism, using in this respect language similar to that used previously by the Nazis.[1] She caused all her satellites (Poland, Jugoslavia, Rumania, Hungary, Bulgaria, Albania, Czechoslovakia) and Finland to reject it, though Czechoslovakia had at first accepted. The representatives of the other states of Europe, however, met in Paris and drew up their plans and made estimates of the amounts of help needed from the United States. Eventually, a vast scheme of American aid to Europe—part by way of loan, part by way of gift—was approved by Congress in 1948. The scheme provided for a sum equivalent to £1,325,000,000 to finance the first year of the plan. As a result of the Russian menace the United States also increased their own defences: a big addition was made to defence expenditure, and compulsory military training was reintroduced.

While America was making her plans to assist, the nations of Europe were doing something to strengthen their own political and military position. In the general elections in Italy the Christian Democrat Party achieved a clear majority in the parliament—this was a political first-fruit of Marshall aid. Belgium, the Netherlands and Luxemburg had already established a limited customs union known as Benelux. Most vital of all, on March 17, 1948, the foreign ministers of Britain,

[1] See for example *Dollar-Imperialismus*, published in 1942 by the Nazi Party in Berlin.

France, Belgium, Holland and Luxemburg met in Brussels and signed a fifty-years pact, which set up a Western European Union (W.E.U.), with machinery for economic and cultural, but more particularly for military, co-operation.   But for any effective security such a union had to look to American military

EAST AND WEST, 1949

support.   This fact was increasingly realised during the ensuing months.   At length on April 4, 1949, the foreign ministers of twelve western nations—the U.S.A., Canada, Great Britain, France, Belgium, the Netherlands, Luxemburg, Norway, Denmark, Iceland, Portugal, and Italy—met in Washington and signed the Atlantic Pact, by which they agreed to recognise aggression against one as aggression against all.

N.A.T.O.

By the North Atlantic Pact or Treaty the signatories provided a Council as the supreme authority of the Organisation.   The creation of N.A.T.O. showed clearly enough that its members felt they could not entrust their security to the U.N. alone—a body in which the Russian veto could prevent effective action from being taken for the defence of the west. U.N. was, and is, a world body including nations committed to either side and to neither. N.A.T.O., on the other hand, was to be a regional association including only those western states which were determined to resist communist aggression, and which felt they could best accomplish this by uniting together against any piecemeal Soviet action. In 1952 Greece and Turkey were also brought into N.A.T.O., and in 1955 the German Federal Republic. All members shared a collective guarantee against any further advance of Russian power in the west, and at the time of its creation such an organisation was clearly needed to meet the Russian threat.

N.A.T.O., with its council of ministers and secretary-general, brought into existence a network of commands, staffs, military plans, and logistical preparations, and installed massive equipment such as airfields and radar installations, with the United States as the paymaster of the coalition. The Supreme Allied Commander, Europe—always an American national, the first being General Eisenhower—had forces assigned to him by member states, and operated from a supreme headquarters (S.H.A.P.E.) near Paris. There was also a Supreme Atlantic Commander to safeguard the western seas. Given whole-hearted participation by the war-weary powers of western Europe, the new set-up might be expected to be increasingly effective as a deterrent to any Russian project for overrunning western Europe at small cost. And in the background there was the American nuclear monopoly.

But in the year in which N.A.T.O. was formed it became clear that Russia was also entering the field of nuclear armament. This new factor in the situation seemed at first to reduce the value of N.A.T.O. Yet, if each side was in a position to destroy the other—and all civilisation with it—by strategic bombing with nuclear weapons of gigantic force, it was rational to suppose that neither side would deliberately resort to such catastrophic and suicidal action—in which case the N.A.T.O. system still had a vital rôle to play. Any Russian advance into the west must be effectively resisted by N.A.T.O. forces using conventional weapons and the smaller, tactical nuclear weapons supplied by America or (from 1954 onwards) manufactured in the United Kingdom. This made it possible to believe as well as to hope that the balance of terror could be preserved, and that neither side would be tempted to try to settle a limited dispute by accepting the illimitable consequences involved in being the first to launch an inter-continental ballistic missile.

Political disharmonies, economic strains, colonial wars, and plain unwillingness to serve all delayed the growth of N.A.T.O. forces, but by 1960 a strength of 30 fully mobilised divisions was within sight of achievement. Meanwhile Russia, too, created international institutions in reply to those of the west. In the years after the war nearly 100,000,000 Europeans had been brought within the Russian orbit. Of the eight countries concerned only Jugoslavia (and, much later, tiny Albania) escaped from Russian control. In 1949 they were linked by a Council for Mutual Economic Aid (COMECON); in 1955 this was followed by the Warsaw Pact, pledging military aid to each other in the event of attack.

European Recovery and Common Institutions

The Brussels Treaty and the N.A.T.O. Pact clearly demonstrated a new initiative among the states of western Europe and a new determination both to defend themselves and to work with the United States and Canada for their common defence. At the same time the advance of communism on the home front —its appeal to the impoverished, the discontented, and the despairing—was effectively driven back by the Marshall Plan and the hopes which it engendered. The Organisation for European Economic Co-operation (O.E.E.C.) [1] was set up in Paris in 1948, so that European Governments and expert civil servants seconded by them might, subject to American approval, spend the American grants to the best advantage. That object was further secured by an arrangement requiring the European countries which participated in Marshall aid to place equivalent sums in a counterpart fund; this, too, was to be used for approved purposes conducive to recovery.

---

[1] Reconstituted in 1961 as the Organisation for Economic Co-operation and Development (O.E.C.D.), having the U.S.A. and Canada as full members and the additional task of co-ordinating aid to under-developed countries outside Europe.

An astonishing transformation followed, as in most parts of western Europe the painful post-war shortages began to disappear; production mounted; and people prospered. From 1952 onwards France, for example, claimed a record rate of industrial growth of 10 per cent per annum. Most remarkable of all was the recovery of the German industrial areas, which the Allies had laid in ruins. American aid gave a stimulus to the native capacity for hard work and industrial 'know-how,' which together overcame all difficulties. Neunkirchen in the Saar may serve as an illustration. In 1939 it was a flourishing coal and iron centre, profiting by Hitler's armament drive, with busy streets, shops, and cafés; in 1946 it was gone—one got down from the train on to the tracks to find that station, streets, and shops had all vanished; by 1950 it was back again, a busy industrial town once more. Over the whole territory of the German Federal Republic industrial production by 1958 was two and a half times as large as before the war.

The economic recovery of western Europe was accompanied by, and related to, the growth of the new European institutions. Such was the Council of Europe, set up in 1949, with an executive committee of ministers, delegated by the governments of member states; an annual consultative assembly; and an international secretariat at its headquarters in Strasbourg. This new body overshadowed the union previously established through the Brussels Treaty, except that the latter was used in 1954 as the basis for an expanded Western European Union, including Germany and Italy, which was formed to allay French fears regarding the re-arming of west Germany as a member of N.A.T.O. The Council of Europe, with fifteen member states, developed important cultural activities, but enthusiasts who looked to it to promote political unification were held in check by less enthusiastic members, such as Great Britain. The main advance came, however, through the cultivation of specifically economic relationships among France, the German Federal Republic, Italy, Belgium, the Netherlands, and Luxemburg, the three last-named having formed their own small customs union as early as January, 1948.

In 1951 these six powers began by placing coal, iron, and steel production under the full control of a High Authority located at Luxemburg, which was to aim at such regulation of prices and output as would be most conducive to the expansion of the whole economy. The results—about which opinion in Britain had been rather sceptical—were such that in 1957 the six states signed the Treaties of Rome, which bound their economies together so closely that national political sovereignty was plainly destined to dwindle and disappear. In the long run the establishment of the European Atomic Energy Community (EURATOM), to develop nuclear power in common for all civil uses, was likely to have great importance. But what had immediate impact was the decision taken at Rome to set up the European Economic Community or Common Market. Its objects comprised the elimination of all customs barriers between member states; the common regulation of tariffs against other states; and the integration of their economies by allowing the free movement of capital and labour from one state to another. The governing institutions of the new Community were to include an assembly of 142 delegates elected by parliaments; a policy-making council of six ministers, one for each country, but with a voting-power which for many purposes varied according to size; and a court of justice charged with the interpretation and enforcement of the terms of agreement. All executive tasks, however, were entrusted to a commission of nine, who were not to be national representatives; and there was also to be a large advisory committee to watch the interests of employers' organisations, trade unions, etc.

Unwilling to accept restrictions upon her absolute sovereignty inside the United Kingdom or to face the probable impairment of her economic relations with other member states of the Commonwealth, Britain turned instead to the formation of a European Free Trade Association (E.F.T.A.) with the remaining, economically less important, states of western Europe. This duly came into existence through the Treaty of Stockholm in 1960. But the Common Market developed with unexpected speed, and by January, 1962, it had reached the point of no return. In American eyes the economic unification of Europe, for which their own continent provided something of a pattern, was clearly desirable. In British eyes participation still seemed no better than a regrettable necessity. But much depended upon what terms Britain might obtain to safeguard rights of sovereignty and Commonwealth relationships; the impact upon her agriculture; and the position of the other members of E.F.T.A. The cost was still uncertain, but a new

Europe was being made, from which Britain could not afford to be excluded.

The Korean War, 1950–53

But before the recovery and reorganisation of Europe had proceeded very far, the general east-west situation deteriorated sharply. In fact, the Cold War suddenly became hot, although in a distant part of the world. In 1949, after China had been racked by civil war or foreign invasion for a period of nearly forty years, the Chinese communists emerged as final victors, a result which slowly endangered the balance of power in the whole world. Immediately, it endangered Korea, a country recovered from the Japanese Empire in 1945. Since then the northern part had been occupied by the Russians, the southern part by the Americans, and these parts had hardened into two Korean states of opposite and hostile political outlook. The withdrawal of American troops was followed in June, 1950, by a well-prepared invasion of the south by the communist North Koreans. Since Russia had probably prepared the move and certainly stood to gain by it, her veto in the Security Council would have been used to prevent any intervention by the U.N. But for tactical reasons she was just then boycotting the meetings of the Council, which enabled the Council to declare that the North Koreans were the aggressors and to authorise the Americans to act on its behalf. American forces were sent to Korea under the U.N. flag, and were in time to turn back the invasion. By October North Korea in turn was being overrun, but the Chinese communists then gave powerful support, so that a long struggle ensued, throughout which the Americans bore the brunt of the fighting on the U.N. side, though there was a Commonwealth Division and smaller units supplied by fifteen other powers. The most significant feature of the war was that it remained localised. The Americans did not invade Manchuria, on which the Chinese operations were based, nor did they resort to nuclear weapons; on the other side, no troops were put in by the Russians. These measures of self-restraint staved off a third world war, and after the war in Korea had dragged on for three years it was terminated by an armistice which recognised approximately the *status quo*. Meanwhile about 3,000,000 Koreans, one-tenth of the population of the country, are believed to have perished.

Two more positive measures were also taken to safeguard the situation in the far east. At Commonwealth instigation, but with the Americans paying more than half the cost, the Colombo Plan made large provision for capital expenditure to help to raise the standard of life in India and elsewhere. Three years after this came into operation, the South-East Asia Treaty Organisation or S.E.A.T.O. was set up to give the same kind of military protection under American leadership as was already enabling communist pressures to be withstood by the N.A.T.O. countries in the west.

Contraction of the European World

Chinese participation in the Korean War was a sharp reminder, if one was still needed, of the rejection of dominance by the white nations of the world, which was a feature of the age. Between 1870 and 1919 peoples of European stock had parcelled out among themselves virtually the whole of the African continent, established their hold upon all the nearer parts of Asia, and left their Japanese imitators as the only serious obstacle to the full economic penetration and exploitation of what had been the Celestial Empire. Now the very word colonialism had become a pejorative expression. There was a general retreat of the European empires from both Asia and Africa. New nations, made up of long submerged peoples, were beginning to take the stage, who might be bitterly in need of economic, technical, and cultural assistance from outside, but who would rather go without than accept any concomitant restraints upon their new-found freedom.

The most spectacular and quite possibly the best conducted retreat was that of the British from India. The Indian demand for independence had become very strong, but the division of the country between two great religious communities, Hindu and Moslem, posed grave difficulties, which the British met by fixing a definite date for the transfer of authority and accepting the abandonment of the unity they had planned for through the creation of the two entirely separate dominions of India and Pakistan. Both countries later adopted republican constitutions, but they remained within the Commonwealth, as did also Ceylon and the Federation of Malaya, though the independence of the last-named was delayed for a further ten years, until 1957, by the needs of a long struggle against communist guerrillas. In the case of each of these countries—and even in Burma, which left the Commonwealth—the end of British rule did not mean a severance of economic and cultural relations. After the British gave up their hold on India, the French handed over Pondicherry and their other tiny settlements in India without much demur. Portugal, however, clung to Goa, which at the close of 1961 was invaded and annexed by Indian forces in direct contravention of traditions of non-violence, which had been preached by Gandhi and in name at least accepted by their prime minister, Nehru.

Both the Dutch and the French lost valuable empires in the Far East, the loss in each case being partly the result of the disruption caused by the Japanese occupation, which had also played havoc with Malaya. When the Dutch returned to Indonesia in 1945, they found that the Japanese had left an Indonesian nationalist government in possession. There followed years of disorder and fighting, in which the Dutch for brief periods had the upper hand, until in 1949 they made an almost complete transfer of sovereignty to the Indonesian Republic. The single exception was Netherlands New Guinea, which by 1962 the Indonesian President was threatening to take by force. The French in Indochina were likewise confronted in 1945 by the menace of revolutionary nationalism. After four years they tried to meet this by granting independence within the French Union—a quasi-federal system established under the Fourth Republic—to Cambodia, Laos, and Vietnam. But meanwhile war had broken out between the French and the communists of north Vietnam, who had Chinese backing. When the Korean War ended, the Chinese were able to divert arms and supplies to Vietnam, but the Americans were understandably unwilling to be committed there. The French army, which in all suffered 234,000 casualties in Indochina, including 92,000 dead, made a last desperate stand at Dienbien-phu, which fell in May, 1954; a conference already in session at Geneva reached a final settlement in July. Vietnam was partitioned, the north going to the communists. The other states of Indochina became completely separated from France, and the task of containing the further advance of communist power in Laos passed in the end to the Americans.

In the Near East, too, the European Powers were obliged to withdraw. Even before the war ended a League of Arab

States had been formed, representing a population of 36,000,000, and the tragic events of the war period had exacerbated the demands of the Jews for complete possession of their National Home in Palestine. Syria, which had been under French mandate since 1920, achieved its independence in 1946. In the next year Britain, after a vain attempt to suppress terrorism and to preserve a balance between Jews and Arabs, gave up the mandate for Palestine. The sequel was a partition proposed by the United Nations; a war between the Jews and the League of Arab States, in which the latter were routed; and the acceptance by the United Nations and world opinion of an Israeli Republic of rather wider dimensions than had originally been offered to the Jews.

Egypt was, however, the most difficult case. The monarchy was overthrown in 1952, and after two years power and the presidency of the new republic were seized by a ruthless army officer, Colonel Nasser, who cast himself for the rôle of leader of Arab nationalism throughout the Near East. He secured an agreement by which British troops were withdrawn from the Suez Canal, which they had safeguarded for more than 70 years, and Britain also gave up its interest in the Anglo-Egyptian Sudan, which opted to become a wholly independent state. But when Nasser made the refusal of mainly American credit facilities for the construction of a new High Dam at Aswan a justification for the seizure of the Suez Canal, in which Britain was the chief shareholder, the Eden government resolved upon his overthrow. Hostilities begun by Israel against Egypt provided a pretext for an Anglo-French ultimatum to both sides and a demand for the temporary reoccupation of the Canal zone, which Nasser refused to accept. Egyptian airfields were then bombed and an Anglo-French force was sent off in a rather dilatory fashion to occupy Port Said and compass the downfall of the Egyptian dictator.

But events did not go according to plan. A hostile vote in the United Nations Assembly was only to be expected, as were also the threats of retaliation by nuclear bombing of London and Paris with which the Russians championed the Egyptian cause. What was unexpected was the sharp division of opinion in Britain, which did not run entirely along party lines; the strength of the opposition in the Commonwealth; and—what was of course of paramount importance—the direct and outspoken hostility of the American government, which was in a position to thwart the action.   Since the British prime minister had begun the operation in the belief that he would receive at least covert support from across the Atlantic, it is reasonable to point not only to Eden's declining health which may have impaired his judgement, but to the exigencies of the American presidential campaign as possibly affecting the judgement of his counterpart.   Be that as it may, Britain and France were compelled to agree to a cease-fire, and a U.N. force took over the positions they had secured at Port Said and along the blocked Canal.   Nasser came out unscathed, and although he did not prove to be the mere Russian puppet Sir Anthony Eden had anticipated, it was significant that within two years the pro-British monarchy in Iraq had been brutally overthrown and a similar dictatorship established there.   Only forty years had passed since Allenby's army had rid the Arab world of a Turkish despotism that had lasted for nearly four centuries.

The Transformation of Africa

In Africa a single decade sufficed to undo the political settlement imposed by a half-century of imperialism.   The result was to confront not only the former colonial powers but the whole civilised world with the difficult problems which arise when economically depressed and culturally backward peoples strive to jump forward to the prosperity and absolute political freedom that they covet.   Even the British colonies, where preparatory institutions of self-rule had long been in existence, passed through the last stages to complete emancipation at a speed determined more by their wishes than their needs.   Great areas were granted their independence: Ghana in 1957, Nigeria in 1960, Tanganyika, as well as some smaller territories, in 1961.   All of them remained in the Commonwealth, but it was partly a consequence of their remaining inside that the South African Republic, with its harsh policy of *apartheid*, preferred to go outside.   Painful conflicts of interest, if not of duty, still faced the British people in other parts of Africa, notably Kenya and Northern Rhodesia, where the surrender of sovereign power to the natives could hardly be accomplished without inflicting severe hardship upon white settlers who had been encouraged to make their homes there under the assured protection of the British flag.// In Kenya the Mau-Mau rebellion of 1952-6 suggested ominous possibilities; in the two Rhodesias the experiment of a federal union involving also Nyasaland provoked native opposition.

The vast French empire in Africa was likewise transformed. After the war colonial ties were first loosened by the formation of a French Union, which in 1958 was renamed the French Community, and the peoples of the various tropical possessions were then invited to decide by referendum whether they wished to belong. With the exception of Guinea, which opted for immediate secession, they all chose to remain in the Community as sovereign republics, twelve in number. In 1956 France recognised the independence of both Tunisia and Morocco (where Spain followed the same policy), though relations remained for a time uneasy. The real problem, however, was that of Algeria, which overturned the Fourth Republic (of 1946) and more than once threatened the stability of the Fifth.

There seems to have been a legacy of hatred there since the original invasion of 1830 and the long and costly French campaigns against Abd-el-Kader. The French settlers or *colons* built up comfortable lives for themselves, while abject poverty continued among the Moslems. In 1940 the latter were tempted to think of Hitler as their prospective liberator; after the war there were demonstrations, race riots in which Europeans were killed, and ruthless repression by the French. In 1954 a guerrilla struggle broke out, which was waged with great ferocity on both sides. The French exerted their full military strength, but were never able to reduce the entire country to order because the 'hard core' of rebels received more or less clandestine support from neighbouring Arab states and the communist world beyond. In May, 1958, a military *coup* in Algiers under the leadership of embittered professional army officers, who saw that Algeria was going the way of Indochina, threatened to bring about civil war in France, which was staved off through the personal ascendancy of General de Gaulle, who became the nearly all-powerful President of the Fifth Republic. But his policy in Algeria disgusted the military faction by its acceptance of the inevitable. By 1962 an Algerian nationalist government was ready to take over, and the prospect before the *colons* in France's last great imperial possession was extremely bleak.

Germany and Italy were perhaps fortunate to have lost their African territories already, as losers in the two world wars. Portugal clung desperately to possessions which she had held since the sixteenth century: the result was a savage outbreak in Angola in 1961, savagely—and perhaps only temporarily—suppressed. Belgium, which was the other small power concerned in African affairs, took the opposite course, again with discreditable consequences. In June, 1960, when administration of their huge Congolese territory was proving troublesome, the Belgians abruptly handed over all authority to an unprepared native government and an undisciplined native army. The result was grave disorders, economic collapse, and provincial or even tribal movements for secession. The central government appealed to the U.N., which promptly dispatched a military force, teams of civilian experts, and much-needed supplies, both for humanitarian reasons and also to prevent the Russians from fishing in troubled waters. But in a large and barbaric country such as the Congo, where the natives had had no experience whatever in the workings of self-government, a quick solution was impossible. The U.N. troops could hardly preserve their own lives, let alone suppress murderous disorders, without being accused of infringing rights of sovereignty. To make matters worse, African secessionists in the province of Katanga, with its rich Belgian-run copper mines still at work, were receiving financial and other forms of support from Belgium and from across the Rhodesian border. It took eighteen months to establish a precarious internal peace and unity, even though the U.N. action had the wholehearted support of America.

Increase of U.N. Activities

Before returning from this brief consideration of the outer continents to our proper subject, the affairs of Europe, it is important to notice that the decline of colonialism helped in the further evolution of the United Nations. The fact that the second Secretary-General, Dag Hammarskjöld (a Swede who had succeeded the Norwegian, Trygve Lie, in 1953), met his death in a flying accident on a visit to the Congo in 1961, was a dramatic reminder of the extent to which it had become usual for this official to take upon himself the rôle of world mediator. Moreover, Hammarskjöld was replaced for his two unexpired years of office by a native of an ex-colonial territory, the Burmese, U Thant. The specialised agencies of the U.N. likewise acquired a wider usefulness through the services they could render to the newly independent states, which were often reluctant to accept help directly from great powers. But the most striking change was in the character of the annual General Assembly.

In the autumn of 1950, when Russia's temporary boycott of the Security Council meetings had enabled the Council to agree upon intervention in Korea, the Assembly took the opportunity to pass a resolution to the effect that, if a Security Council veto prevented action for dealing with an aggressor, such action could be taken by a two-thirds majority of the Assembly. This considerably enhanced the practical authority of the Assembly, but its moral authority was still seriously limited by the dependence, or in some cases supposed dependence, of a majority of its members upon the goodwill of the United States. The fragmentation of what had been the colonial empires ended this. By 1961 the 50 states which had originally signed the U.N. Charter had doubled in number. Other things being equal, the newer members desired nothing more than the chance to play off America and Russia against each other in the name of liberty, and the effort to show that things were not equal involved the great powers in something like a genuine appeal to world opinion. The Afro-Asians were becoming an important factor—and since Stalin's death Russia, too, was not indifferent to their suffrage.

Death of Stalin (1953): Changes in Russia and Satellite States

It is often suggested by democrats and optimists that even the strongest of dictatorships will not outlive its founder. Nevertheless, just as Stalin had secured the succession to Lenin, so once again, when Stalin was gone, there was no breakdown, no counter-revolution, no civil war. His death occurred, indeed, at a moment when the medical staff of the Kremlin had been under arrest for two months on a never-cleared-up charge of conspiracy to murder, but it is generally accepted that the all-powerful Georgian died naturally of a cerebral hemorrhage. As prime minister Stalin was succeeded by Malenkov, as Communist Party Secretary by Khrushchev, while behind the scenes Beria, Molotov, and others joined in the struggle for power. Beria, who as head of the dead dictator's police and security services had been the chief instrument of tyranny, was arrested and shot before the end of the year. Malenkov remained at the head of a kind of collective leadership until 1955, when he stepped down to the position of a deputy premier, having vainly urged that the time had come to give consumer goods precedence over the claims of heavy industry. The new prime minister was Marshal Bulganin, but there was a further struggle behind the scenes, in which Khrushchev worsted Molotov; Malenkov and he were then relegated to quite minor posts. Finally, in 1958 the Supreme Soviet formally replaced Bulganin by Khrushchev, so that, as holding both premiership and party secretaryship, he was now the undisputed leader of the country—but a leader of a very different type from Stalin.

Stalin's death had been followed by a slight immediate thaw in the Cold War and a considerable relaxation of the regime inside Russia. Support was given to the negotiations which terminated the Korean War, and two years later Russia joined the other powers in signing a treaty of peace with Austria. The four-power occupation, which had been very profitable to the Russians, was at last brought to an end; the frontiers of 1937 were re-established; and the restored state made a pledge of complete neutrality. It was implied in various ways that the change of rulers had introduced a new flexibility into Soviet policy. Khrushchev spoke at various times of war with the capitalist states as not being inevitable, of socialism as being in some cases attainable by non-revolutionary action, and of the possibility of peaceful co-existence for communism and capitalism. He put the stress on economic development: communist production, he maintained, would outpace capitalist and show its superiority. In July, 1955, Bulganin and Khrushchev attended a Summit Conference at Geneva, the first meeting of heads of government since Potsdam. No important concrete results were achieved, but Bulganin reported to the Supreme Soviet that all four powers had shown their desire to end the Cold War. It also seemed significant that Soviet leaders began to travel abroad, Khrushchev himself paying much publicised visits to Britain, to India, and to the United States.

Domestic changes included an amnesty for political prisoners and the release of many other unfortunates from forced-labour camps. It became notably easier for foreigners to gain admission to Russia and for Russians to spend periods of study in the outside world. Free discussion and even criticism began to be in evidence from time to time on the Soviet scene. Most remarkable of all was Khrushchev's denunciation of Stalin at a secret session of the Party Congress in 1956, when he accused his late master of the tyrannical conduct of purges, of the torture and shooting of Party leaders and members whom he suspected of daring to criticise him, and even of being himself to blame for Russia's military setbacks in the early years of the war. The violent reaction against Stalin and Stalinism ('the cult of personality') soon became public and went even further in subsequent years. In 1961 the embalmed body was officially removed from its place of honour alongside that of Lenin in the Red Square at Moscow, and the city of Stalingrad, where that iron will had been most memorably asserted, was renamed Volgagrad.

The changes in Russia had important repercussions in the satellite states—reaction against Stalinism and those who had supported it, and hopes of greater liberty. In June, 1953, there were risings in East Germany, and especially in East Berlin, suppressed by Russian tanks. More serious disturbances broke out three years later in Poland, and then in Hungary. The Russians avoided any direct conflict with the Poles: an alternative and more popular communist leader, Gomulka, was placed in power, under whom his fellow-countrymen enjoyed some degree of freedom. But in Hungary a popular revolt overthrew the communist government by force, induced the Russian garrison to withdraw from Budapest, and appealed to the United Nations for support. It was all in vain. World opinion was distracted at this juncture by the Suez crisis, but in any case a third world war seemed to most people too high a price to offer for the liberation of Hungary. On November 4, 1956, Russian armoured columns were directed against Budapest and other urban centres and stamped out the revolt in blood. Many communists appear to have been disgusted by the cynical disregard of the will of the people; the non-communist world salved its conscience as best it could, by a generous reception of refugees.

Nevertheless, when this eventful decade closed, Soviet Russia no less than her opponents had serious problems to face. The satellite states were not unaware of the extent to which their relationship with the Soviet Union still exposed them to crude economic exploitation. It was significant that Jugoslavia, having once made good her escape from the Soviet *bloc*, though remaining staunchly communist in doctrine and economy, was never tempted to rejoin. By 1960 Albania was likewise beginning to follow an independent course. Behind Albania loomed the figure of the Chinese People's Republic, with a far greater population and presumably far greater potential resources than the U.S.S.R., discordantly denouncing the policy of possible co-existence proclaimed by Khrushchev. This was one reason why relations between east and west suffered a swift deterioration over the problem of the future of Berlin.

Germany and the Problem of Berlin

The Cold War had particularly important effects on the development of Germany throughout these years, because the inability of Russia and the Western Allies to find a common policy left it permanently divided. West Germany and the Allies were increasingly driven to work together, a situation which enabled the former to make a rapid recovery. In 1948 a stable currency was created, and in the following year the three western zones of occupation became the German Federal Republic, with Bonn for capital and the veteran Dr. Conrad Adenauer as federal chancellor. The regime of disarmament, demilitarisation, and occupation by Allied forces continued, however, until 1955, when the Federal Republic was recognised by treaty with the western allies to be a sovereign state. The Allied troops stayed on—but as guests, to encourage resistance to Soviet pressure. At the same time the Federal Republic was brought into Western European Union and N.A.T.O., in order that she might make a major contribution to the military manpower still lacking for the defence of western Europe. Thus once more, as after the First World War, the permanent disarmament of Germany was proposed, imposed, and abandoned.

Meanwhile Russia had turned her zone into the German Democratic Republic, set up by proclamation in 1949 and made into a sovereign state in 1955. West Germany and the western Allies alike refused recognition, on the grounds that this state was not based on any free elections, such as had been held in the *Länder* of West Germany, whose representatives had originally formed the Federal Republic. But Russia's German satellite also had its armed forces, backed by the Russian counterpart to N.A.T.O. under a unified command set up by the Warsaw Pact. Such a division at the heart of Europe was bound to be extremely dangerous. It was made worse by the steady flow of refugees across the frontier from east to west; by the often provocative refusal of West Germans to admit the finality of the Oder-Neisse frontier; and by the endless provocative incidents arising from the position of West Berlin as an enclave in East Germany.

From the time of the failure of the Berlin blockade in 1949, hardly a year passed without some kind of interference by the Russians with Allied rights in Berlin as provided by the Potsdam Agreement. But it was not until the summer of 1961 that a second dangerous crisis arose there. Khrushchev announced his intention of making a separate peace treaty with the German Democratic Republic, to which he would hand over any responsibility to the western Allies regarding rights of communication with Berlin, as they arose out of a war situation which Russia had now terminated. The Allies, for their part, were unwilling to recognise East Germany, reluctant to desert their friends in West Berlin, and unable to disregard the damage to their prestige in other parts of the world which would follow the abandonment of this exposed position. The American army called up some of its reserves, and the Berlin garrison was reinforced. The East Germans built a wall right across the city, which not only stopped the flight of hapless refugees but might eventually atrophy the economic life of West Berlin, which had never caught up with the prosperity of the rest of western Germany.[1] At the close of 1961 the situation over Berlin was still tense and potentially very dangerous, though some comfort was derived from the fact that the autumn months had passed without either side provoking a

[1] In 1959 two-fifths of the West Berlin population of 2,200,000 were wholly or partly dependent on public assistance, although 75 per cent of the refugees arriving there were flown out to West Germany. The figures are taken from *Meet Germany*, a booklet published by Atlantik-Brücke, Hamburg, 'to introduce Germany to Americans.'

showdown. But the Russians had shocked even the uncommitted powers, such as India, by deciding at this juncture to resume experimental nuclear explosions involving pollution of the atmosphere, which had been suspended since November, 1958, by a self-imposed moratorium among the three nuclear powers.[1] In particular, a bomb of 50 (or possibly 57) megatons —that is to say, one with an explosive force at least 2,500 times as great as that which destroyed Hiroshima—was exploded on October 30, 1961, and was described by Khrushchev as a warning to the west.

Science and the Future

The giant bomb was indeed a warning—but a warning to the whole world of the fact that scientific advances will serve the purposes of peace or war. Science offers mankind the alternatives of material progress beyond the wildest dreams of yesterday and, on the other hand, self-annihilation which human insanity could bring. The twentieth century has already witnessed the growth of amenities, especially in America, which could be applied to the amelioration of the human condition everywhere—if only the statesmen could settle the political problems. But man's power over nature has developed much faster than his power of self-control. This is strikingly illustrated if one considers the impact of the two world wars: on the one hand, the faltering and imperfectly successful efforts to devise the political means of avoiding further international conflicts; on the other hand, the way in which the wartime advances of applied science have been systematically exploited to produce further discoveries and practical applications.

Until very recently the aeroplane appeared to be the most spectacular of all human inventions. It was during the second world war that the principle of jet propulsion was applied to military aircraft: by 1948 jet planes were beginning to be able on occasion to exceed the speed of sound, and within another decade civil air liners of gigantic size were providing jet services between the continents.

[1] British megaton weapons were being produced by February, 1958 (see Cmd. 363), as a sequel to tests conducted the previous year in the vicinity of Christmas Island. French tests in the Sahara in 1960–1 were on a very much smaller scale.

Radar, which Britain was developing for her air defences before the actual outbreak of war in 1939, and the important wartime uses of transistor radio equipment speeded up the elaboration of electronic devices and equipment of all kinds, which has helped to make the construction of complicated types of computer and the spread of automation in general among the most significant post-war changes. The chemistry of synthetic materials, such as plastics in innumerable variety, clearly owes much to the frantic search during both world wars for substitutes by means of which to resist the pressure of blockade measures. Lastly, we must at least mention the wartime advances in surgery, psychiatry, and medicine, including the introduction of marvellous new drugs such as penicillin. The results by 1961 included a definite reduction in the more extreme forms of physical suffering, an increase in longevity, and biological researches leading to a closer approach to the understanding of the ultimate structure of living material.

The early achievements of atomic physics in Cambridge and elsewhere, including the first 'splitting of the atom,' were not of course related to the needs of war. But the race to develop nuclear fission as a means of destruction, crowned as it was with success at Hiroshima and Nagasaki, was a wartime expedient which aroused great stirrings of conscience as soon as its results became known, though condoned by many as a desperate remedy in a situation that would never recur. By 1945, too, the peaceful uses of nuclear power were beginning to be more readily available to man, so that the next fifteen years witnessed an important growth of atomic power stations in Britain, the building of the first atom-powered submarines in America, and some exploitation of medical and other possibilities. The military use, however, was not allowed to fade into the background, as had been hoped, since the Cold War provided the Russians with an incentive to challenge the American monopoly, while a variety of factors, ranging from the ability to concentrate a large part of their economy upon a single project to the capture of German nuclear scientists in 1945, made rapid progress possible for them. Within four years the Russians were known to have made the nuclear-fission bomb, but the Americans by then possessed the nuclear-fusion or hydrogen bomb, which was vastly more powerful. When the Russians surprised the world by exploding their own first hydrogen bomb as early as November, 1952, it became clear that all-out war between America and Russia would destroy civilisation as we know it and might even—through long-term radiation effects—destroy the human race.

There is something ironical in the fact that the technology which may at any moment be employed to render our world uninhabitable, in the meantime beguiles us with the prospect of visits to other worlds. For the rocket, which contains within itself the means of its propulsion, is the chosen instrument for conveying the nuclear bomb from continent to continent and landing it with presumed accuracy in the target area; it is also the instrument which, because it does not require the oxygen of the air to effect combustion, is the chosen instrument for exploring outer space. It was on October 4, 1957, that the Russians put the first artificial earth satellite successfully into orbit, the actual *sputnik* (Russian for 'travelling-companion') being launched from the third stage of a rocket. In intense rivalry, the Americans put up their first satellite the following year. Then in 1959 the Russians sent out a moon probe, which passed the moon and went into orbit round the sun, thus becoming the first artificial planet; again the Americans were fairly quick to achieve a similar result. But before the end of the year the Russians had contrived to hit the moon with one of their *luniks* and to use another for photographing its hidden side. Throughout 1960 the competition continued, watched by the whole of the civilised world, with scientific exploration of space as the prime motive but with very considerable general prestige accruing to the Russians, who clearly retained the lead. Finally, on April 12, 1961, the Russians achieved the first manned space flight, when a multi-stage rocket sent up a five-ton spaceship which orbited the earth and brought back in safety its passenger, Major Gagarin, 'the Columbus of inter-planetary space'. Both sides then planned to send men to the moon, the American proposal being to land a whole team of astronauts there before 1970.

Europe and the World

From the Battle of Sedan to projected moon-flights in only 100 years! It might well seem that, with space travel, with the world stage occupied by the world powers of America and

Russia, and with China as a potential third, Europe has been reduced to a minor role. But this is not necessarily so. For the old Europe has great resources on which to fall back—in experience, in tradition and culture, and in intellectual power as well as technical 'know-how.' Economically, too, she has immense strength that still awaits mobilisation. In his 1962 Message on the State of the Union, President Kennedy spoke of the European Common Market as 'the greatest challenge of all. Assuming the accession of the United Kingdom,' he continued, 'there will arise across the Atlantic a trading partner behind a single external tariff similar to ours with an economy which nearly equals our own.' The future is still a challenge.

Suggestions for Further Reading

Special studies of very recent events are liable to be over-burdened with detail or distorted by polemics. It is safer to rely upon standard works of reference, such as *The Annual Register*, *The Statesman's Year Book*, *The Encyclopedia Britannica Book of the Year*, and *Keesing's Contemporary Archives*.

DATES OF SOME IMPORTANT
INTERNATIONAL EVENTS

1871: January 17. Conference of London opened.
January 28. Capitulation of France to Germany.
May 10. Treaty of Frankfort signed.

1872: September 6. Meeting of the Three Emperors in Berlin (originating the *Dreikaiserbund*).

1875: April 8. War scare inspired by German Press.

1876: June 30. Serbian declaration of war against Turkey.

1877: April 24. Russian declaration of war against Turkey.
December 10. Fall of Plevna.

1878: March 3. Treaty of San Stefano signed.
June 13. Congress of Berlin opened.

1879: October 7. Dual Alliance of Germany and Austria-Hungary formed.

1881: May 12. Treaty of Bardo signed.
June 18. League of the Three Emperors (*Dreikaiserbund*) reaffirmed and formalised.

1882: May 20. Triple Alliance of Germany, Austria-Hungary, and Italy formed.
July 11. British bombardment of Alexandria.

1884: April 24. German protectorate proclaimed in Southwest Africa.
November 15. Conference of Berlin opened.

1885: September 18. Union of Eastern Rumelia with Bulgaria proclaimed.
November 19. Bulgarian victory at Slivnitsa completed.

1887: April 20. Arrest of Schnaebele.
June 18. 'Reinsurance' Treaty between Germany and Russia signed.
December 12. Near Eastern Agreement between Britain, Austria-Hungary, and Italy signed.

1890: July 1. Anglo-German Colonial Agreement signed.

1891: August 27. Dual Alliance of Russia and France formed (signature of Political Convention).

1893: December 27. Military Convention between Russia and France adopted.

1895: April 17. Treaty of Shimonoseki signed.
December 17. President Cleveland's Message to Congress upon the Venezuela boundary dispute.

1896: January 3. German Emperor's telegram sent to Krüger.

March 1. Battle of Adowa.

1897: April 17. Turkish declaration of war against Greece.

1898: March 27. Port Arthur leased to Russia.

April 24. War declared by Spain against America.

September 18. British confront French forces at Fashoda.

1899: May 18. First Hague Conference opened.

October 11. Outbreak of the Boer War.

1900: June 12. Second German Navy Law passed.

October 16. China Agreement between Britain and Germany signed.

1902: January 30. Alliance of Britain and Japan formed.

May 31. Treaty of Vereeniging signed.

1904: April 8. *Entente Cordiale* created by Franco-British Declaration upon Egypt and Morocco.

October 21. Dogger Bank incident.

1905: March 31. Landing of the German Emperor at Tangier.

July 25. Treaty of Björkö signed.

September 5. Treaty of Portsmouth signed.

1906: January 16. Algeciras Conference opened.

February 10. *H.M.S. Dreadnought* launched.

1907: June 15. Second Hague Conference opened.

August 31. Triple *Entente* created by Russo-British Convention on Persia.

1908: October 6. Annexation of Bosnia-Herzegovina by Austria-Hungary announced.

1911: July 1. Announcement of the despatch of the *Panther* to Agadir.

September 29. War between Italy and Turkey begun.

November 4. Franco-German negotiations on Morocco and French Congo completed.

1912: October 8. First Balkan War begun.

October 24. Bulgarian victory at Kirk Kilisse and Serbian victory at Kumanovo completed.

1913: May 30. Treaty of London signed, ending First Balkan War.

June 29. Second Balkan War begun.

August 10. Treaty of Bucharest signed.

✗ 1914: June 28. Assassination of Archduke Franz Ferdinand.
   ✗ July 28. Austrian Declaration of War against Serbia.
      August 4. British Declaration of War against Germany
        (11 p.m.).
      August 30. Completion of the German victory at
        Tannenberg.
      September 6. Allied counter-attack launched on the
        Marne.
      November 5. Allied Declaration of War against
        Turkey.
1915: April 26. Treaty of London signed.
1916: January 9. Evacuation of Gallipoli Peninsula com-
      pleted.
      February 21. Battle of Verdun begun.
      May 31. Battle of Jutland.
      July 1. Battle of the Somme begun.
1917: February 1. 'Unlimited' submarine warfare begun by
      Germany.
      March 8. Outbreak of 'February' revolution in Russia.
      April 6. American Declaration of War against
      Germany.
      October 24. Italian Army broken at Caporetto.
      November 7. Outbreak of 'October' Revolution in
      Russia.
✗ 1918: March 3. Treaty of Brest-Litovsk signed.
      March 21. Opening of great German offensive in the
      West.
      August 8. Decisive British attack in front of Amiens.
      November 11. Armistice came into force.
1919: January 18. Paris Peace Conference opened.
   ✗ June 28. Treaty of Versailles signed.
1920: August 14. Polish counter-offensive at Warsaw begun.
   ✗ November 15. First League of Nations Assembly opened.
1921: November 12. Washington Conference opened.
1922: April 16. Russo-German Treaty of Rapallo signed.
   ✗ August 26. Greek Army overwhelmed by the Turks.
      September 23. Turkish confront British forces at
      Chanak.
✗ 1923: January 11. French occupation of the Ruhr begun.
      July 24. Treaty of Lausanne signed.
      August 31. Italian bombardment of Corfu.

1924: August 30. Final acceptance of the Dawes Plan for reparations.

1925: December 1. Locarno Treaties signed.

1926: September 8. Admission of Germany to the League of Nations.

1928: August 27. Kellogg Pact (Pact of Paris) signed.

1929: February 11. Concordat between Italy and the Papacy signed.

August 28. Final acceptance of the Young Plan for reparations at The Hague Conference.

October 24. American Stock Exchange collapse.

1931: May 11. Collapse of the *Kreditanstalt* in Austria.

September 18. Japanese attack on Manchuria.

1932: February 2. World Disarmament Conference opened.

1933: January 30. Hitler becomes Chancellor.

July 27. 'Adjournment' of the World Economic Conference.

October 14. Withdrawal of Germany from the Disarmament Conference and from the League of Nations.

1934: September 16. Entry of Russia into the League of Nations.

1935: January 13. Saar Plebiscite held.

June 18. Anglo-German Naval Agreement signed.

October 3. Italian declaration of War against Abyssinia.

1936: March 7. German military reoccupation of the Rhineland.

July 18. Outbreak of the Spanish Civil War.

1937: July 7. Renewal of Japanese aggression in China.

1938: March 11. German occupation of Austria begun.

September 30. Munich Agreement completed.

1939: March 15. German occupation of Prague.

April 7. Italian invasion of Albania.

September 1. German invasion of Poland begun.

1940: April 9. German invasion of Denmark and Norway.

May 10. Opening of the German attack in the West.

June 10. Italian Declaration of War.

June 21. Armistice between France and Germany signed.

1941: March 11. Lend-Lease Bill signed by President
Roosevelt.
April 6. German invasion of Jugoslavia and Greece.
June 22. German invasion of Russia.
August 14. 'Atlantic Charter' announced.
December 7. Japanese attack on Pearl Harbour.
1942: February 15. Fall of Singapore.
November 2. British victory at El Alamein completed.
1943: January 31. Surrender of von Paulus before Stalin-
grad.
July 10. Invasion of Sicily.
July 23. Main Russian counter-attack begun.
September 3. Armistice signed by Italian non-Fascist
Government.
1944: June 4. Capture of Rome.
June 6. Allied landings in Normandy ('D'-day).
August 23. Liberation of Paris.
September 26. British advance checked at Arnhem.
1945: March 7. First passage of the Rhine at Remagen.
May 7. Unconditional surrender terms signed for all
German forces.
June 26. United Nations Charter signed at San
Francisco.
July 17. Potsdam Conference begun.
August 6. Atomic bomb dropped on Hiroshima.
August 14. Unconditional surrender of Japan.
1946: October 13. Constitution of Fourth Republic adopted
in France.
October 16. Leading war criminals hanged at
Nuremberg.
1947: February 10. Peace Treaties with Italy, etc., signed
at Paris.
June 5. Marshall Plan proposed.
August 15. End of British rule in India.
1948: February 25. Communist *coup* in Czechoslovakia.
March 17. Treaty of Brussels signed (W.E.U.).
June 24. Start of Berlin Blockade by Russians.
1949: April 4. Atlantic Pact signed at Washington.
May 5. Statute of the Council of Europe signed.
May 11. New State of Israel admitted to U.N.

May 23.   Federal German Republic established (non-sovereign).

October 1.   People's Republic of China formally proclaimed.

1950:   June 25.   South Korea invaded by North Koreans.

1951:   April 18.   Signature of agreement for European Coal and Steel Community.

1952:   November 1.   First Russian H-bomb exploded (announced 8 August 1953).

1953:   March 5.   Death of Stalin.

July 27.   Armistice terminating hostilities in Korea.

1954:   May 7.   Fall of Dien-bien-phu.

September 8.   SEATO pact signed at Manila.

1955:   May 9.   Federal German Republic admitted as sovereign power to NATO.

May 13.   Warsaw Treaty Organisation established by Russia.

May 15.   Treaty of peace signed with Austria.

July 23.   End of 6-day Summit Conference at Geneva.

1956:   June 28.   Start of riots in Poland.

October 22–November 8.   Anti-Russian revolt in Hungary and its suppression.

October 31–November 6.   Anglo-French Suez Canal operations.

1957:   March 25.   Signature of Treaties of Rome (start of Common Market and Euratom, 1 January 1958).

October 4.   Launching of first Sputnik (weight 83·6 Kg.).

1958:   March 27.   Khrushchev became President of the Council of Ministers, U.S.S.R.

May 13.   Military *coup* in Algeria, demanding power for de Gaulle.

September 28.   Constitution of Fifth Republic adopted in France.

1959:   November 20.   Signature of Treaty of Stockholm (EFTA).

December 14.   Establishment of Organisation for Economic Co-operation and Development (OECD).

1960:   March 15.   South Africa announced its withdrawal from the Commonwealth.

June 30.   Belgian Congo became independent.

1961: April 12.   First successful launching of man into space.

June 15.   Berlin Crisis, resulting from announced Russian intention to sign separate peace treaty with East German government.

October 30.   Explosion of 50–57 megaton bomb in Russian test series.

INDEX

Names of Battles and Treaties will be found under those headings

France—*continued*
Agadir crisis, 125-8; the Dreyfus case, 132-3; socialism, and separation of Church and State, 133-5; trade unionism in, 135; pre-war defence, 136; and the First World War, 202 f.; and the Rhineland, 243-4; and the Reparations question, 256-9; and the Locarno Pact, 267-8; improved relations with Germany, 1925-30, 276; internal politics, 1925-30, 277-8; the *Front Populaire* Government, 368-9; and the Second World War, 383-4; 'D' Day, 401-2; liberation of, 402-3; and the occupation of Germany and Austria, 408-13; post-war conditions in, 420, 433; external links, 430, 433; colonial policy, 437-8, 440; Fifth Republic, 440
Francis Joseph, Emperor, 7, 8, 161
Franco, General, 340, 361-3, 420
Franco-Prussian War, 1-2, 24, 39-40
Franz Ferdinand, Archduke, 162, 196-7
Fraser, Sir J. G., 147
Frederick, Emperor, 148
Free French, the, 396
Freud, S., 147

GAGARIN, Major, 449
Galicia, 153
Galliéni, General, 203
Gallipoli campaign, 210
Galsworthy, John, 146
Gambetta, L., 2, 39, 44, 47, 133
Gapon, Father, 155
Gas, poison, 207
Geneva Protocol, 266
George, Crown Prince, 123
George, Henry, 304
George V, King, 199
German Democratic Republic. *See* East Germany.
German Federal Republic, 431, 433, 445-6
Germany: economic ascendancy of, 21, 28-31; population of, 35; the Bismarckian era, 49-50; constitution of Second Reich, 51-3; minorities and Catholics, 53-6; Bismarck's later domestic policy, 56-9; and the Reinsurance Treaty, 73-6; imperialism in Africa, 82, 86; in the Pacific, 87-8; negotiations of 1898-1901 with Britain, 102-6; character of, 109, 348-9; and first Moroccan crisis, 113-16; and British naval rivalry, 118-20; the Agadir Crisis, 125-8; the Wilhelmine era, 148-50; the naval budget, 150-1; treatment of minorities,

151-2; rapprochement with Turkey over Balkans, 193-4; declaration of war, 1914, 199; the First World War, 202 f.; Russia and the Treaty of Brest-Litovsk, 228-9; the Treaty of Versailles, 240-6; the Weimar Republic, 253-6; French demand for reparations, 257-9; admission into League of Nations, 269; improved relations with France 1925-30, 276; centre coalition governments and evasions of disarmament clauses, 278-9; establishment of dictatorship, 342; financial crisis, 345; causes of rise of Hitlerism, 346-50; Hitler becomes chancellor, 350-1; the Nazi revolution, 352-5; the Nazi policy of expansion, 363-5; non-aggression pact with Poland, 365; the Saar plebiscite, 366; building-up for war, 366-9; naval agreement with Britain, 367, 373; the Rome-Berlin Axis, 368; annexes Austria, 369-70; Czechoslovakia and the Munich settlement, 370-2; attacks Poland, 373-4; the conquest of Europe and the New Order, 375-7; the Second World War, 378 f.; end of Hitler's Germany, 403-5; four-power occupation of, 408-13
Gilbert Islands, 400
Giolitti, 138, 261
Gladstone, W. E., 18, 37, 64, 66, 82
Goa, 437
Göbbels, Dr., 412
Gomułka, 444
Gordon, General, 91
Göring, Hermann, 321, 412
Gorki, Maxim, 146, 308
Gortchakoff, Prince, 19, 62, 63, 69
Gotthard, St., 37
Greece: nationalism in, 11; claims to Crete, 164-5; joins Bulgaria and Serbia, 188; gains after Second Balkan War, 191-2; entry into First World War, 215; gains after First World War, 248-9; war with Turkey, 252; and the Treaty of Lausanne, 259-60; dispute with Bulgaria, 273-4; republicanism and dictatorship in, 286; since 1940, 387-8, 418, 429, 431
Greek Church. *See* Religion.
Grévy, 47, 48
Grey, Sir Edward (later Viscount), 109, 116, 117, 122, 126, 195, 199-200
Guam, 89
Gustav V, King of Sweden, 144

HAAKON VII, KING OF NORWAY, 144
Hacha, President, 372

Russia—*continued*
agreement with Austria over Macedonia, 121; and Bosnian crisis, 122-4; the Racconigi Agreement, 124-5; and Teheran, 126; under Alexander III and Pobiedonostzeff, 152 f.; economic development under Witte, 154; growth of Bolshevism, and the first Revolution, 154-8; the Dumas and the land reforms, 156-8; and the Balkan League, 187, 189, 194; mobilisation after Serajevo, 198-9; defeated at Tannenberg and Masurian Lakes, 204-5; campaigns in Balkans and victories over Turkey, 210-12; collapse of, and the Revolution, 213-14; the February Revolution, 219-21; the provisional governments, 221-2; the theory of Communism, 222-4; the October Revolution, 224-7; Communist seizure of land, 227-8; Germany and the Treaty of Brest Litovsk, 228-9; triumph of the Communists, 229-31; the Civil War and foreign intervention, 231-3; war with Poland, 233-4; treaty with Turkey, 234; the great famine, 234-5, 307-8; excluded from League of Nations, 265; develops in isolation, 314-17; the New Economic Policy and the five-year plans, 316-25; federal dictatorship, and constitution of, 325-8; struggle for power inside Communist Party, 328-9; foreign policy, 329-31; features of Soviet régime, 331-2; admitted into League of Nations, 355; overtures by Britain and France, 373-4; pact with Germany, 374; occupation of eastern Poland, 378; attacks Finland, 380; German attack on, 389; Stalingrad, 392, 393; recovery on eastern front, 398-9; declares war on Japan, 406; and the occupation of Germany and Austria, 408-13; post-war conditions in, 417-18; conception of democracy, 426-8; and U.N., 423-4, 435, 442, 444

SAAR, THE, 241-2, 272, 366, 433
Sacred Heart, cult of the, 47
Sakhalin, 111
Salazar, Dr., 341
Salisbury, Lord, 75, 99, 101, 102, 103
Salonika, 68, 191, 211, 215
Salter, Sir Arthur, 237, 344
Salvation Army, 173
Samoa, 88, 296-7
Sanders, General Liman von, 194

Sazanoff, 124
Schacht, Dr., 267
Schleicher, General von, 351, 354
Schleswig, North, 151, 240
Schleswig-Holstein, 14, 53, 145
Schlieffen, 113, 202
Schmitt, Professor Bernadotte E., 196
Schnaebele, 48, 73
Schönbrunn Convention, 62 n.
Schuschnigg, Dr., 356
Science: in the 1870's, 31; latest developments of, 447-9
SEATO, 436
Senegal, 84
Separation Law, 134, 135
Serajevo, 196
Serbia: rivalry with Bulgaria, 72; and the Bosnian crisis, 121, 123; the alternation of democracy and autocracy, 162-3; alliance with Bulgaria, 187-8; attacked by Bulgaria, 189-90; fails to gain from Second Balkan War, 192-3; enmity of Austria-Hungary, 194-5; Serajevo and the Austrian ultimatum, 196-8; attacked by Austria, 205; obliteration of, 211
Seyss-Inquart, 370
Shaw, Bernard, 146
Siam, 92
Sicily, 397
Siegfried Line, 367, 404
Siemens, 22, 30
Silesia, Upper, 242, 264
Simon, Sir John (later Viscount), 367
Sinclair, Upton, 312
Skobelev, General, 92
Slavery, African, 79
Slavs: pan-Slavism, 10-11; under the Dual Monarchy, 161. *See also* Jugoslavia.
Smuts, General, 291
Socialism: beginnings of modern, 36-7; in pre-war France, 133-4; and internationalism, 183-5
Solomon Islands, 88
Somaliland, 388
South Africa, 100, 104, 439
South America, European expansion in, 89-90
Spain: in 1870, 13; railways, iron and steel, 31; Pacific colonies of, 88-9; pre-war régime, 138-40; war with U.S.A., 297-9; growth of fascism, 339-40; the Civil War, 360-3; Franco régime, 420, 440
Spanish-American War, 88, 297-9
Spencer, Herbert, 16
Sputnik, 449
Stahremberg, Prince, 355
Stakhanov, 324

Tukhachevsky, Marshal, 329
Tunis, 47
Tunisia, 71, 80, 81, 84, 440
Turkestan, 76
Turkey: and Bulgaria, 12; not desired
in Europe, 17; war with Russia, 64-7;
massacres by, 99; pro-German atti-
tude, 121; decline of, in Europe,
165-6, 190; Young Turk Revolution,
166-7; and the Balkan League, 187-
8; *rapprochement* with Germany over
Balkans, 193-4; joins Central Powers,
205, 215; treaty with Russia, 234;
Allied terms to, 248; under Kemal
Ataturk, 249, 289-90; war with
Greece, 252; and the Treaty of
Lausanne, 259-60; the Mosul ques-
tion, 273; pacts with Britain and
France, 372; after Second World
War, 429, 431
Tyrol, the, 69

U Thant, 442
Umberto, King, 420
Unamuno, 146
Unemployment in world economic
crisis, 345
United Kingdom: free trade in, 23;
railways, 27, 31; coal, iron and steel,
31; population, 35; and Russia, 67,
72; and Bismarck's overtures, 74;
agreement with Italy, 74; imperialism
in Africa, 80, 83-4, 85-6; colonial
rivalries with France, 84-5; imperialism in the Pacific, 87, 88; and
development of S. America, 89-90;
and China, 91-2; alarm at Dual
Alliance, and diplomatic isolation,
98-101; rivalry with Russia in Far
East, 101; negotiations of 1898-
1901 with Germany, 102-6; alliance
with Japan, 106; *Entente Cordiale* with
France, 106-10; and first Moroccan
crisis, 113-16; *entente* with Russia,
116-18; and German naval rivalry,
118-20; and Bosnian crisis, 122-4;
and Agadir crisis, 126-8; naval
guarantee to France, 128; literature
of pre-war era, 146; rising standard
of life, 167; the *Alabama* case, 178;
and the Balkan situation, 193-4,
195-6; the decision to declare war,
1914, 199-200; and the First World
War, 203 f.; and the Turco-Greek
conflict, 260; rejects Treaty of
Mutual Assistance, 266; and the
Spanish Civil War, 362; naval
agreement with Germany, 367, 373;
complacency of, 369; guarantee to

Poland, 372; and the Second World
War, 378 f.; and the occupation of
Germany and Austria, 408-13; and
nuclear armament, 431-2, 447
United Nations: organisation, 421-4;
interventions, 435, 438, 441; expan-
sion, 441-2; failure in Hungary, 444
United States. *See* America.
Urban life, growth of, 36-7

Van Gogh, 37
Vandervelde, 142
Vatican Council of 1870, 2-3
Venezuela, 99, 107, 295-6
Venizelos, 165, 188, 215, 248, 249,
286
Victor Emmanuel II, King, 2
Victor Emmanuel III, King, 138, 262
Victoria, Queen, 62
Villari, Professor, 263
Vilna, 264
Vladivostok, 77

Wagner, 16
Waldeck-Rousseau, 133
Walloons, 280
Wangenheim, von, 193
Washington, George, 294
Wavell, General, 387, 388
Weimar Republic, 253-6, 348
Wells, H. G., 146, 240, 291
West Germany, *see* German Federal
Republic.
Western European Union, 430, 433
Weygand, General, 234, 383
Wilder, Thornton, 312
Wilhelmina, Queen, 143
William I, Kaiser, 95, 96, 148
William II, Kaiser: personal rule of,
148-50; abdication of, 254; other
references, 39, 51, 75, 96, 103, 105,
108, 111-12, 113, 116, 120, 177,
192 n., 193, 194, 197, 298
William of Wied, Prince, 193
Wilson, Daniel, 48
Wilson, President, 236, 238, 240, 242,
244, 250, 305-6
Witos, Polish Prime Minister, 284
Witte, Count, 112, 154, 155, 156, 157
World Economic Conference, 356-7
Wrangel, General, 234

Yalta Conference, 408
Young Plan, the, 276
Younghusband, Sir F., 117